W9-BVW-195

WITHDRAWN
No longer the property of the
Boston Public Library.
Sale of this material benefits the Library

BATMAN
vs
Ra's al Ghul

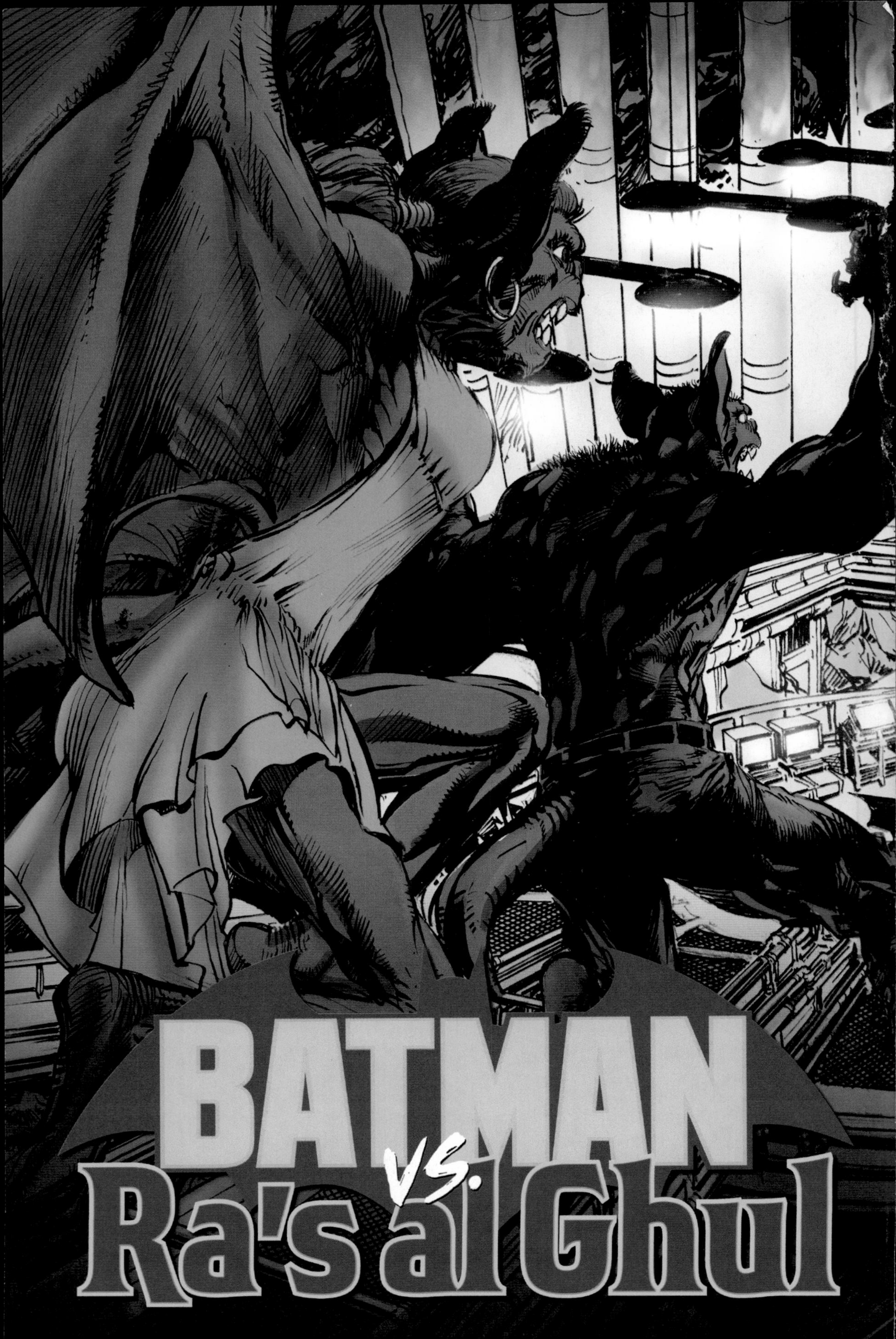
BATMAN
VS.
Ra's al Ghul

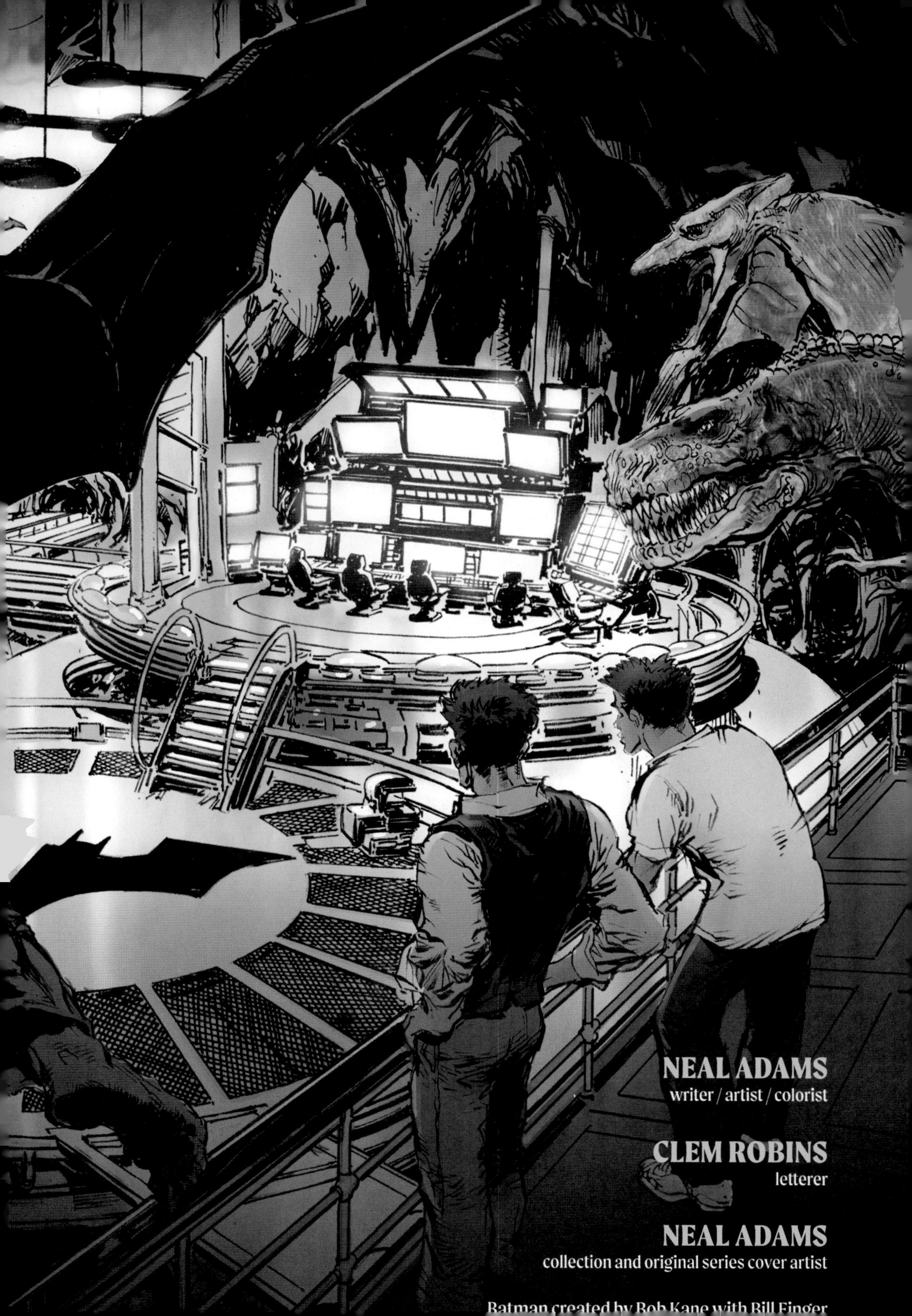

NEAL ADAMS
writer / artist / colorist

CLEM ROBINS
letterer

NEAL ADAMS
collection and original series cover artist

Batman created by Bob Kane with Bill Finger

Kristy Quinn
Editor – Original Series & Collected Edition

Liz Erickson
Assistant Editor – Original Series

Steve Cook
Design Director – Books

Megen Bellersen
Publication Design

Erin Vanover
Publication Production

Marie Javins
Editor-in-Chief, DC Comics

Anne DePies
Senior VP – General Manager

Jim Lee
Publisher & Chief Creative Officer

Don Falletti
VP – Manufacturing Operations & Workflow Management

Lawrence Ganem
VP – Talent Services

Alison Gill
Senior VP – Manufacturing & Operations

Jeffrey Kaufman
VP – Editorial Strategy & Programming

Nick J. Napolitano
VP – Manufacturing Administration & Design

Nancy Spears
VP – Revenue

BATMAN VS. RA'S AL GHUL

Published by DC Comics. Compilation and all new material Copyright © 2022 DC Comics. All Rights Reserved. Originally published in single magazine form in *Batman vs. Ra's al Ghul* 1-6. Copyright © 2019, 2020, 2021 DC Comics. All Rights Reserved. All characters, their distinctive likenesses, and related elements featured in this publication are trademarks of DC Comics. The stories, characters, and incidents featured in this publication are entirely fictional. DC Comics does not read or accept unsolicited submissions of ideas, stories, or artwork.

DC Comics, 4000 Warner Blvd., Bldg. 700, 2nd Floor, Burbank, CA 91522
Printed by Transcontinental Printing Interweb Montreal, a division of Transcontinental Printing Inc., Boucherville, QC, Canada. 11/18/22. First Printing.
ISBN: 978-1-77951-828-6

Library of Congress Cataloging-in-Publication Data is available.

PEFC Certified
This product is from sustainably managed forests and controlled sources
PEFC/01-31-106   www.pefc.org

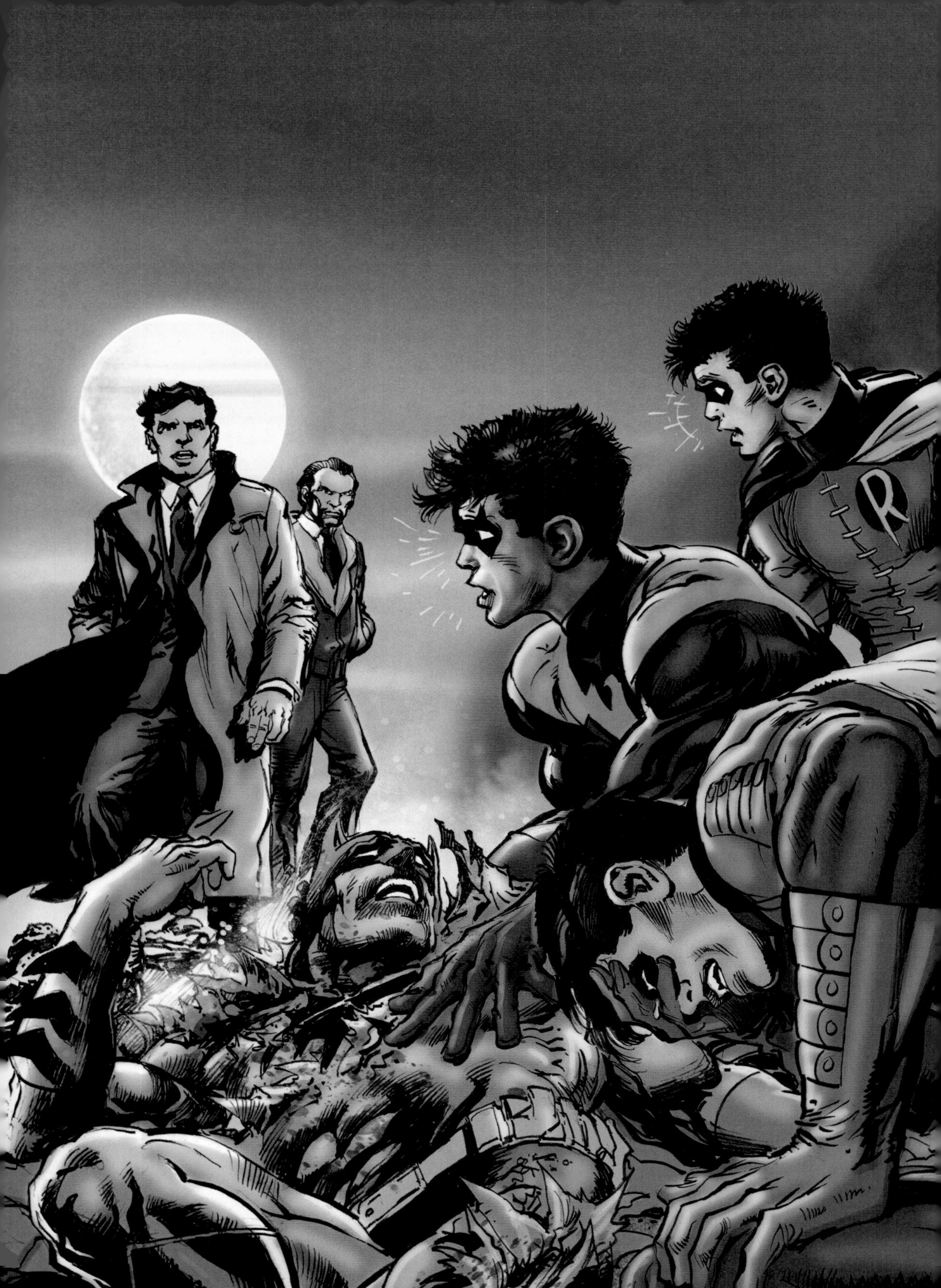

Chapter 1

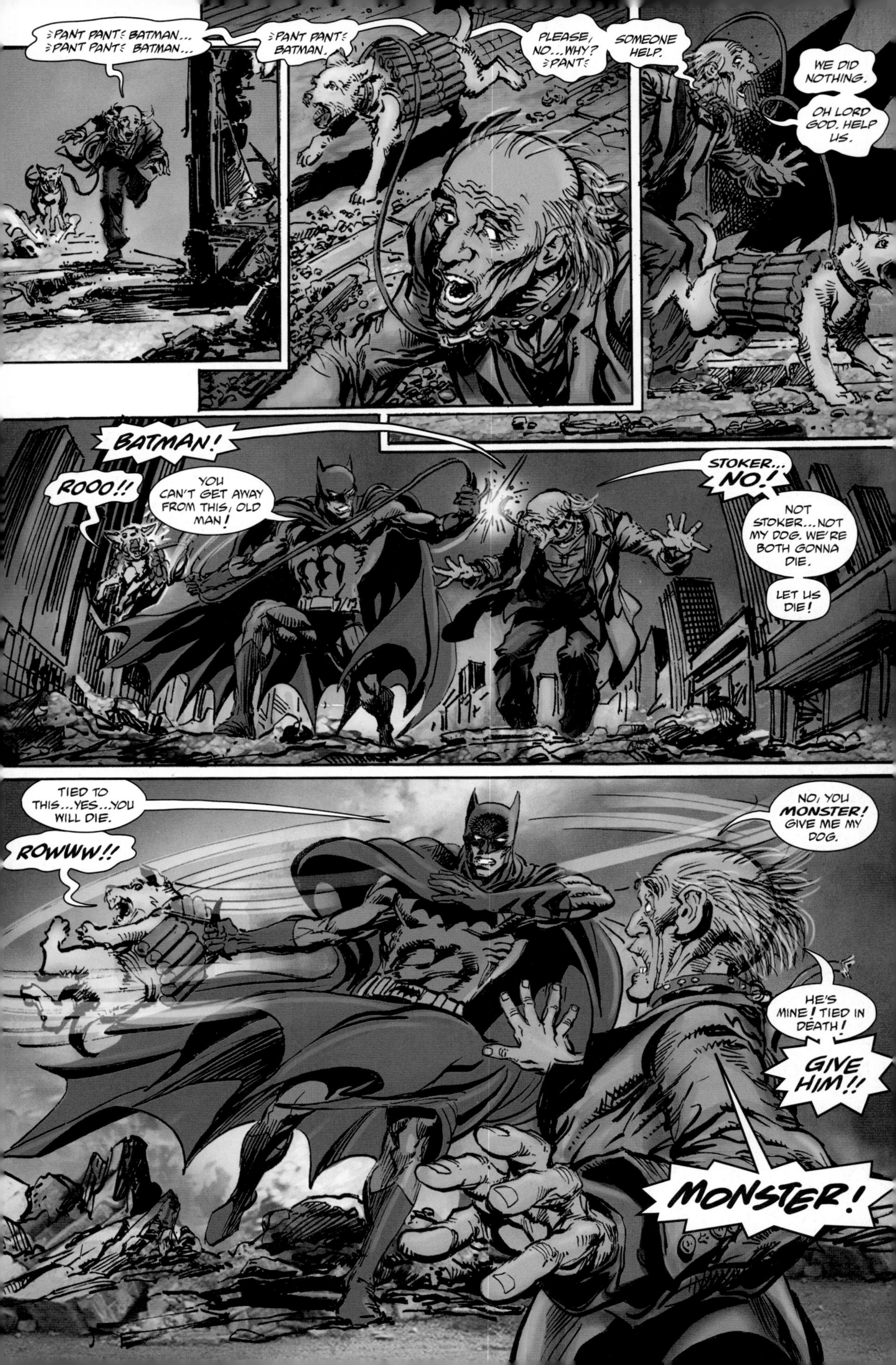

≷PANT PANT≶ BATMAN... ≷PANT PANT≶ BATMAN...
≷PANT PANT≶ BATMAN.
PLEASE, NO...WHY? ≷PANT≶
SOMEONE HELP.
WE DID NOTHING.
OH LORD GOD. HELP US.
BATMAN!
ROOO!!
YOU CAN'T GET AWAY FROM THIS, OLD MAN!
STOKER... NO!
NOT STOKER...NOT MY DOG. WE'RE BOTH GONNA DIE.
LET US DIE!
TIED TO THIS...YES...YOU WILL DIE.
ROWWW!!
NO, YOU MONSTER! GIVE ME MY DOG.
HE'S MINE! TIED IN DEATH!
GIVE HIM!!
MONSTER!

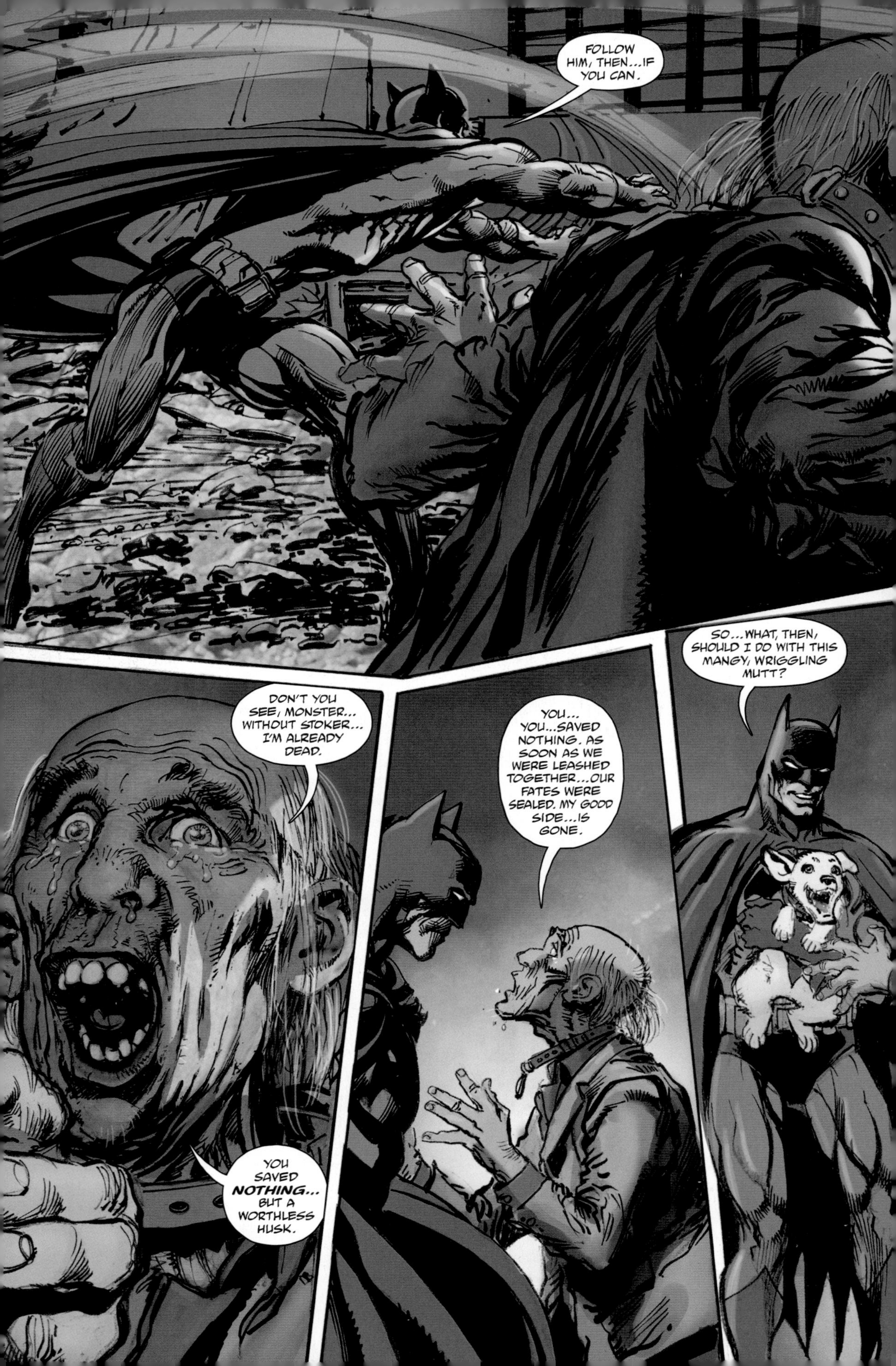
FOLLOW HIM, THEN...IF YOU CAN.
DON'T YOU SEE, MONSTER... WITHOUT STOKER... I'M ALREADY DEAD.
YOU SAVED **NOTHING...** BUT A WORTHLESS HUSK.
YOU... YOU...SAVED NOTHING. AS SOON AS WE WERE LEASHED TOGETHER...OUR FATES WERE SEALED. MY GOOD SIDE...IS GONE.
SO...WHAT, THEN, SHOULD I DO WITH THIS MANGY, WRIGGLING MUTT?

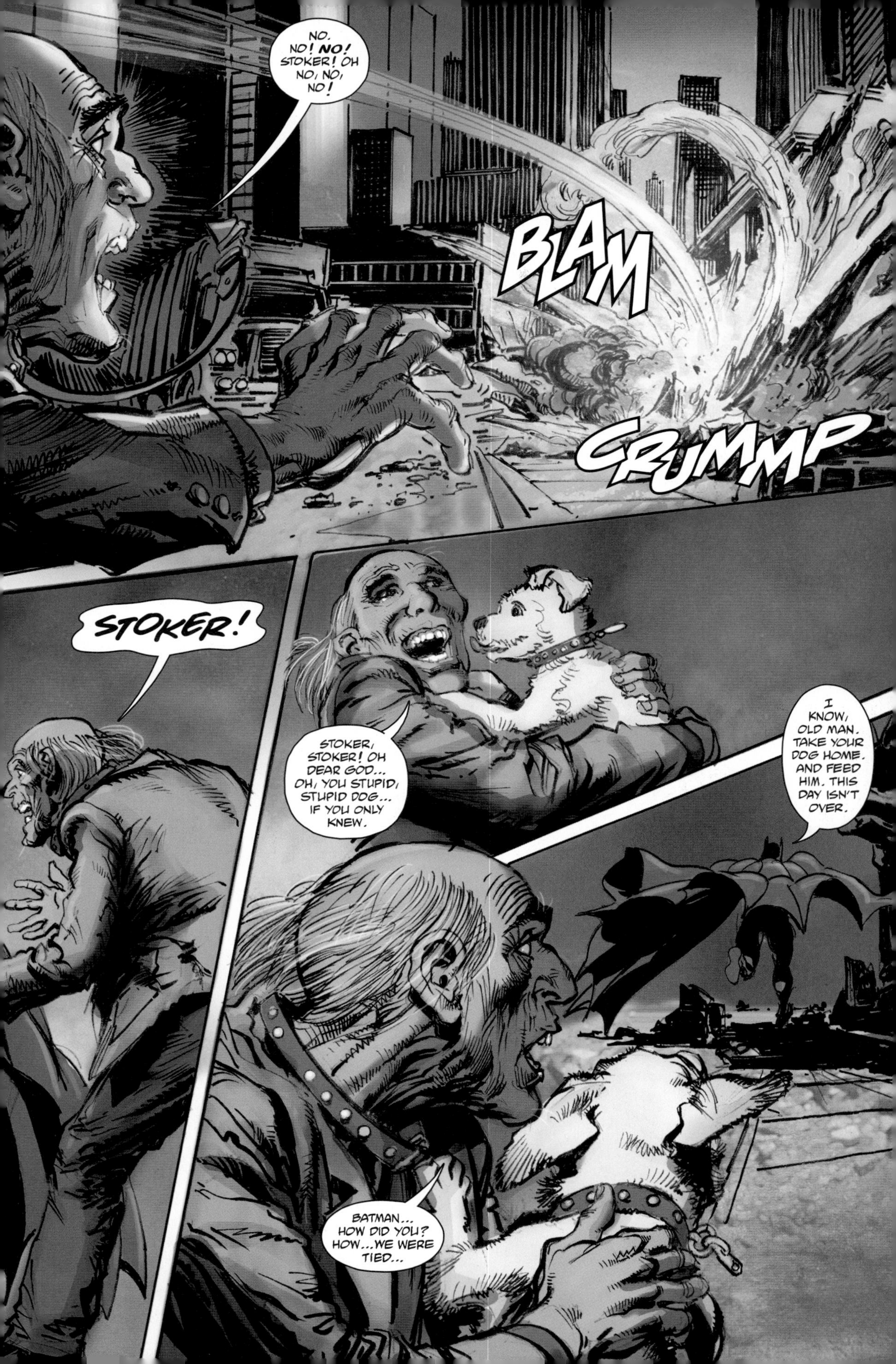
NO. NO! NO! STOKER! OH NO, NO, NO!
BLAM
CRUMMP
STOKER!
STOKER, STOKER! OH DEAR GOD... OH, YOU STUPID, STUPID DOG... IF YOU ONLY KNEW.
I KNOW, OLD MAN. TAKE YOUR DOG HOME. AND FEED HIM. THIS DAY ISN'T OVER.
BATMAN... HOW DID YOU? HOW...WE WERE TIED...

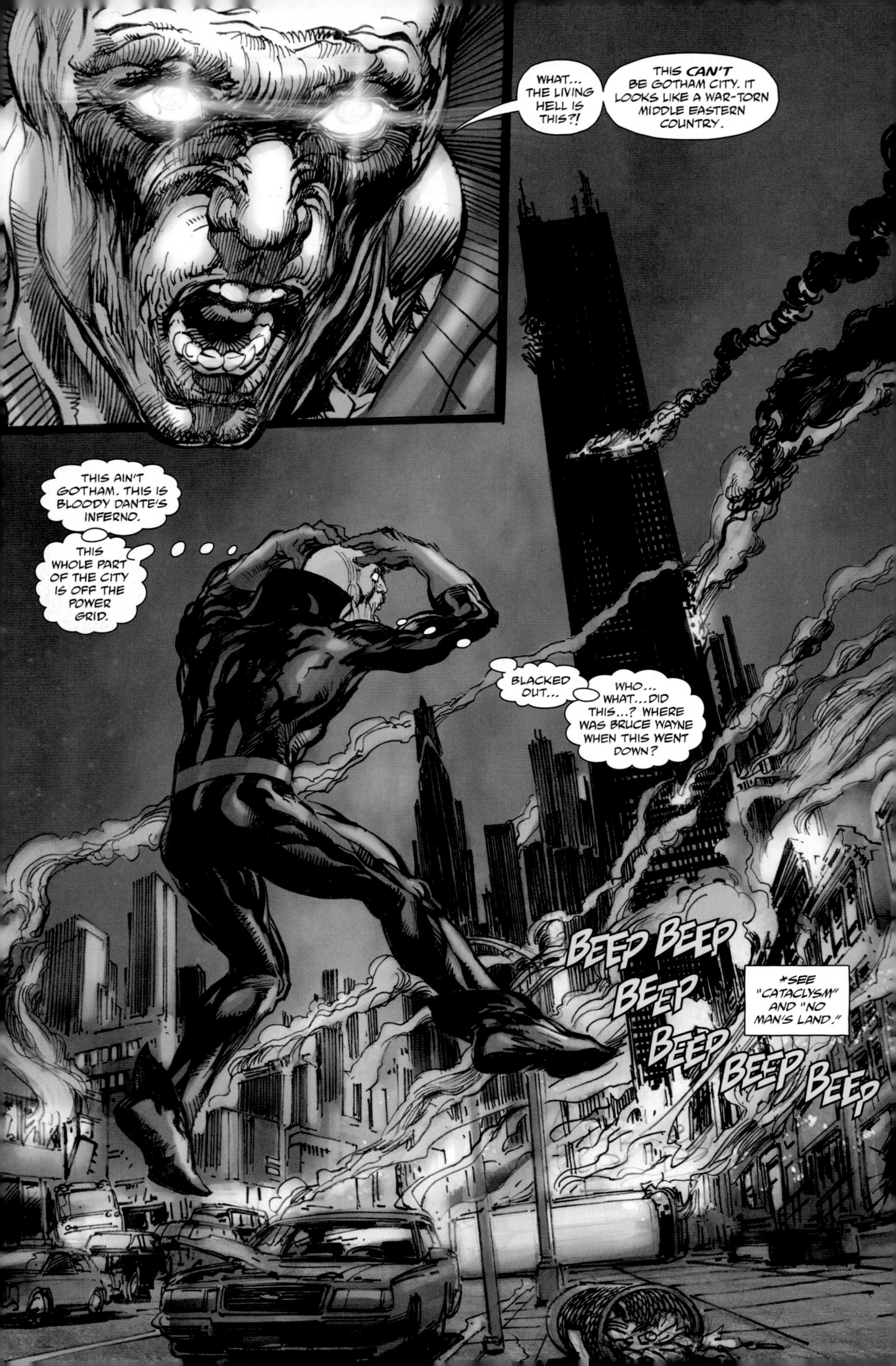

WHAT... THE LIVING HELL IS THIS?!
THIS CAN'T BE GOTHAM CITY. IT LOOKS LIKE A WAR-TORN MIDDLE EASTERN COUNTRY.
THIS AIN'T GOTHAM. THIS IS BLOODY DANTE'S INFERNO.
THIS WHOLE PART OF THE CITY IS OFF THE POWER GRID.
BLACKED OUT...
WHO... WHAT...DID THIS...? WHERE WAS BRUCE WAYNE WHEN THIS WENT DOWN?
BEEP BEEP BEEP BEEP BEEP BEEP
*SEE "CATACLYSM" AND "NO MAN'S LAND."

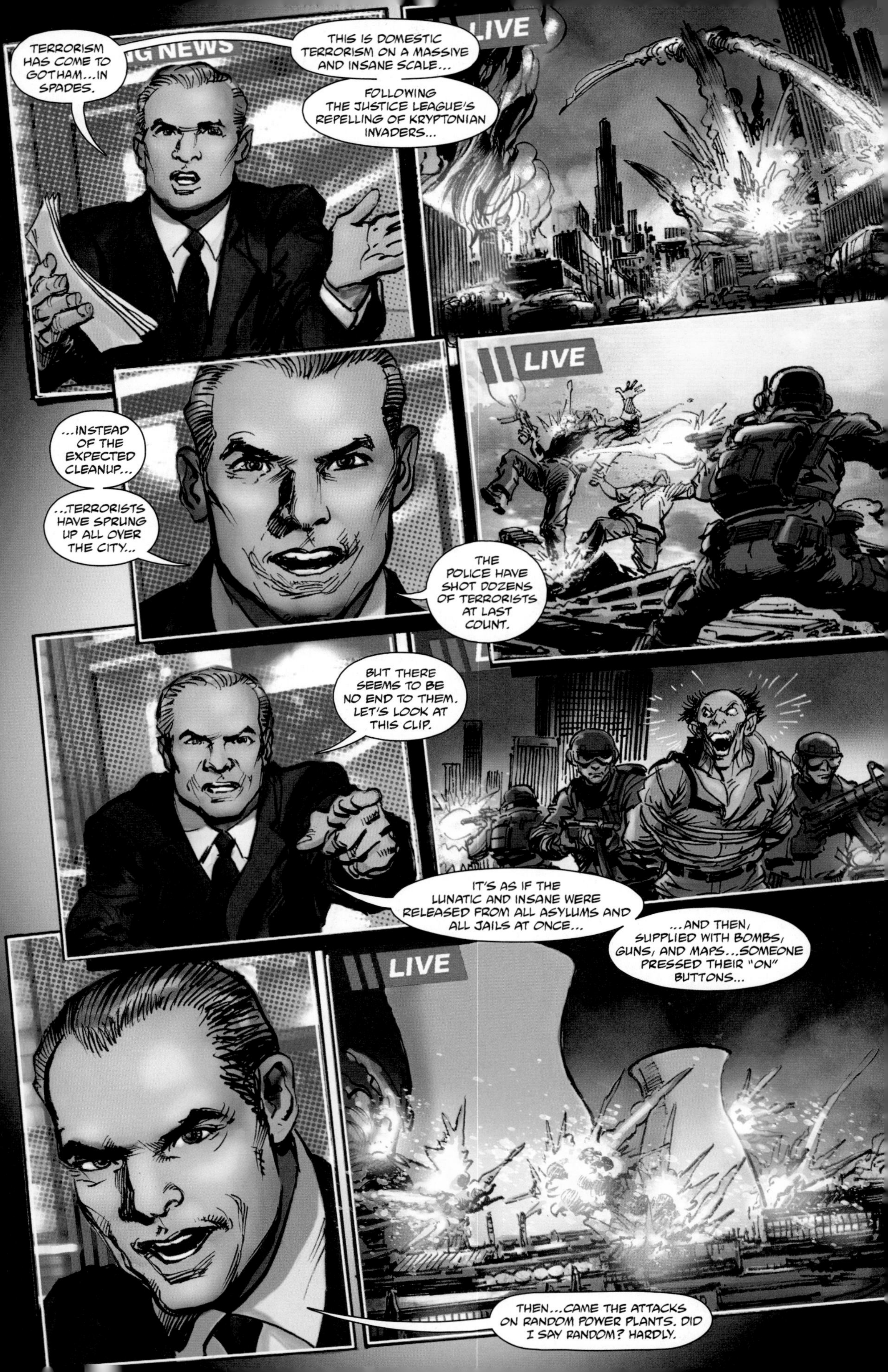
IG NEWS
TERRORISM HAS COME TO GOTHAM...IN SPADES.
THIS IS DOMESTIC TERRORISM ON A MASSIVE AND INSANE SCALE...
FOLLOWING THE JUSTICE LEAGUE'S REPELLING OF KRYPTONIAN INVADERS...
LIVE
...INSTEAD OF THE EXPECTED CLEANUP...
...TERRORISTS HAVE SPRUNG UP ALL OVER THE CITY...
LIVE
THE POLICE HAVE SHOT DOZENS OF TERRORISTS AT LAST COUNT.
BUT THERE SEEMS TO BE NO END TO THEM. LET'S LOOK AT THIS CLIP.
IT'S AS IF THE LUNATIC AND INSANE WERE RELEASED FROM ALL ASYLUMS AND ALL JAILS AT ONCE...
...AND THEN, SUPPLIED WITH BOMBS, GUNS, AND MAPS...SOMEONE PRESSED THEIR "ON" BUTTONS...
LIVE
THEN...CAME THE ATTACKS ON RANDOM POWER PLANTS. DID I SAY RANDOM? HARDLY.

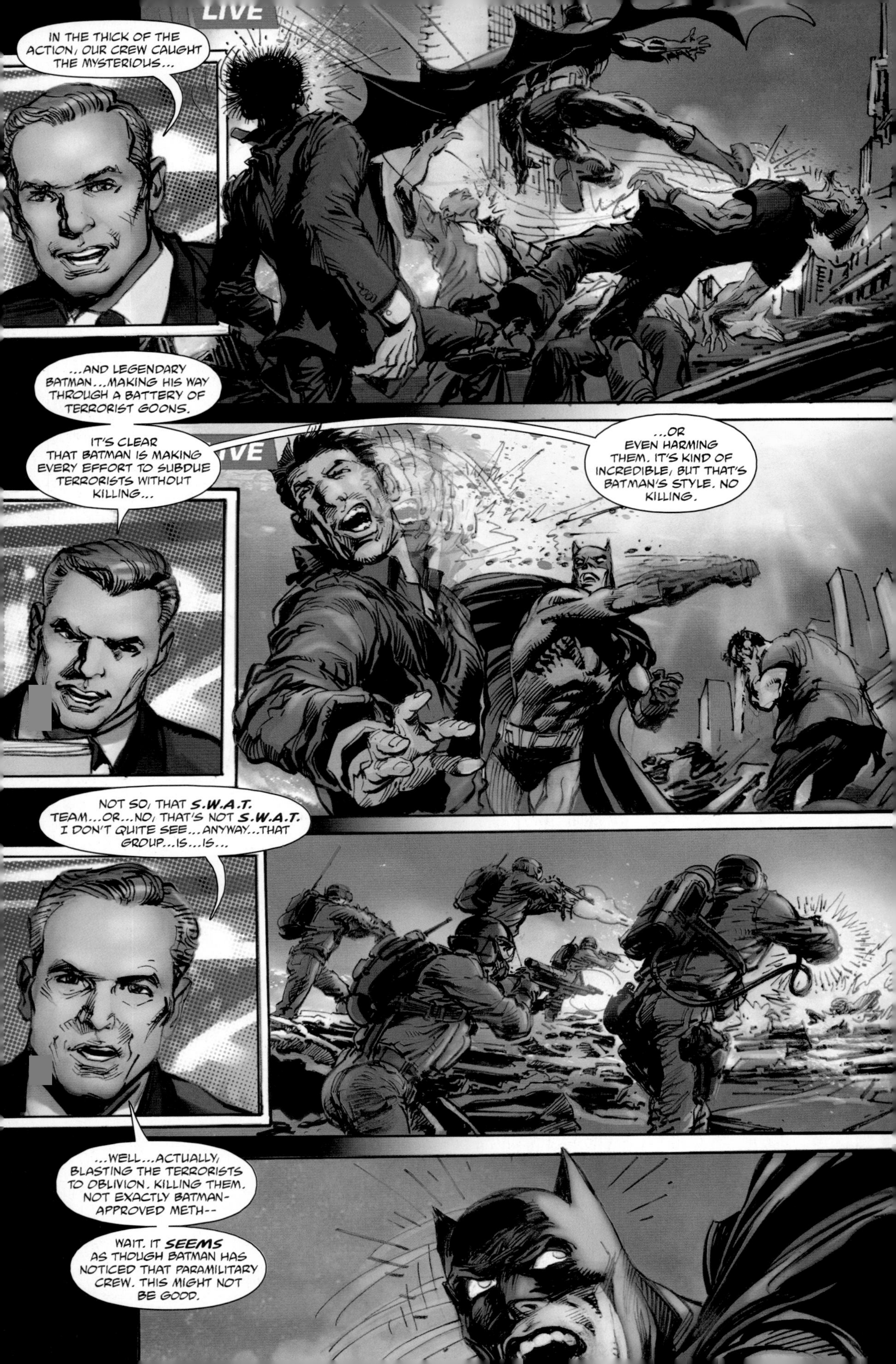
LIVE
IN THE THICK OF THE ACTION, OUR CREW CAUGHT THE MYSTERIOUS...
...AND LEGENDARY BATMAN...MAKING HIS WAY THROUGH A BATTERY OF TERRORIST GOONS.
LIVE
IT'S CLEAR THAT BATMAN IS MAKING EVERY EFFORT TO SUBDUE TERRORISTS WITHOUT KILLING...
...OR EVEN HARMING THEM. IT'S KIND OF INCREDIBLE, BUT THAT'S BATMAN'S STYLE. NO KILLING.
NOT SO, THAT S.W.A.T. TEAM...OR...NO, THAT'S NOT S.W.A.T. I DON'T QUITE SEE...ANYWAY...THAT GROUP...IS...IS...
...WELL...ACTUALLY, BLASTING THE TERRORISTS TO OBLIVION. KILLING THEM. NOT EXACTLY BATMAN-APPROVED METH--
WAIT. IT SEEMS AS THOUGH BATMAN HAS NOTICED THAT PARAMILITARY CREW. THIS MIGHT NOT BE GOOD.

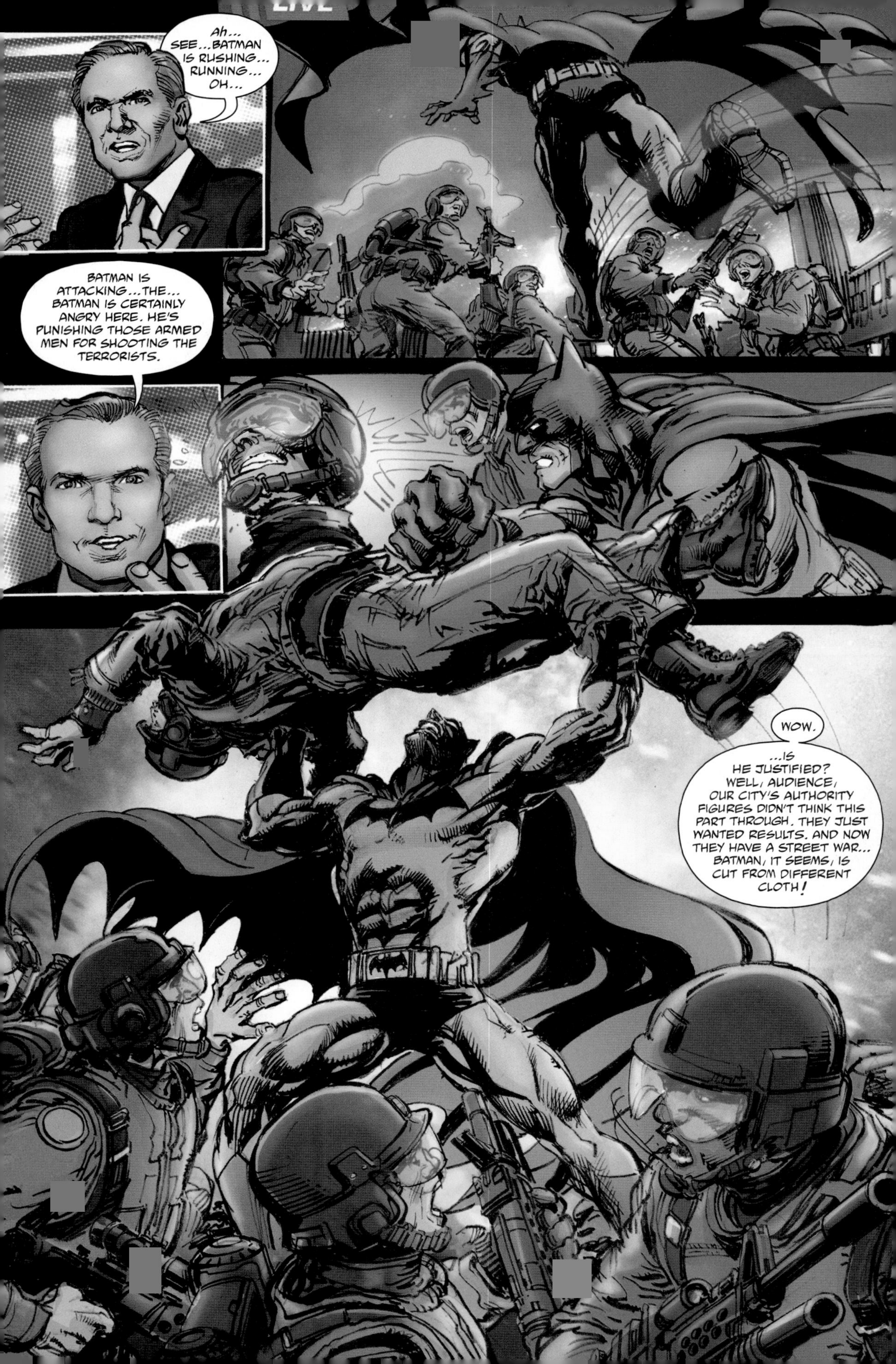
LIVE
Ah... SEE...BATMAN IS RUSHING... RUNNING... OH...
BATMAN IS ATTACKING...THE... BATMAN IS CERTAINLY ANGRY HERE. HE'S PUNISHING THOSE ARMED MEN FOR SHOOTING THE TERRORISTS.
WOW.
...IS HE JUSTIFIED? WELL, AUDIENCE, OUR CITY'S AUTHORITY FIGURES DIDN'T THINK THIS PART THROUGH. THEY JUST WANTED RESULTS. AND NOW THEY HAVE A STREET WAR... BATMAN, IT SEEMS, IS CUT FROM DIFFERENT CLOTH!

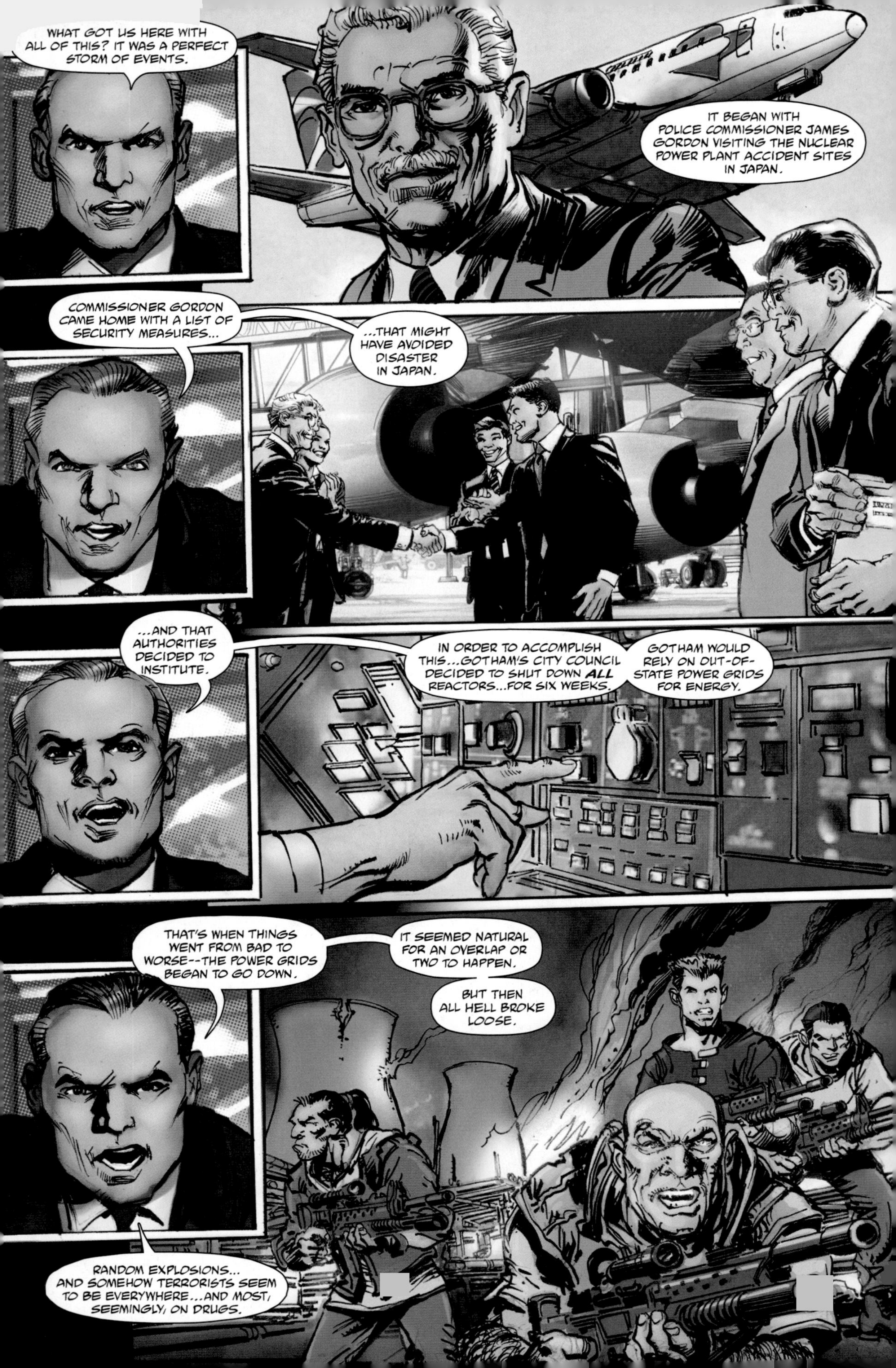
WHAT GOT US HERE WITH ALL OF THIS? IT WAS A PERFECT STORM OF EVENTS.
IT BEGAN WITH POLICE COMMISSIONER JAMES GORDON VISITING THE NUCLEAR POWER PLANT ACCIDENT SITES IN JAPAN.
COMMISSIONER GORDON CAME HOME WITH A LIST OF SECURITY MEASURES...
...THAT MIGHT HAVE AVOIDED DISASTER IN JAPAN.
...AND THAT AUTHORITIES DECIDED TO INSTITUTE.
IN ORDER TO ACCOMPLISH THIS...GOTHAM'S CITY COUNCIL DECIDED TO SHUT DOWN ALL REACTORS...FOR SIX WEEKS.
GOTHAM WOULD RELY ON OUT-OF-STATE POWER GRIDS FOR ENERGY.
THAT'S WHEN THINGS WENT FROM BAD TO WORSE--THE POWER GRIDS BEGAN TO GO DOWN.
IT SEEMED NATURAL FOR AN OVERLAP OR TWO TO HAPPEN.
BUT THEN ALL HELL BROKE LOOSE.
RANDOM EXPLOSIONS... AND SOMEHOW TERRORISTS SEEM TO BE EVERYWHERE...AND MOST, SEEMINGLY, ON DRUGS.

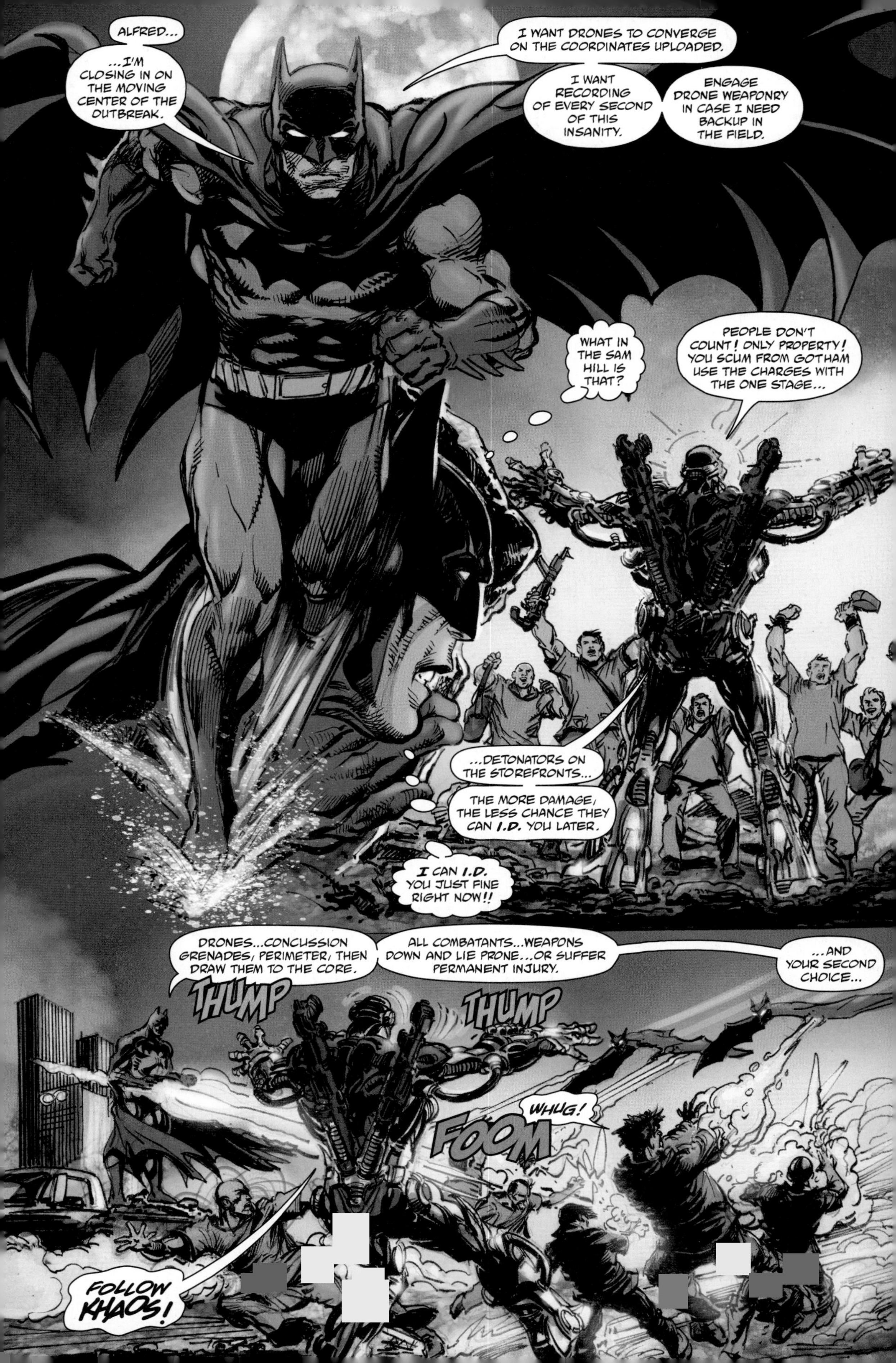
ALFRED...
...I'M CLOSING IN ON THE MOVING CENTER OF THE OUTBREAK.
I WANT DRONES TO CONVERGE ON THE COORDINATES UPLOADED.
I WANT RECORDING OF EVERY SECOND OF THIS INSANITY.
ENGAGE DRONE WEAPONRY IN CASE I NEED BACKUP IN THE FIELD.
WHAT IN THE SAM HILL IS THAT?
PEOPLE DON'T COUNT! ONLY PROPERTY! YOU SCUM FROM GOTHAM USE THE CHARGES WITH THE ONE STAGE...
...DETONATORS ON THE STOREFRONTS...
THE MORE DAMAGE, THE LESS CHANCE THEY CAN I.D. YOU LATER.
I CAN I.D. YOU JUST FINE RIGHT NOW!!
DRONES...CONCUSSION GRENADES, PERIMETER, THEN DRAW THEM TO THE CORE.
ALL COMBATANTS...WEAPONS DOWN AND LIE PRONE...OR SUFFER PERMANENT INJURY.
...AND YOUR SECOND CHOICE...
THUMP
THUMP
WHUG!
FOOM
FOLLOW KHAOS!

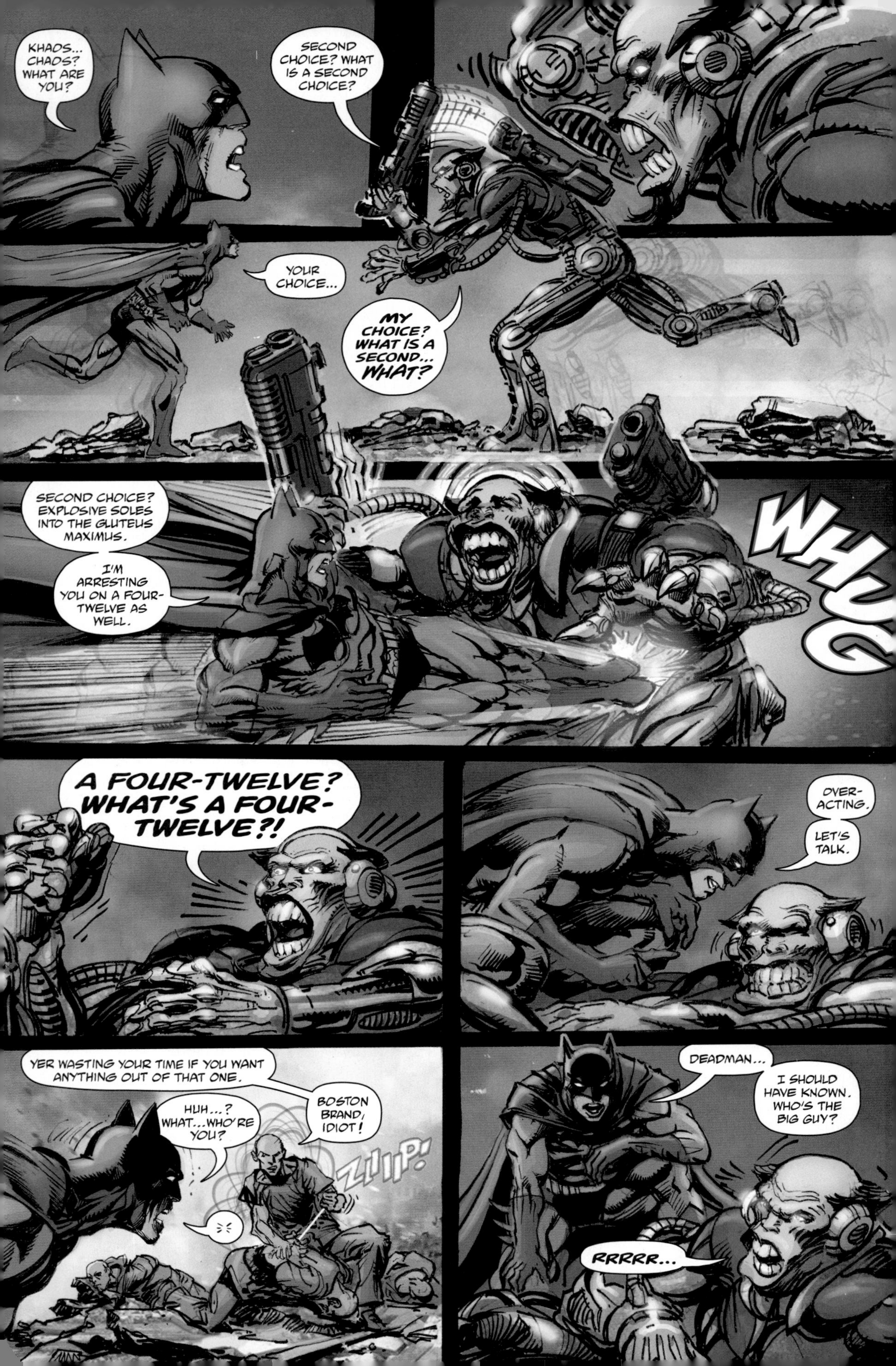
KHAOS... CHAOS? WHAT ARE YOU?
SECOND CHOICE? WHAT IS A SECOND CHOICE?
YOUR CHOICE...
MY CHOICE? WHAT IS A SECOND... WHAT?
SECOND CHOICE? EXPLOSIVE SOLES INTO THE GLUTEUS MAXIMUS.
I'M ARRESTING YOU ON A FOUR-TWELVE AS WELL.
WHUG
A FOUR-TWELVE? WHAT'S A FOUR-TWELVE?!
OVER-ACTING.
LET'S TALK.
YER WASTING YOUR TIME IF YOU WANT ANYTHING OUT OF THAT ONE.
HUH...? WHAT...WHO'RE YOU?
BOSTON BRAND, IDIOT!
ZIIIP!
DEADMAN...
I SHOULD HAVE KNOWN. WHO'S THE BIG GUY?
RRRRR...

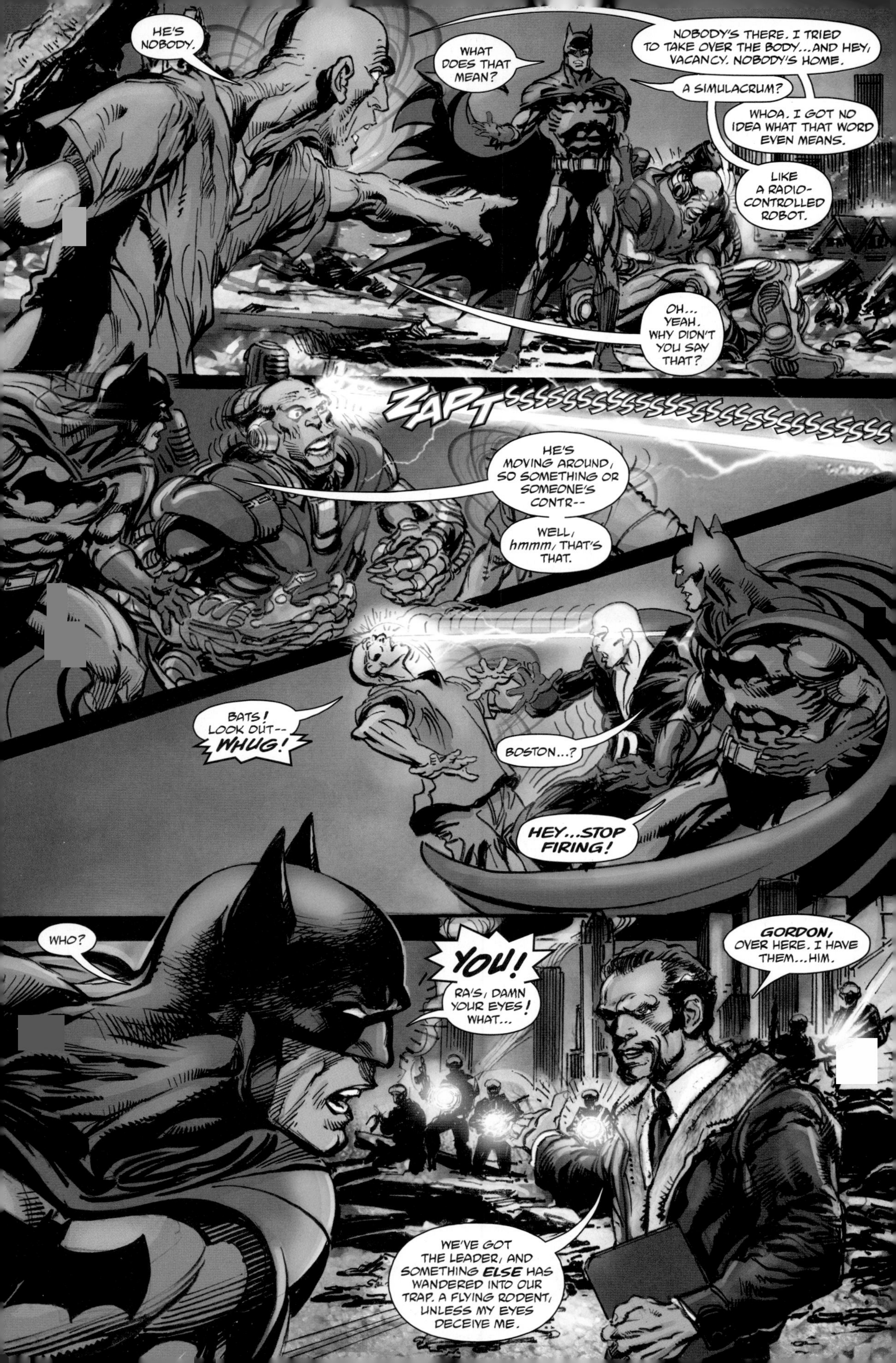
HE'S NOBODY.
WHAT DOES THAT MEAN?
NOBODY'S THERE. I TRIED TO TAKE OVER THE BODY...AND HEY, VACANCY. NOBODY'S HOME.
A SIMULACRUM?
WHOA. I GOT NO IDEA WHAT THAT WORD EVEN MEANS.
LIKE A RADIO-CONTROLLED ROBOT.
OH... YEAH. WHY DIDN'T YOU SAY THAT?
ZAPT SSSSSSSSSSSSSSSSSSSSSSSSSS
HE'S MOVING AROUND, SO SOMETHING OR SOMEONE'S CONTR--
WELL, *hmmm*, THAT'S THAT.
BATS! LOOK OUT-- **WHUG!**
BOSTON...?
HEY...STOP FIRING!
WHO?
YOU!
RA'S, DAMN YOUR EYES! WHAT...
GORDON, OVER HERE. I HAVE THEM...HIM.
WE'VE GOT THE LEADER, AND SOMETHING **ELSE** HAS WANDERED INTO OUR TRAP. A FLYING RODENT, UNLESS MY EYES DECEIVE ME.

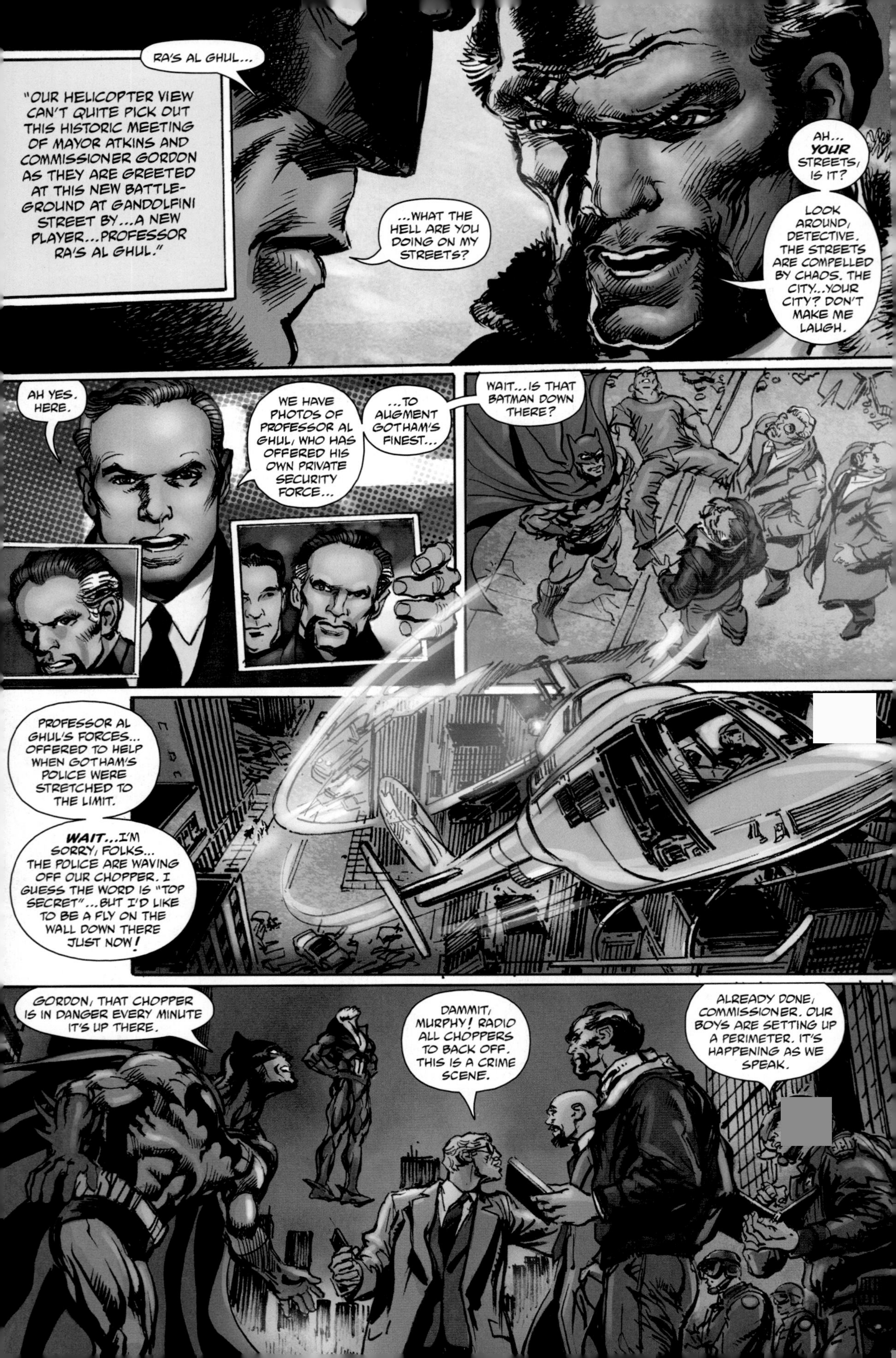
RA'S AL GHUL...
"OUR HELICOPTER VIEW CAN'T QUITE PICK OUT THIS HISTORIC MEETING OF MAYOR ATKINS AND COMMISSIONER GORDON AS THEY ARE GREETED AT THIS NEW BATTLE-GROUND AT GANDOLFINI STREET BY...A NEW PLAYER...PROFESSOR RA'S AL GHUL."
...WHAT THE HELL ARE YOU DOING ON MY STREETS?
AH... YOUR STREETS, IS IT?
LOOK AROUND, DETECTIVE. THE STREETS ARE COMPELLED BY CHAOS. THE CITY...YOUR CITY? DON'T MAKE ME LAUGH.
AH YES. HERE.
WE HAVE PHOTOS OF PROFESSOR AL GHUL, WHO HAS OFFERED HIS OWN PRIVATE SECURITY FORCE...
...TO AUGMENT GOTHAM'S FINEST...
WAIT...IS THAT BATMAN DOWN THERE?
PROFESSOR AL GHUL'S FORCES... OFFERED TO HELP WHEN GOTHAM'S POLICE WERE STRETCHED TO THE LIMIT.
WAIT...I'M SORRY, FOLKS... THE POLICE ARE WAVING OFF OUR CHOPPER. I GUESS THE WORD IS "TOP SECRET"...BUT I'D LIKE TO BE A FLY ON THE WALL DOWN THERE JUST NOW!
GORDON, THAT CHOPPER IS IN DANGER EVERY MINUTE IT'S UP THERE.
DAMMIT, MURPHY! RADIO ALL CHOPPERS TO BACK OFF. THIS IS A CRIME SCENE.
ALREADY DONE, COMMISSIONER. OUR BOYS ARE SETTING UP A PERIMETER. IT'S HAPPENING AS WE SPEAK.

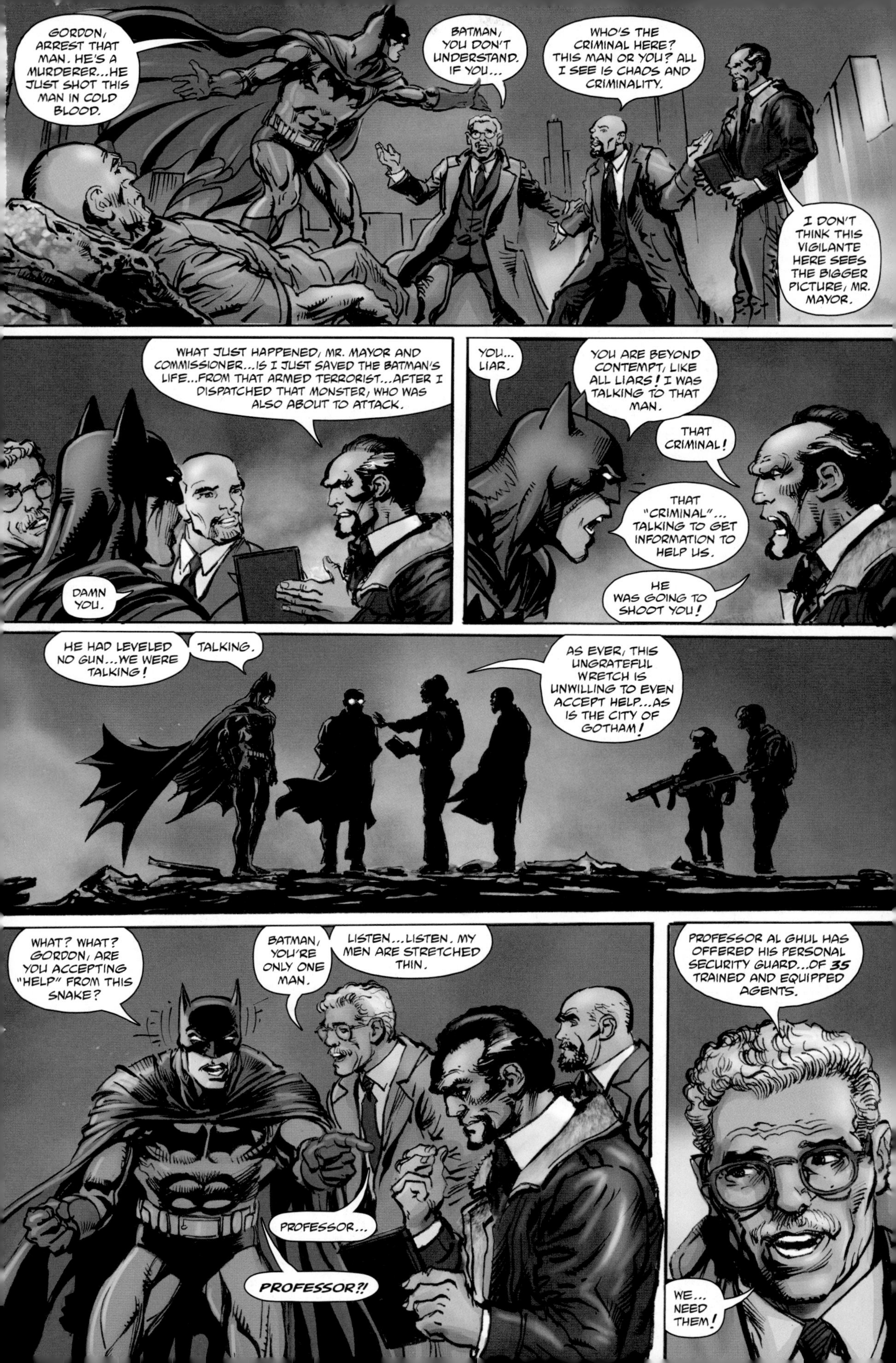
GORDON, ARREST THAT MAN. HE'S A MURDERER...HE JUST SHOT THIS MAN IN COLD BLOOD.
BATMAN, YOU DON'T UNDERSTAND. IF YOU...
WHO'S THE CRIMINAL HERE? THIS MAN OR YOU? ALL I SEE IS CHAOS AND CRIMINALITY.
I DON'T THINK THIS VIGILANTE HERE SEES THE BIGGER PICTURE, MR. MAYOR.
WHAT JUST HAPPENED, MR. MAYOR AND COMMISSIONER...IS I JUST SAVED THE BATMAN'S LIFE...FROM THAT ARMED TERRORIST...AFTER I DISPATCHED THAT MONSTER, WHO WAS ALSO ABOUT TO ATTACK.
DAMN YOU.
YOU... LIAR.
YOU ARE BEYOND CONTEMPT, LIKE ALL LIARS! I WAS TALKING TO THAT MAN.
THAT CRIMINAL!
THAT "CRIMINAL"... TALKING TO GET INFORMATION TO HELP US.
HE WAS GOING TO SHOOT YOU!
HE HAD LEVELED NO GUN...WE WERE TALKING!
TALKING.
AS EVER, THIS UNGRATEFUL WRETCH IS UNWILLING TO EVEN ACCEPT HELP...AS IS THE CITY OF GOTHAM!
WHAT? WHAT? GORDON, ARE YOU ACCEPTING "HELP" FROM THIS SNAKE?
BATMAN, YOU'RE ONLY ONE MAN.
LISTEN...LISTEN. MY MEN ARE STRETCHED THIN.
PROFESSOR...
PROFESSOR?!
PROFESSOR AL GHUL HAS OFFERED HIS PERSONAL SECURITY GUARD...OF 35 TRAINED AND EQUIPPED AGENTS.
WE... NEED THEM!

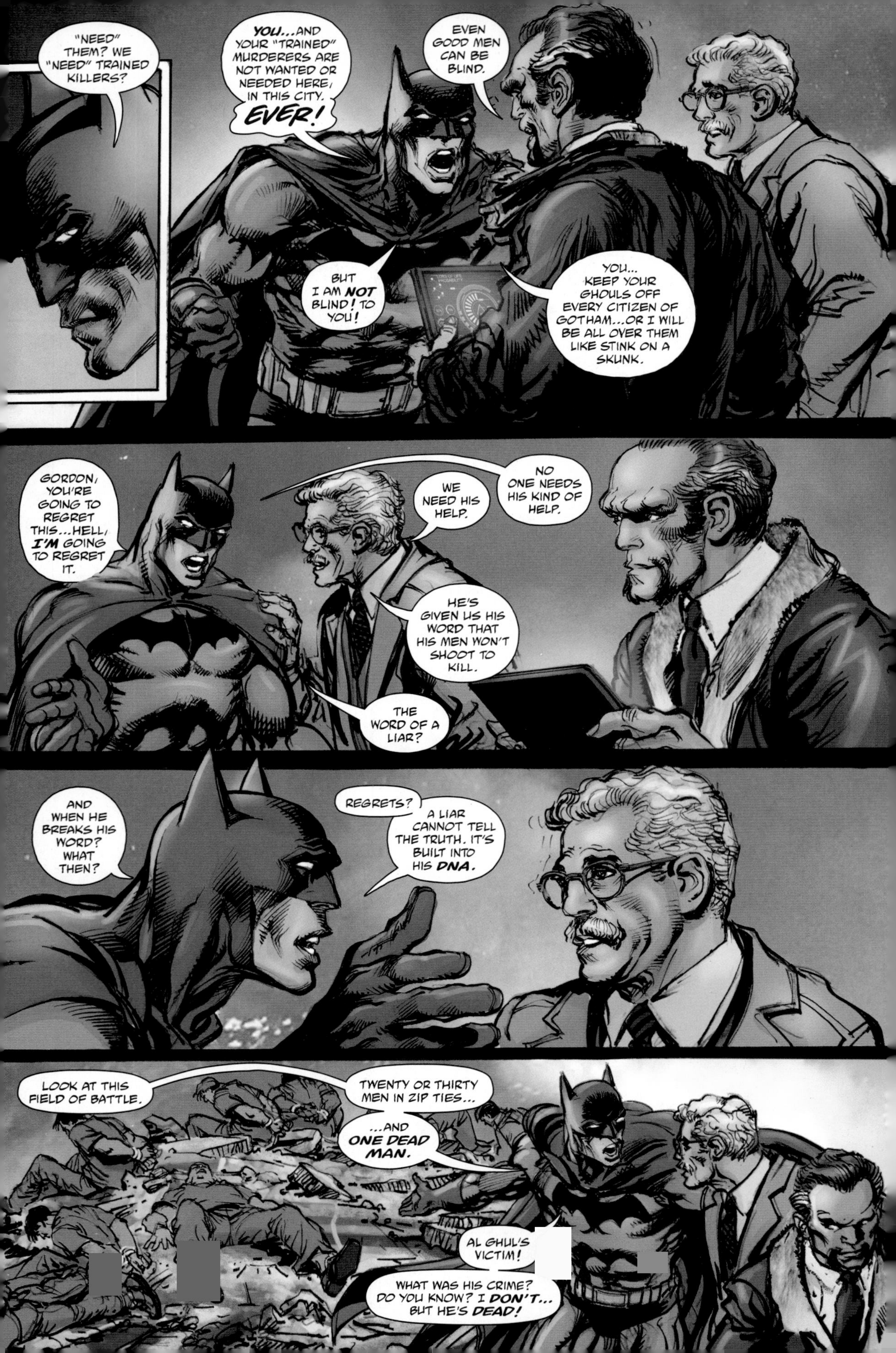
"NEED" THEM? WE "NEED" TRAINED KILLERS?
YOU...AND YOUR "TRAINED" MURDERERS ARE NOT WANTED OR NEEDED HERE, IN THIS CITY. EVER!
EVEN GOOD MEN CAN BE BLIND.
BUT I AM NOT BLIND! TO YOU!
YOU... KEEP YOUR GHOULS OFF EVERY CITIZEN OF GOTHAM...OR I WILL BE ALL OVER THEM LIKE STINK ON A SKUNK.
GORDON, YOU'RE GOING TO REGRET THIS...HELL, I'M GOING TO REGRET IT.
WE NEED HIS HELP.
NO ONE NEEDS HIS KIND OF HELP.
HE'S GIVEN US HIS WORD THAT HIS MEN WON'T SHOOT TO KILL.
THE WORD OF A LIAR?
AND WHEN HE BREAKS HIS WORD? WHAT THEN?
REGRETS?
A LIAR CANNOT TELL THE TRUTH. IT'S BUILT INTO HIS DNA.
LOOK AT THIS FIELD OF BATTLE.
TWENTY OR THIRTY MEN IN ZIP TIES...
...AND ONE DEAD MAN.
AL GHUL'S VICTIM!
WHAT WAS HIS CRIME? DO YOU KNOW? I DON'T... BUT HE'S DEAD!

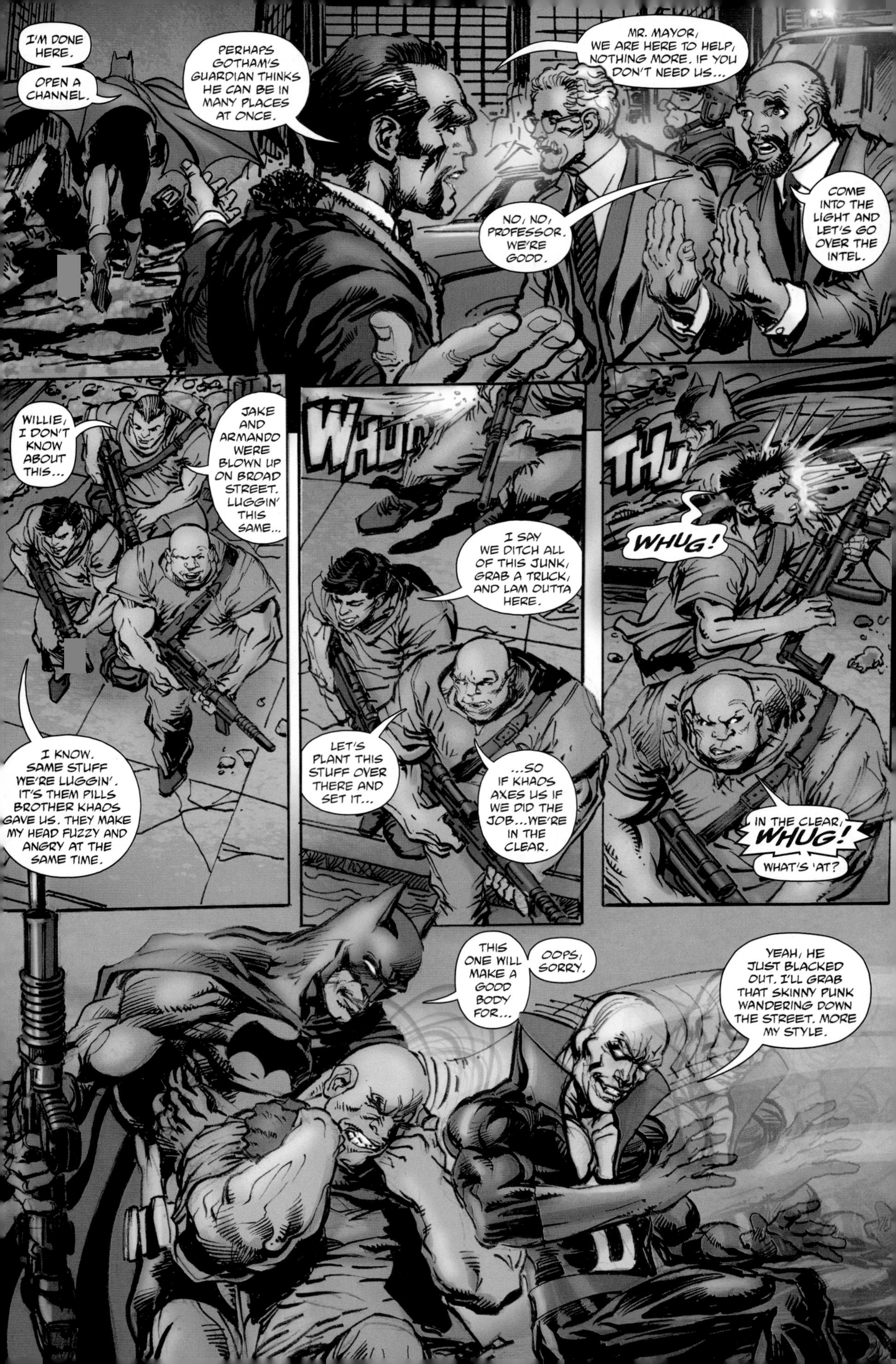
I'M DONE HERE.
OPEN A CHANNEL.
PERHAPS GOTHAM'S GUARDIAN THINKS HE CAN BE IN MANY PLACES AT ONCE.
MR. MAYOR, WE ARE HERE TO HELP, NOTHING MORE. IF YOU DON'T NEED US...
NO, NO, PROFESSOR. WE'RE GOOD.
COME INTO THE LIGHT AND LET'S GO OVER THE INTEL.
WILLIE, I DON'T KNOW ABOUT THIS...
JAKE AND ARMANDO WERE BLOWN UP ON BROAD STREET. LUGGIN' THIS SAME...
I KNOW. SAME STUFF WE'RE LUGGIN'. IT'S THEM PILLS BROTHER KHAOS GAVE US. THEY MAKE MY HEAD FUZZY AND ANGRY AT THE SAME TIME.
WHU
I SAY WE DITCH ALL OF THIS JUNK, GRAB A TRUCK, AND LAM OUTTA HERE.
LET'S PLANT THIS STUFF OVER THERE AND SET IT...
...SO IF KHAOS AXES US IF WE DID THE JOB...WE'RE IN THE CLEAR.
THU
WHUG!
IN THE CLEAR, WHUG! WHAT'S 'AT?
THIS ONE WILL MAKE A GOOD BODY FOR...
OOPS, SORRY.
YEAH, HE JUST BLACKED OUT. I'LL GRAB THAT SKINNY PUNK WANDERING DOWN THE STREET. MORE MY STYLE.

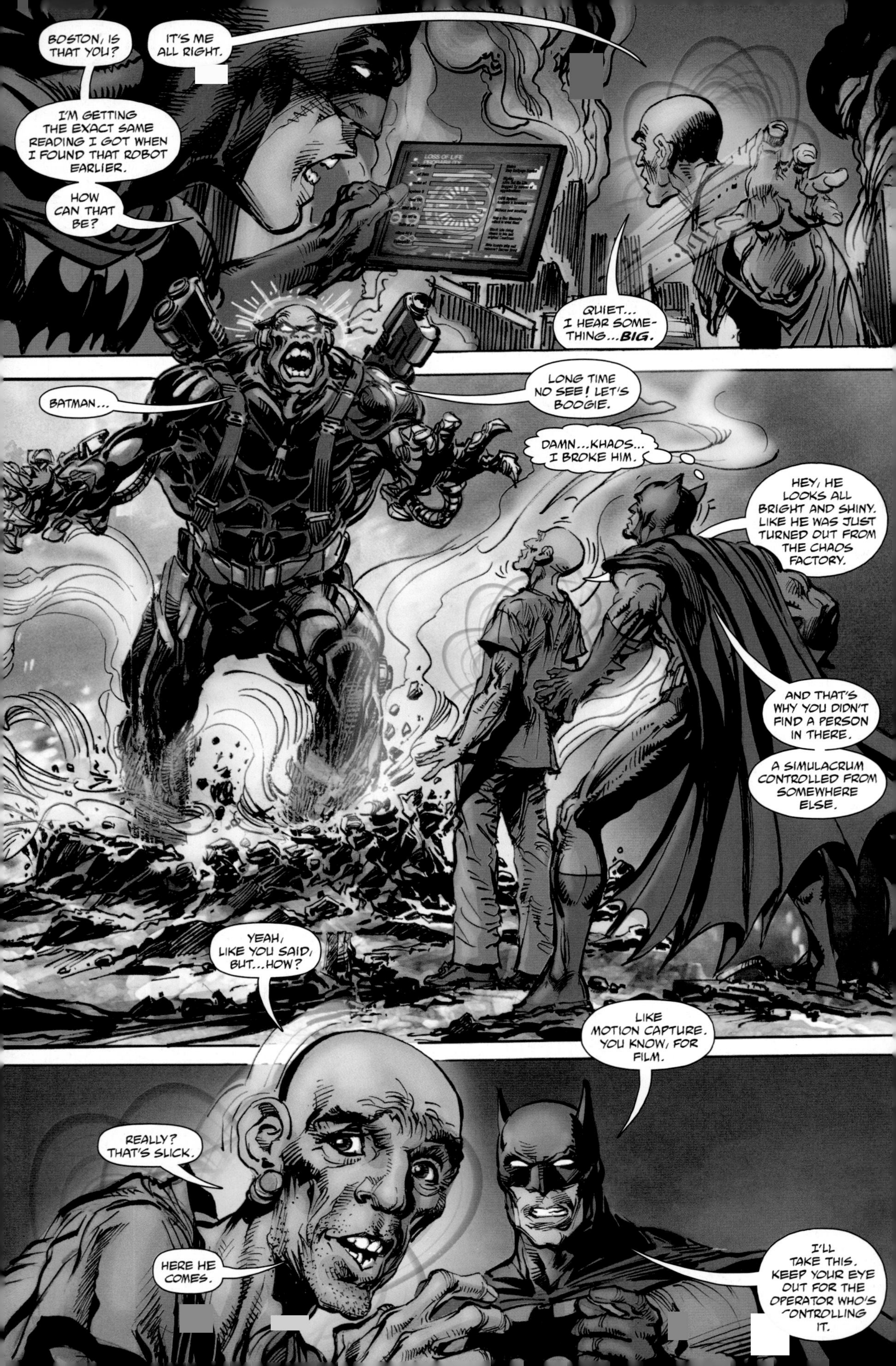
BOSTON, IS THAT YOU?
IT'S ME ALL RIGHT.
I'M GETTING THE EXACT SAME READING I GOT WHEN I FOUND THAT ROBOT EARLIER.
HOW CAN THAT BE?
QUIET... I HEAR SOME-THING...BIG.
BATMAN...
LONG TIME NO SEE! LET'S BOOGIE.
DAMN...KHAOS... I BROKE HIM.
HEY, HE LOOKS ALL BRIGHT AND SHINY. LIKE HE WAS JUST TURNED OUT FROM THE CHAOS FACTORY.
AND THAT'S WHY YOU DIDN'T FIND A PERSON IN THERE.
A SIMULACRUM CONTROLLED FROM SOMEWHERE ELSE.
YEAH, LIKE YOU SAID, BUT...HOW?
LIKE MOTION CAPTURE. YOU KNOW, FOR FILM.
REALLY? THAT'S SLICK.
HERE HE COMES.
I'LL TAKE THIS. KEEP YOUR EYE OUT FOR THE OPERATOR WHO'S CONTROLLING IT.

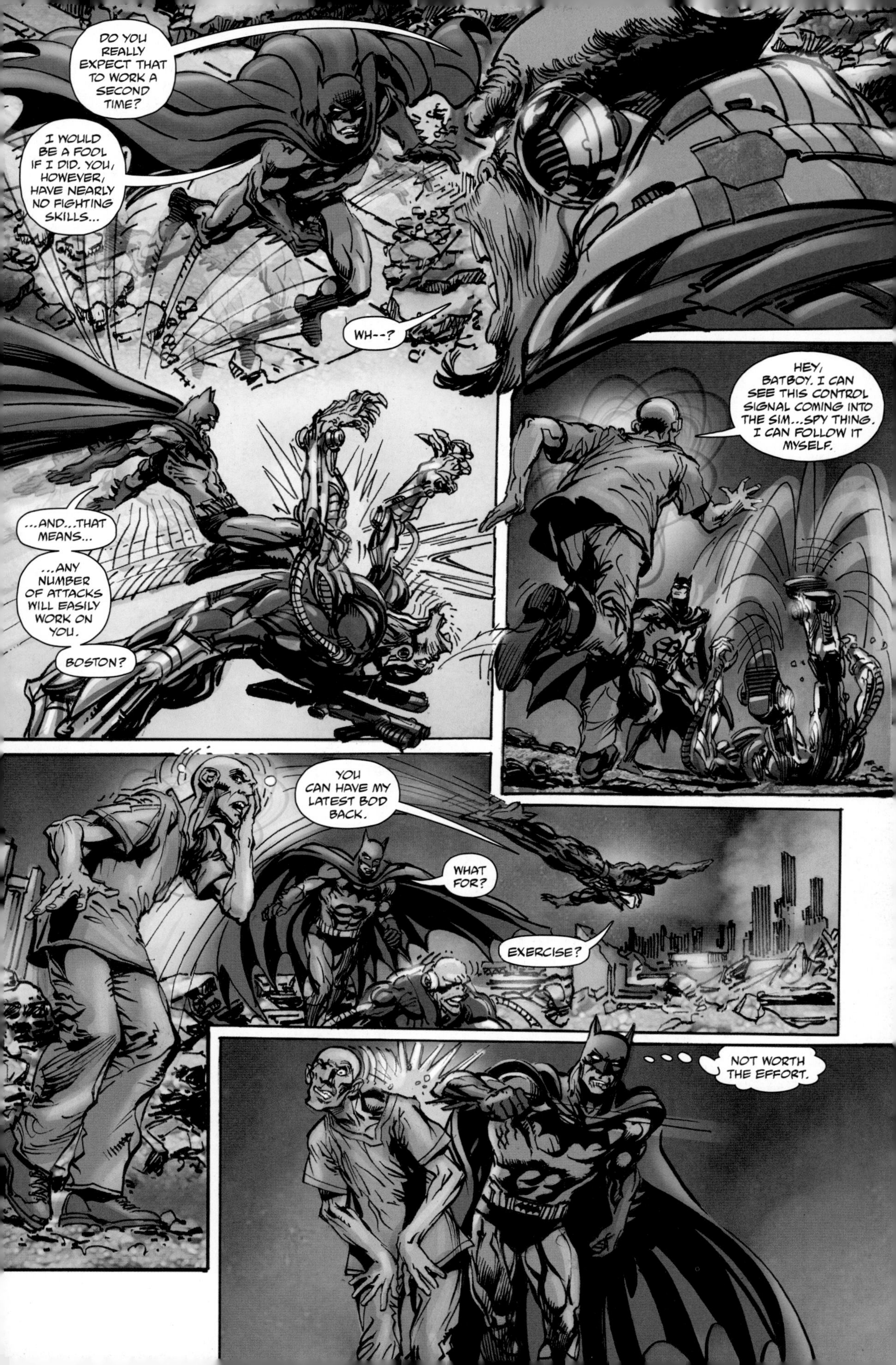

DO YOU REALLY EXPECT THAT TO WORK A SECOND TIME?
I WOULD BE A FOOL IF I DID. YOU, HOWEVER, HAVE NEARLY NO FIGHTING SKILLS...
WH--?
...AND...THAT MEANS...
...ANY NUMBER OF ATTACKS WILL EASILY WORK ON YOU.
BOSTON?
HEY, BATBOY. I CAN SEE THIS CONTROL SIGNAL COMING INTO THE SIM...SPY THING. I CAN FOLLOW IT MYSELF.
YOU CAN HAVE MY LATEST BOD BACK.
WHAT FOR?
EXERCISE?
NOT WORTH THE EFFORT.

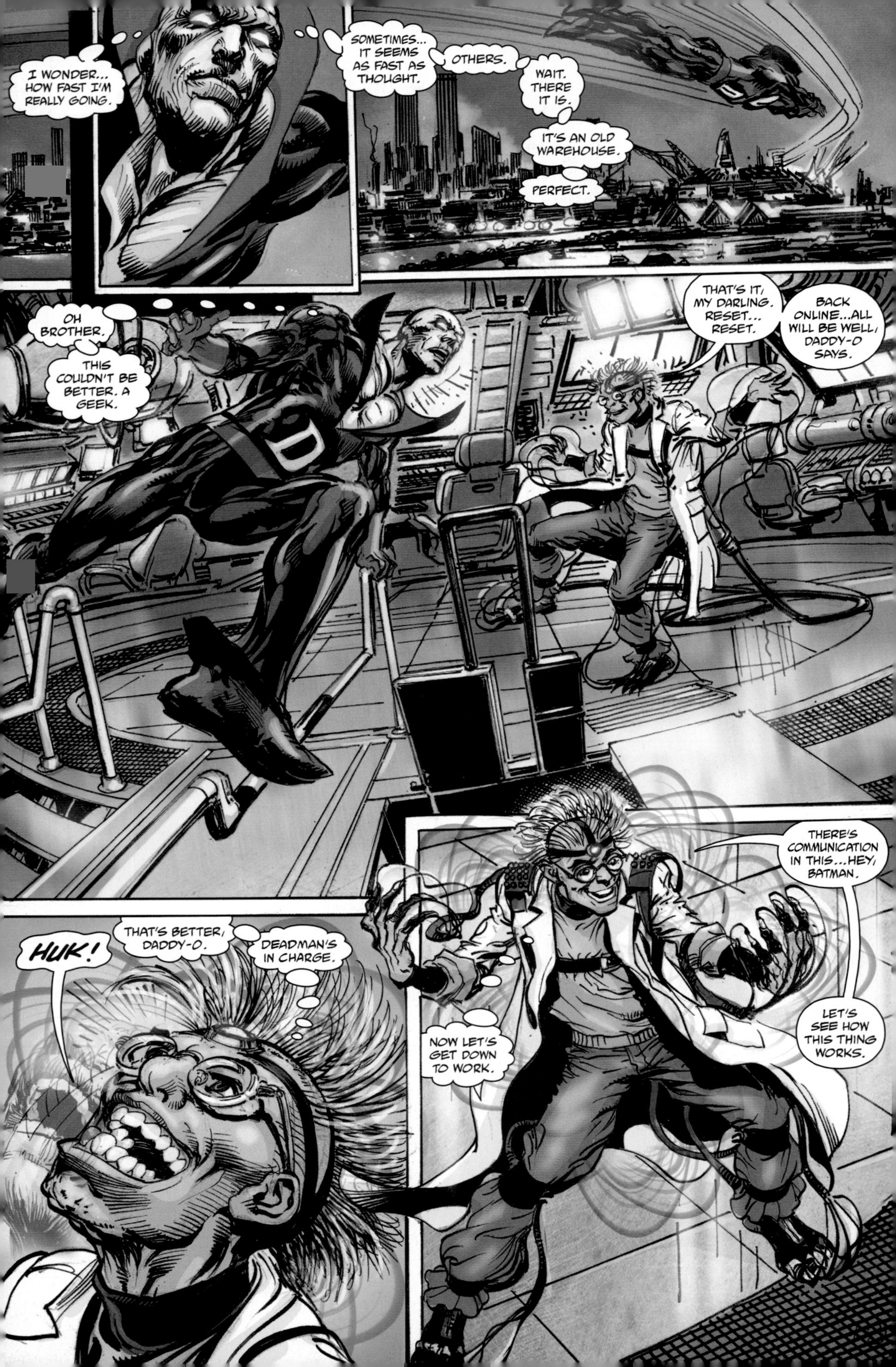
I WONDER... HOW FAST I'M REALLY GOING.
SOMETIMES... IT SEEMS AS FAST AS THOUGHT.
OTHERS.
WAIT. THERE IT IS.
IT'S AN OLD WAREHOUSE.
PERFECT.
OH BROTHER.
THIS COULDN'T BE BETTER. A GEEK.
THAT'S IT, MY DARLING. RESET... RESET.
BACK ONLINE...ALL WILL BE WELL, DADDY-O SAYS.
HUK!
THAT'S BETTER, DADDY-O.
DEADMAN'S IN CHARGE.
NOW LET'S GET DOWN TO WORK.
THERE'S COMMUNICATION IN THIS...HEY, BATMAN.
LET'S SEE HOW THIS THING WORKS.

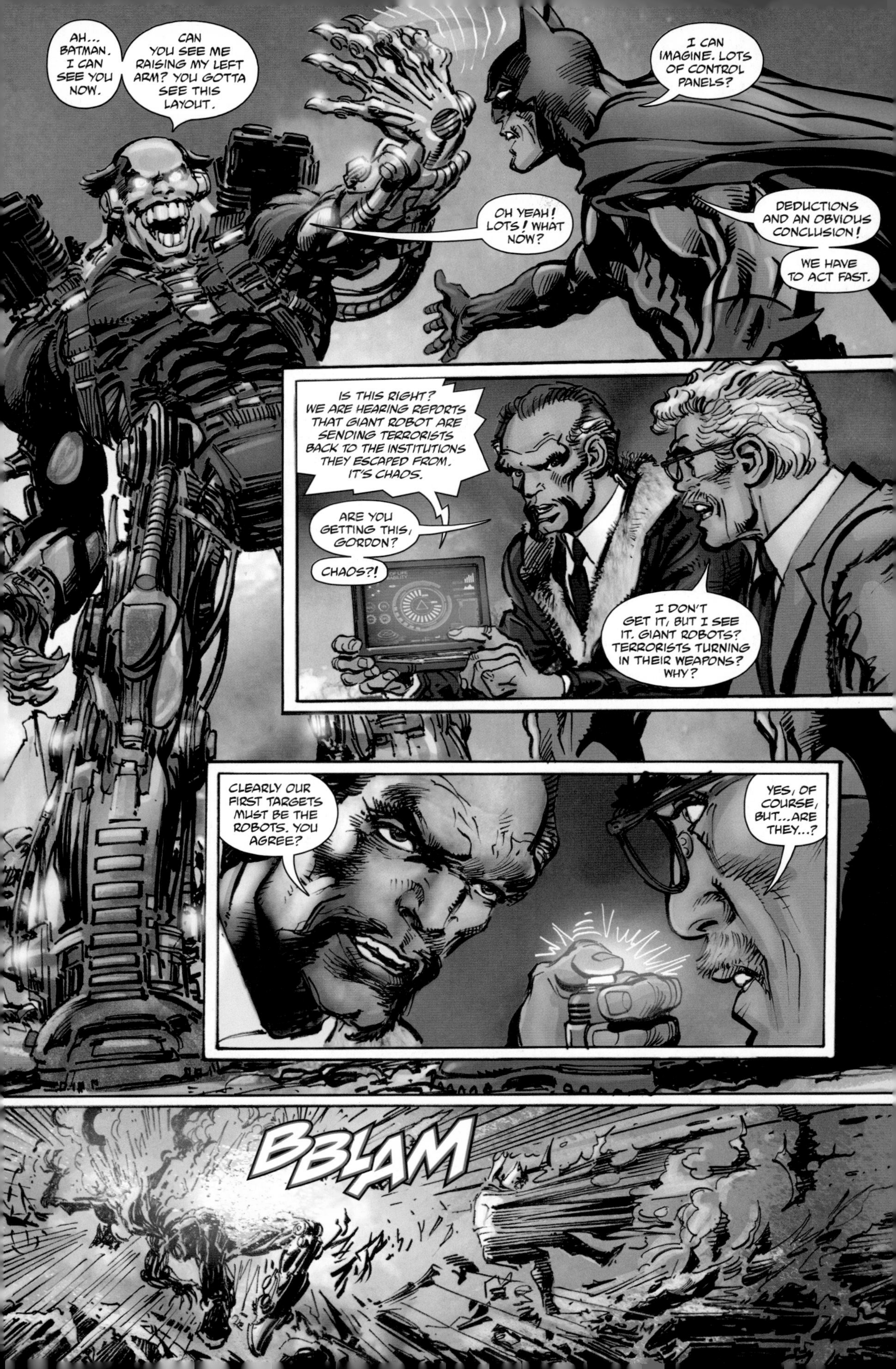
AH... BATMAN. I CAN SEE YOU NOW.
CAN YOU SEE ME RAISING MY LEFT ARM? YOU GOTTA SEE THIS LAYOUT.
I CAN IMAGINE. LOTS OF CONTROL PANELS?
OH YEAH! LOTS! WHAT NOW?
DEDUCTIONS AND AN OBVIOUS CONCLUSION!
WE HAVE TO ACT FAST.
IS THIS RIGHT? WE ARE HEARING REPORTS THAT GIANT ROBOT ARE SENDING TERRORISTS BACK TO THE INSTITUTIONS THEY ESCAPED FROM. IT'S CHAOS.
ARE YOU GETTING THIS, GORDON?
CHAOS?!
I DON'T GET IT, BUT I SEE IT. GIANT ROBOTS? TERRORISTS TURNING IN THEIR WEAPONS? WHY?
CLEARLY OUR FIRST TARGETS MUST BE THE ROBOTS. YOU AGREE?
YES, OF COURSE, BUT...ARE THEY...?
BBLAM

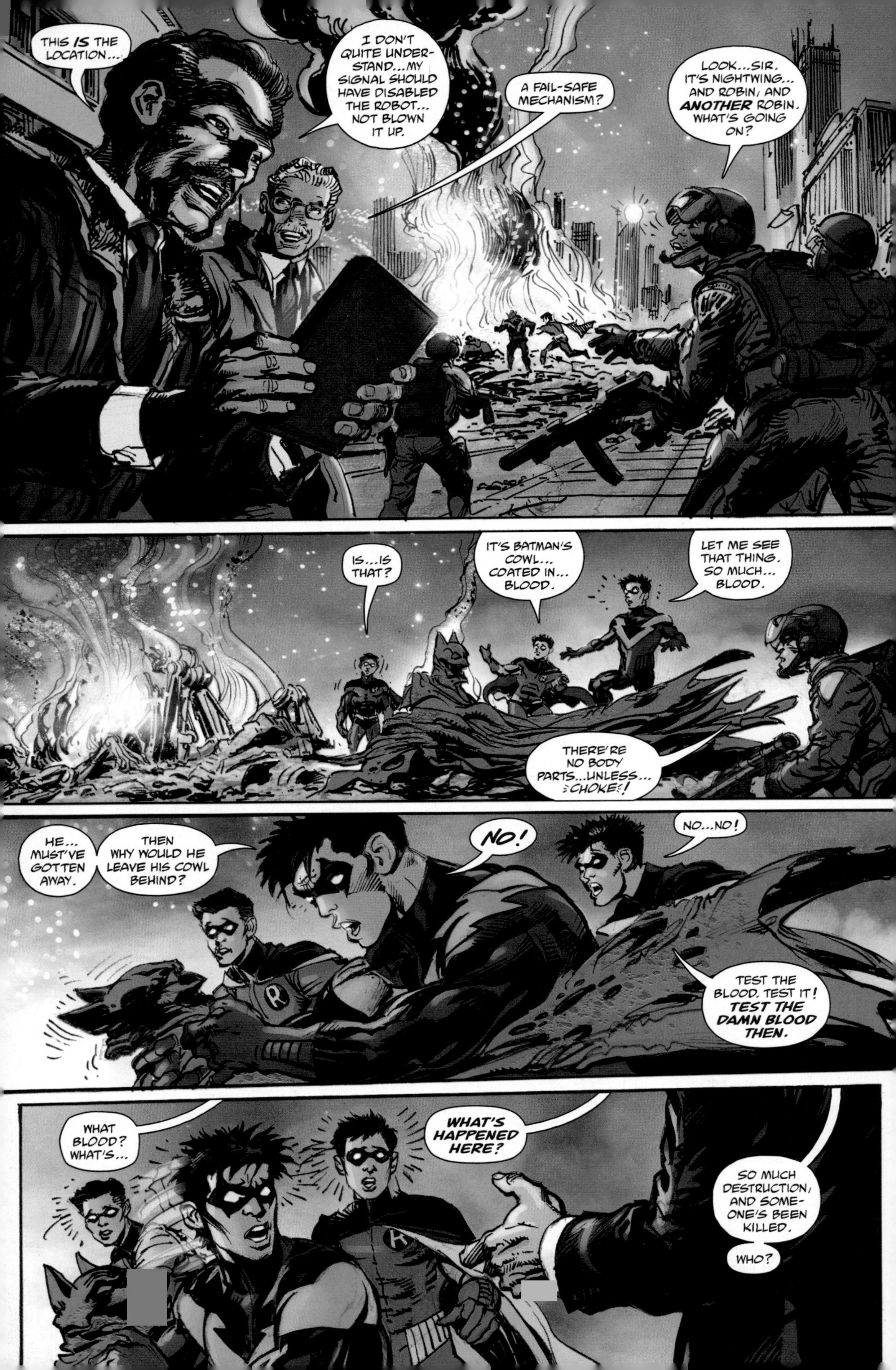
THIS IS THE LOCATION...
I DON'T QUITE UNDER-STAND...MY SIGNAL SHOULD HAVE DISABLED THE ROBOT... NOT BLOWN IT UP.
A FAIL-SAFE MECHANISM?
LOOK...SIR. IT'S NIGHTWING... AND ROBIN, AND ANOTHER ROBIN. WHAT'S GOING ON?
IS...IS THAT?
IT'S BATMAN'S COWL... COATED IN... BLOOD.
LET ME SEE THAT THING. SO MUCH... BLOOD.
THERE'RE NO BODY PARTS...UNLESS... CHOKE!
HE... MUST'VE GOTTEN AWAY.
THEN WHY WOULD HE LEAVE HIS COWL BEHIND?
NO!
NO...NO!
TEST THE BLOOD. TEST IT! TEST THE DAMN BLOOD THEN.
WHAT BLOOD? WHAT'S...
WHAT'S HAPPENED HERE?
SO MUCH DESTRUCTION, AND SOME-ONE'S BEEN KILLED.
WHO?

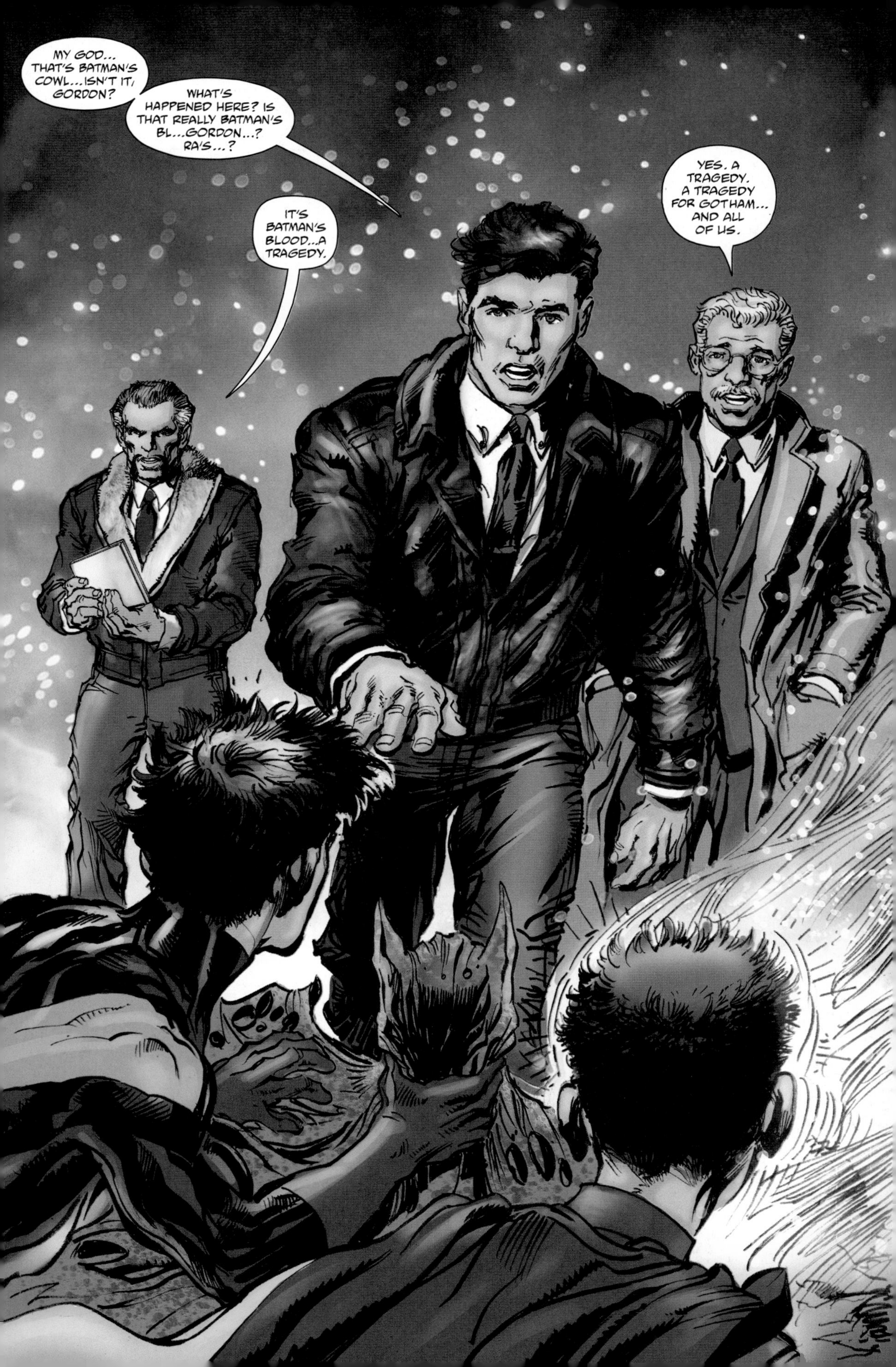
MY GOD... THAT'S BATMAN'S COWL...ISN'T IT, GORDON?
WHAT'S HAPPENED HERE? IS THAT REALLY BATMAN'S BL...GORDON...? RA'S...?
IT'S BATMAN'S BLOOD...A TRAGEDY.
YES. A TRAGEDY. A TRAGEDY FOR GOTHAM... AND ALL OF US.

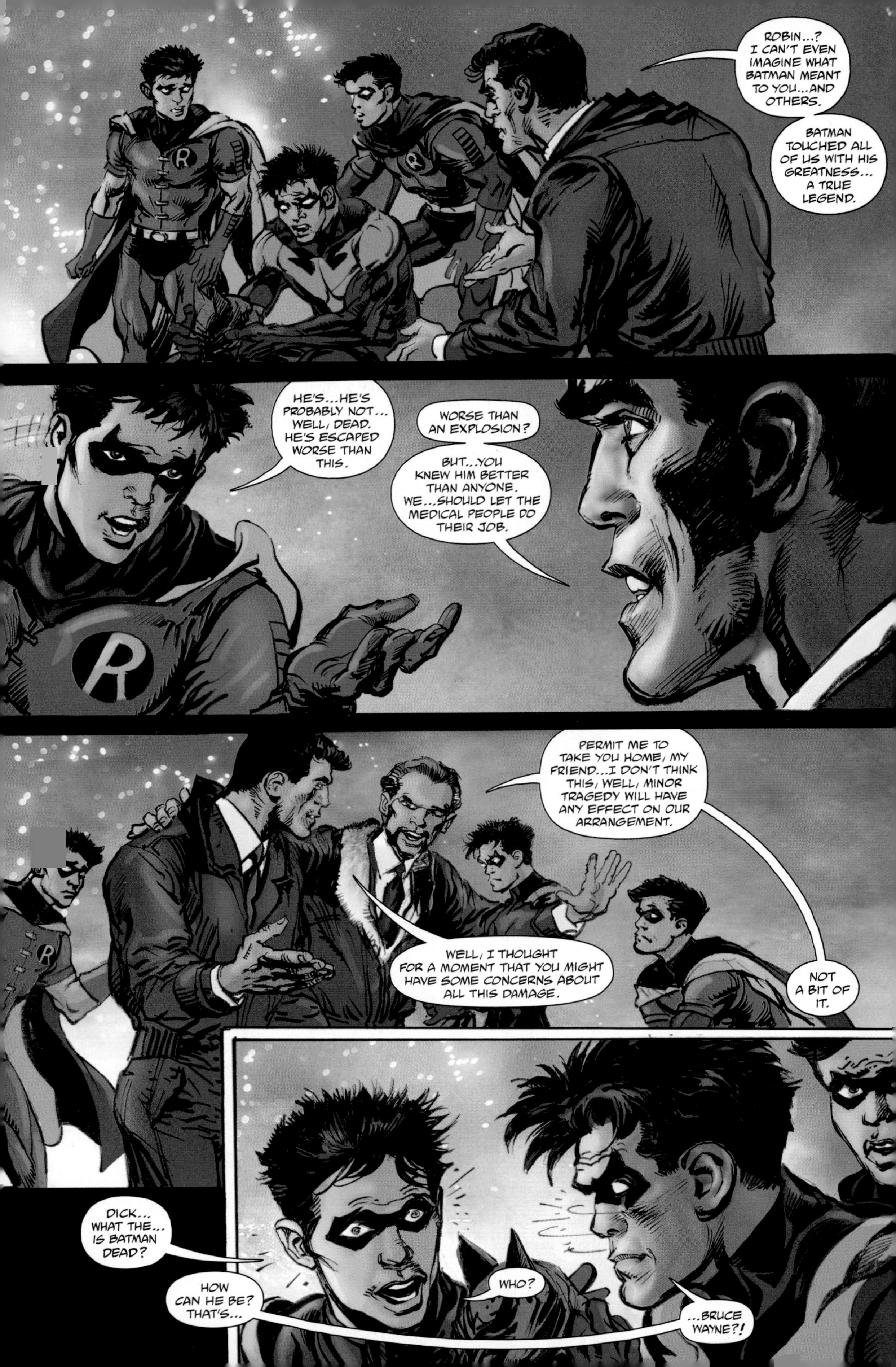
ROBIN...? I CAN'T EVEN IMAGINE WHAT BATMAN MEANT TO YOU...AND OTHERS.
BATMAN TOUCHED ALL OF US WITH HIS GREATNESS... A TRUE LEGEND.
HE'S...HE'S PROBABLY NOT... WELL, DEAD. HE'S ESCAPED WORSE THAN THIS.
WORSE THAN AN EXPLOSION?
BUT...YOU KNEW HIM BETTER THAN ANYONE. WE...SHOULD LET THE MEDICAL PEOPLE DO THEIR JOB.
PERMIT ME TO TAKE YOU HOME, MY FRIEND...I DON'T THINK THIS, WELL, MINOR TRAGEDY WILL HAVE ANY EFFECT ON OUR ARRANGEMENT.
WELL, I THOUGHT FOR A MOMENT THAT YOU MIGHT HAVE SOME CONCERNS ABOUT ALL THIS DAMAGE.
NOT A BIT OF IT.
DICK... WHAT THE... IS BATMAN DEAD?
HOW CAN HE BE? THAT'S...
WHO?
...BRUCE WAYNE?!

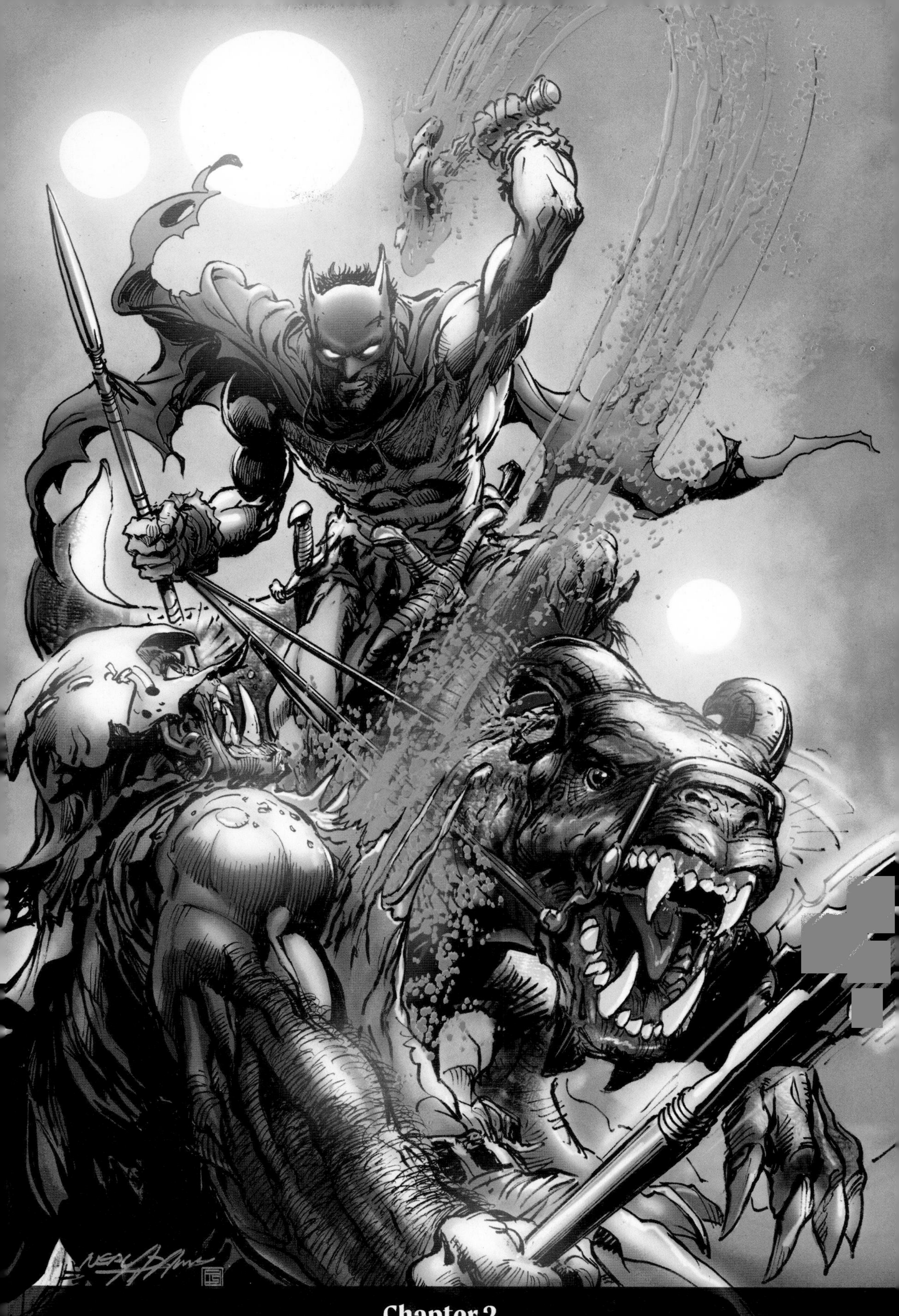

Chapter 2

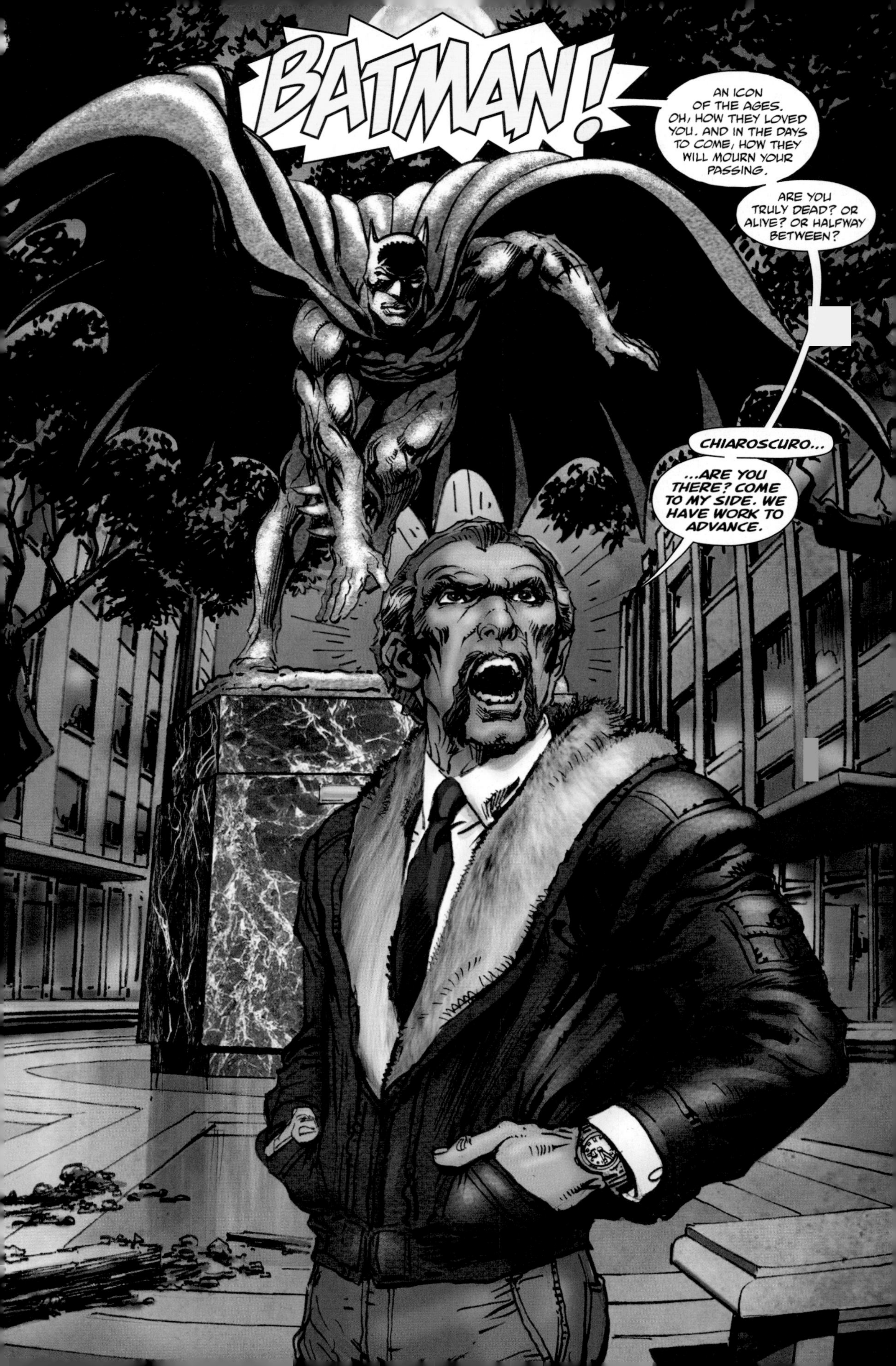
BATMAN!
AN ICON OF THE AGES. OH, HOW THEY LOVED YOU. AND IN THE DAYS TO COME, HOW THEY WILL MOURN YOUR PASSING.
ARE YOU TRULY DEAD? OR ALIVE? OR HALFWAY BETWEEN?
CHIAROSCURO...
...ARE YOU THERE? COME TO MY SIDE. WE HAVE WORK TO ADVANCE.

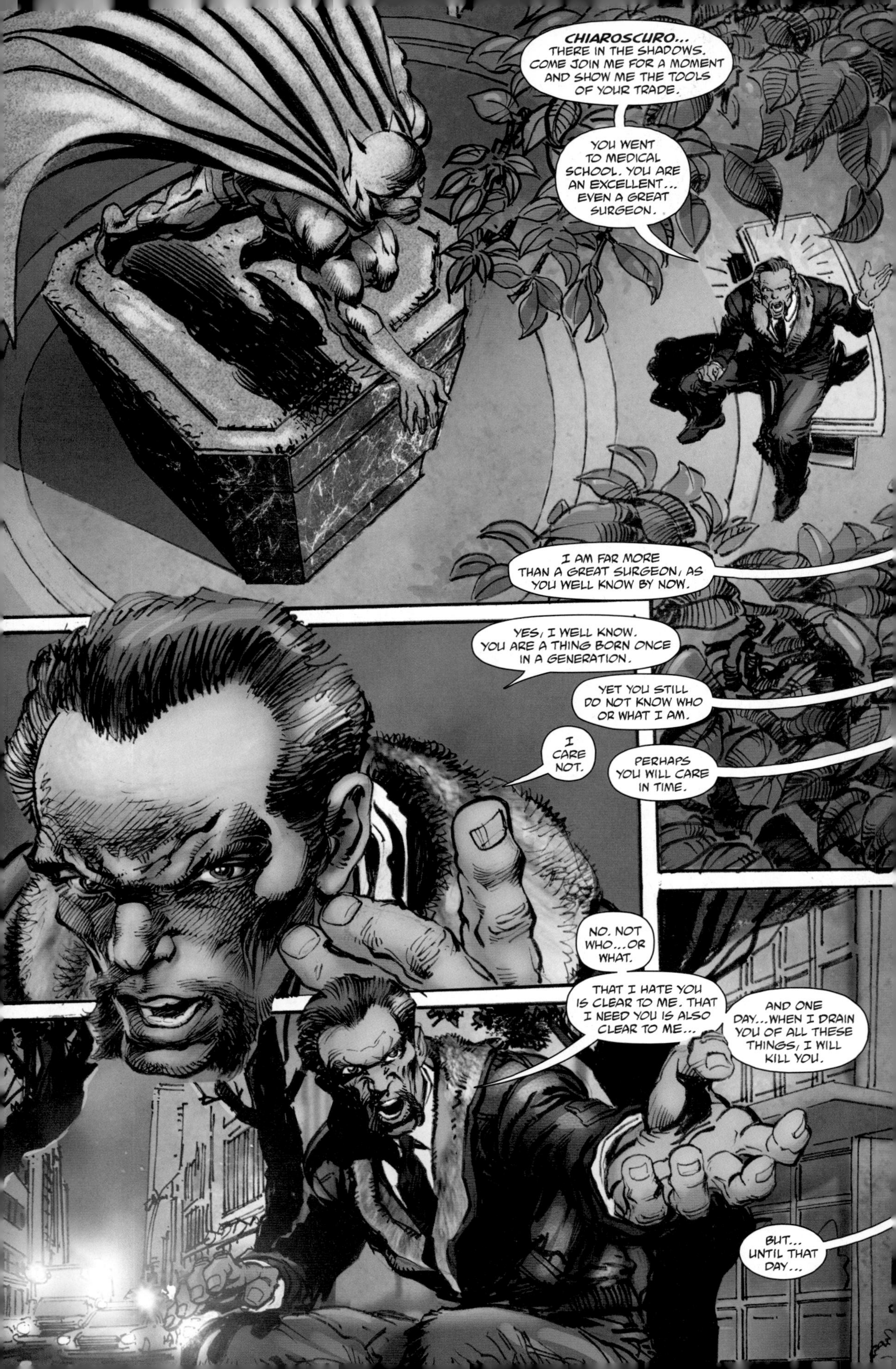

CHIAROSCURO... THERE IN THE SHADOWS. COME JOIN ME FOR A MOMENT AND SHOW ME THE TOOLS OF YOUR TRADE.
YOU WENT TO MEDICAL SCHOOL. YOU ARE AN EXCELLENT... EVEN A GREAT SURGEON.
I AM FAR MORE THAN A GREAT SURGEON, AS YOU WELL KNOW BY NOW.
YES, I WELL KNOW. YOU ARE A THING BORN ONCE IN A GENERATION.
YET YOU STILL DO NOT KNOW WHO OR WHAT I AM.
I CARE NOT.
PERHAPS YOU WILL CARE IN TIME.
NO. NOT WHO...OR WHAT.
THAT I HATE YOU IS CLEAR TO ME. THAT I NEED YOU IS ALSO CLEAR TO ME...
AND ONE DAY...WHEN I DRAIN YOU OF ALL THESE THINGS, I WILL KILL YOU.
BUT... UNTIL THAT DAY...

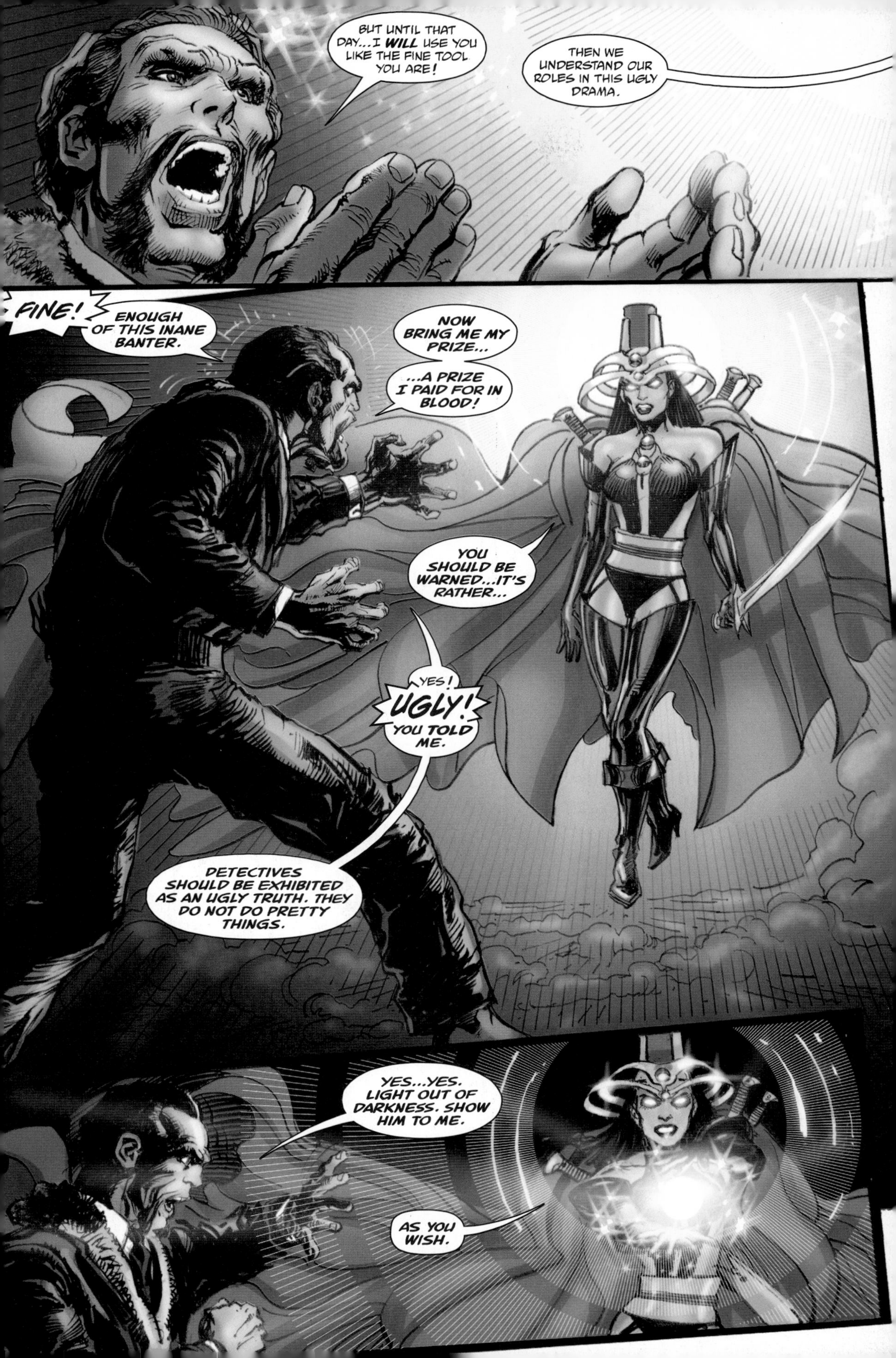
BUT UNTIL THAT DAY...I WILL USE YOU LIKE THE FINE TOOL YOU ARE!
THEN WE UNDERSTAND OUR ROLES IN THIS UGLY DRAMA.
FINE!
ENOUGH OF THIS INANE BANTER.
NOW BRING ME MY PRIZE...
...A PRIZE I PAID FOR IN BLOOD!
YOU SHOULD BE WARNED...IT'S RATHER...
YES!
UGLY!
YOU TOLD ME.
DETECTIVES SHOULD BE EXHIBITED AS AN UGLY TRUTH. THEY DO NOT DO PRETTY THINGS.
YES...YES. LIGHT OUT OF DARKNESS. SHOW HIM TO ME.
AS YOU WISH.

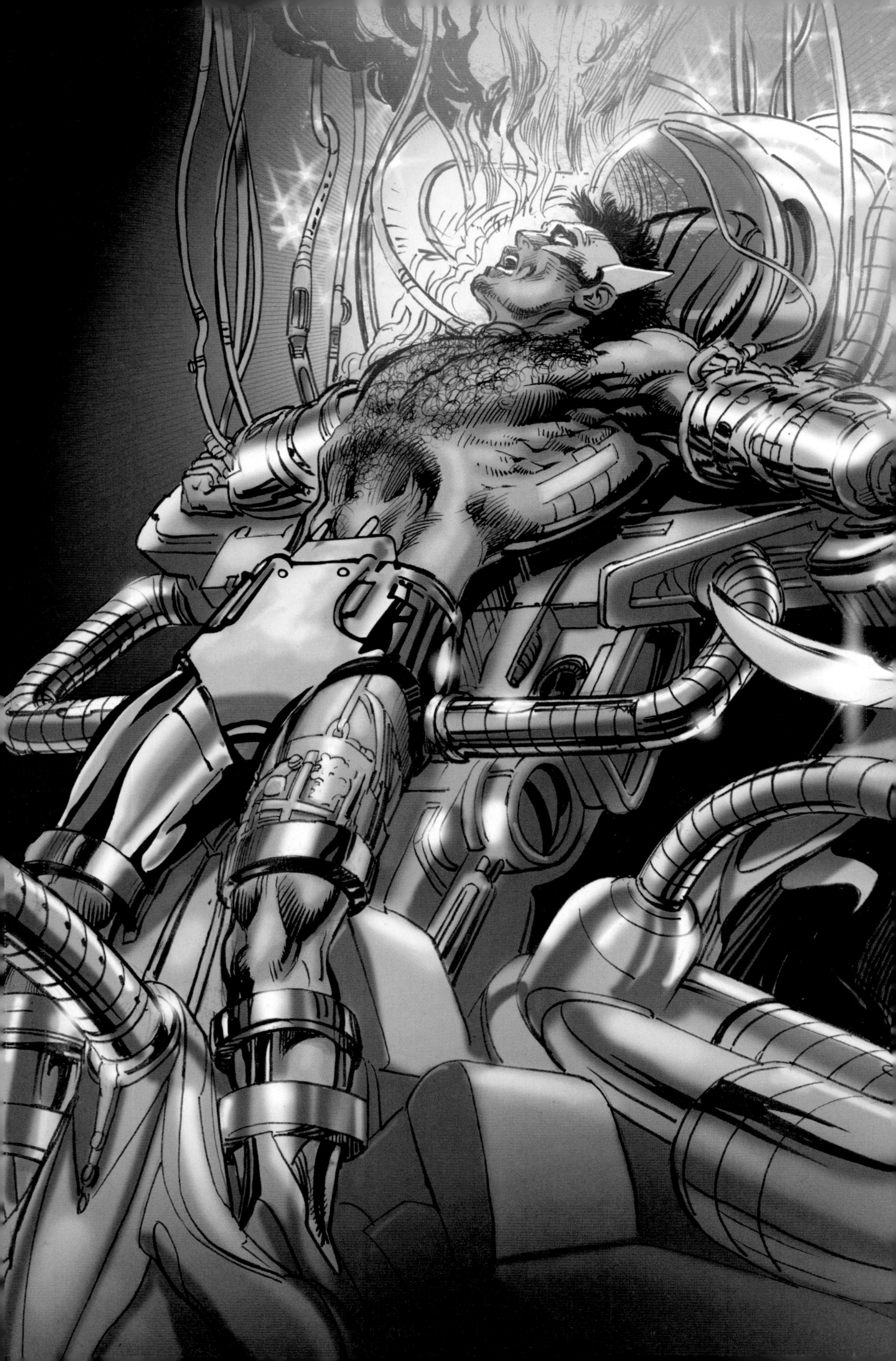

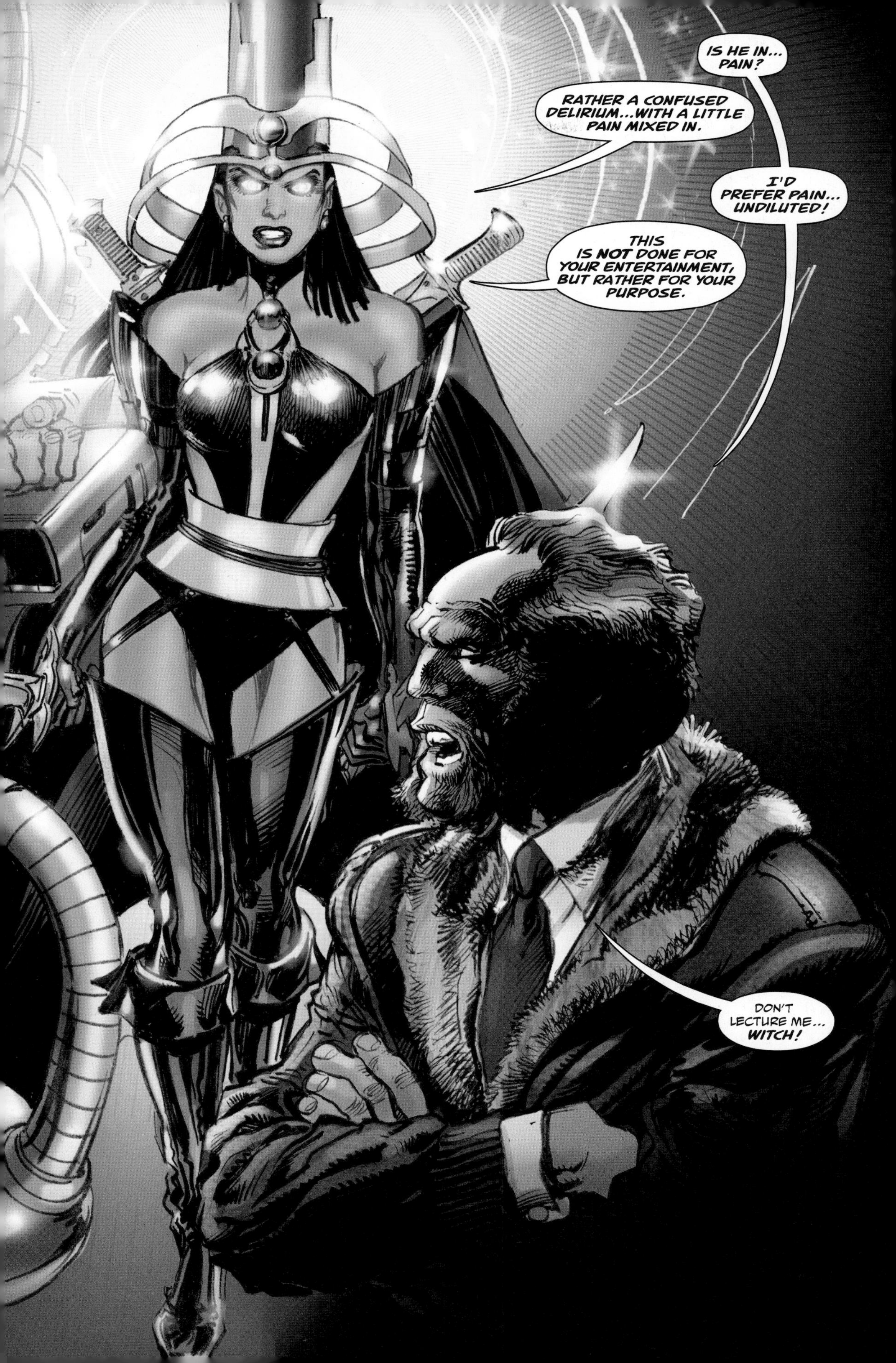
IS HE IN... PAIN?
RATHER A CONFUSED DELIRIUM...WITH A LITTLE PAIN MIXED IN.
I'D PREFER PAIN... UNDILUTED!
THIS IS NOT DONE FOR YOUR ENTERTAINMENT, BUT RATHER FOR YOUR PURPOSE.
DON'T LECTURE ME... WITCH!

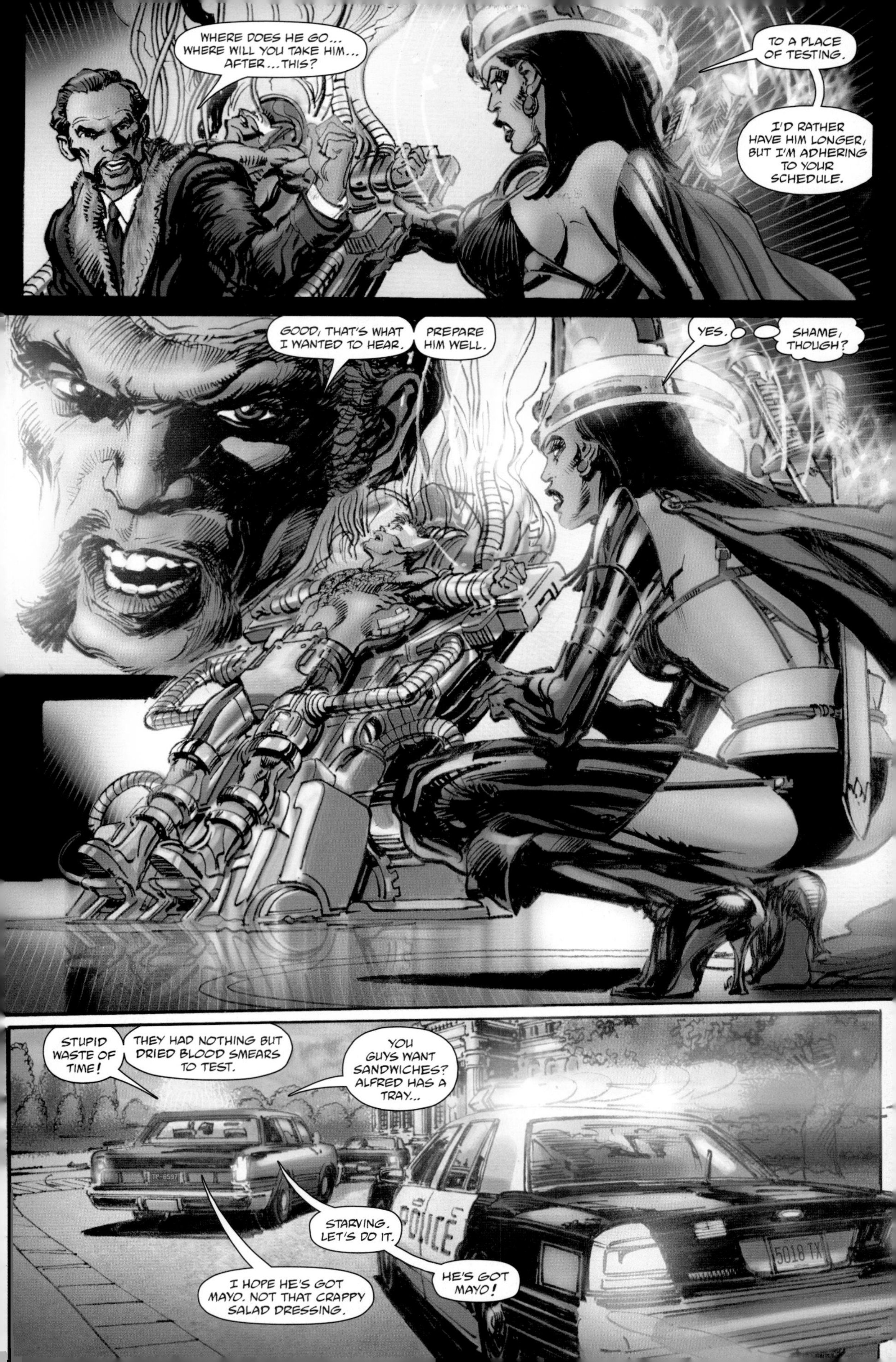

WHERE DOES HE GO... WHERE WILL YOU TAKE HIM... AFTER...THIS?
TO A PLACE OF TESTING.
I'D RATHER HAVE HIM LONGER, BUT I'M ADHERING TO YOUR SCHEDULE.
GOOD, THAT'S WHAT I WANTED TO HEAR.
PREPARE HIM WELL.
YES.
SHAME, THOUGH?
STUPID WASTE OF TIME!
THEY HAD NOTHING BUT DRIED BLOOD SMEARS TO TEST.
YOU GUYS WANT SANDWICHES? ALFRED HAS A TRAY...
STARVING. LET'S DO IT.
I HOPE HE'S GOT MAYO. NOT THAT CRAPPY SALAD DRESSING.
HE'S GOT MAYO!
POLICE
5018 TX

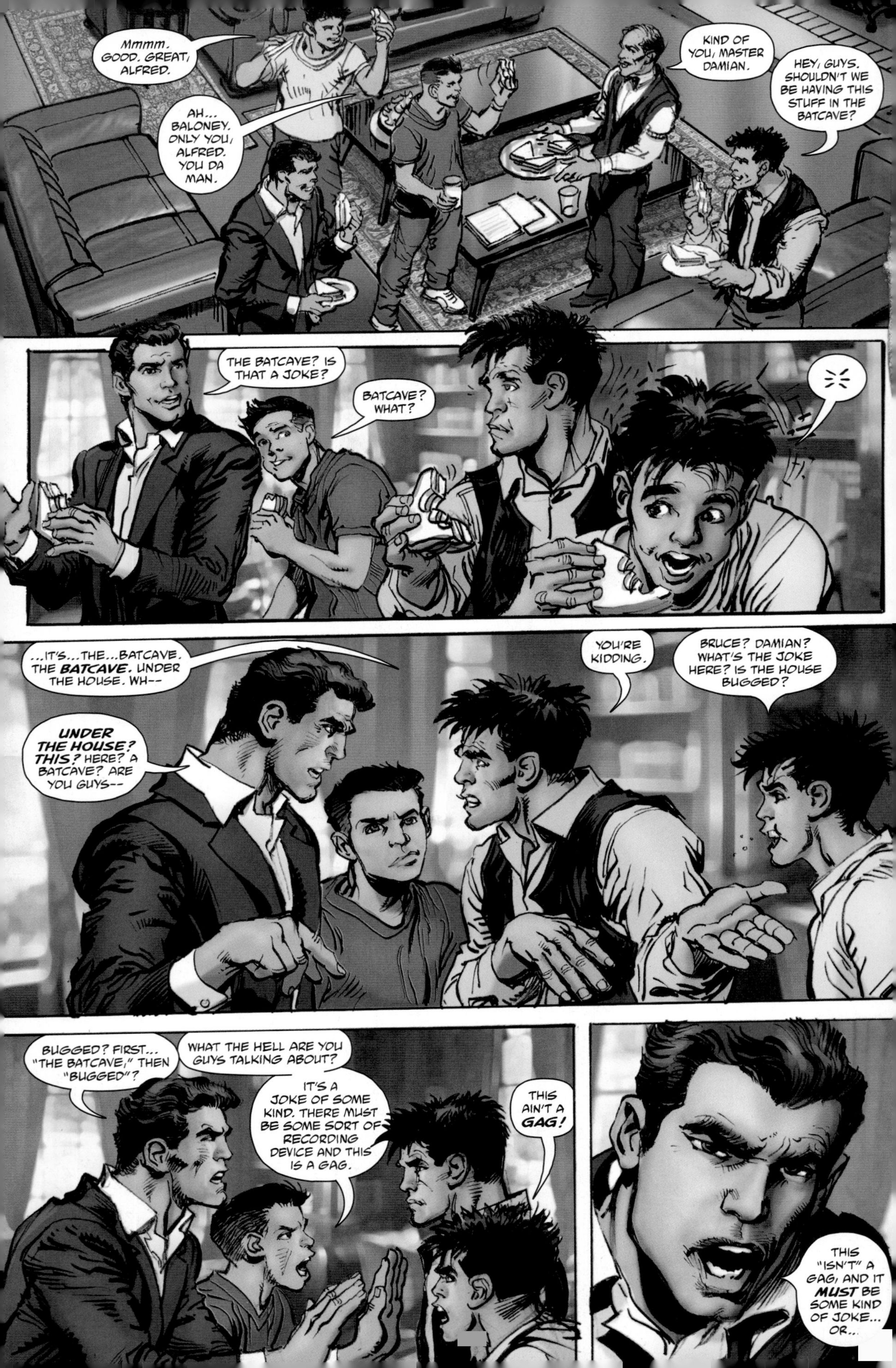
Mmmm. GOOD. GREAT, ALFRED.
AH... BALONEY. ONLY YOU, ALFRED. YOU DA MAN.
KIND OF YOU, MASTER DAMIAN.
HEY, GUYS. SHOULDN'T WE BE HAVING THIS STUFF IN THE BATCAVE?
THE BATCAVE? IS THAT A JOKE?
BATCAVE? WHAT?
...IT'S...THE...BATCAVE. THE **BATCAVE.** UNDER THE HOUSE. WH--
YOU'RE KIDDING.
BRUCE? DAMIAN? WHAT'S THE JOKE HERE? IS THE HOUSE BUGGED?
UNDER THE HOUSE? THIS? HERE? A BATCAVE? ARE YOU GUYS--
BUGGED? FIRST... "THE BATCAVE," THEN "BUGGED"?
WHAT THE HELL ARE YOU GUYS TALKING ABOUT?
IT'S A JOKE OF SOME KIND. THERE MUST BE SOME SORT OF RECORDING DEVICE AND THIS IS A GAG.
THIS AIN'T A ***GAG!***
THIS "ISN'T" A GAG, AND IT ***MUST*** BE SOME KIND OF JOKE... OR...

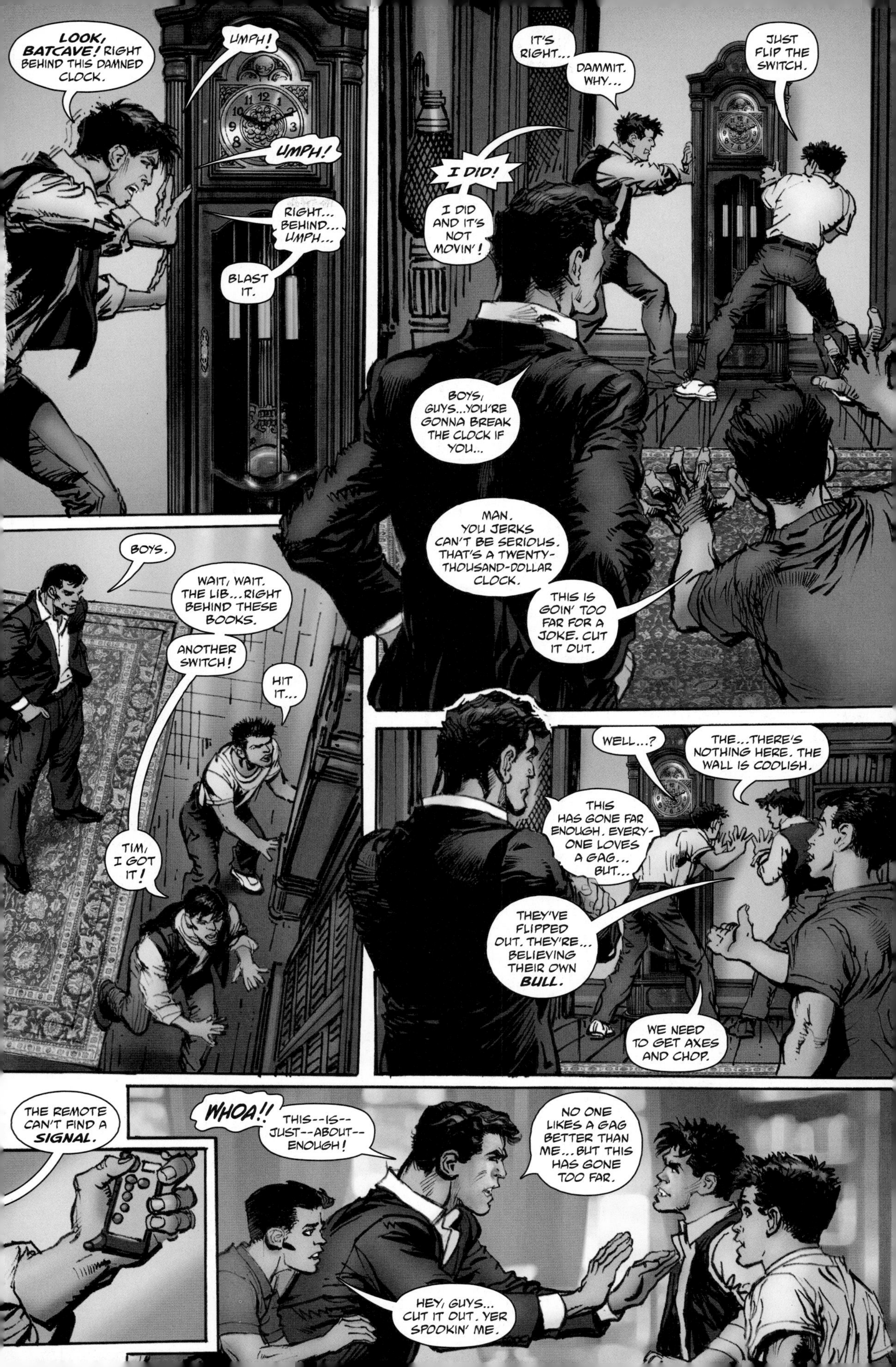
LOOK, BATCAVE! RIGHT BEHIND THIS DAMNED CLOCK.
UMPH!
UMPH!
RIGHT... BEHIND... UMPH...
BLAST IT.
IT'S RIGHT...
DAMMIT. WHY...
JUST FLIP THE SWITCH.
I DID!
I DID AND IT'S NOT MOVIN'!
BOYS, GUYS...YOU'RE GONNA BREAK THE CLOCK IF YOU...
MAN. YOU JERKS CAN'T BE SERIOUS. THAT'S A TWENTY-THOUSAND-DOLLAR CLOCK.
THIS IS GOIN' TOO FAR FOR A JOKE. CUT IT OUT.
BOYS.
WAIT, WAIT. THE LIB...RIGHT BEHIND THESE BOOKS.
ANOTHER SWITCH!
HIT IT...
TIM, I GOT IT!
WELL...?
THE...THERE'S NOTHING HERE. THE WALL IS COOLISH.
THIS HAS GONE FAR ENOUGH. EVERY-ONE LOVES A GAG... BUT...
THEY'VE FLIPPED OUT. THEY'RE... BELIEVING THEIR OWN BULL.
WE NEED TO GET AXES AND CHOP.
THE REMOTE CAN'T FIND A SIGNAL.
WHOA!!
THIS--IS--JUST--ABOUT--ENOUGH!
NO ONE LIKES A GAG BETTER THAN ME...BUT THIS HAS GONE TOO FAR.
HEY, GUYS... CUT IT OUT. YER SPOOKIN' ME.

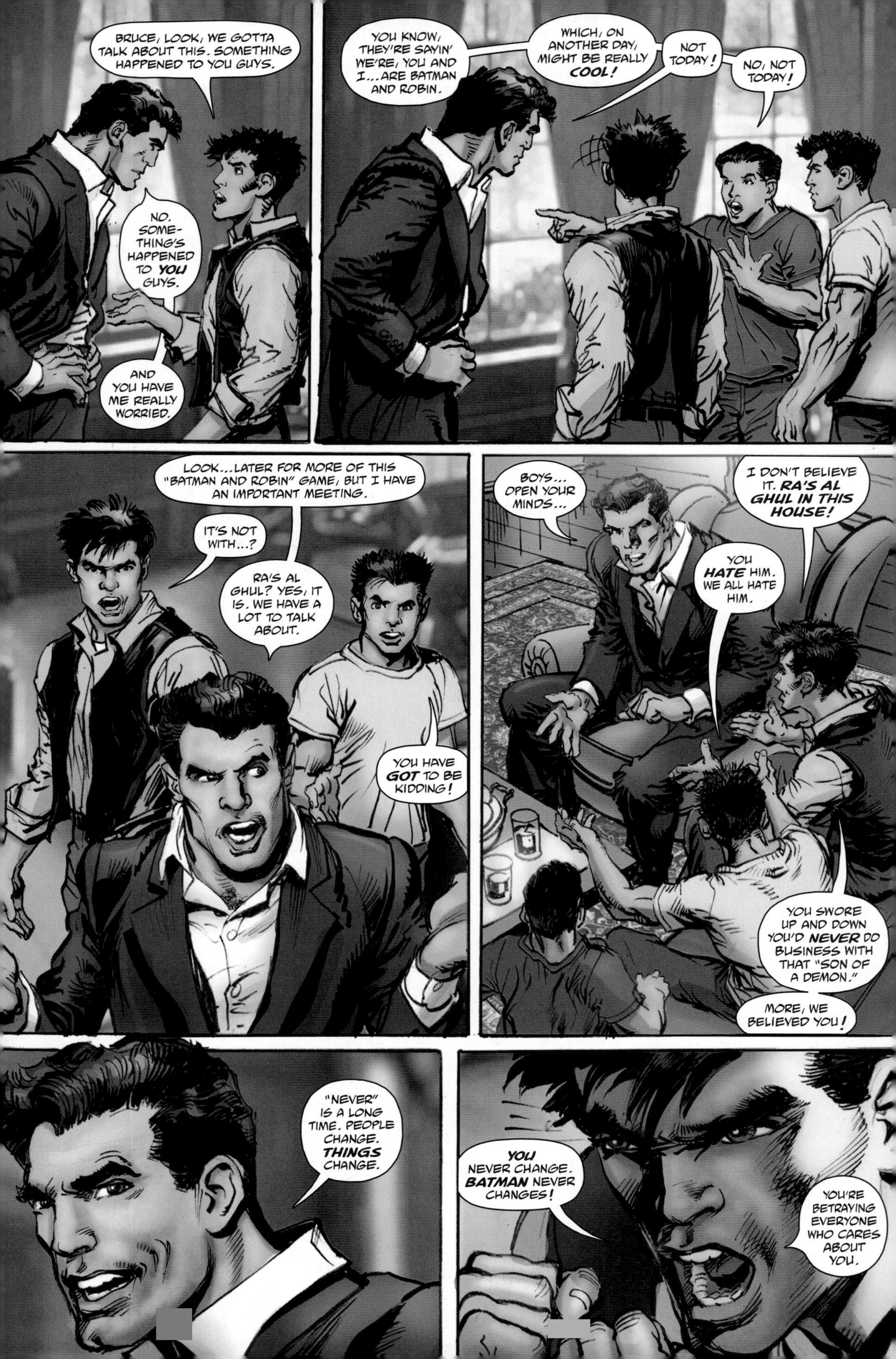
BRUCE, LOOK, WE GOTTA TALK ABOUT THIS. SOMETHING HAPPENED TO YOU GUYS.
NO. SOME-THING'S HAPPENED TO **YOU** GUYS.
AND YOU HAVE ME REALLY WORRIED.
YOU KNOW, THEY'RE SAYIN' WE'RE, YOU AND I... ARE BATMAN AND ROBIN.
WHICH, ON ANOTHER DAY, MIGHT BE REALLY **COOL!**
NOT TODAY!
NO, NOT TODAY!
LOOK...LATER FOR MORE OF THIS "BATMAN AND ROBIN" GAME, BUT I HAVE AN IMPORTANT MEETING.
IT'S NOT WITH...?
RA'S AL GHUL? YES, IT IS. WE HAVE A LOT TO TALK ABOUT.
YOU HAVE **GOT** TO BE KIDDING!
BOYS... OPEN YOUR MINDS...
I DON'T BELIEVE IT. **RA'S AL GHUL IN THIS HOUSE!**
YOU **HATE** HIM. WE ALL HATE HIM.
YOU SWORE UP AND DOWN YOU'D **NEVER** DO BUSINESS WITH THAT "SON OF A DEMON."
MORE, WE BELIEVED YOU!
"NEVER" IS A LONG TIME. PEOPLE CHANGE. **THINGS** CHANGE.
YOU NEVER CHANGE. **BATMAN** NEVER CHANGES!
YOU'RE BETRAYING EVERYONE WHO CARES ABOUT YOU.

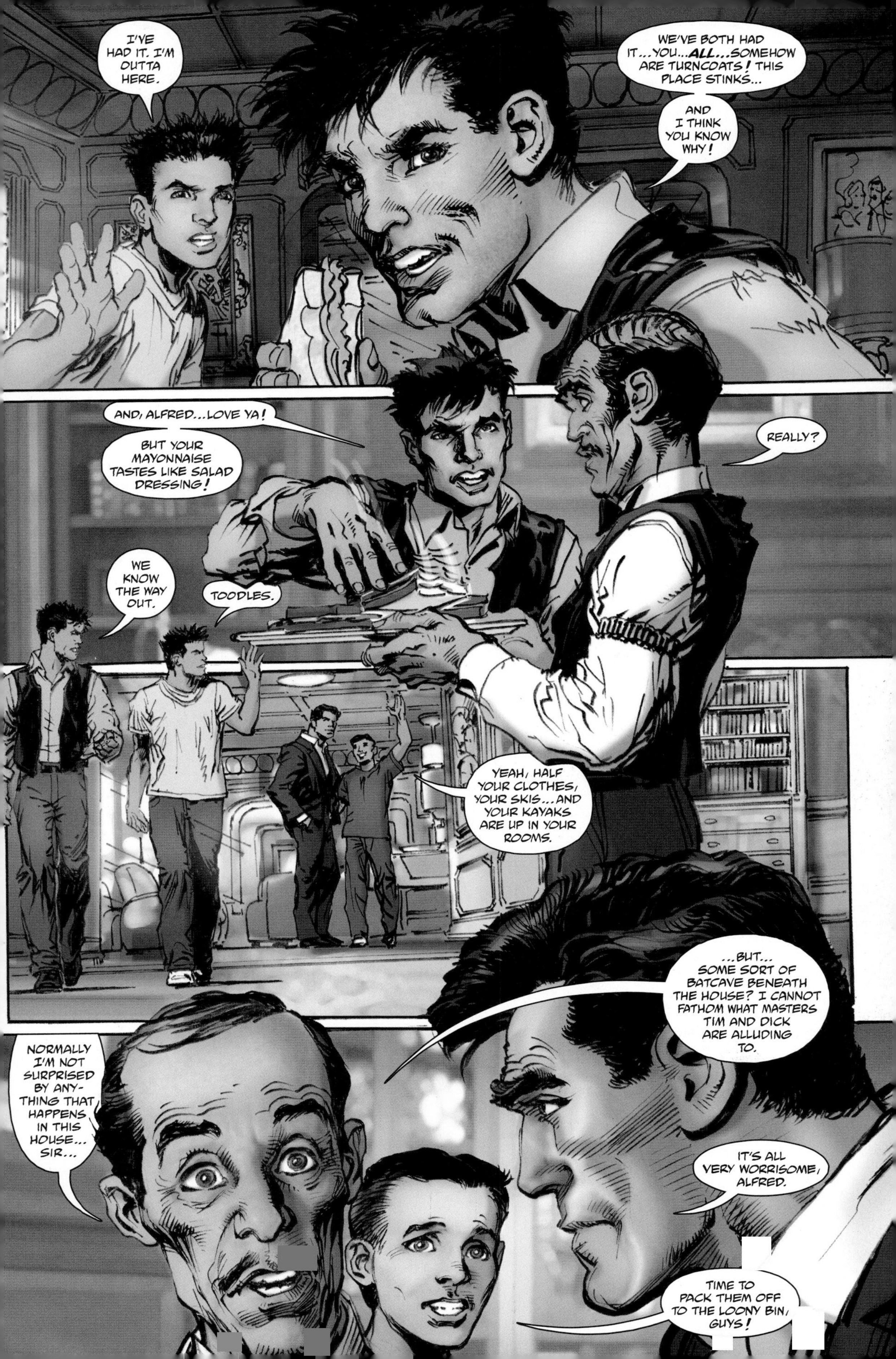
I'VE HAD IT. I'M OUTTA HERE.
WE'VE BOTH HAD IT...YOU...ALL...SOMEHOW ARE TURNCOATS! THIS PLACE STINKS...
AND I THINK YOU KNOW WHY!
AND, ALFRED...LOVE YA!
BUT YOUR MAYONNAISE TASTES LIKE SALAD DRESSING!
REALLY?
WE KNOW THE WAY OUT.
TOODLES.
YEAH, HALF YOUR CLOTHES, YOUR SKIS...AND YOUR KAYAKS ARE UP IN YOUR ROOMS.
NORMALLY I'M NOT SURPRISED BY ANY-THING THAT HAPPENS IN THIS HOUSE... SIR...
...BUT... SOME SORT OF BATCAVE BENEATH THE HOUSE? I CANNOT FATHOM WHAT MASTERS TIM AND DICK ARE ALLUDING TO.
IT'S ALL VERY WORRISOME, ALFRED.
TIME TO PACK THEM OFF TO THE LOONY BIN, GUYS!

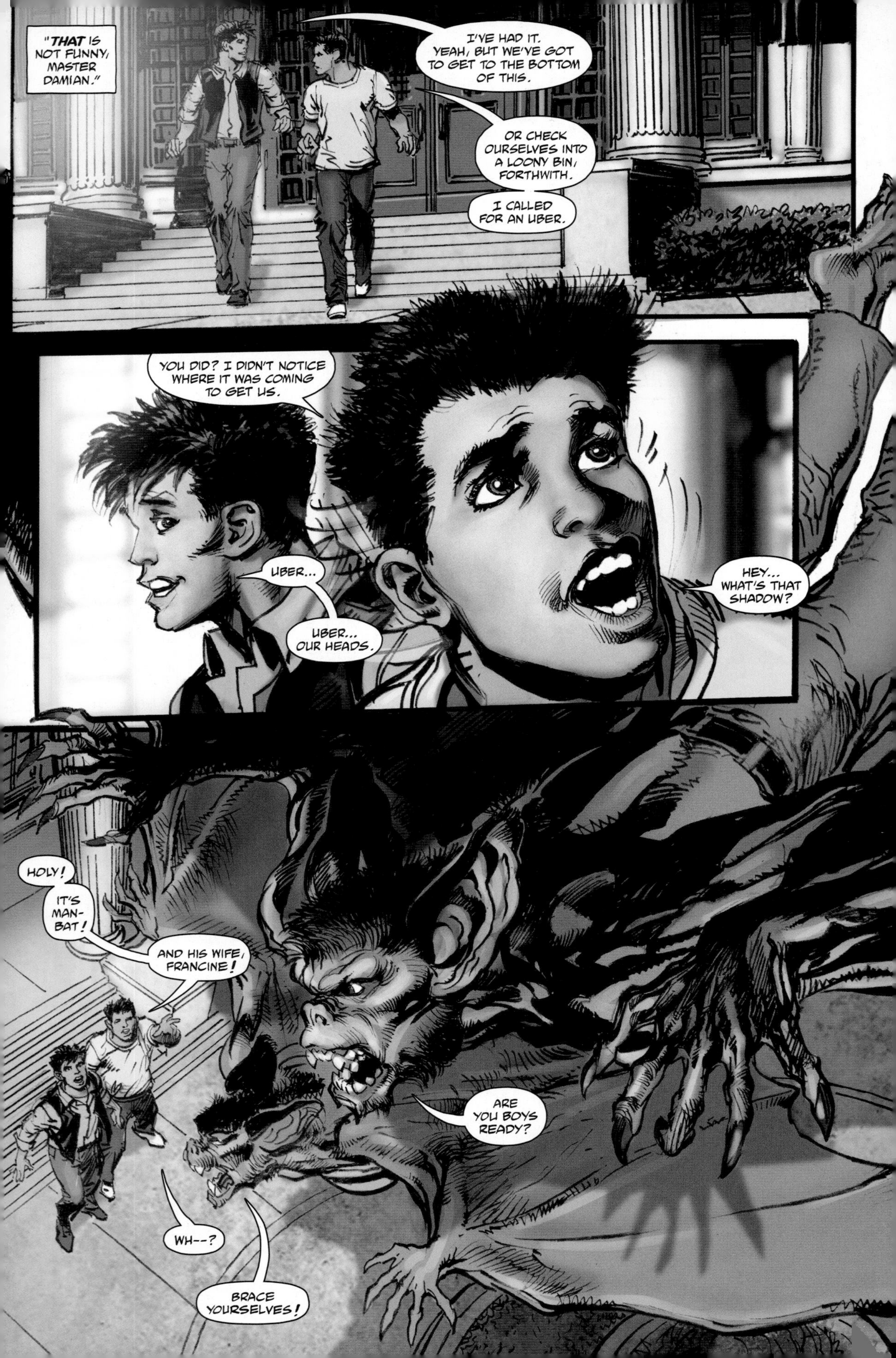
"THAT IS NOT FUNNY, MASTER DAMIAN."
I'VE HAD IT. YEAH, BUT WE'VE GOT TO GET TO THE BOTTOM OF THIS.
OR CHECK OURSELVES INTO A LOONY BIN, FORTHWITH.
I CALLED FOR AN UBER.
YOU DID? I DIDN'T NOTICE WHERE IT WAS COMING TO GET US.
UBER...
UBER... OUR HEADS.
HEY... WHAT'S THAT SHADOW?
HOLY!
IT'S MAN-BAT!
AND HIS WIFE, FRANCINE!
ARE YOU BOYS READY?
WH--?
BRACE YOURSELVES!

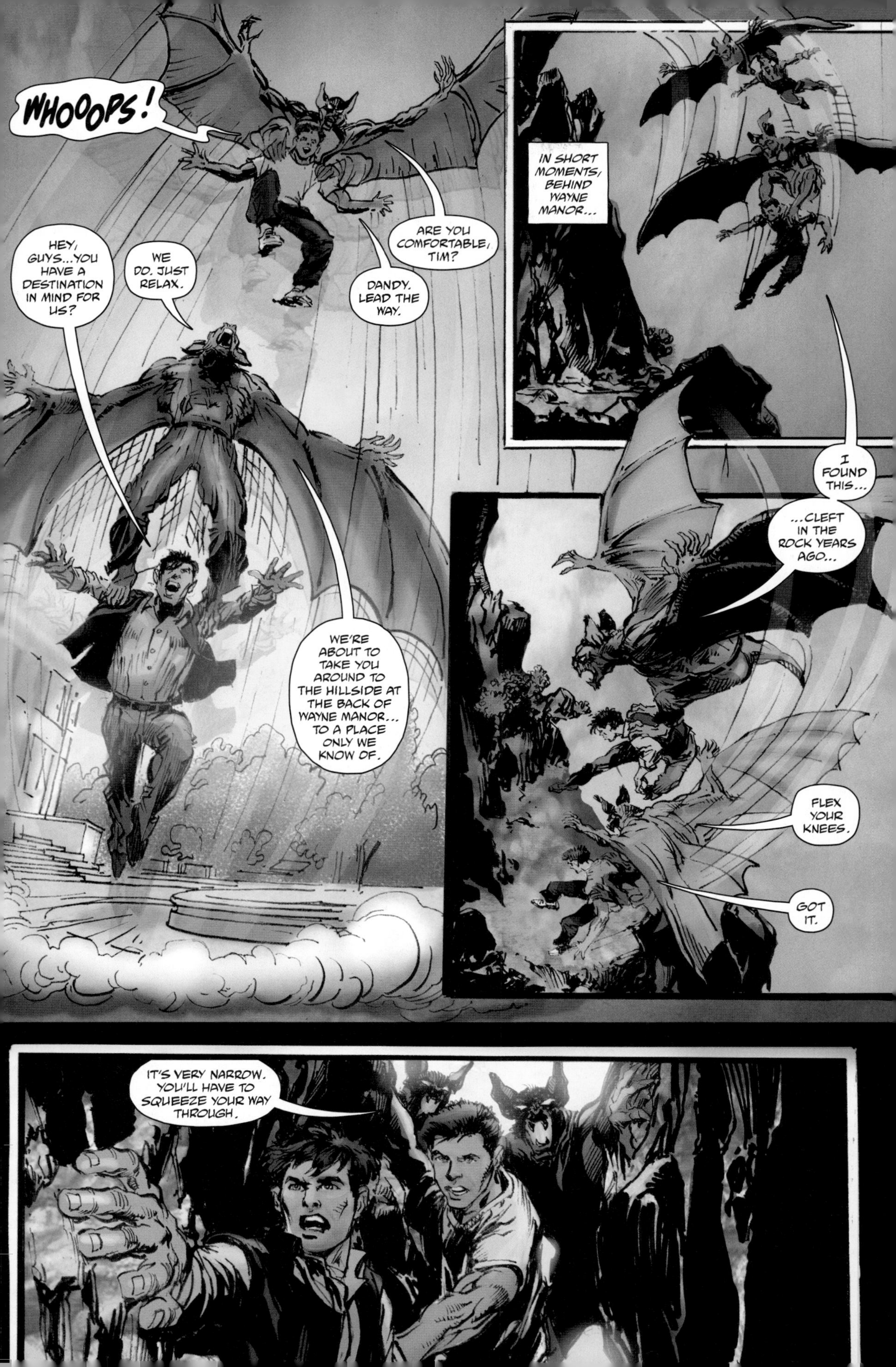
WHOOOPS!
ARE YOU COMFORTABLE, TIM?
DANDY. LEAD THE WAY.
HEY, GUYS...YOU HAVE A DESTINATION IN MIND FOR US?
WE DO. JUST RELAX.
WE'RE ABOUT TO TAKE YOU AROUND TO THE HILLSIDE AT THE BACK OF WAYNE MANOR... TO A PLACE ONLY WE KNOW OF.
IN SHORT MOMENTS, BEHIND WAYNE MANOR...
I FOUND THIS...
...CLEFT IN THE ROCK YEARS AGO...
FLEX YOUR KNEES.
GOT IT.
IT'S VERY NARROW. YOU'LL HAVE TO SQUEEZE YOUR WAY THROUGH.

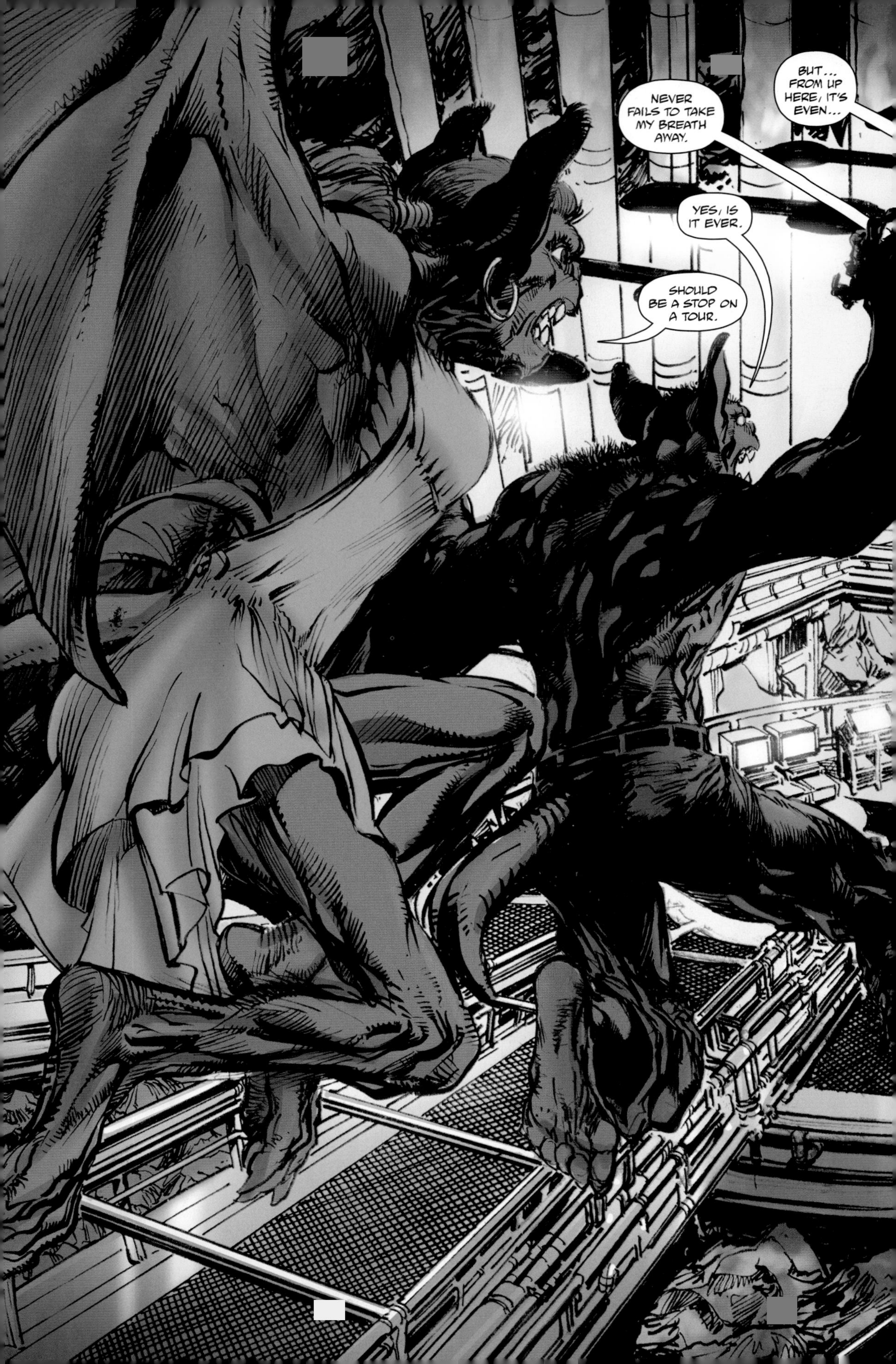
NEVER FAILS TO TAKE MY BREATH AWAY.
BUT... FROM UP HERE, IT'S EVEN...
YES, IS IT EVER.
SHOULD BE A STOP ON A TOUR.

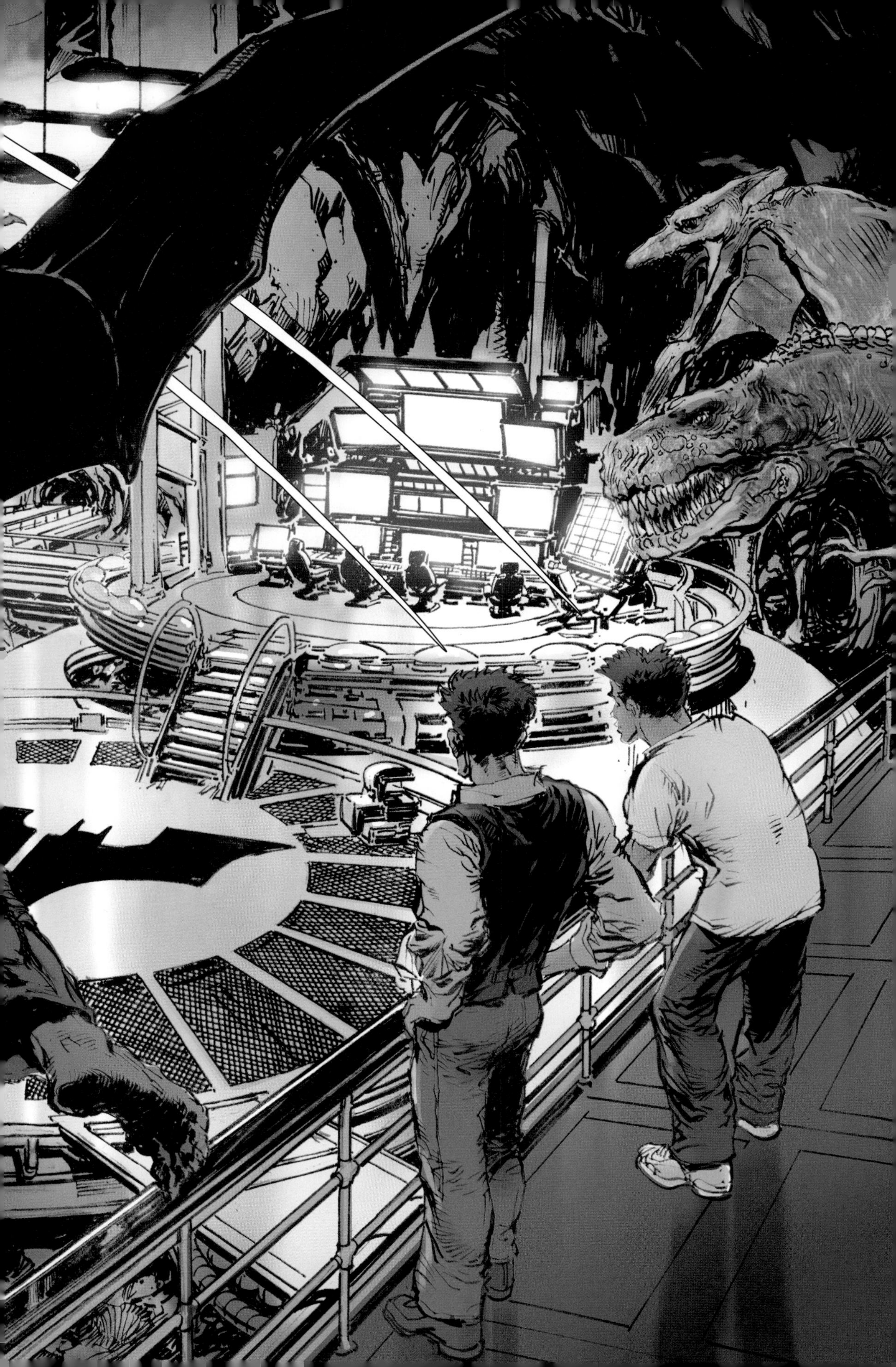

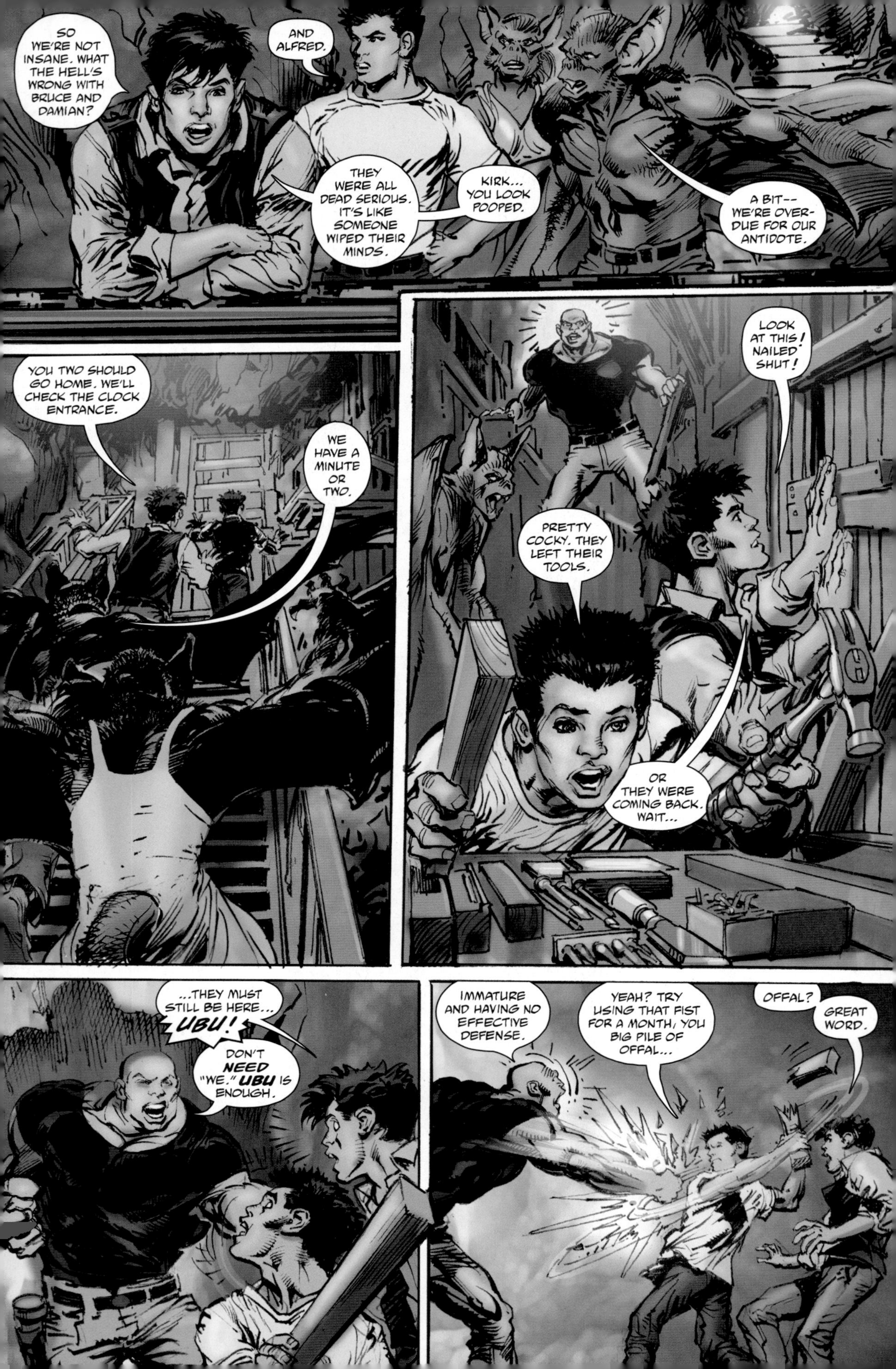
SO WE'RE NOT INSANE. WHAT THE HELL'S WRONG WITH BRUCE AND DAMIAN?
AND ALFRED.
THEY WERE ALL DEAD SERIOUS. IT'S LIKE SOMEONE WIPED THEIR MINDS.
KIRK... YOU LOOK POOPED.
A BIT-- WE'RE OVER-DUE FOR OUR ANTIDOTE.
YOU TWO SHOULD GO HOME. WE'LL CHECK THE CLOCK ENTRANCE.
WE HAVE A MINUTE OR TWO.
LOOK AT THIS! NAILED SHUT!
PRETTY COCKY. THEY LEFT THEIR TOOLS.
OR THEY WERE COMING BACK. WAIT...
...THEY MUST STILL BE HERE... UBU!
DON'T NEED "WE." UBU IS ENOUGH.
IMMATURE AND HAVING NO EFFECTIVE DEFENSE.
YEAH? TRY USING THAT FIST FOR A MONTH, YOU BIG PILE OF OFFAL...
OFFAL?
GREAT WORD.

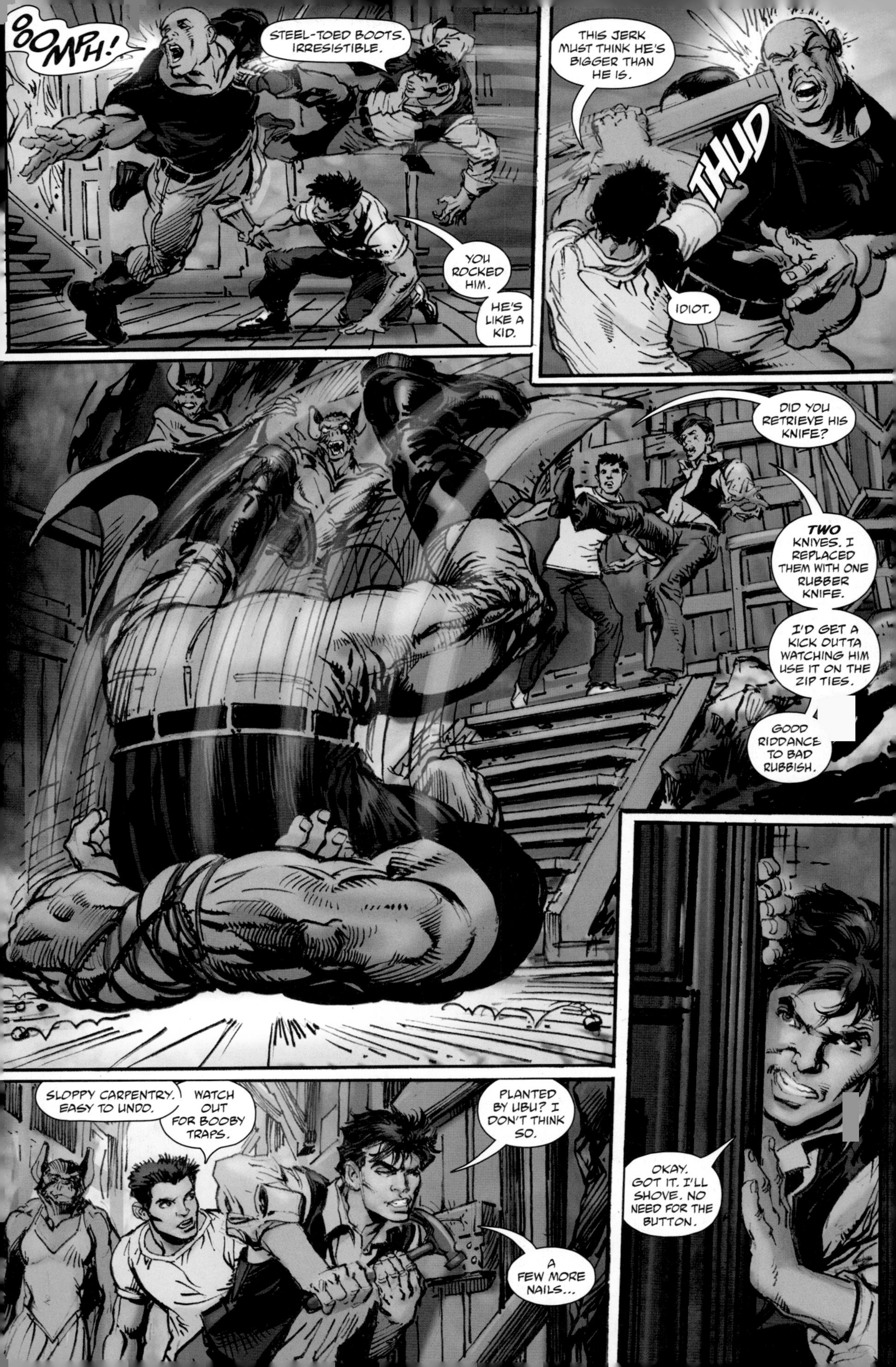
OOOMPH!
STEEL-TOED BOOTS. IRRESISTIBLE.
YOU ROCKED HIM.
HE'S LIKE A KID.
THIS JERK MUST THINK HE'S BIGGER THAN HE IS.
THUD
IDIOT.
DID YOU RETRIEVE HIS KNIFE?
TWO KNIVES. I REPLACED THEM WITH ONE RUBBER KNIFE.
I'D GET A KICK OUTTA WATCHING HIM USE IT ON THE ZIP TIES.
GOOD RIDDANCE TO BAD RUBBISH.
SLOPPY CARPENTRY. EASY TO UNDO.
WATCH OUT FOR BOOBY TRAPS.
PLANTED BY UBU? I DON'T THINK SO.
A FEW MORE NAILS...
OKAY. GOT IT. I'LL SHOVE. NO NEED FOR THE BUTTON.

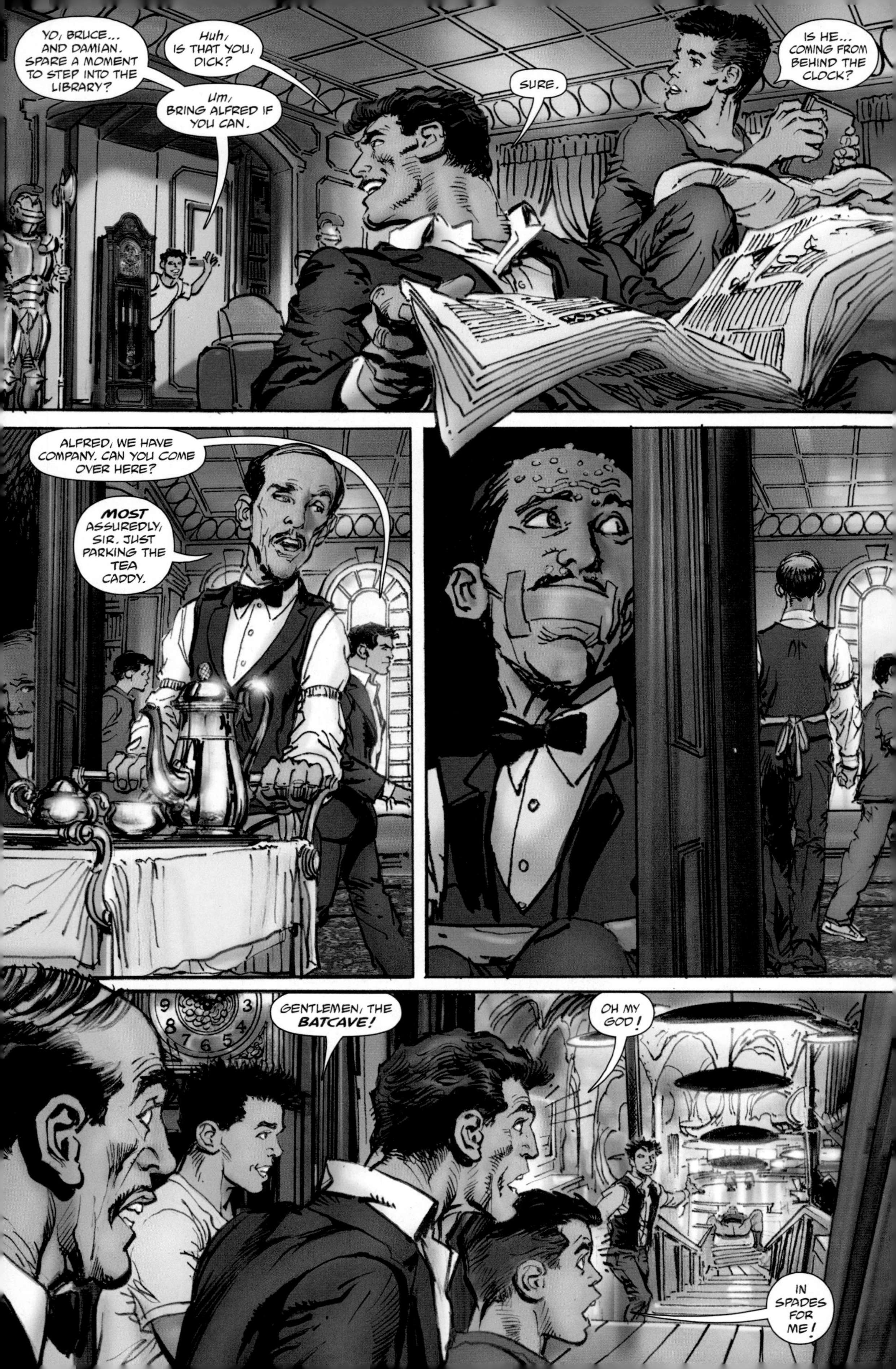
YO, BRUCE... AND DAMIAN. SPARE A MOMENT TO STEP INTO THE LIBRARY?
HUH, IS THAT YOU, DICK?
UM, BRING ALFRED IF YOU CAN.
SURE.
IS HE... COMING FROM BEHIND THE CLOCK?
ALFRED, WE HAVE COMPANY. CAN YOU COME OVER HERE?
MOST ASSUREDLY, SIR. JUST PARKING THE TEA CADDY.
GENTLEMEN, THE BATCAVE!
OH MY GOD!
IN SPADES FOR ME!

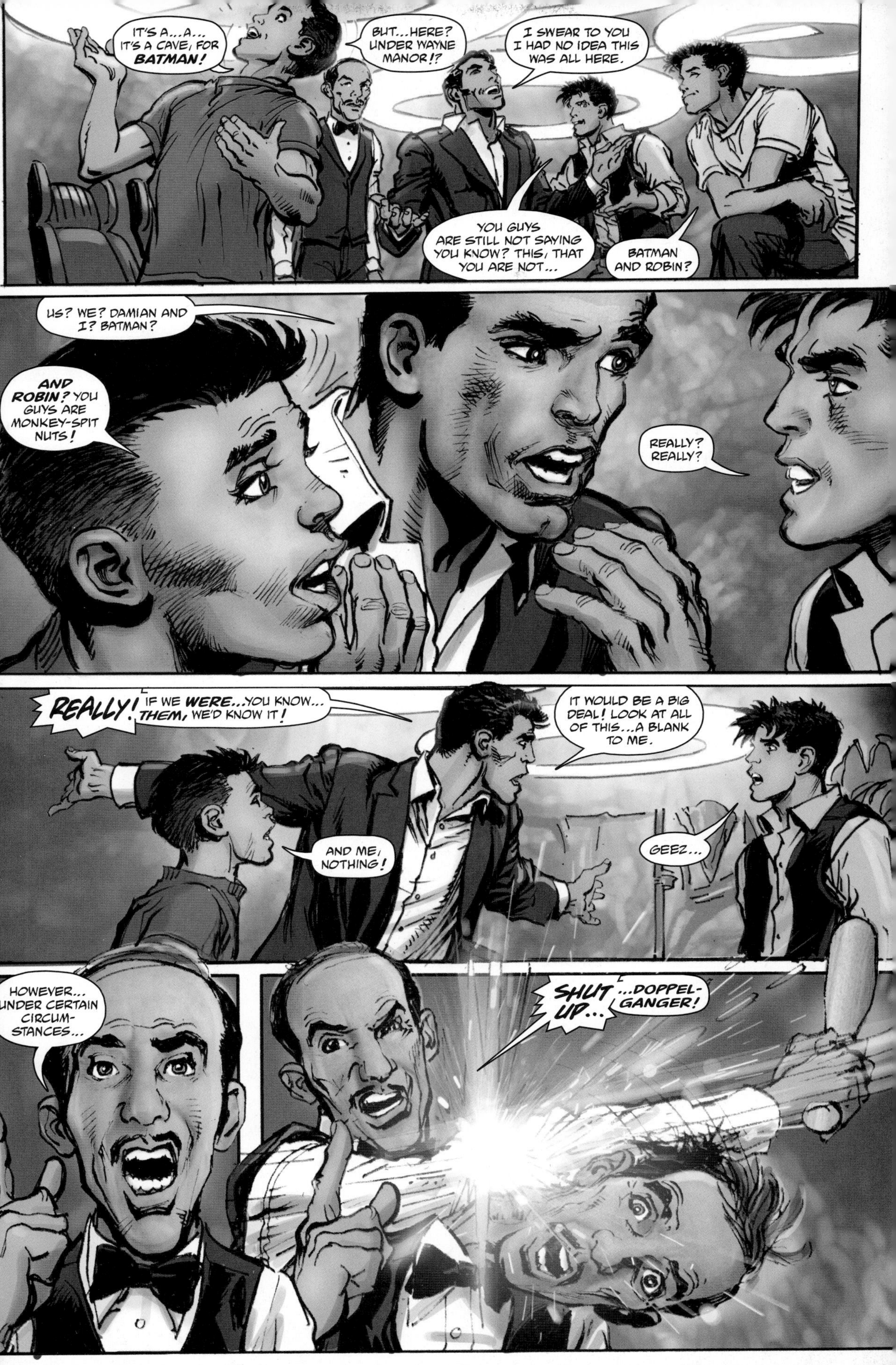

IT'S A...A... IT'S A CAVE, FOR BATMAN!
BUT...HERE? UNDER WAYNE MANOR!?
I SWEAR TO YOU I HAD NO IDEA THIS WAS ALL HERE.
YOU GUYS ARE STILL NOT SAYING YOU KNOW? THIS, THAT YOU ARE NOT...
BATMAN AND ROBIN?
US? WE? DAMIAN AND I? BATMAN?
AND ROBIN? YOU GUYS ARE MONKEY-SPIT NUTS!
REALLY? REALLY?
REALLY! IF WE WERE...YOU KNOW... THEM, WE'D KNOW IT!
IT WOULD BE A BIG DEAL! LOOK AT ALL OF THIS...A BLANK TO ME.
AND ME, NOTHING!
GEEZ...
HOWEVER... UNDER CERTAIN CIRCUM-STANCES...
SHUT UP...
...DOPPEL-GANGER!

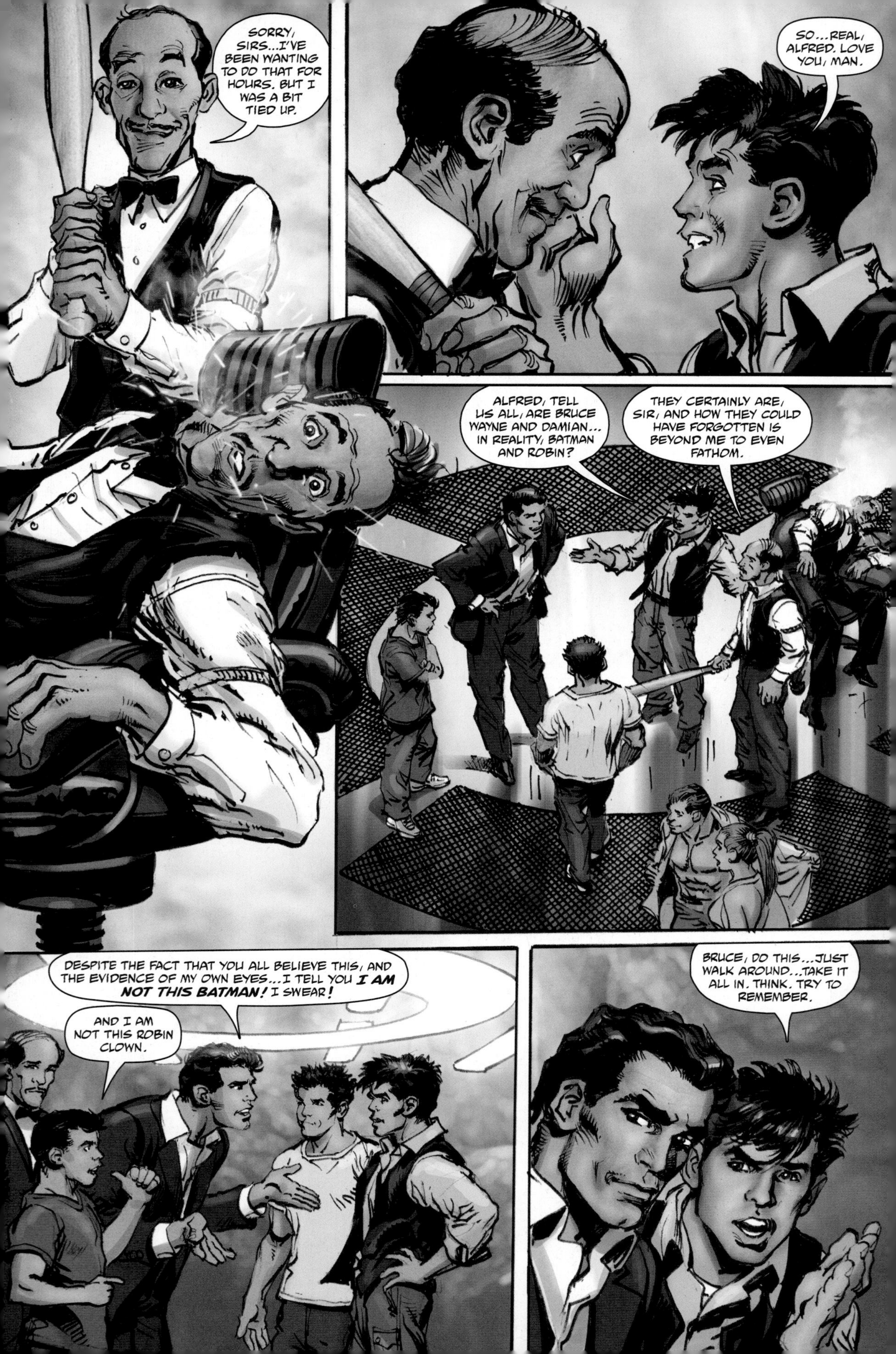
SORRY, SIRS...I'VE BEEN WANTING TO DO THAT FOR HOURS. BUT I WAS A BIT TIED UP.
SO...REAL, ALFRED. LOVE YOU, MAN.
ALFRED, TELL US ALL, ARE BRUCE WAYNE AND DAMIAN... IN REALITY, BATMAN AND ROBIN?
THEY CERTAINLY ARE, SIR, AND HOW THEY COULD HAVE FORGOTTEN IS BEYOND ME TO EVEN FATHOM.
DESPITE THE FACT THAT YOU ALL BELIEVE THIS, AND THE EVIDENCE OF MY OWN EYES...I TELL YOU **I AM NOT THIS BATMAN!** I SWEAR!
AND I AM NOT THIS ROBIN CLOWN.
BRUCE, DO THIS...JUST WALK AROUND...TAKE IT ALL IN. THINK. TRY TO REMEMBER.

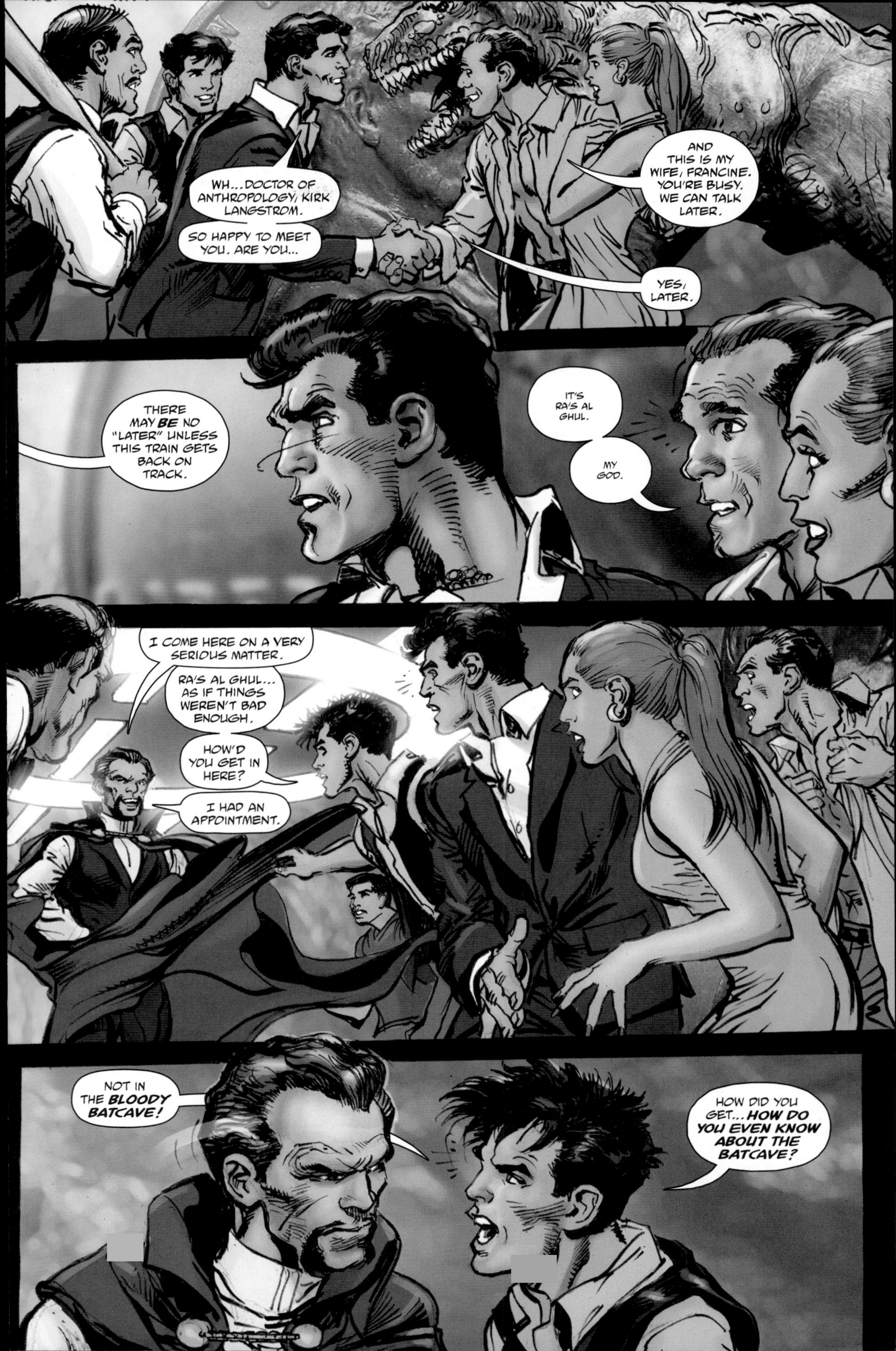
WH...DOCTOR OF ANTHROPOLOGY, KIRK LANGSTROM.
SO HAPPY TO MEET YOU. ARE YOU...
AND THIS IS MY WIFE, FRANCINE. YOU'RE BUSY. WE CAN TALK LATER.
YES, LATER.
THERE MAY **BE** NO "LATER" UNLESS THIS TRAIN GETS BACK ON TRACK.
IT'S RA'S AL GHUL.
MY GOD.
I COME HERE ON A VERY SERIOUS MATTER.
RA'S AL GHUL... AS IF THINGS WEREN'T BAD ENOUGH.
HOW'D YOU GET IN HERE?
I HAD AN APPOINTMENT.
NOT IN THE ***BLOODY BATCAVE!***
HOW DID YOU GET... ***HOW DO YOU EVEN KNOW ABOUT THE BATCAVE?***

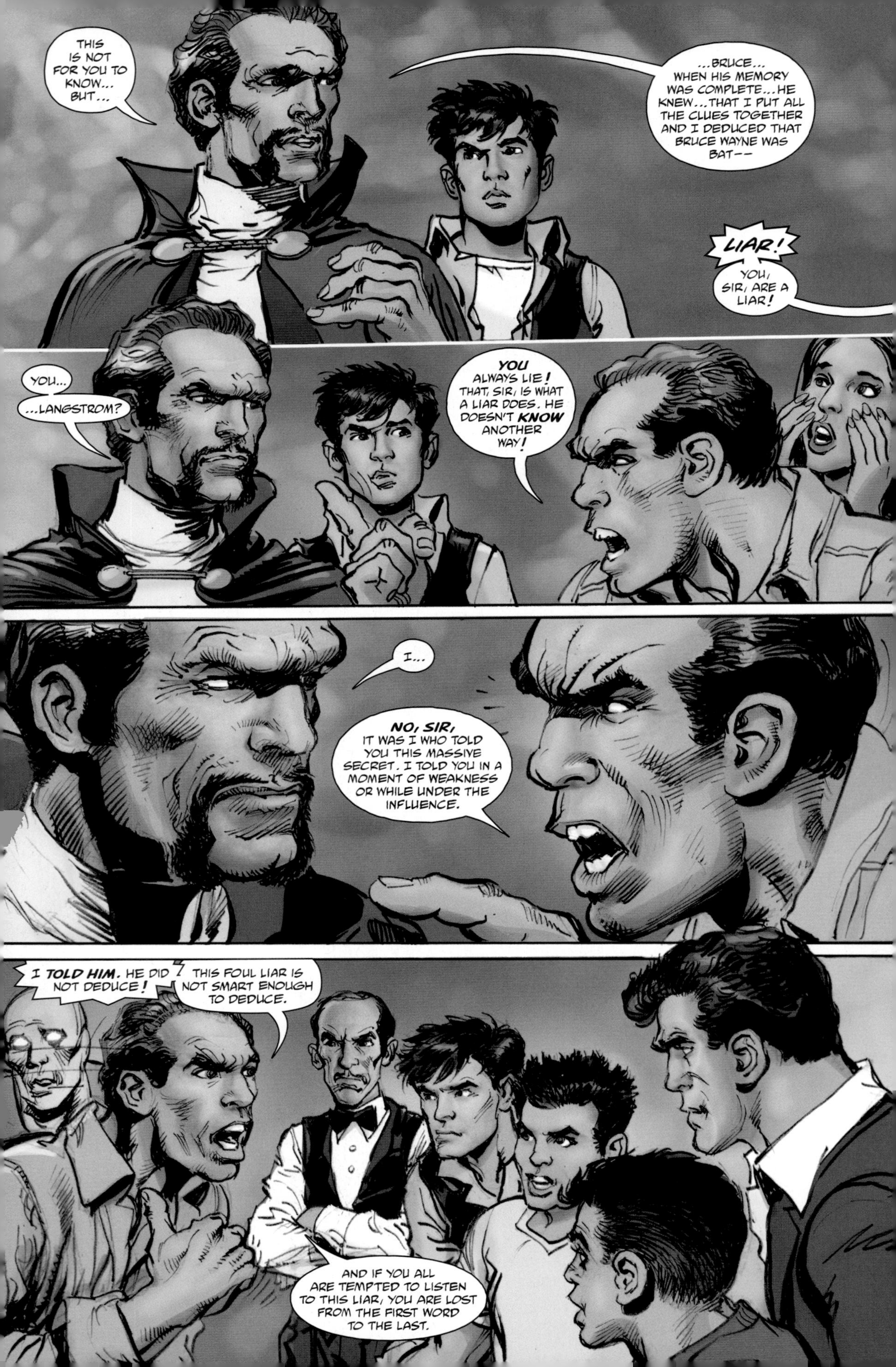
THIS IS NOT FOR YOU TO KNOW... BUT...
...BRUCE... WHEN HIS MEMORY WAS COMPLETE...HE KNEW...THAT I PUT ALL THE CLUES TOGETHER AND I DEDUCED THAT BRUCE WAYNE WAS BAT--
LIAR!
YOU, SIR, ARE A LIAR!
YOU...
...LANGSTROM?
YOU ALWAYS LIE! THAT, SIR, IS WHAT A LIAR DOES. HE DOESN'T KNOW ANOTHER WAY!
I...
NO, SIR, IT WAS I WHO TOLD YOU THIS MASSIVE SECRET. I TOLD YOU IN A MOMENT OF WEAKNESS OR WHILE UNDER THE INFLUENCE.
I TOLD HIM. HE DID NOT DEDUCE!
THIS FOUL LIAR IS NOT SMART ENOUGH TO DEDUCE.
AND IF YOU ALL ARE TEMPTED TO LISTEN TO THIS LIAR, YOU ARE LOST FROM THE FIRST WORD TO THE LAST.

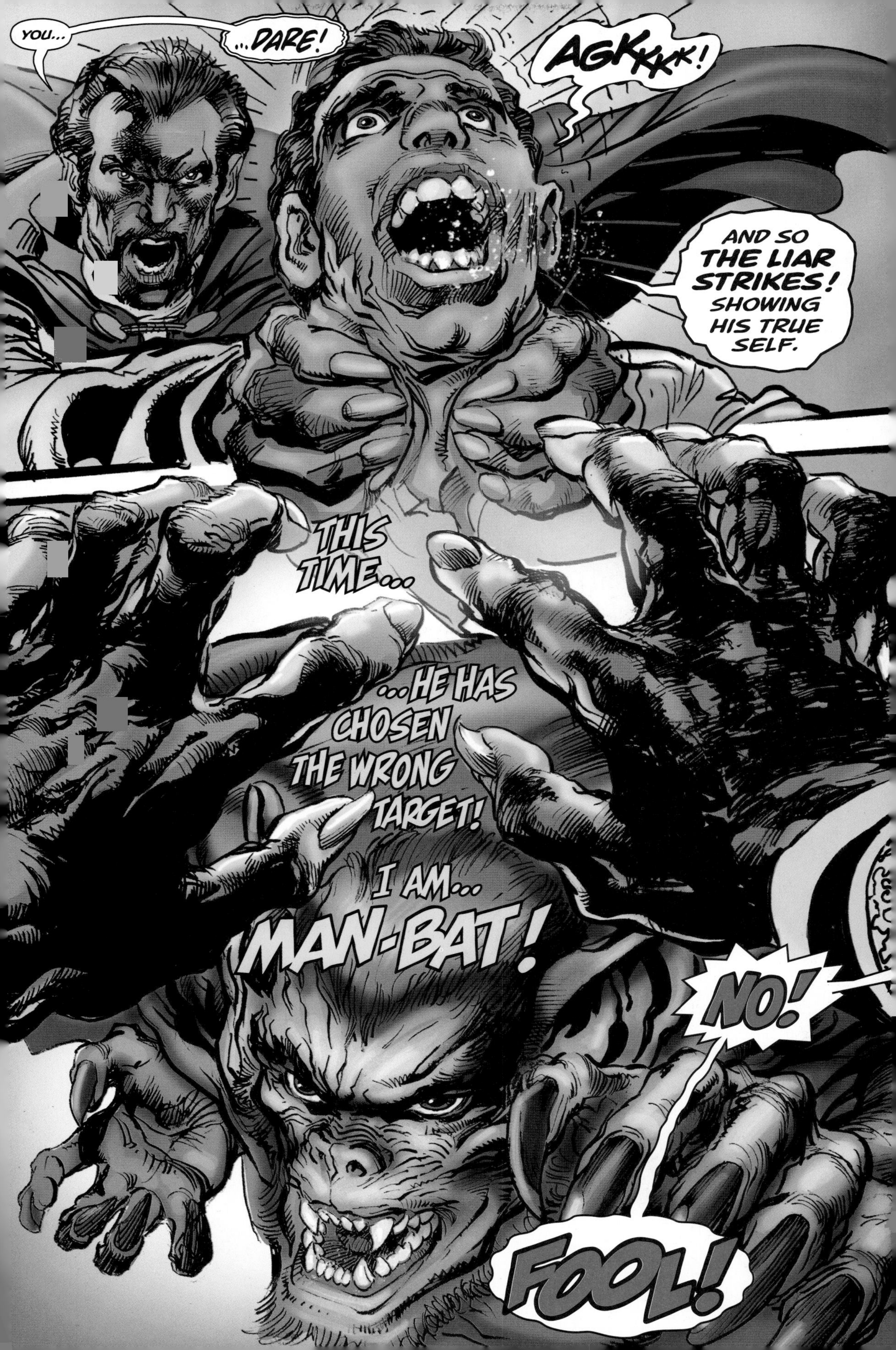
YOU...
...DARE!
AGKKKK!
AND SO THE LIAR STRIKES! SHOWING HIS TRUE SELF.
THIS TIME...
...HE HAS CHOSEN THE WRONG TARGET!
I AM... MAN-BAT!
NO!
FOOL!

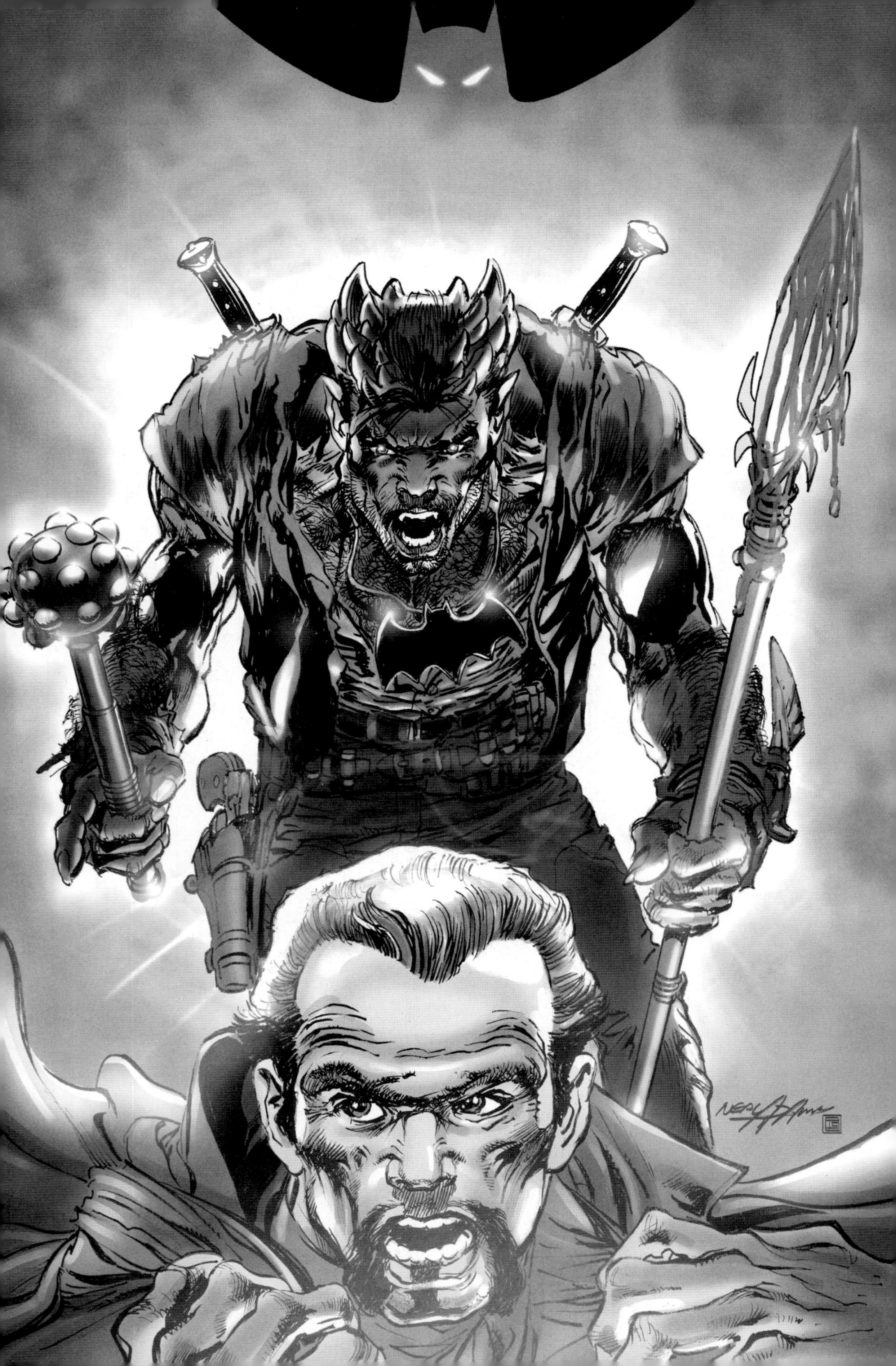

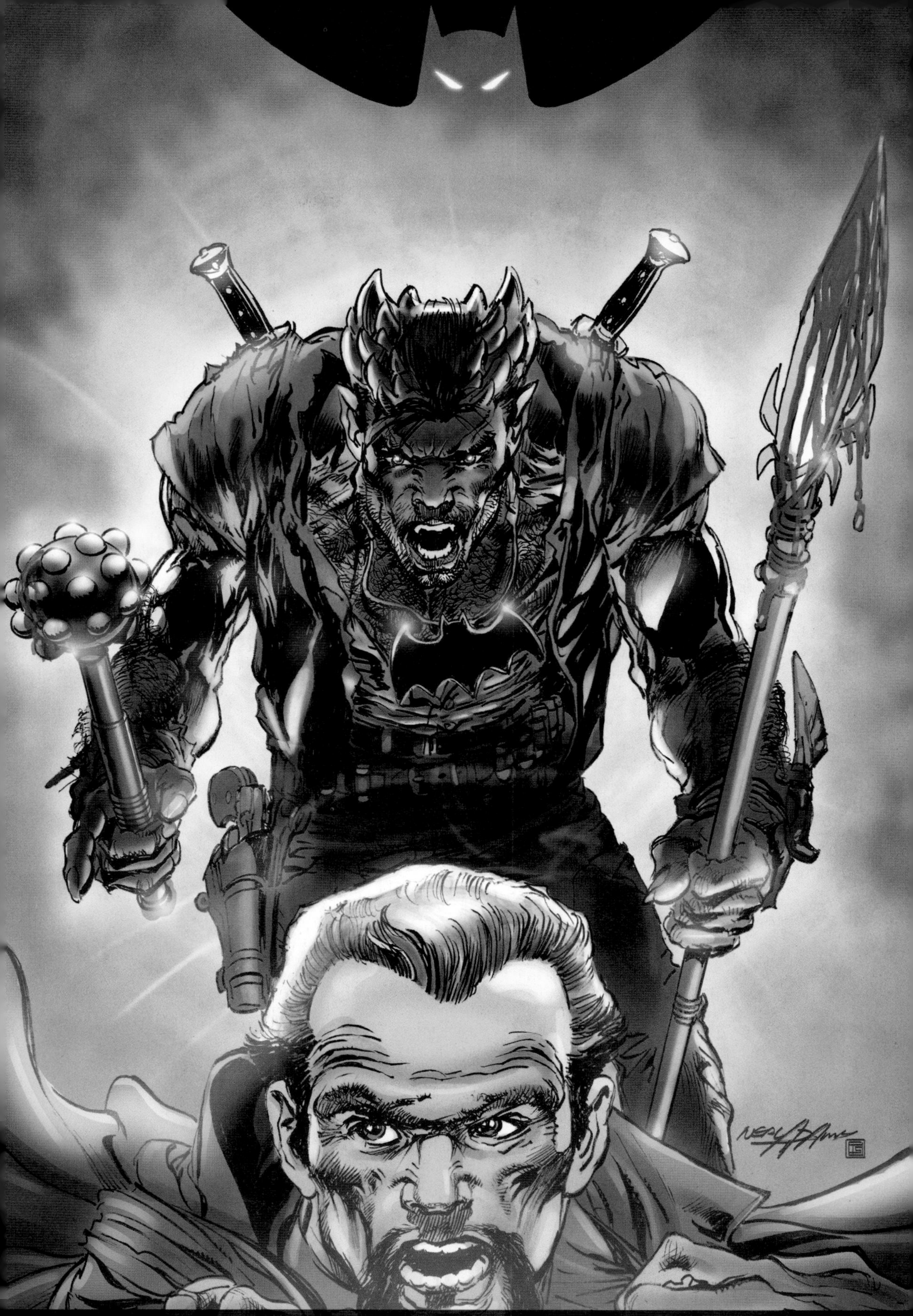

Chapter 3

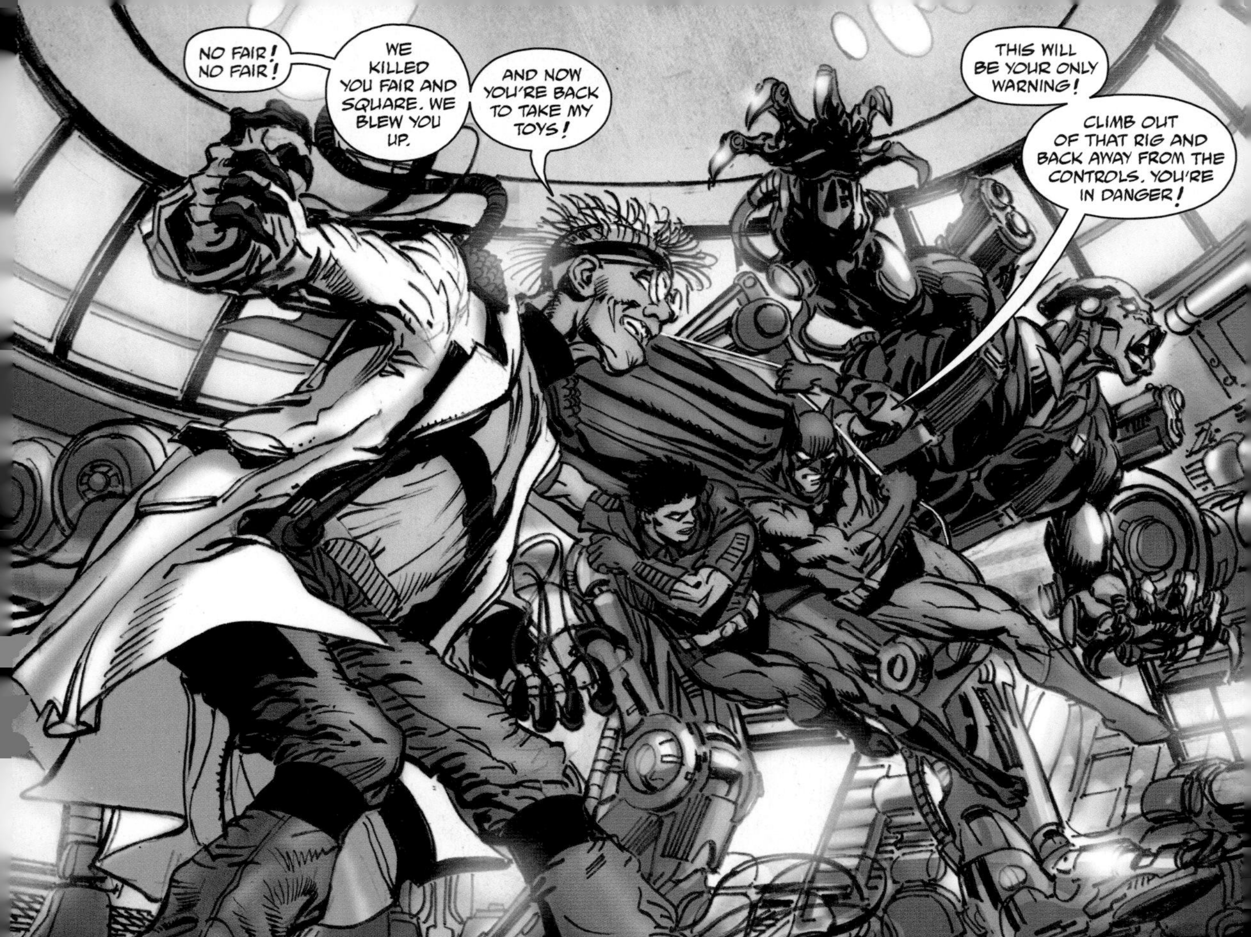
NO FAIR! NO FAIR!
WE KILLED YOU FAIR AND SQUARE. WE BLEW YOU UP.
AND NOW YOU'RE BACK TO TAKE MY TOYS!
THIS WILL BE YOUR ONLY WARNING!
CLIMB OUT OF THAT RIG AND BACK AWAY FROM THE CONTROLS. YOU'RE IN DANGER!

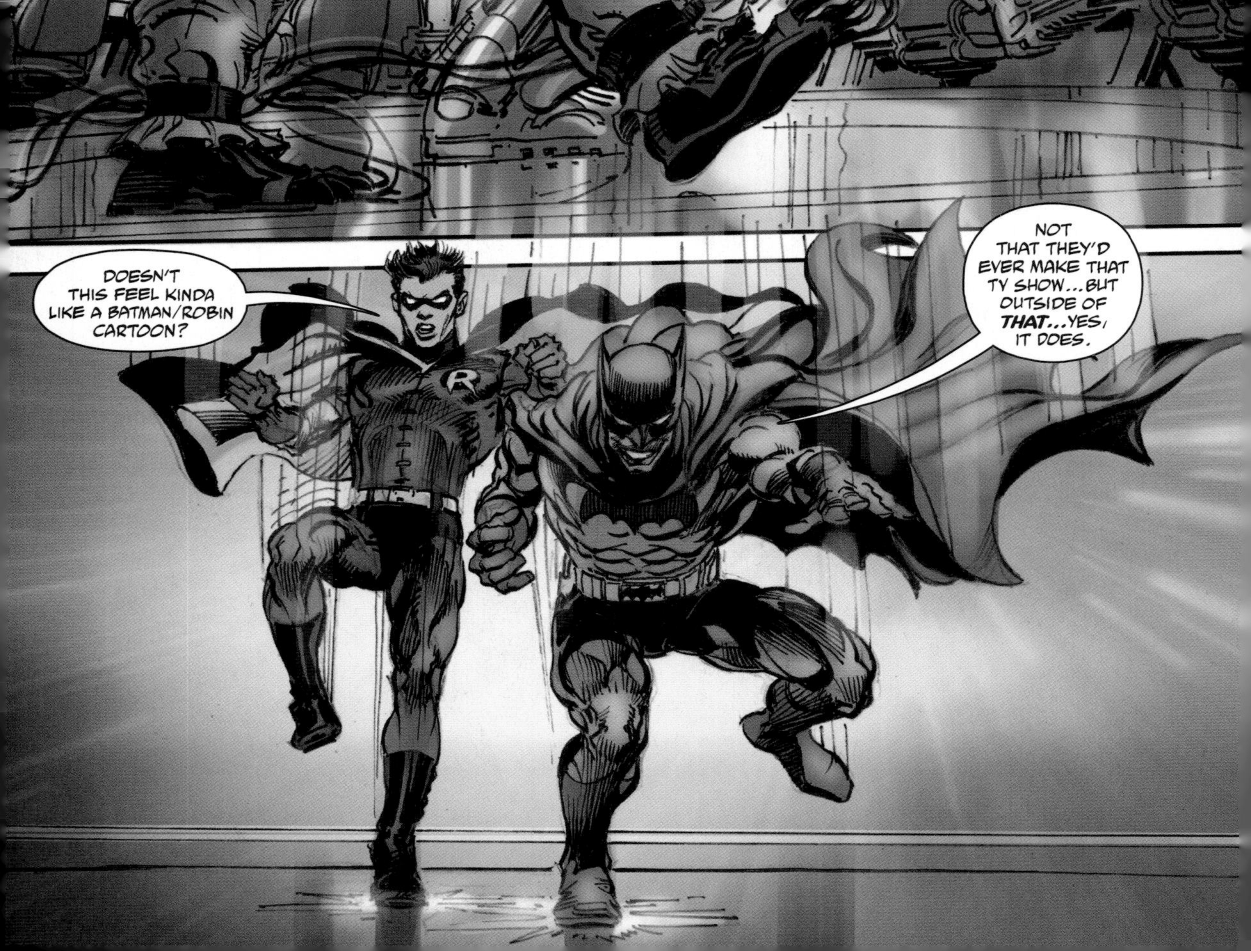
DOESN'T THIS FEEL KINDA LIKE A BATMAN/ROBIN CARTOON?
NOT THAT THEY'D EVER MAKE THAT TV SHOW...BUT OUTSIDE OF THAT...YES, IT DOES.

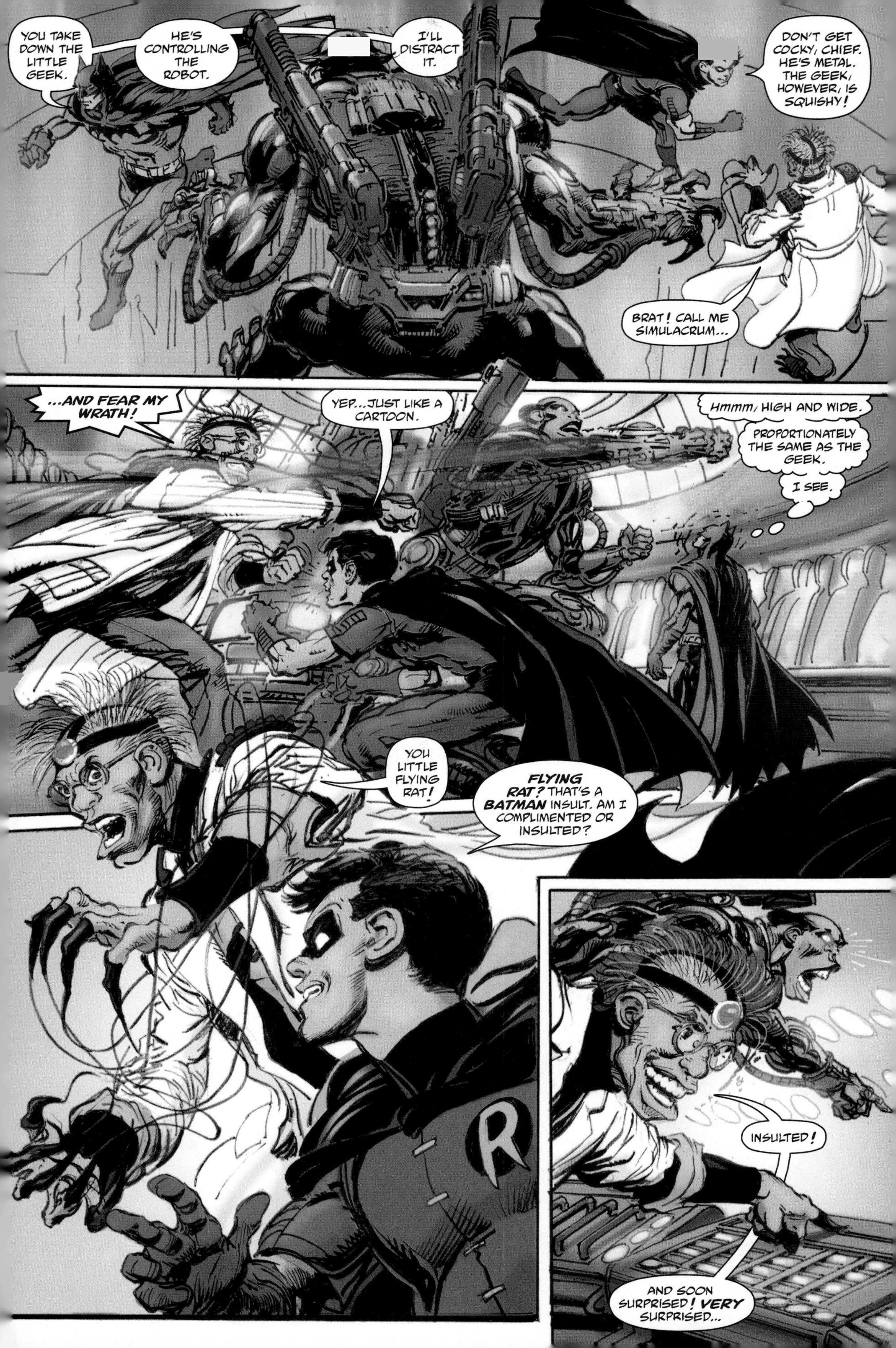

YOU TAKE DOWN THE LITTLE GEEK.
HE'S CONTROLLING THE ROBOT.
I'LL DISTRACT IT.
DON'T GET COCKY, CHIEF. HE'S METAL. THE GEEK, HOWEVER, IS SQUISHY!
BRAT! CALL ME SIMULACRUM...
...AND FEAR MY WRATH!
YEP...JUST LIKE A CARTOON.
Hmmm, HIGH AND WIDE.
PROPORTIONATELY THE SAME AS THE GEEK.
I SEE.
YOU LITTLE FLYING RAT!
FLYING RAT? THAT'S A BATMAN INSULT. AM I COMPLIMENTED OR INSULTED?
INSULTED!
AND SOON SURPRISED! VERY SURPRISED...

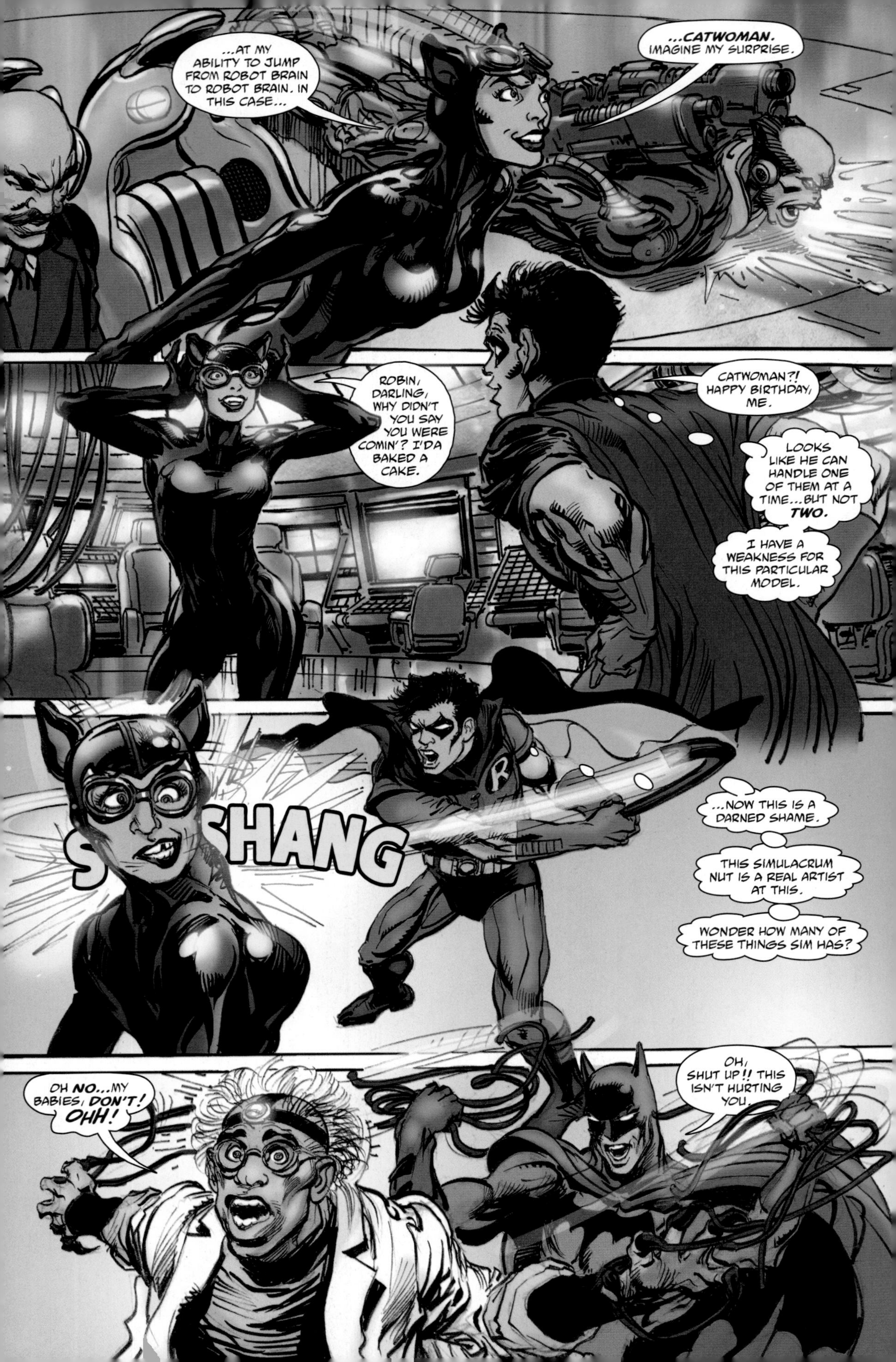
...AT MY ABILITY TO JUMP FROM ROBOT BRAIN TO ROBOT BRAIN. IN THIS CASE...
...CATWOMAN. IMAGINE MY SURPRISE.
ROBIN, DARLING, WHY DIDN'T YOU SAY YOU WERE COMIN'? I'DA BAKED A CAKE.
CATWOMAN?! HAPPY BIRTHDAY, ME.
LOOKS LIKE HE CAN HANDLE ONE OF THEM AT A TIME...BUT NOT TWO.
I HAVE A WEAKNESS FOR THIS PARTICULAR MODEL.
SHANG
...NOW THIS IS A DARNED SHAME.
THIS SIMULACRUM NUT IS A REAL ARTIST AT THIS.
WONDER HOW MANY OF THESE THINGS SIM HAS?
OH NO...MY BABIES, DON'T! OHH!
OH, SHUT UP!! THIS ISN'T HURTING YOU.

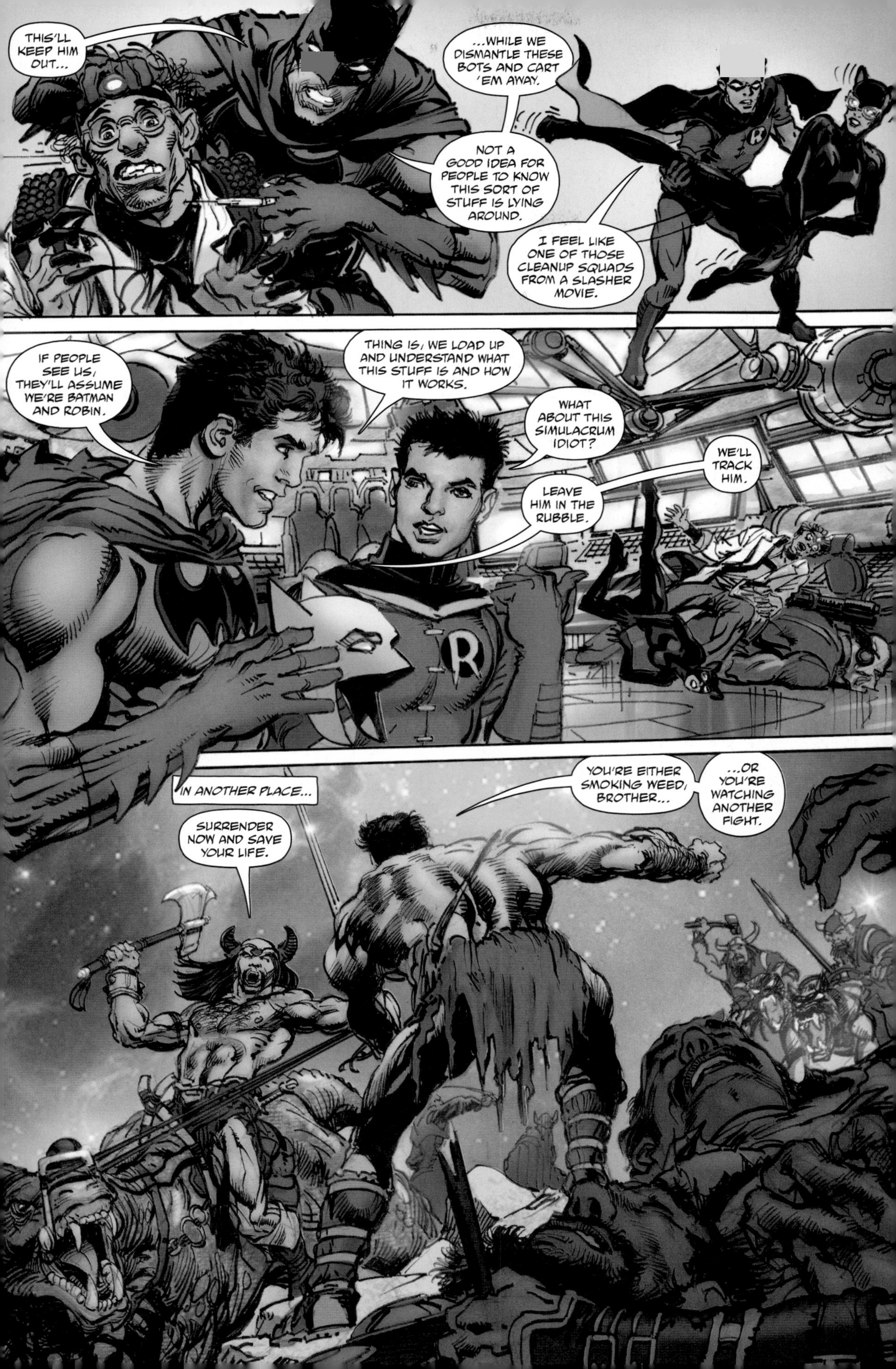
THIS'LL KEEP HIM OUT...
...WHILE WE DISMANTLE THESE BOTS AND CART 'EM AWAY.
NOT A GOOD IDEA FOR PEOPLE TO KNOW THIS SORT OF STUFF IS LYING AROUND.
I FEEL LIKE ONE OF THOSE CLEANUP SQUADS FROM A SLASHER MOVIE.
IF PEOPLE SEE US, THEY'LL ASSUME WE'RE BATMAN AND ROBIN.
THING IS, WE LOAD UP AND UNDERSTAND WHAT THIS STUFF IS AND HOW IT WORKS.
WHAT ABOUT THIS SIMULACRUM IDIOT?
WE'LL TRACK HIM.
LEAVE HIM IN THE RUBBLE.
IN ANOTHER PLACE...
SURRENDER NOW AND SAVE YOUR LIFE.
YOU'RE EITHER SMOKING WEED, BROTHER...
...OR YOU'RE WATCHING ANOTHER FIGHT.

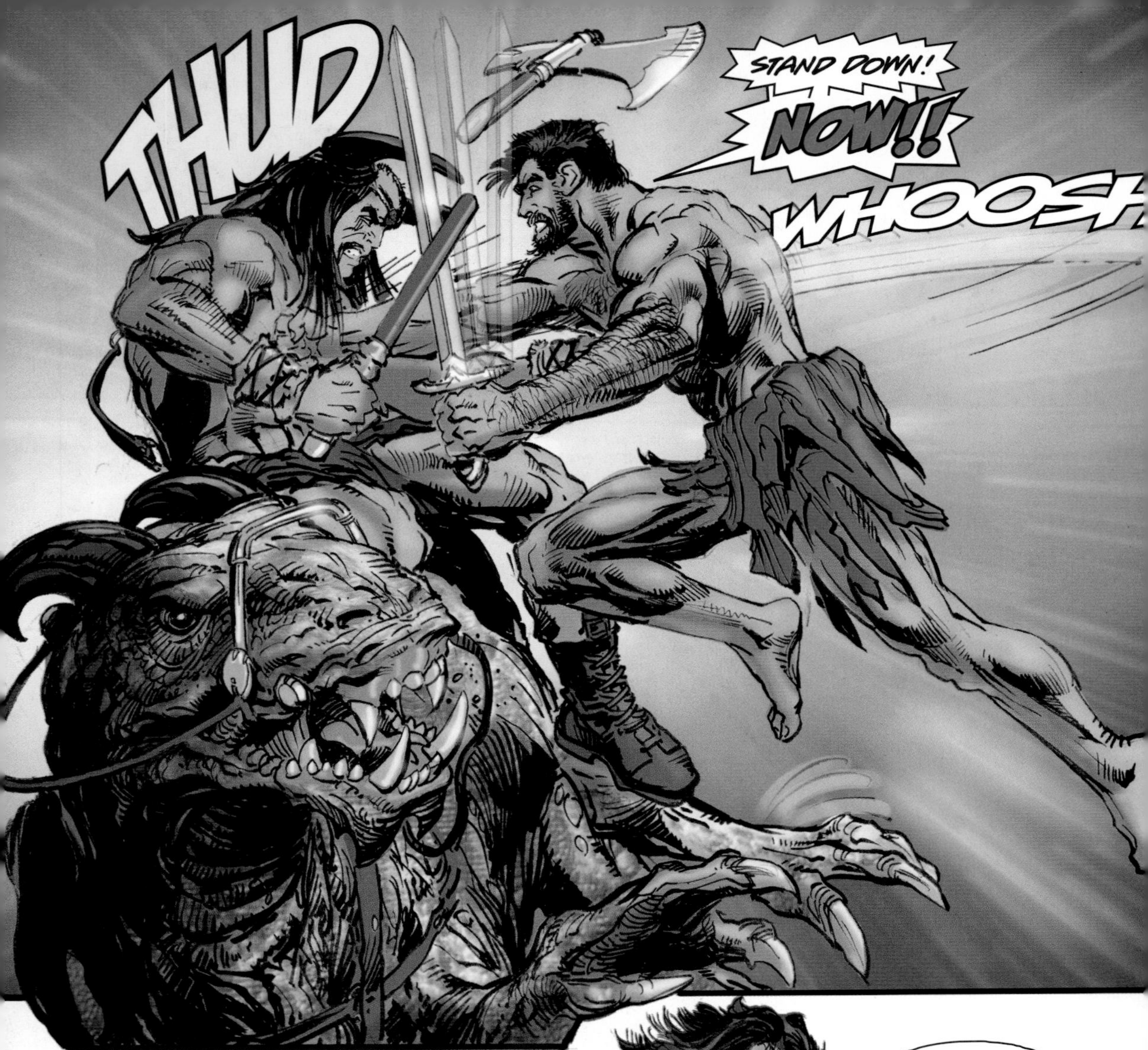
THUD
STAND DOWN!
NOW!!
WHOOSH

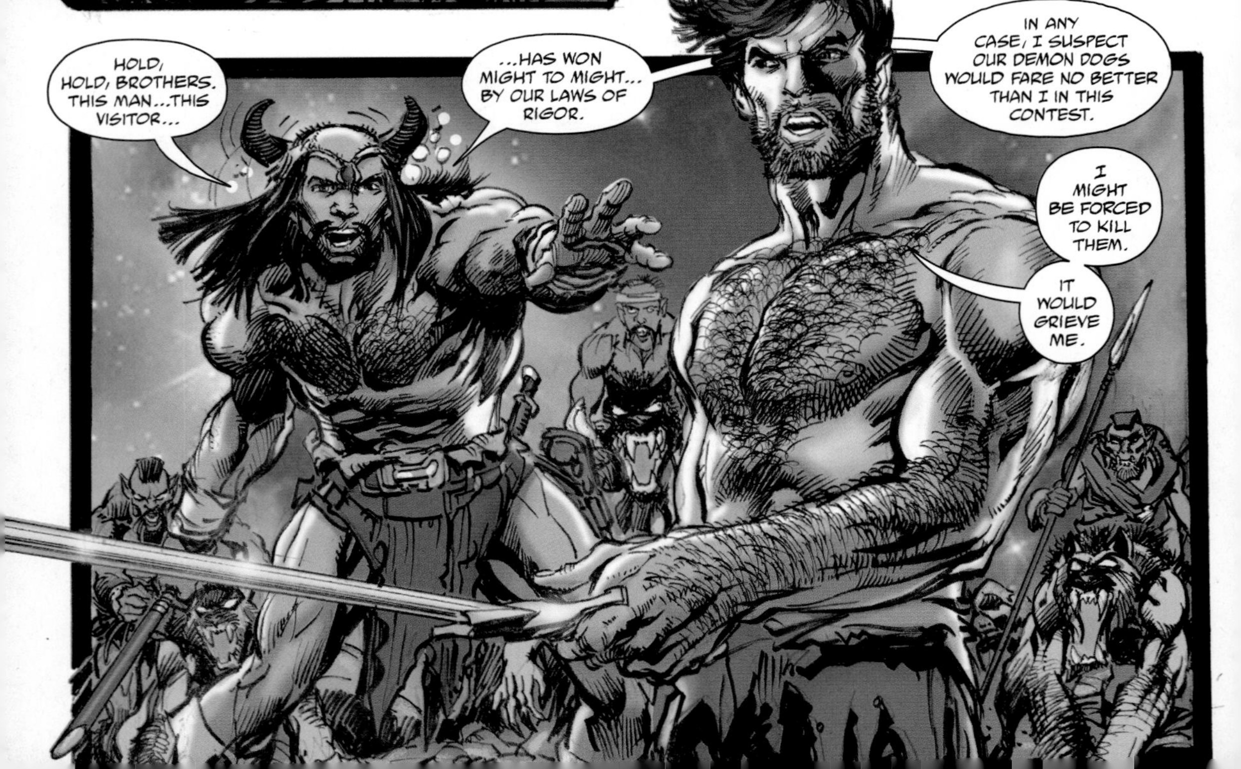
HOLD, HOLD, BROTHERS. THIS MAN...THIS VISITOR...
...HAS WON MIGHT TO MIGHT... BY OUR LAWS OF RIGOR.
IN ANY CASE, I SUSPECT OUR DEMON DOGS WOULD FARE NO BETTER THAN I IN THIS CONTEST.
I MIGHT BE FORCED TO KILL THEM.
IT WOULD GRIEVE ME.

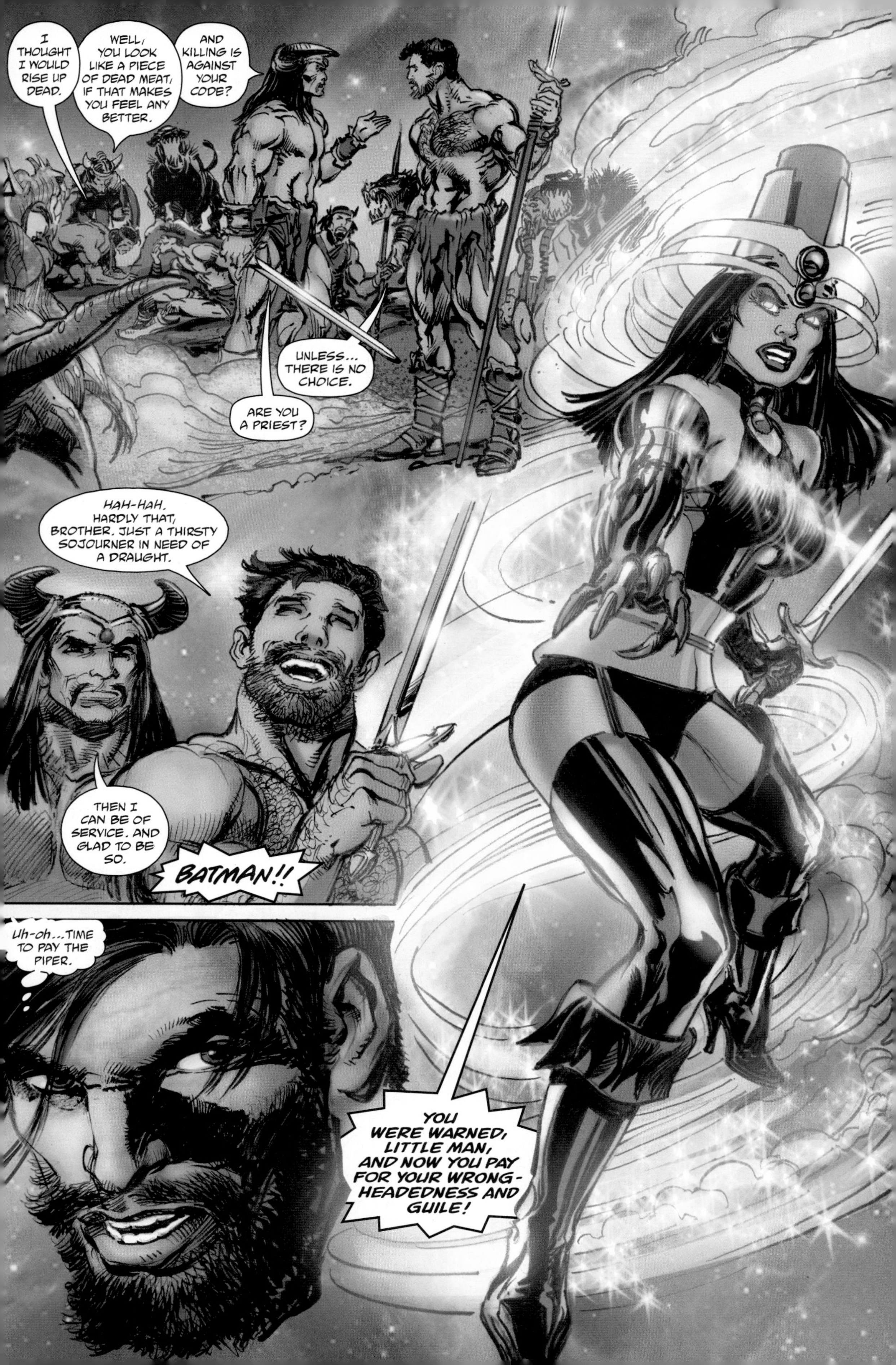
I THOUGHT I WOULD RISE UP DEAD.
WELL, YOU LOOK LIKE A PIECE OF DEAD MEAT, IF THAT MAKES YOU FEEL ANY BETTER.
AND KILLING IS AGAINST YOUR CODE?
UNLESS... THERE IS NO CHOICE.
ARE YOU A PRIEST?
HAH-HAH. HARDLY THAT, BROTHER. JUST A THIRSTY SOJOURNER IN NEED OF A DRAUGHT.
THEN I CAN BE OF SERVICE. AND GLAD TO BE SO.
BATMAN!!
Uh-oh... TIME TO PAY THE PIPER.
YOU WERE WARNED, LITTLE MAN, AND NOW YOU PAY FOR YOUR WRONG-HEADEDNESS AND GUILE!

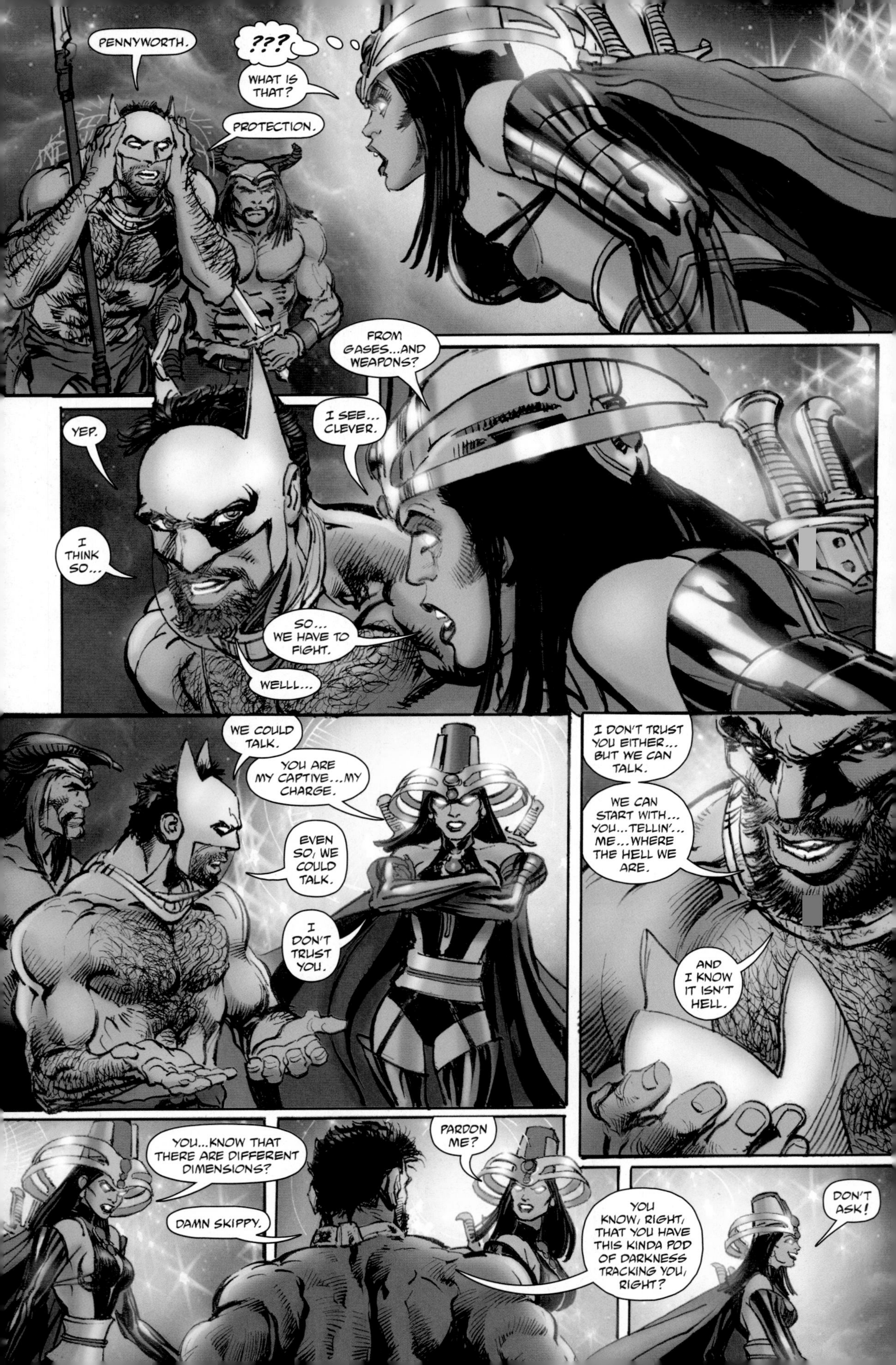
PENNYWORTH.
???
WHAT IS THAT?
PROTECTION.
FROM GASES...AND WEAPONS?
I SEE... CLEVER.
YEP.
I THINK SO...
SO... WE HAVE TO FIGHT.
WELLL...
WE COULD TALK.
YOU ARE MY CAPTIVE...MY CHARGE.
EVEN SO, WE COULD TALK.
I DON'T TRUST YOU.
I DON'T TRUST YOU EITHER... BUT WE CAN TALK.
WE CAN START WITH... YOU...TELLIN'... ME...WHERE THE HELL WE ARE.
AND I KNOW IT ISN'T HELL.
YOU...KNOW THAT THERE ARE DIFFERENT DIMENSIONS?
DAMN SKIPPY.
PARDON ME?
YOU KNOW, RIGHT, THAT YOU HAVE THIS KINDA POD OF DARKNESS TRACKING YOU, RIGHT?
DON'T ASK!

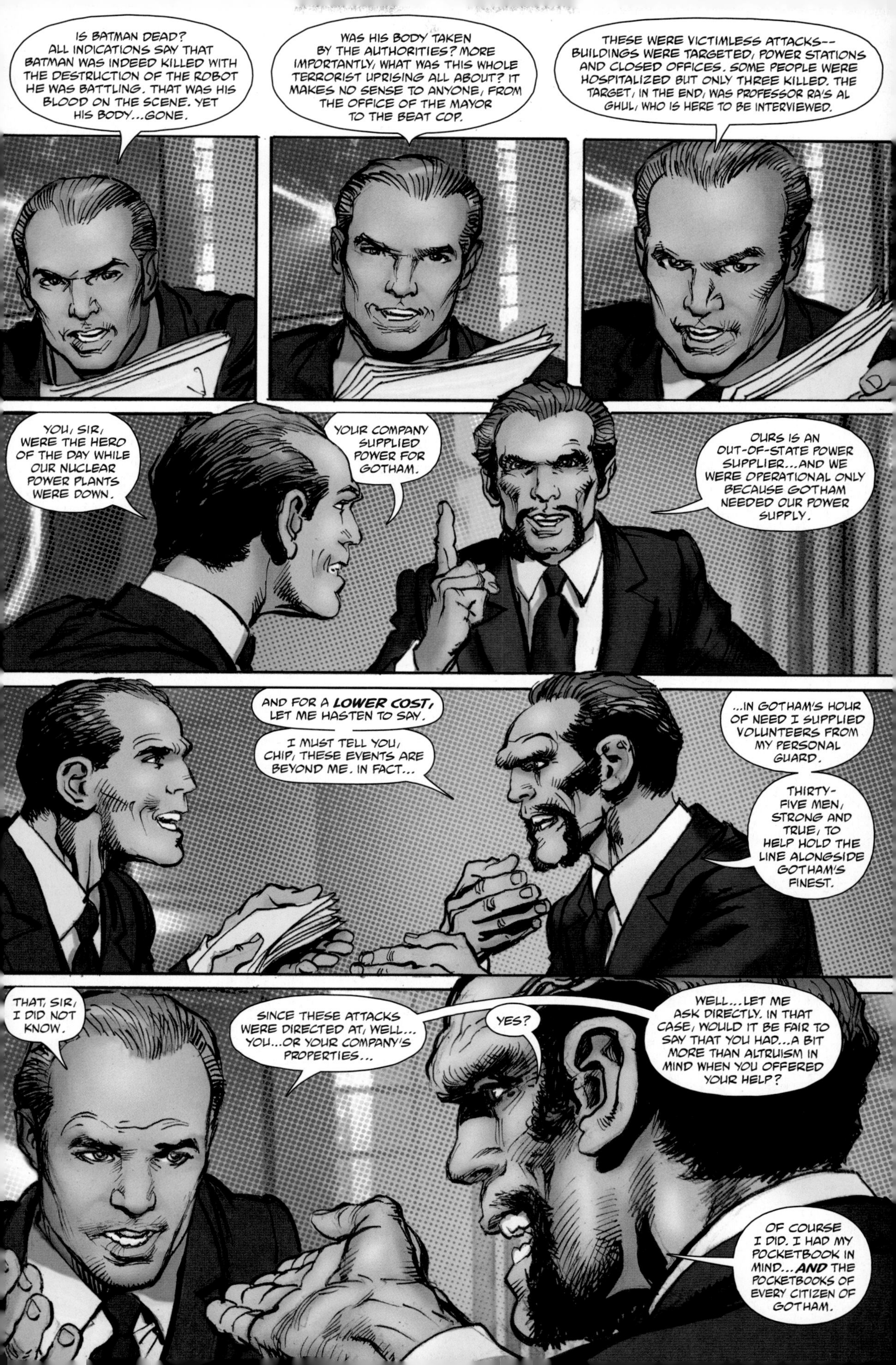
IS BATMAN DEAD? ALL INDICATIONS SAY THAT BATMAN WAS INDEED KILLED WITH THE DESTRUCTION OF THE ROBOT HE WAS BATTLING. THAT WAS HIS BLOOD ON THE SCENE. YET HIS BODY...GONE.
WAS HIS BODY TAKEN BY THE AUTHORITIES? MORE IMPORTANTLY, WHAT WAS THIS WHOLE TERRORIST UPRISING ALL ABOUT? IT MAKES NO SENSE TO ANYONE, FROM THE OFFICE OF THE MAYOR TO THE BEAT COP.
THESE WERE VICTIMLESS ATTACKS-- BUILDINGS WERE TARGETED, POWER STATIONS AND CLOSED OFFICES. SOME PEOPLE WERE HOSPITALIZED BUT ONLY THREE KILLED. THE TARGET, IN THE END, WAS PROFESSOR RA'S AL GHUL, WHO IS HERE TO BE INTERVIEWED.
YOU, SIR, WERE THE HERO OF THE DAY WHILE OUR NUCLEAR POWER PLANTS WERE DOWN.
YOUR COMPANY SUPPLIED POWER FOR GOTHAM.
OURS IS AN OUT-OF-STATE POWER SUPPLIER...AND WE WERE OPERATIONAL ONLY BECAUSE GOTHAM NEEDED OUR POWER SUPPLY.
AND FOR A **LOWER COST,** LET ME HASTEN TO SAY.
I MUST TELL YOU, CHIP, THESE EVENTS ARE BEYOND ME. IN FACT...
...IN GOTHAM'S HOUR OF NEED I SUPPLIED VOLUNTEERS FROM MY PERSONAL GUARD.
THIRTY-FIVE MEN, STRONG AND TRUE, TO HELP HOLD THE LINE ALONGSIDE GOTHAM'S FINEST.
THAT, SIR, I DID NOT KNOW.
SINCE THESE ATTACKS WERE DIRECTED AT, WELL... YOU...OR YOUR COMPANY'S PROPERTIES...
YES?
WELL...LET ME ASK DIRECTLY. IN THAT CASE, WOULD IT BE FAIR TO SAY THAT YOU HAD...A BIT MORE THAN ALTRUISM IN MIND WHEN YOU OFFERED YOUR HELP?
OF COURSE I DID. I HAD MY POCKETBOOK IN MIND...**AND** THE POCKETBOOKS OF EVERY CITIZEN OF GOTHAM.

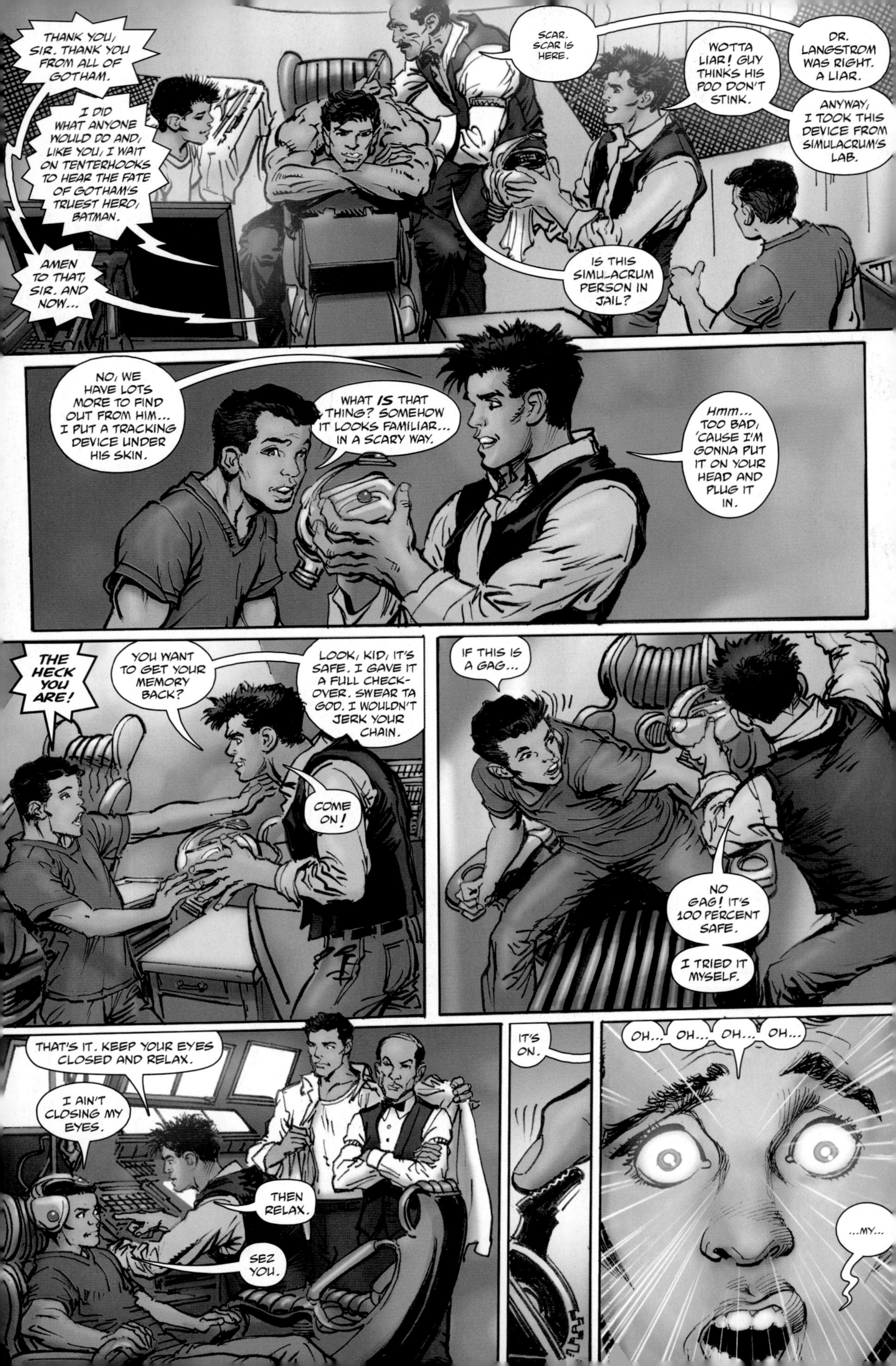
THANK YOU, SIR. THANK YOU FROM ALL OF GOTHAM.
I DID WHAT ANYONE WOULD DO AND, LIKE YOU, I WAIT ON TENTERHOOKS TO HEAR THE FATE OF GOTHAM'S TRUEST HERO, BATMAN.
AMEN TO THAT, SIR. AND NOW...
SCAR. SCAR IS HERE.
WOTTA LIAR! GUY THINKS HIS POO DON'T STINK.
DR. LANGSTROM WAS RIGHT. A LIAR.
ANYWAY, I TOOK THIS DEVICE FROM SIMULACRUM'S LAB.
IS THIS SIMULACRUM PERSON IN JAIL?
NO, WE HAVE LOTS MORE TO FIND OUT FROM HIM... I PUT A TRACKING DEVICE UNDER HIS SKIN.
WHAT IS THAT THING? SOMEHOW IT LOOKS FAMILIAR... IN A SCARY WAY.
Hmm... TOO BAD, 'CAUSE I'M GONNA PUT IT ON YOUR HEAD AND PLUG IT IN.
THE HECK YOU ARE!
YOU WANT TO GET YOUR MEMORY BACK?
LOOK, KID, IT'S SAFE. I GAVE IT A FULL CHECK-OVER. SWEAR TA GOD. I WOULDN'T JERK YOUR CHAIN.
COME ON!
IF THIS IS A GAG...
NO GAG! IT'S 100 PERCENT SAFE.
I TRIED IT MYSELF.
THAT'S IT. KEEP YOUR EYES CLOSED AND RELAX.
I AIN'T CLOSING MY EYES.
THEN RELAX.
SEZ YOU.
IT'S ON.
OH... OH... OH... OH...
...MY...

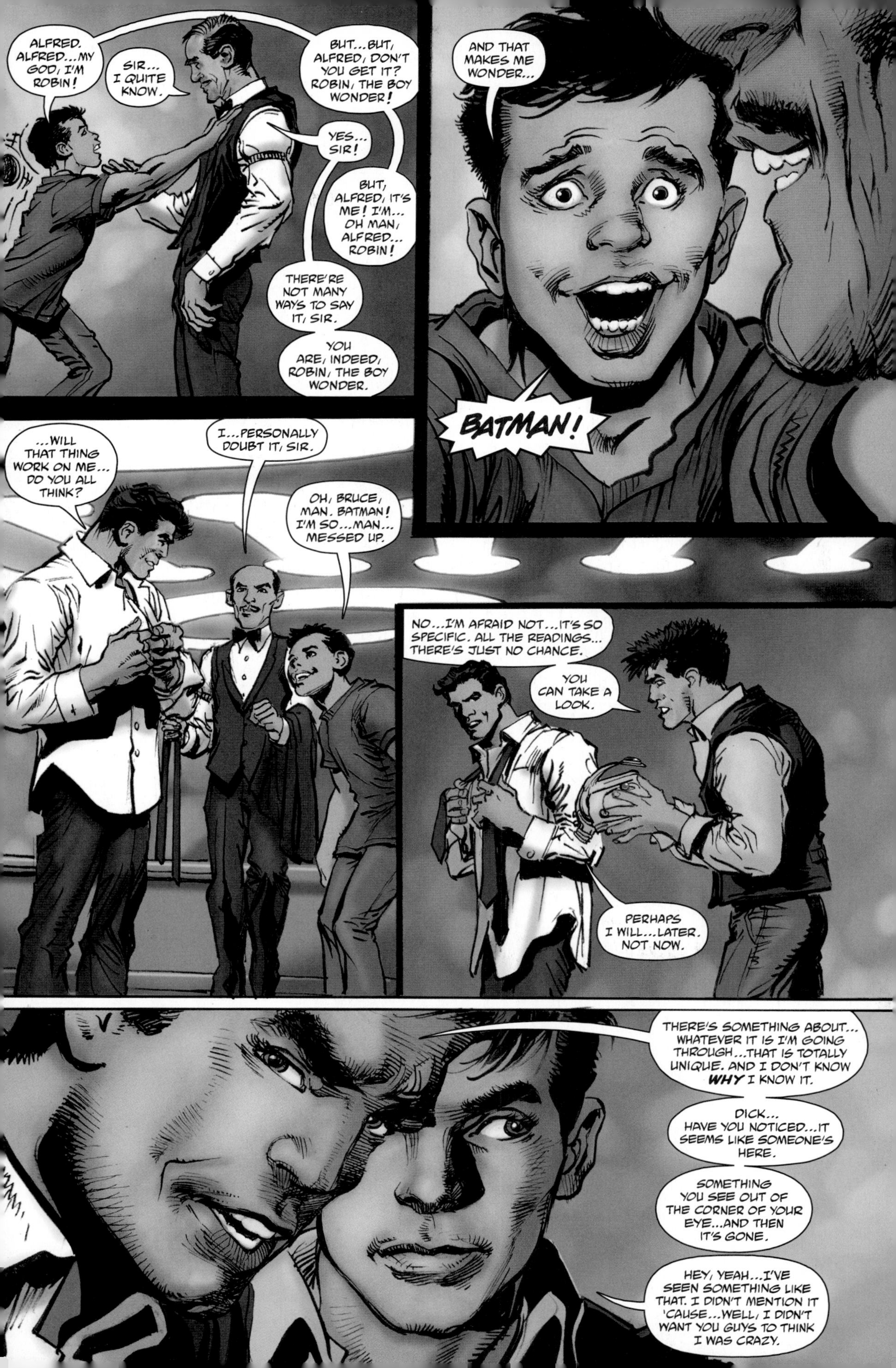
ALFRED. ALFRED...MY GOD, I'M ROBIN!
SIR... I QUITE KNOW.
BUT...BUT, ALFRED, DON'T YOU GET IT? ROBIN, THE BOY WONDER!
YES... SIR!
BUT, ALFRED, IT'S ME! I'M... OH MAN, ALFRED... ROBIN!
THERE'RE NOT MANY WAYS TO SAY IT, SIR.
YOU ARE, INDEED, ROBIN, THE BOY WONDER.
AND THAT MAKES ME WONDER...
BATMAN!
...WILL THAT THING WORK ON ME... DO YOU ALL THINK?
I...PERSONALLY DOUBT IT, SIR.
OH, BRUCE, MAN. BATMAN! I'M SO...MAN... MESSED UP.
NO...I'M AFRAID NOT...IT'S SO SPECIFIC. ALL THE READINGS... THERE'S JUST NO CHANCE.
YOU CAN TAKE A LOOK.
PERHAPS I WILL...LATER. NOT NOW.
THERE'S SOMETHING ABOUT... WHATEVER IT IS I'M GOING THROUGH...THAT IS TOTALLY UNIQUE. AND I DON'T KNOW WHY I KNOW IT.
DICK... HAVE YOU NOTICED...IT SEEMS LIKE SOMEONE'S HERE.
SOMETHING YOU SEE OUT OF THE CORNER OF YOUR EYE...AND THEN IT'S GONE.
HEY, YEAH...I'VE SEEN SOMETHING LIKE THAT. I DIDN'T MENTION IT 'CAUSE...WELL, I DIDN'T WANT YOU GUYS TO THINK I WAS CRAZY.

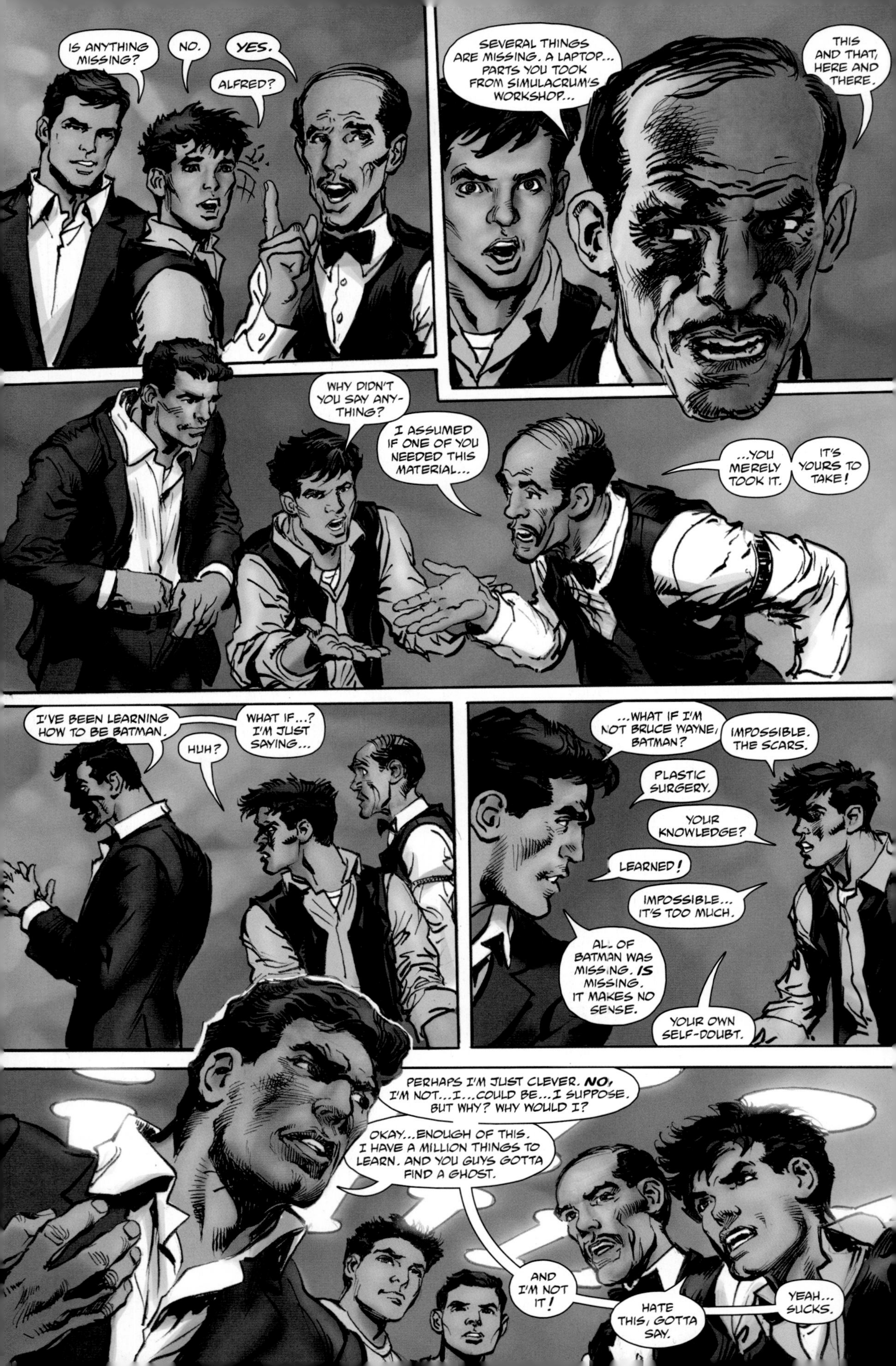
IS ANYTHING MISSING?
NO.
YES.
ALFRED?
SEVERAL THINGS ARE MISSING. A LAPTOP... PARTS YOU TOOK FROM SIMULACRUM'S WORKSHOP...
THIS AND THAT, HERE AND THERE.
WHY DIDN'T YOU SAY ANY-THING?
I ASSUMED IF ONE OF YOU NEEDED THIS MATERIAL...
...YOU MERELY TOOK IT.
IT'S YOURS TO TAKE!
I'VE BEEN LEARNING HOW TO BE BATMAN.
HUH?
WHAT IF...? I'M JUST SAYING...
...WHAT IF I'M NOT BRUCE WAYNE, BATMAN?
IMPOSSIBLE. THE SCARS.
PLASTIC SURGERY.
YOUR KNOWLEDGE?
LEARNED!
IMPOSSIBLE... IT'S TOO MUCH.
ALL OF BATMAN WAS MISSING. IS MISSING. IT MAKES NO SENSE.
YOUR OWN SELF-DOUBT.
PERHAPS I'M JUST CLEVER. NO, I'M NOT...I...COULD BE...I SUPPOSE. BUT WHY? WHY WOULD I?
OKAY...ENOUGH OF THIS. I HAVE A MILLION THINGS TO LEARN. AND YOU GUYS GOTTA FIND A GHOST.
AND I'M NOT IT!
HATE THIS, GOTTA SAY.
YEAH... SUCKS.

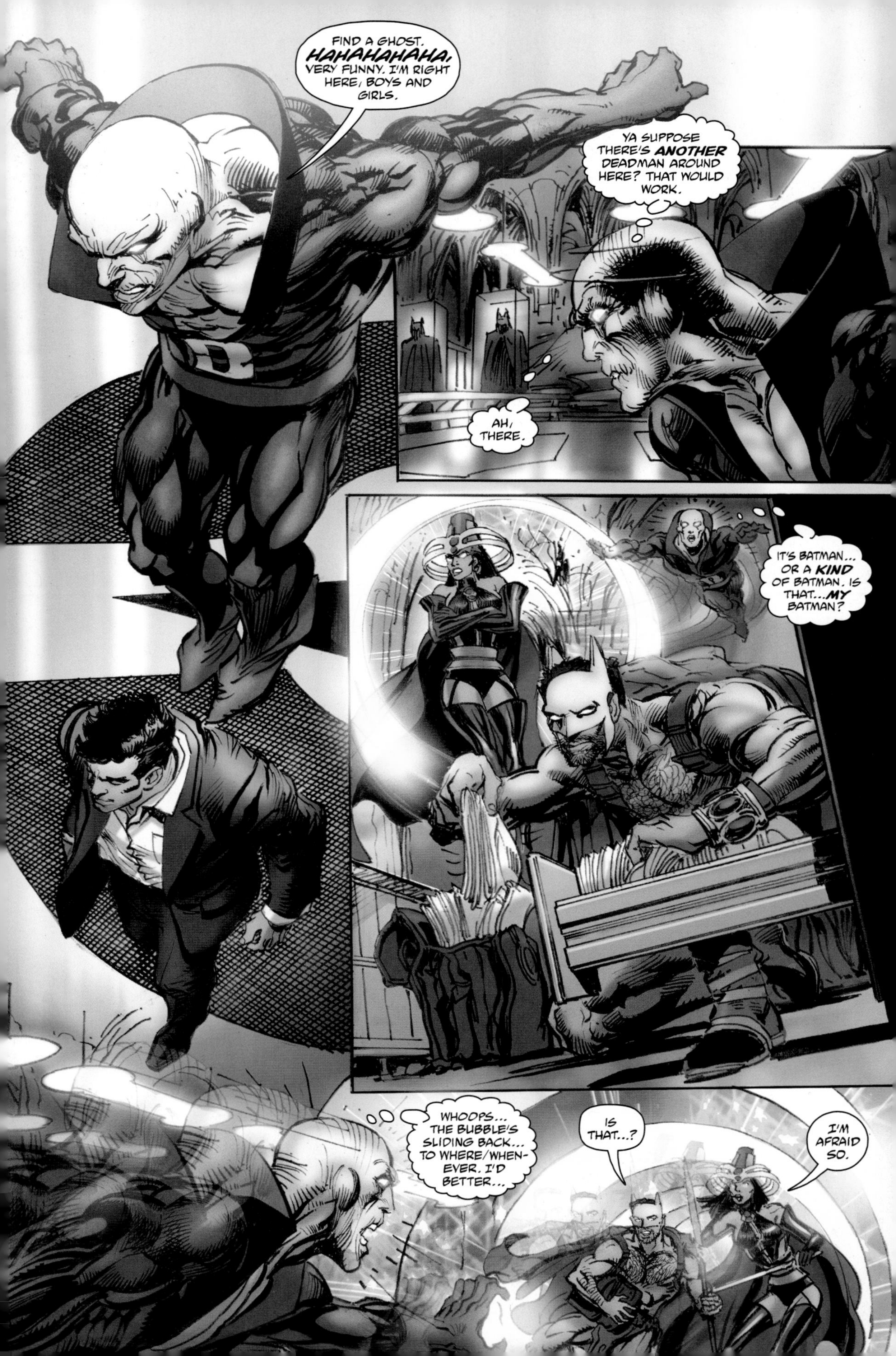
FIND A GHOST. HAHAHAHAHA, VERY FUNNY. I'M RIGHT HERE, BOYS AND GIRLS.
YA SUPPOSE THERE'S ANOTHER DEADMAN AROUND HERE? THAT WOULD WORK.
AH, THERE.
IT'S BATMAN... OR A KIND OF BATMAN. IS THAT...MY BATMAN?
WHOOPS... THE BUBBLE'S SLIDING BACK... TO WHERE/WHEN-EVER. I'D BETTER...
IS THAT...?
I'M AFRAID SO.

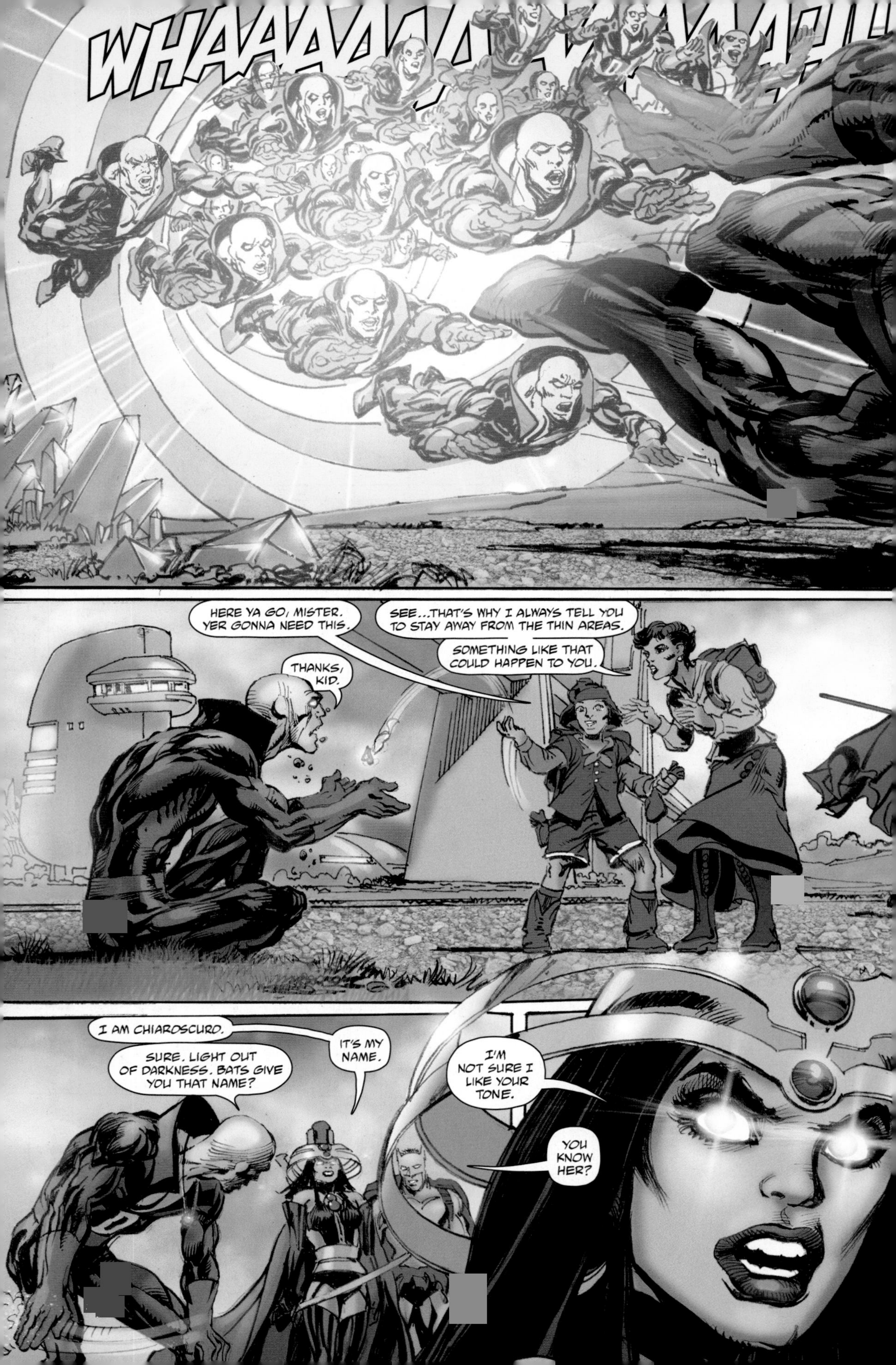
WHAAAA
HERE YA GO, MISTER. YER GONNA NEED THIS.
THANKS, KID.
SEE...THAT'S WHY I ALWAYS TELL YOU TO STAY AWAY FROM THE THIN AREAS.
SOMETHING LIKE THAT COULD HAPPEN TO YOU.
I AM CHIAROSCURO.
IT'S MY NAME.
SURE. LIGHT OUT OF DARKNESS. BATS GIVE YOU THAT NAME?
I'M NOT SURE I LIKE YOUR TONE.
YOU KNOW HER?

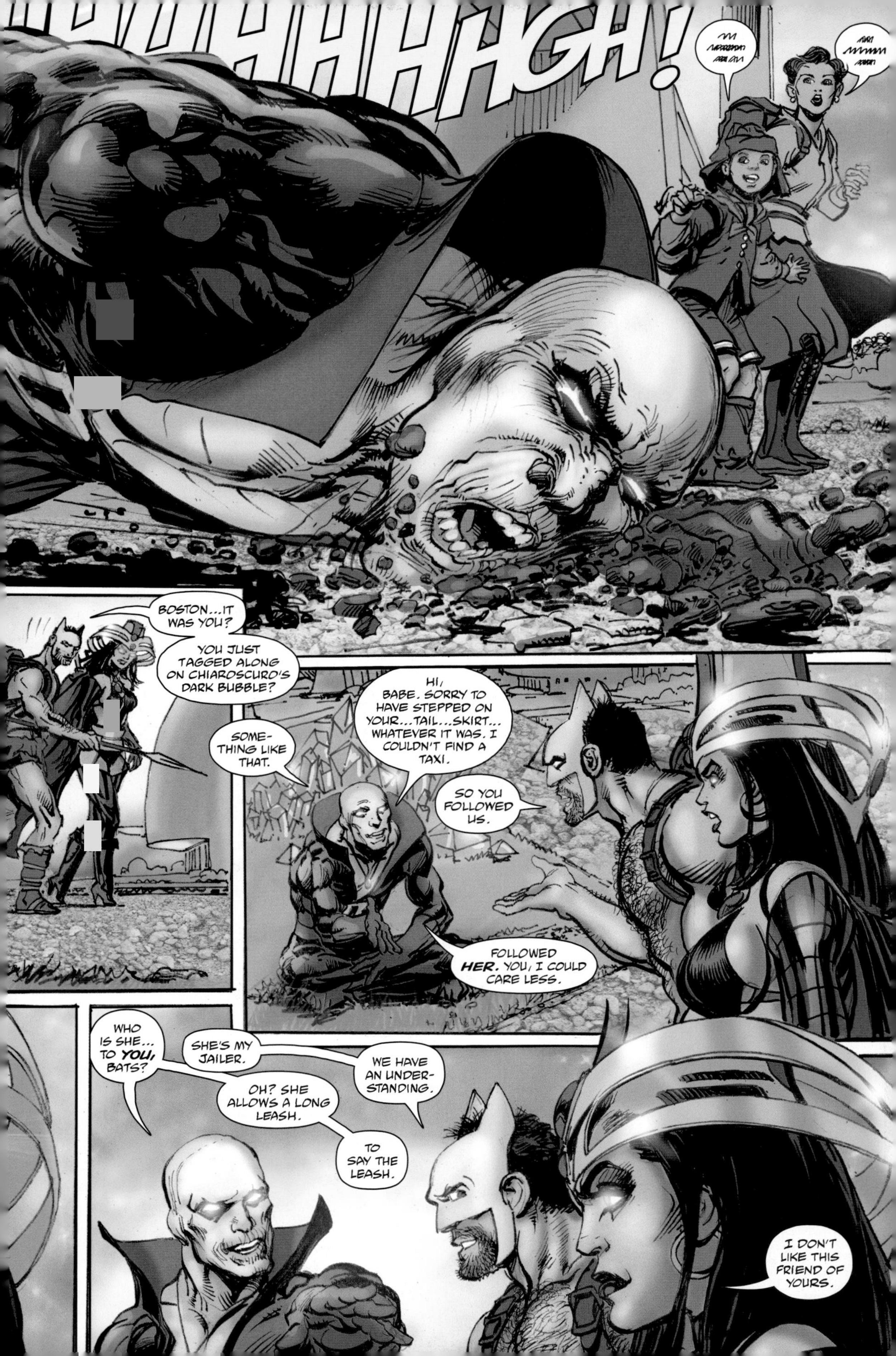

HHHHHGH!
BOSTON...IT WAS YOU?
YOU JUST TAGGED ALONG ON CHIAROSCURO'S DARK BUBBLE?
SOME-THING LIKE THAT.
HI, BABE. SORRY TO HAVE STEPPED ON YOUR...TAIL...SKIRT... WHATEVER IT WAS. I COULDN'T FIND A TAXI.
SO YOU FOLLOWED US.
FOLLOWED **HER.** YOU, I COULD CARE LESS.
WHO IS SHE... TO **YOU,** BATS?
SHE'S MY JAILER.
WE HAVE AN UNDER-STANDING.
OH? SHE ALLOWS A LONG LEASH.
TO SAY THE LEASH.
I DON'T LIKE THIS FRIEND OF YOURS.

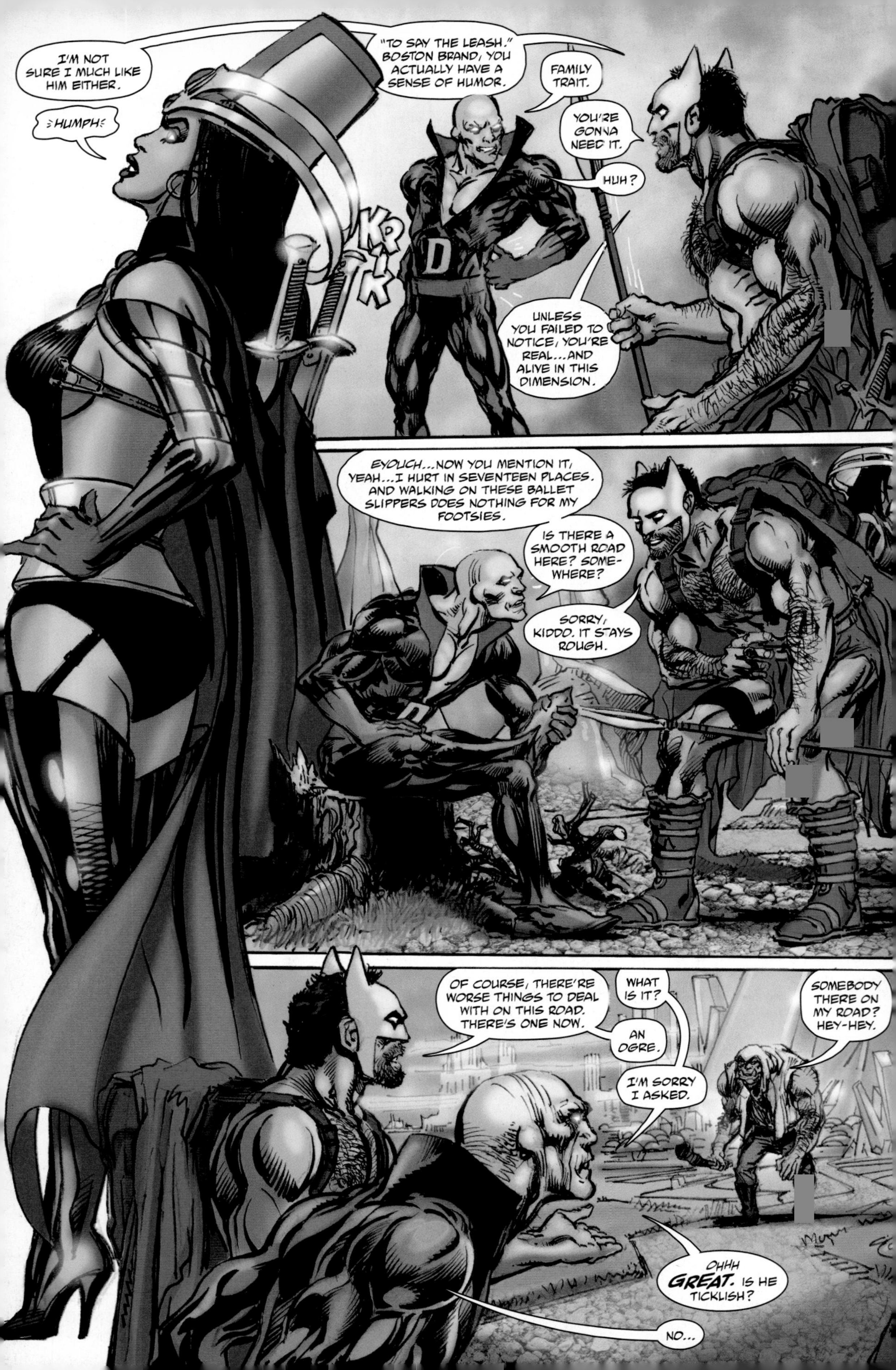

I'M NOT SURE I MUCH LIKE HIM EITHER.
"TO SAY THE LEASH." BOSTON BRAND, YOU ACTUALLY HAVE A SENSE OF HUMOR.
FAMILY TRAIT.
YOU'RE GONNA NEED IT.
HUH?
UNLESS YOU FAILED TO NOTICE, YOU'RE REAL...AND ALIVE IN THIS DIMENSION.
HUMPH
KRIK
EYOUCH...NOW YOU MENTION IT, YEAH...I HURT IN SEVENTEEN PLACES. AND WALKING ON THESE BALLET SLIPPERS DOES NOTHING FOR MY FOOTSIES.
IS THERE A SMOOTH ROAD HERE? SOME-WHERE?
SORRY, KIDDO. IT STAYS ROUGH.
OF COURSE, THERE'RE WORSE THINGS TO DEAL WITH ON THIS ROAD. THERE'S ONE NOW.
WHAT IS IT?
AN OGRE.
I'M SORRY I ASKED.
SOMEBODY THERE ON MY ROAD? HEY-HEY.
OHHH GREAT. IS HE TICKLISH?
NO...

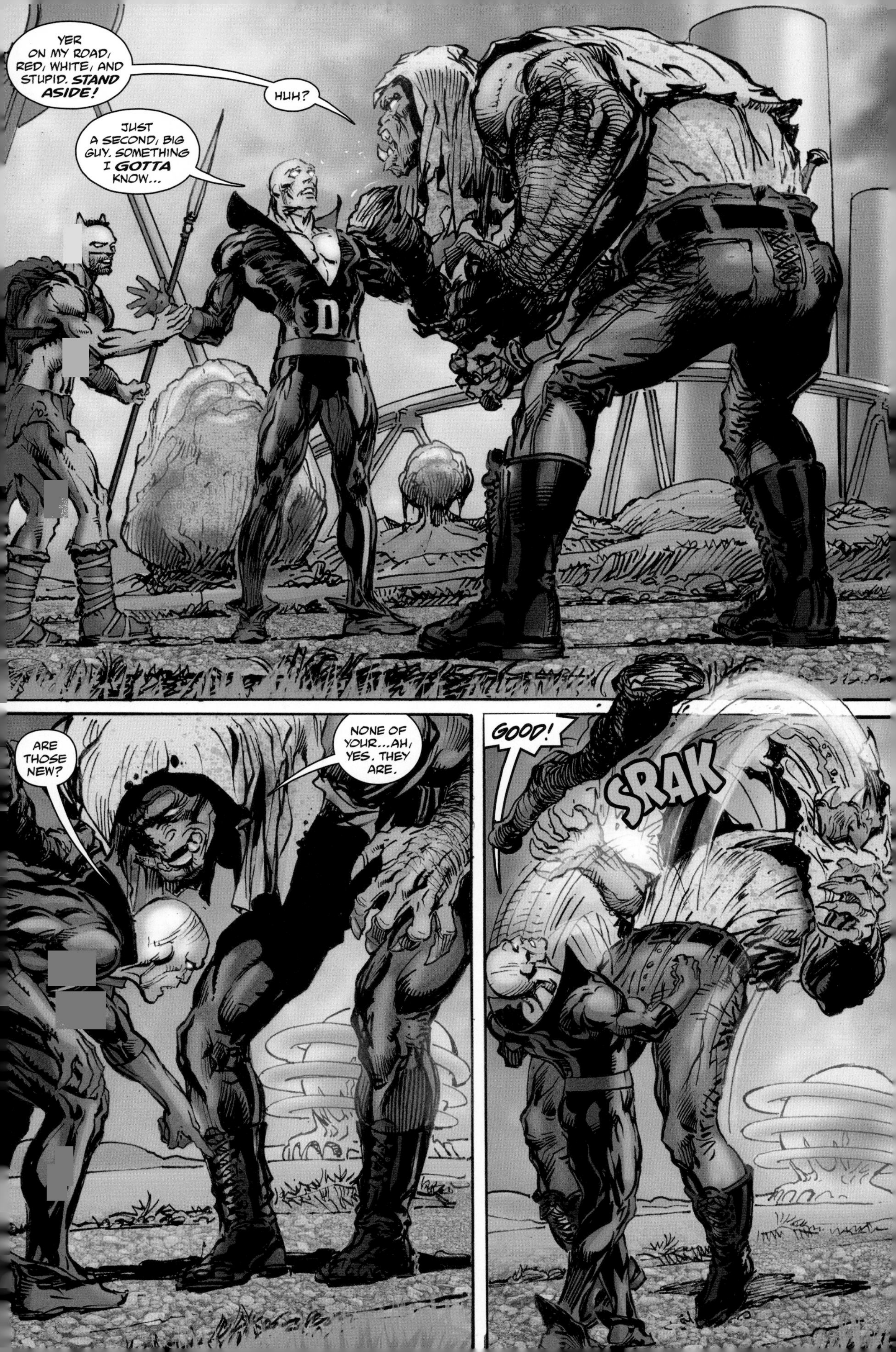
YER ON MY ROAD, RED, WHITE, AND STUPID. STAND ASIDE!
HUH?
JUST A SECOND, BIG GUY. SOMETHING I GOTTA KNOW...
ARE THOSE NEW?
NONE OF YOUR...AH, YES. THEY ARE.
GOOD!
SRAK

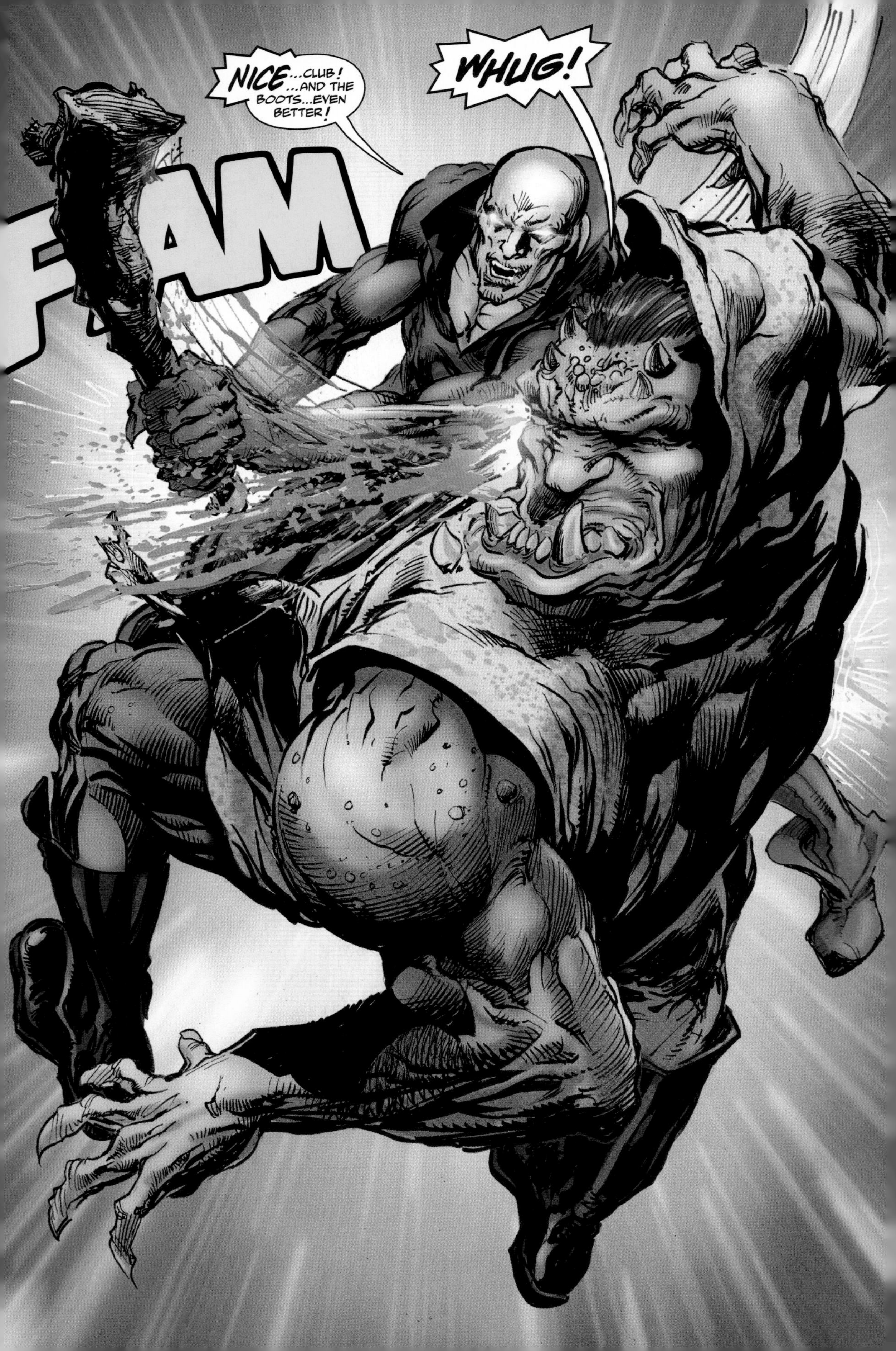
NICE...CLUB! ...AND THE BOOTS...EVEN BETTER!
WHUG!

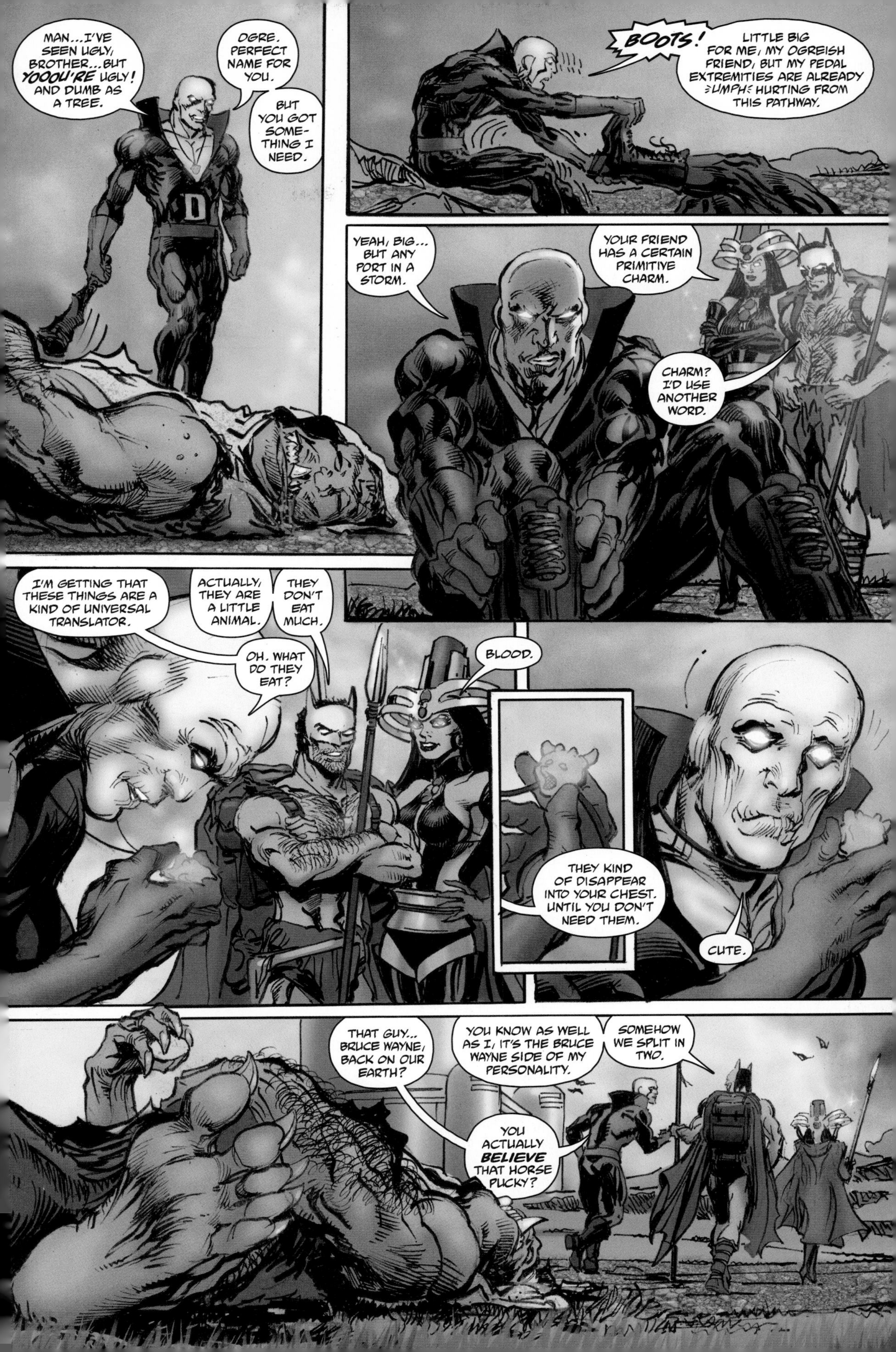
MAN...I'VE SEEN UGLY, BROTHER...BUT YOOOU'RE UGLY! AND DUMB AS A TREE.
OGRE. PERFECT NAME FOR YOU.
BUT YOU GOT SOME-THING I NEED.
BOOTS!
LITTLE BIG FOR ME, MY OGREISH FRIEND, BUT MY PEDAL EXTREMITIES ARE ALREADY =UMPH= HURTING FROM THIS PATHWAY.
YEAH, BIG... BUT ANY PORT IN A STORM.
YOUR FRIEND HAS A CERTAIN PRIMITIVE CHARM.
CHARM? I'D USE ANOTHER WORD.
I'M GETTING THAT THESE THINGS ARE A KIND OF UNIVERSAL TRANSLATOR.
ACTUALLY, THEY ARE A LITTLE ANIMAL.
THEY DON'T EAT MUCH.
OH. WHAT DO THEY EAT?
BLOOD.
THEY KIND OF DISAPPEAR INTO YOUR CHEST. UNTIL YOU DON'T NEED THEM.
CUTE.
THAT GUY... BRUCE WAYNE, BACK ON OUR EARTH?
YOU KNOW AS WELL AS I, IT'S THE BRUCE WAYNE SIDE OF MY PERSONALITY.
SOMEHOW WE SPLIT IN TWO.
YOU ACTUALLY BELIEVE THAT HORSE PUCKY?

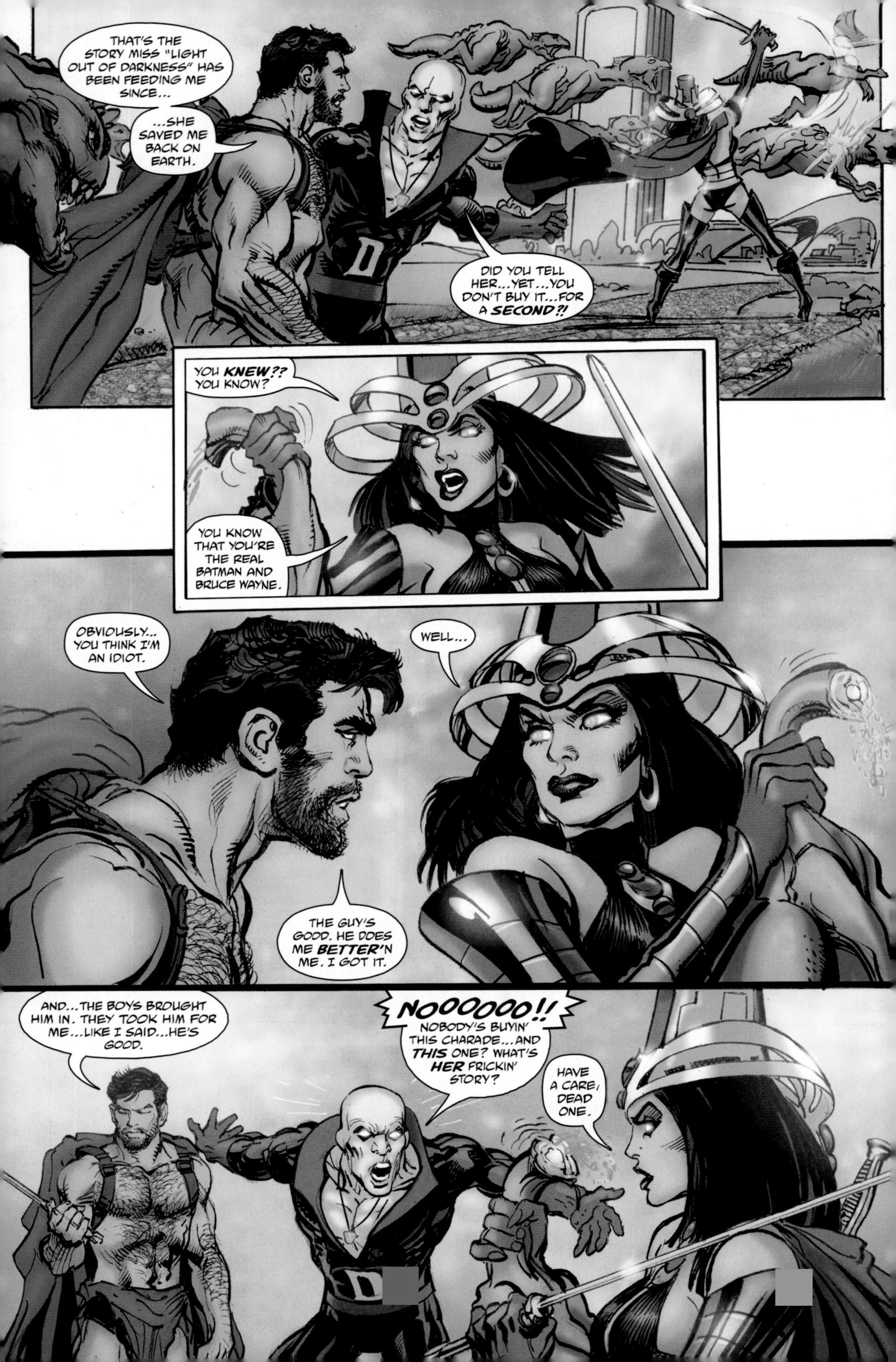
THAT'S THE STORY MISS "LIGHT OUT OF DARKNESS" HAS BEEN FEEDING ME SINCE...
...SHE SAVED ME BACK ON EARTH.
DID YOU TELL HER...YET...YOU DON'T BUY IT...FOR A SECOND?!
YOU KNEW?? YOU KNOW?
YOU KNOW THAT YOU'RE THE REAL BATMAN AND BRUCE WAYNE.
OBVIOUSLY... YOU THINK I'M AN IDIOT.
WELL...
THE GUY'S GOOD. HE DOES ME BETTER'N ME. I GOT IT.
AND...THE BOYS BROUGHT HIM IN. THEY TOOK HIM FOR ME...LIKE I SAID...HE'S GOOD.
NOOOOOO!! NOBODY'S BUYIN' THIS CHARADE...AND THIS ONE? WHAT'S HER FRICKIN' STORY?
HAVE A CARE, DEAD ONE.

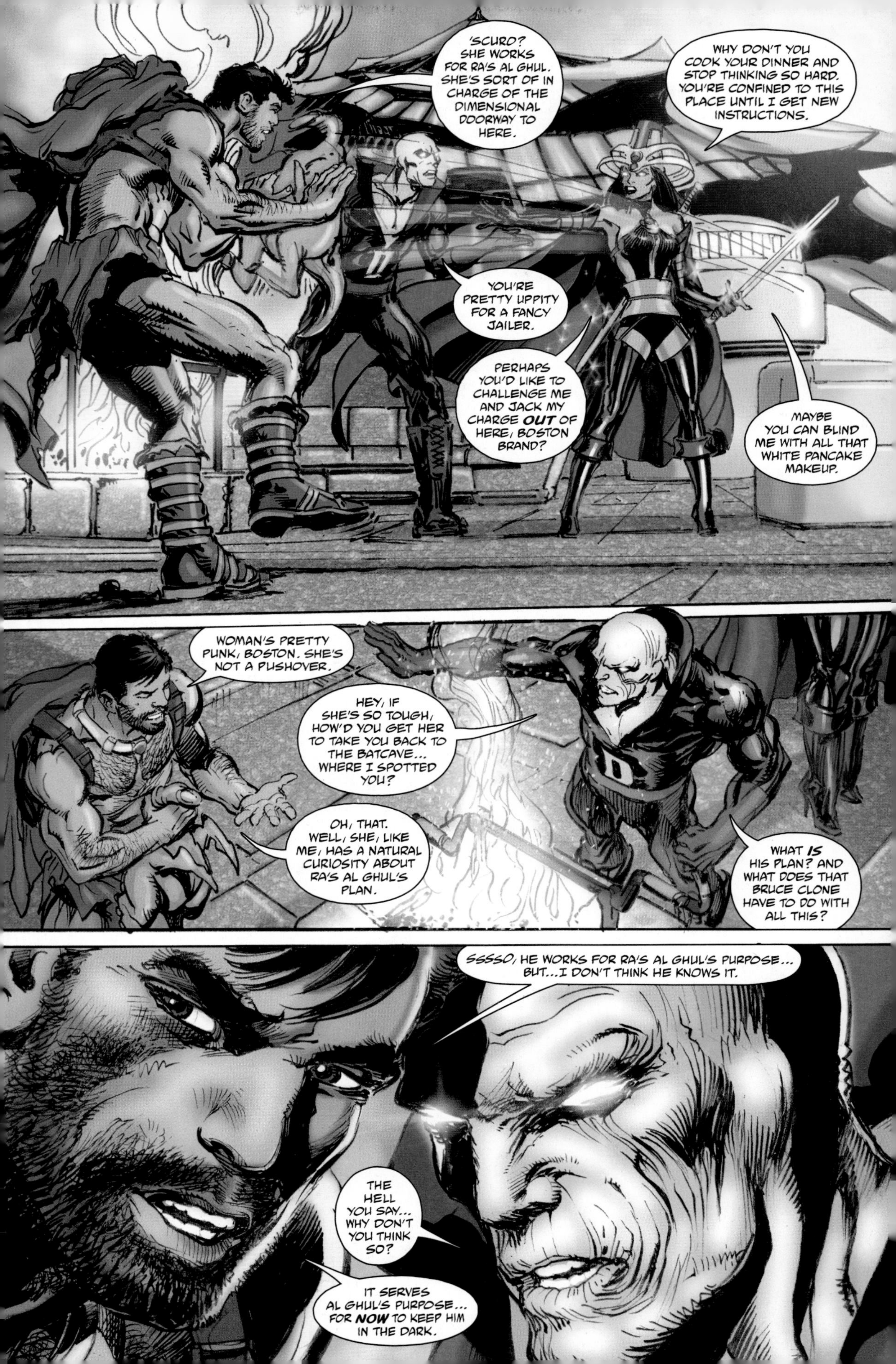
'SCURO? SHE WORKS FOR RA'S AL GHUL. SHE'S SORT OF IN CHARGE OF THE DIMENSIONAL DOORWAY TO HERE.
WHY DON'T YOU COOK YOUR DINNER AND STOP THINKING SO HARD. YOU'RE CONFINED TO THIS PLACE UNTIL I GET NEW INSTRUCTIONS.
YOU'RE PRETTY UPPITY FOR A FANCY JAILER.
PERHAPS YOU'D LIKE TO CHALLENGE ME AND JACK MY CHARGE OUT OF HERE, BOSTON BRAND?
MAYBE YOU CAN BLIND ME WITH ALL THAT WHITE PANCAKE MAKEUP.
WOMAN'S PRETTY PUNK, BOSTON. SHE'S NOT A PUSHOVER.
HEY, IF SHE'S SO TOUGH, HOW'D YOU GET HER TO TAKE YOU BACK TO THE BATCAVE... WHERE I SPOTTED YOU?
OH, THAT. WELL, SHE, LIKE ME, HAS A NATURAL CURIOSITY ABOUT RA'S AL GHUL'S PLAN.
WHAT IS HIS PLAN? AND WHAT DOES THAT BRUCE CLONE HAVE TO DO WITH ALL THIS?
SSSSO, HE WORKS FOR RA'S AL GHUL'S PURPOSE... BUT... I DON'T THINK HE KNOWS IT.
THE HELL YOU SAY... WHY DON'T YOU THINK SO?
IT SERVES AL GHUL'S PURPOSE... FOR NOW TO KEEP HIM IN THE DARK.

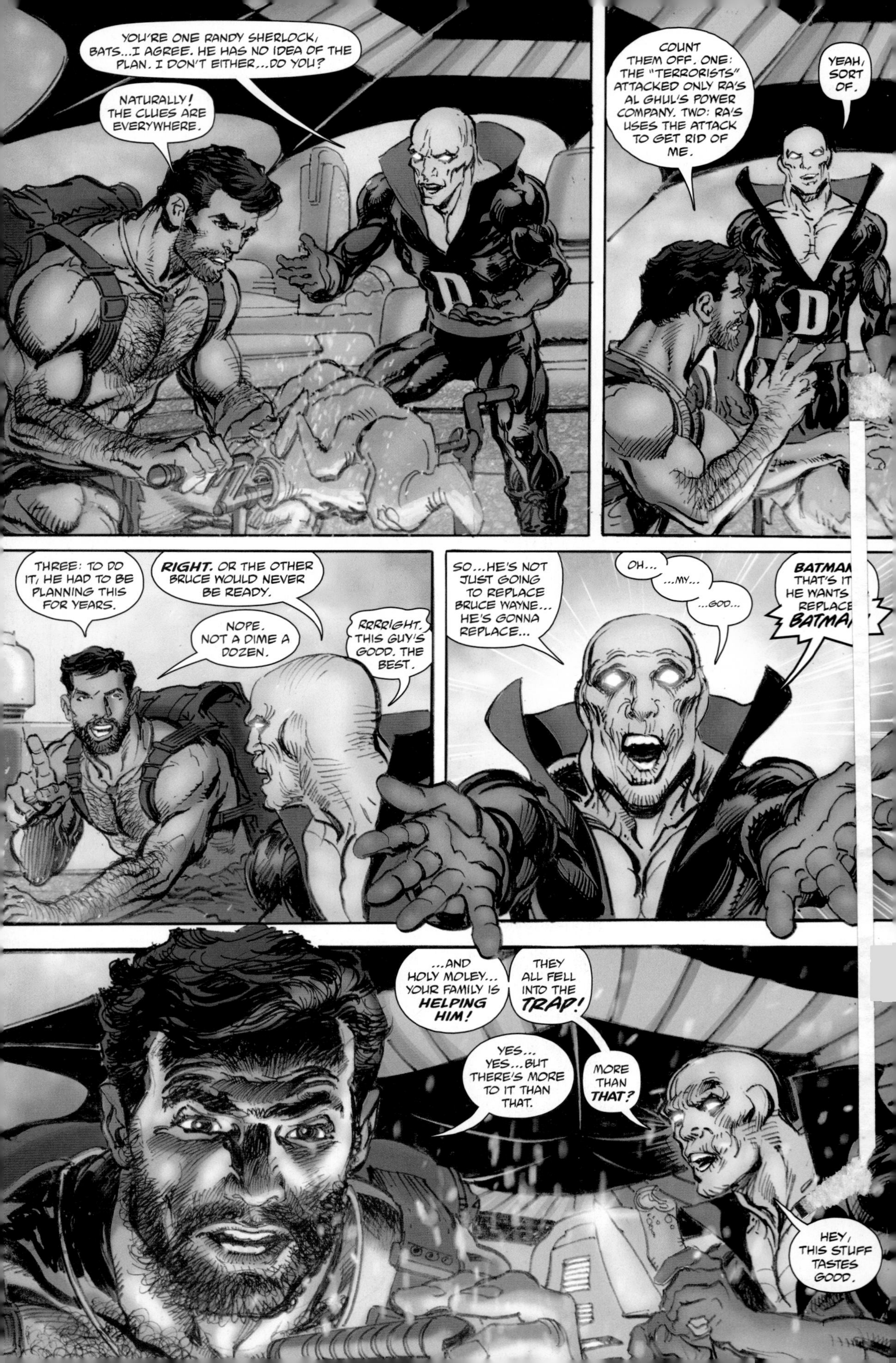
YOU'RE ONE RANDY SHERLOCK, BATS...I AGREE. HE HAS NO IDEA OF THE PLAN. I DON'T EITHER...DO YOU?
NATURALLY! THE CLUES ARE EVERYWHERE.
COUNT THEM OFF. ONE: THE "TERRORISTS" ATTACKED ONLY RA'S AL GHUL'S POWER COMPANY. TWO: RA'S USES THE ATTACK TO GET RID OF ME.
YEAH, SORT OF.
THREE: TO DO IT, HE HAD TO BE PLANNING THIS FOR YEARS.
RIGHT. OR THE OTHER BRUCE WOULD NEVER BE READY.
NOPE. NOT A DIME A DOZEN.
RRRRIGHT. THIS GUY'S GOOD. THE BEST.
SO...HE'S NOT JUST GOING TO REPLACE BRUCE WAYNE... HE'S GONNA REPLACE...
OH... ...MY... ...GOD...
BATMAN THAT'S IT HE WANTS REPLACE BATMAN
...AND HOLY MOLEY... YOUR FAMILY IS HELPING HIM!
THEY ALL FELL INTO THE TRAP!
YES... YES...BUT THERE'S MORE TO IT THAN THAT.
MORE THAN THAT?
HEY, THIS STUFF TASTES GOOD.

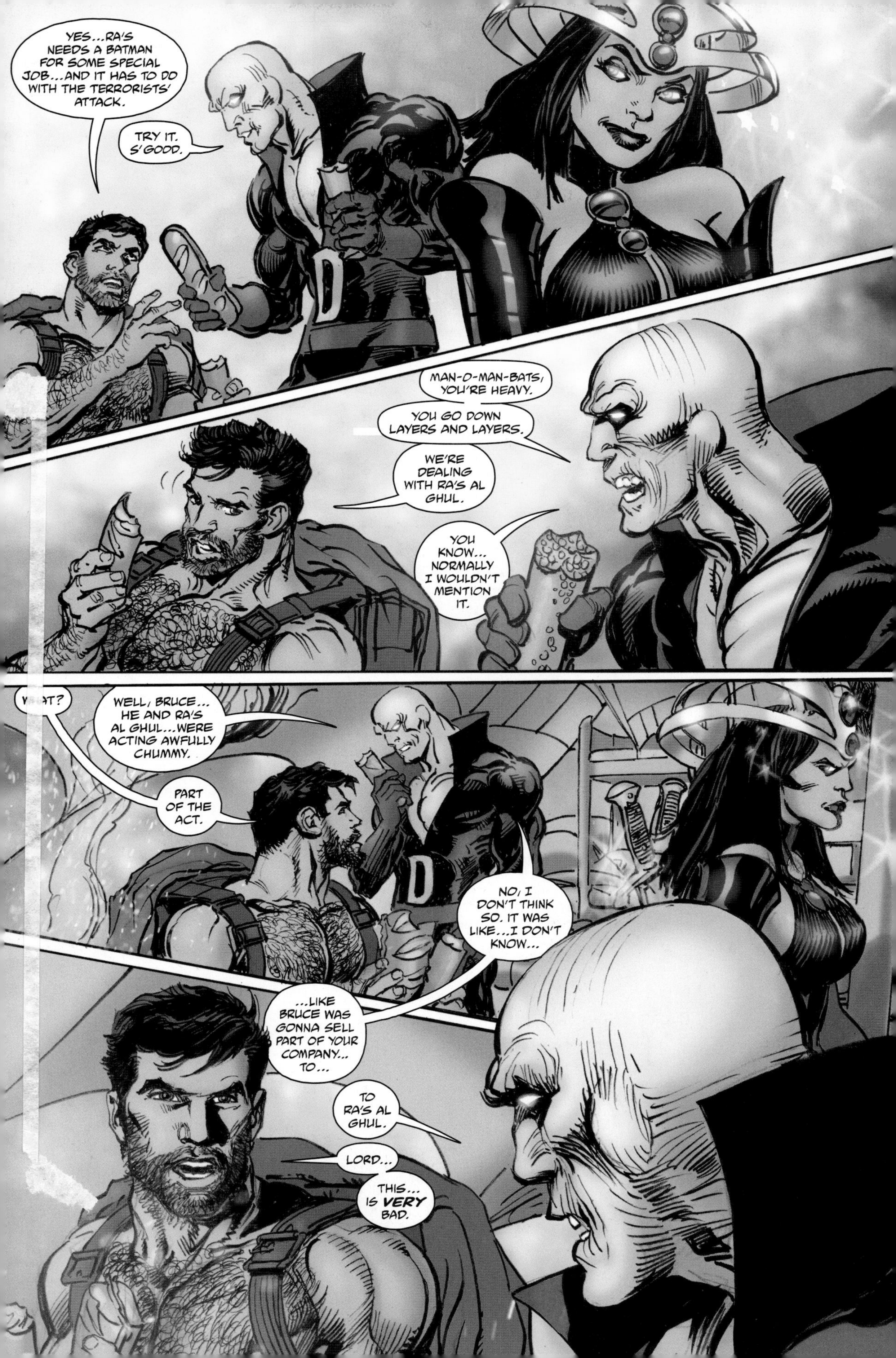

YES...RA'S NEEDS A BATMAN FOR SOME SPECIAL JOB...AND IT HAS TO DO WITH THE TERRORISTS' ATTACK.
TRY IT. S'GOOD.
MAN-O-MAN-BATS, YOU'RE HEAVY.
YOU GO DOWN LAYERS AND LAYERS.
WE'RE DEALING WITH RA'S AL GHUL.
YOU KNOW... NORMALLY I WOULDN'T MENTION IT.
WHAT?
WELL, BRUCE... HE AND RA'S AL GHUL...WERE ACTING AWFULLY CHUMMY.
PART OF THE ACT.
NO, I DON'T THINK SO. IT WAS LIKE...I DON'T KNOW...
...LIKE BRUCE WAS GONNA SELL PART OF YOUR COMPANY... TO...
TO RA'S AL GHUL.
LORD...
THIS... IS **VERY** BAD.

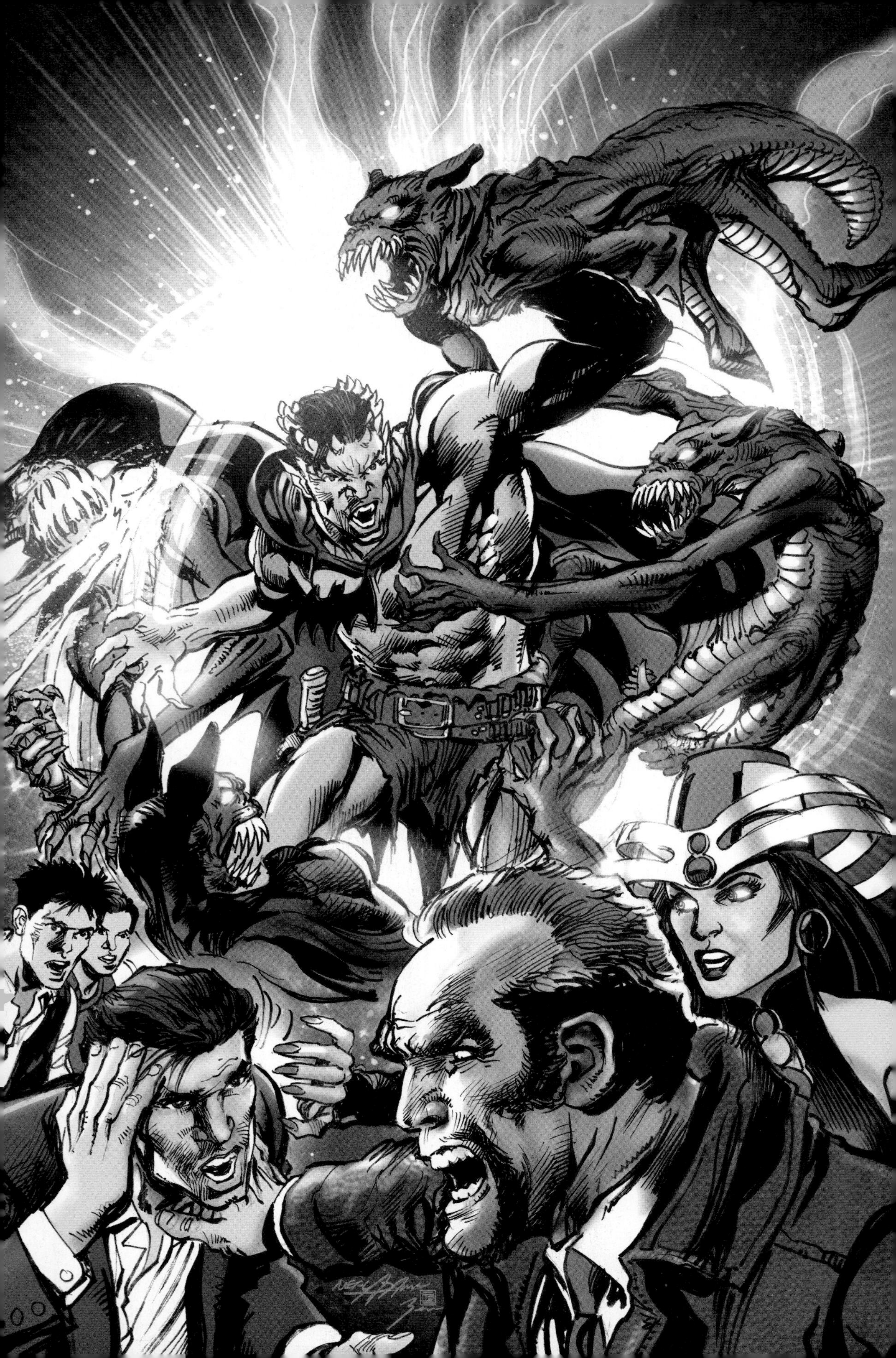

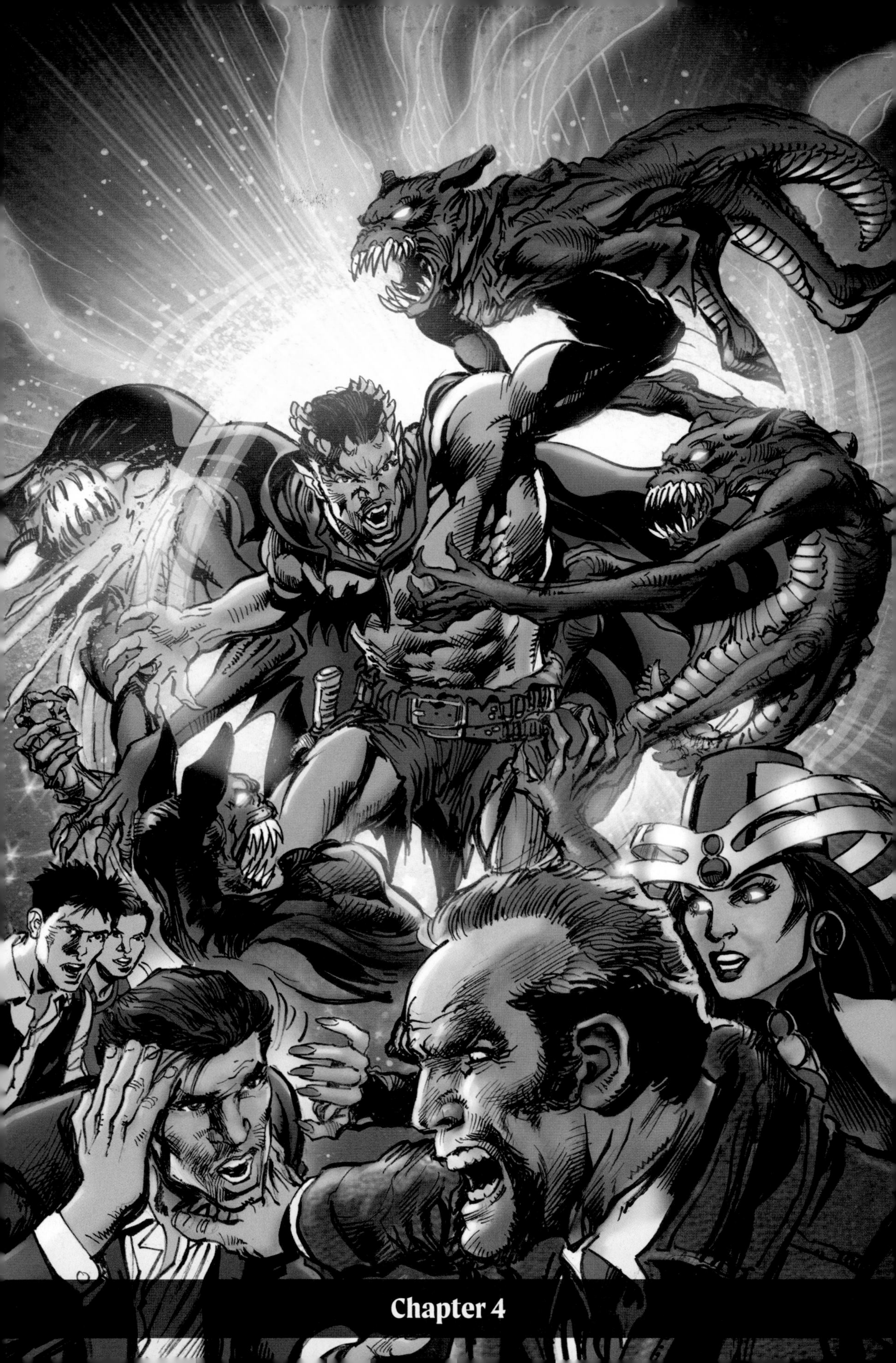

Chapter 4

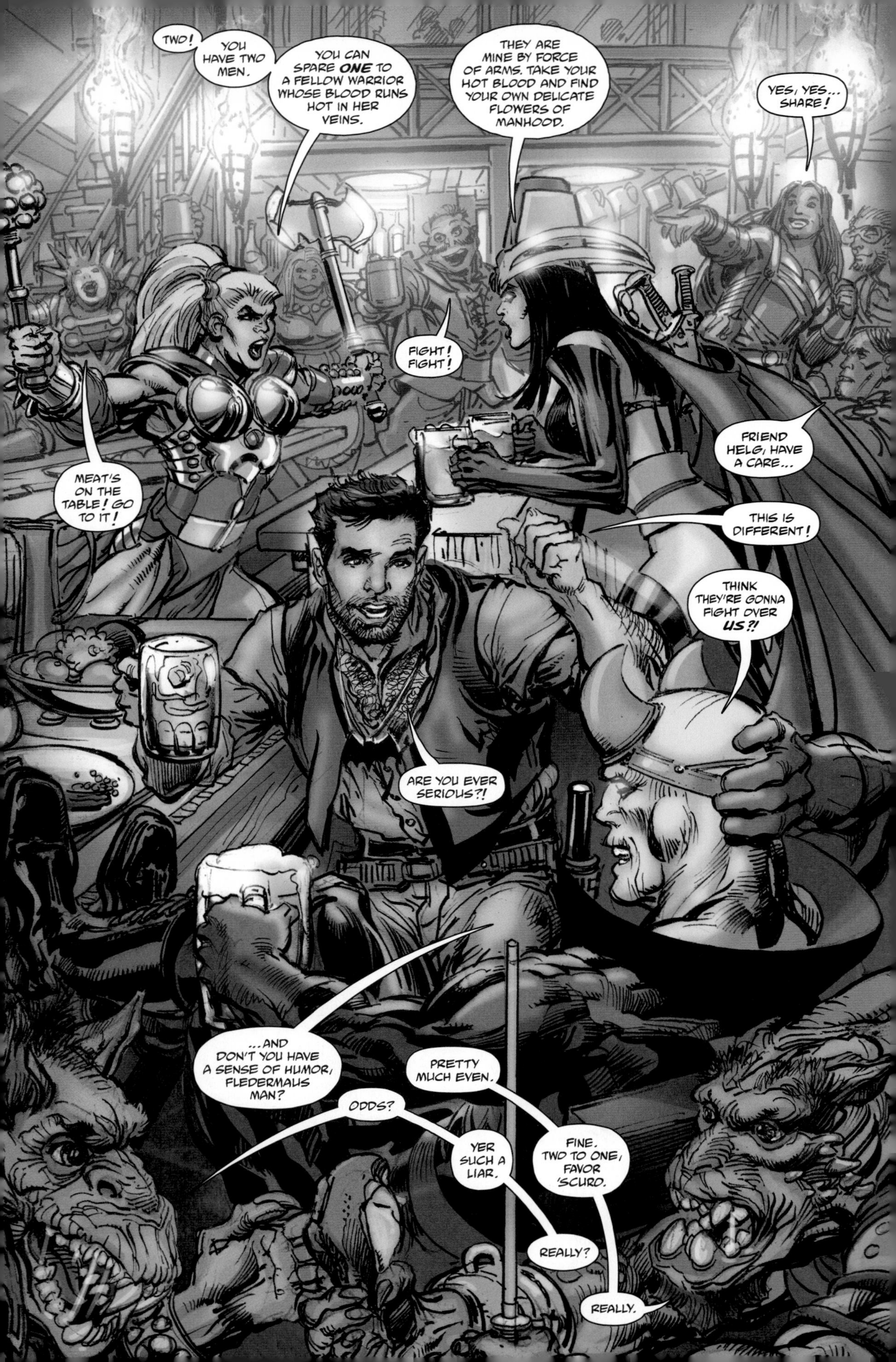
TWO!
YOU HAVE TWO MEN.
YOU CAN SPARE ONE TO A FELLOW WARRIOR WHOSE BLOOD RUNS HOT IN HER VEINS.
THEY ARE MINE BY FORCE OF ARMS. TAKE YOUR HOT BLOOD AND FIND YOUR OWN DELICATE FLOWERS OF MANHOOD.
YES, YES... SHARE!
FIGHT! FIGHT!
MEAT'S ON THE TABLE! GO TO IT!
FRIEND HELG, HAVE A CARE...
THIS IS DIFFERENT!
THINK THEY'RE GONNA FIGHT OVER US?!
ARE YOU EVER SERIOUS?!
...AND DON'T YOU HAVE A SENSE OF HUMOR, FLEDERMAUS MAN?
PRETTY MUCH EVEN.
ODDS?
YER SUCH A LIAR.
FINE. TWO TO ONE, FAVOR 'SCURO.
REALLY?
REALLY.

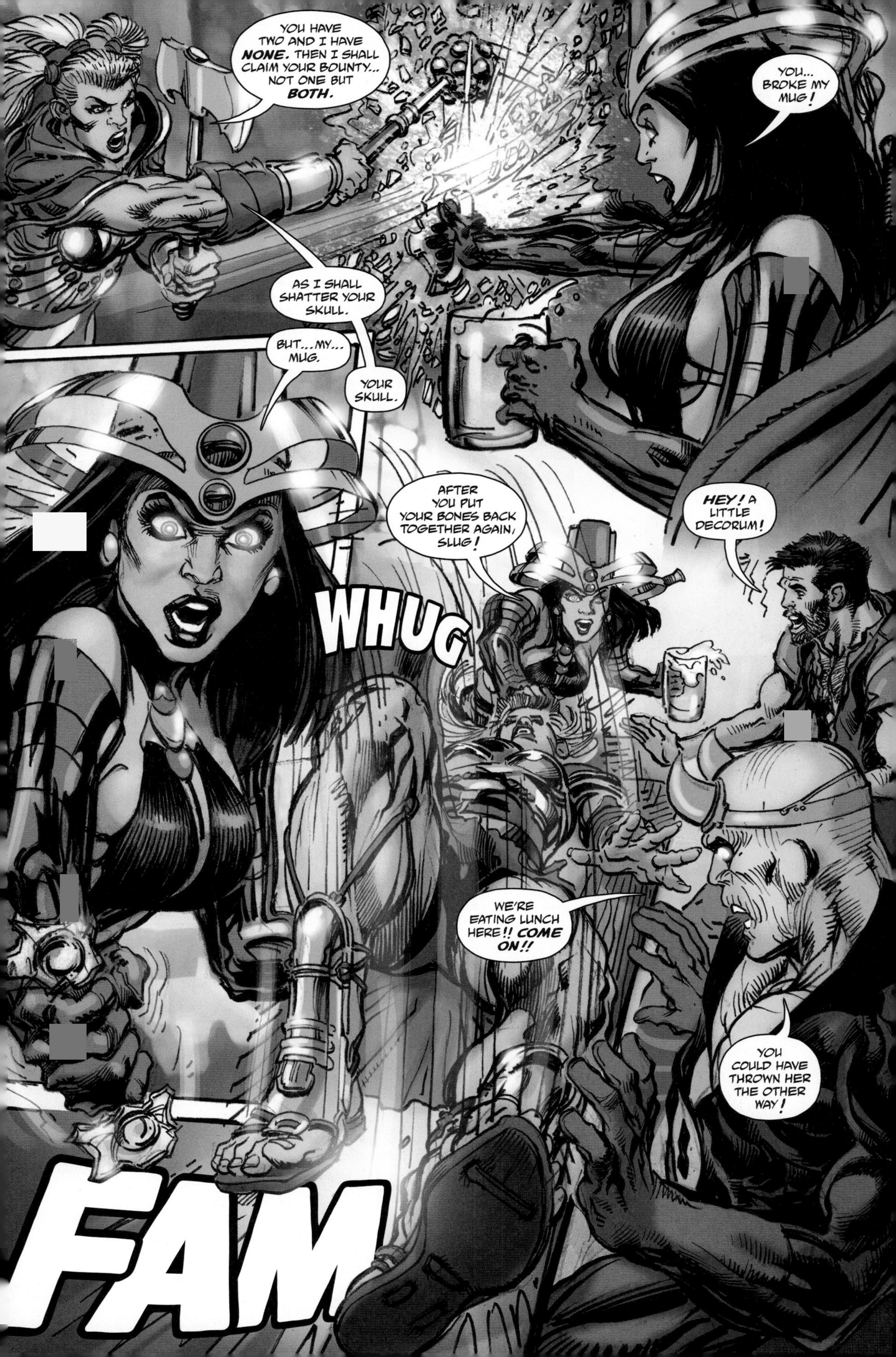
YOU HAVE TWO AND I HAVE NONE. THEN I SHALL CLAIM YOUR BOUNTY... NOT ONE BUT BOTH.
YOU... BROKE MY MUG!
AS I SHALL SHATTER YOUR SKULL.
BUT...MY... MUG.
YOUR SKULL.
AFTER YOU PUT YOUR BONES BACK TOGETHER AGAIN, SLUG!
HEY! A LITTLE DECORUM!
WHUG
WE'RE EATING LUNCH HERE!! COME ON!!
YOU COULD HAVE THROWN HER THE OTHER WAY!
FAM

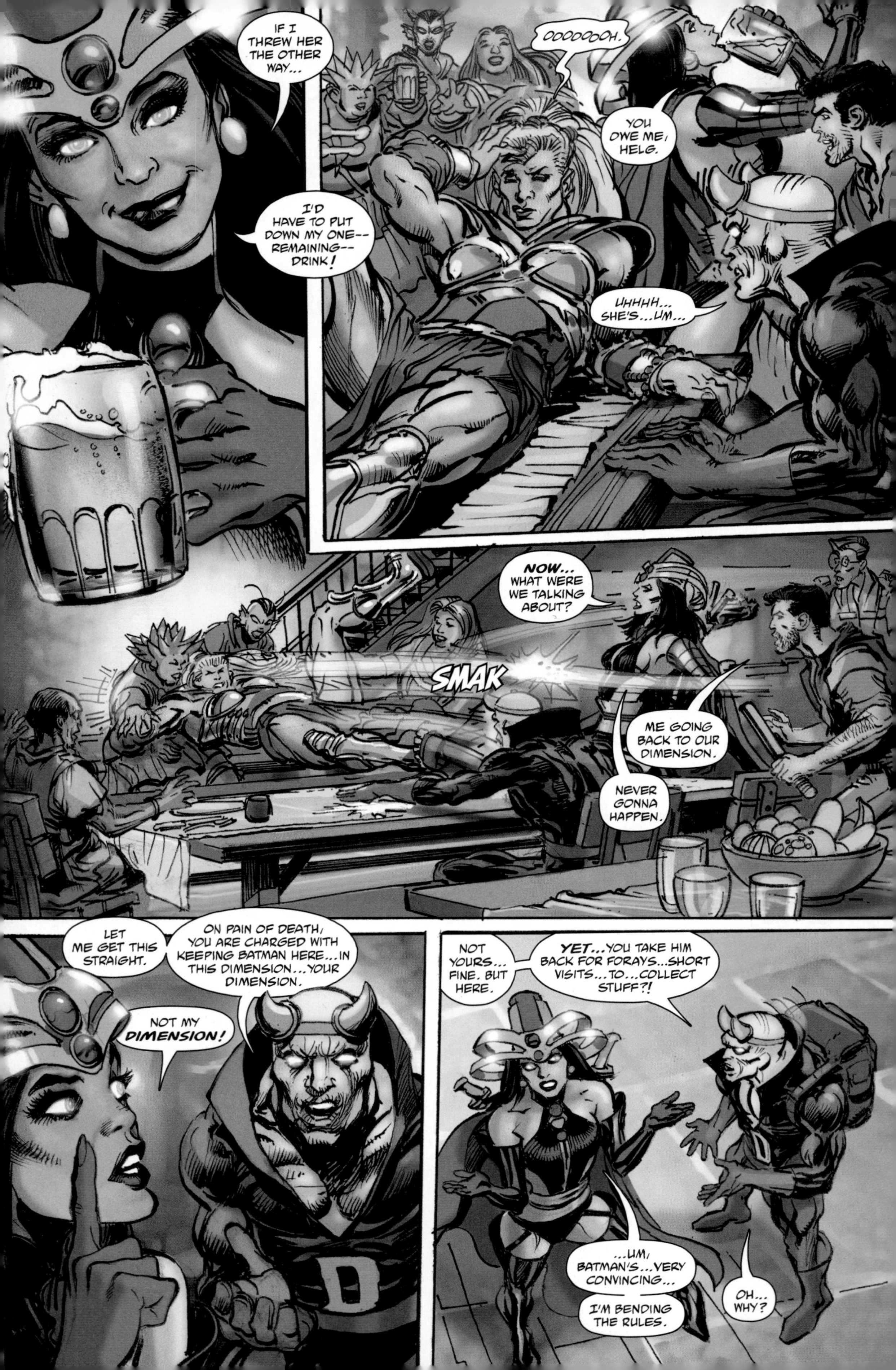
IF I THREW HER THE OTHER WAY...
I'D HAVE TO PUT DOWN MY ONE--REMAINING--DRINK!
OOOOOOOH.
YOU OWE ME, HELG.
UHHHH... SHE'S...UM...
NOW... WHAT WERE WE TALKING ABOUT?
SMAK
ME GOING BACK TO OUR DIMENSION.
NEVER GONNA HAPPEN.
LET ME GET THIS STRAIGHT.
ON PAIN OF DEATH, YOU ARE CHARGED WITH KEEPING BATMAN HERE...IN THIS DIMENSION...YOUR DIMENSION.
NOT MY DIMENSION!
NOT YOURS... FINE. BUT HERE.
YET...YOU TAKE HIM BACK FOR FORAYS...SHORT VISITS...TO...COLLECT STUFF?!
...UM, BATMAN'S...VERY CONVINCING...
I'M BENDING THE RULES.
OH... WHY?

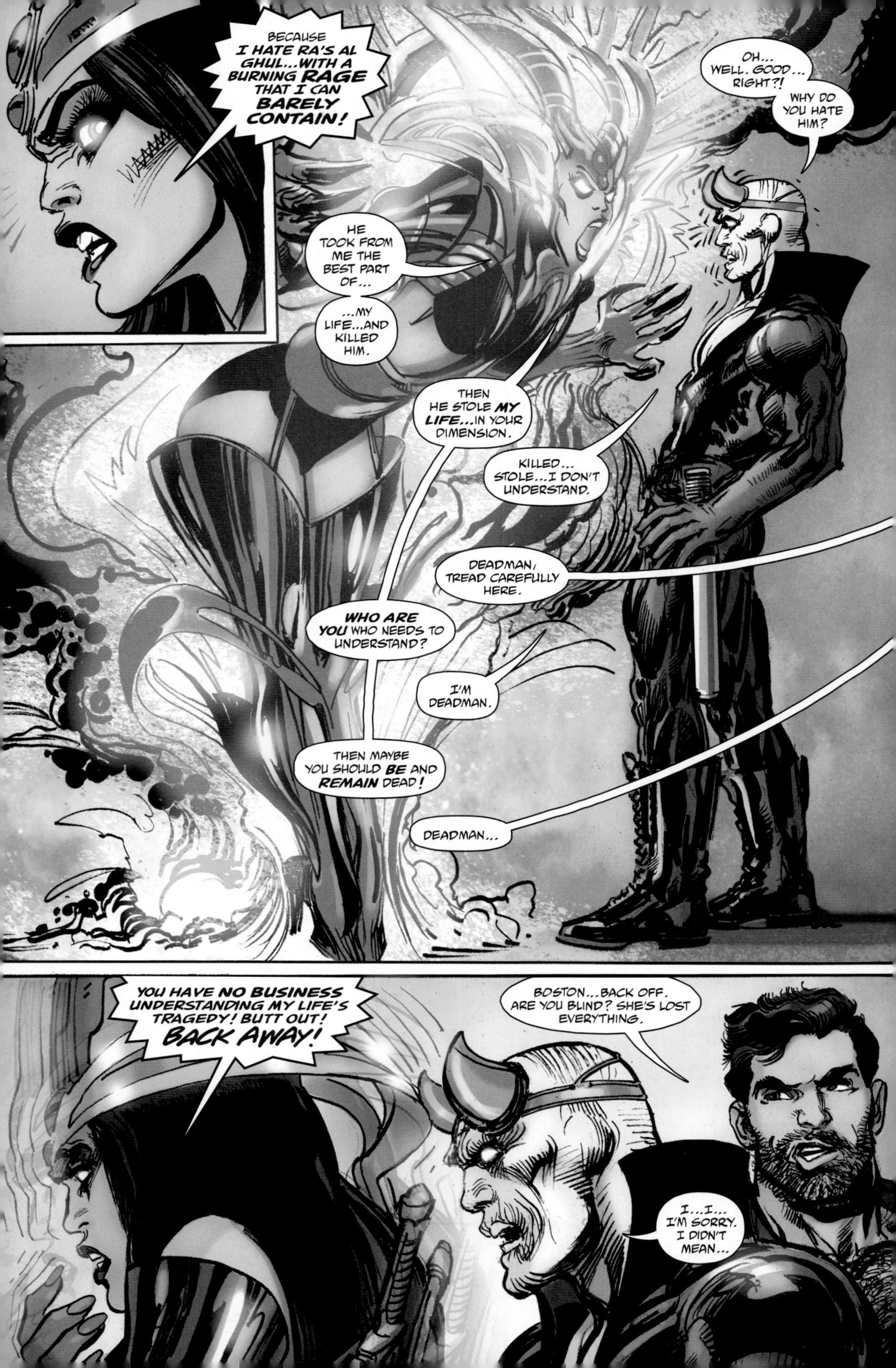

BECAUSE I HATE RA'S AL GHUL...WITH A BURNING RAGE THAT I CAN BARELY CONTAIN!
OH... WELL. GOOD... RIGHT?!
WHY DO YOU HATE HIM?
HE TOOK FROM ME THE BEST PART OF...
...MY LIFE...AND KILLED HIM.
THEN HE STOLE MY LIFE...IN YOUR DIMENSION.
KILLED... STOLE...I DON'T UNDERSTAND.
DEADMAN, TREAD CAREFULLY HERE.
WHO ARE YOU WHO NEEDS TO UNDERSTAND?
I'M DEADMAN.
THEN MAYBE YOU SHOULD BE AND REMAIN DEAD!
DEADMAN...
YOU HAVE NO BUSINESS UNDERSTANDING MY LIFE'S TRAGEDY! BUTT OUT! BACK AWAY!
BOSTON...BACK OFF. ARE YOU BLIND? SHE'S LOST EVERYTHING.
I...I... I'M SORRY. I DIDN'T MEAN...

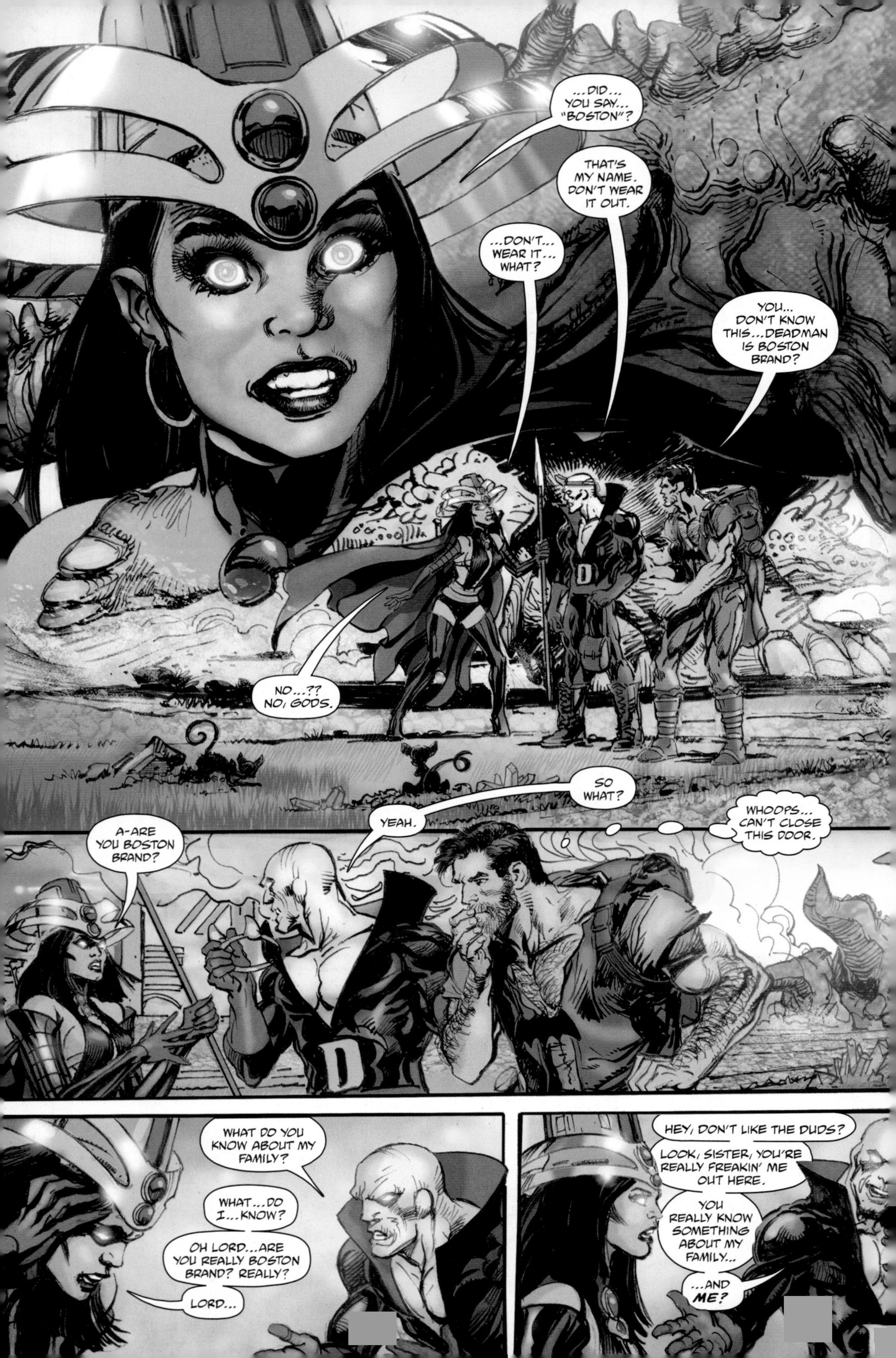
...DID... YOU SAY... "BOSTON"?
THAT'S MY NAME. DON'T WEAR IT OUT.
...DON'T... WEAR IT... WHAT?
YOU... DON'T KNOW THIS...DEADMAN IS BOSTON BRAND?
NO...?? NO, GODS.
A-ARE YOU BOSTON BRAND?
YEAH.
SO WHAT?
WHOOPS... CAN'T CLOSE THIS DOOR.
WHAT DO YOU KNOW ABOUT MY FAMILY?
WHAT...DO I...KNOW?
OH LORD...ARE YOU REALLY BOSTON BRAND? REALLY?
LORD...
HEY, DON'T LIKE THE DUDS?
LOOK, SISTER, YOU'RE REALLY FREAKIN' ME OUT HERE.
YOU REALLY KNOW SOMETHING ABOUT MY FAMILY...
...AND ME?

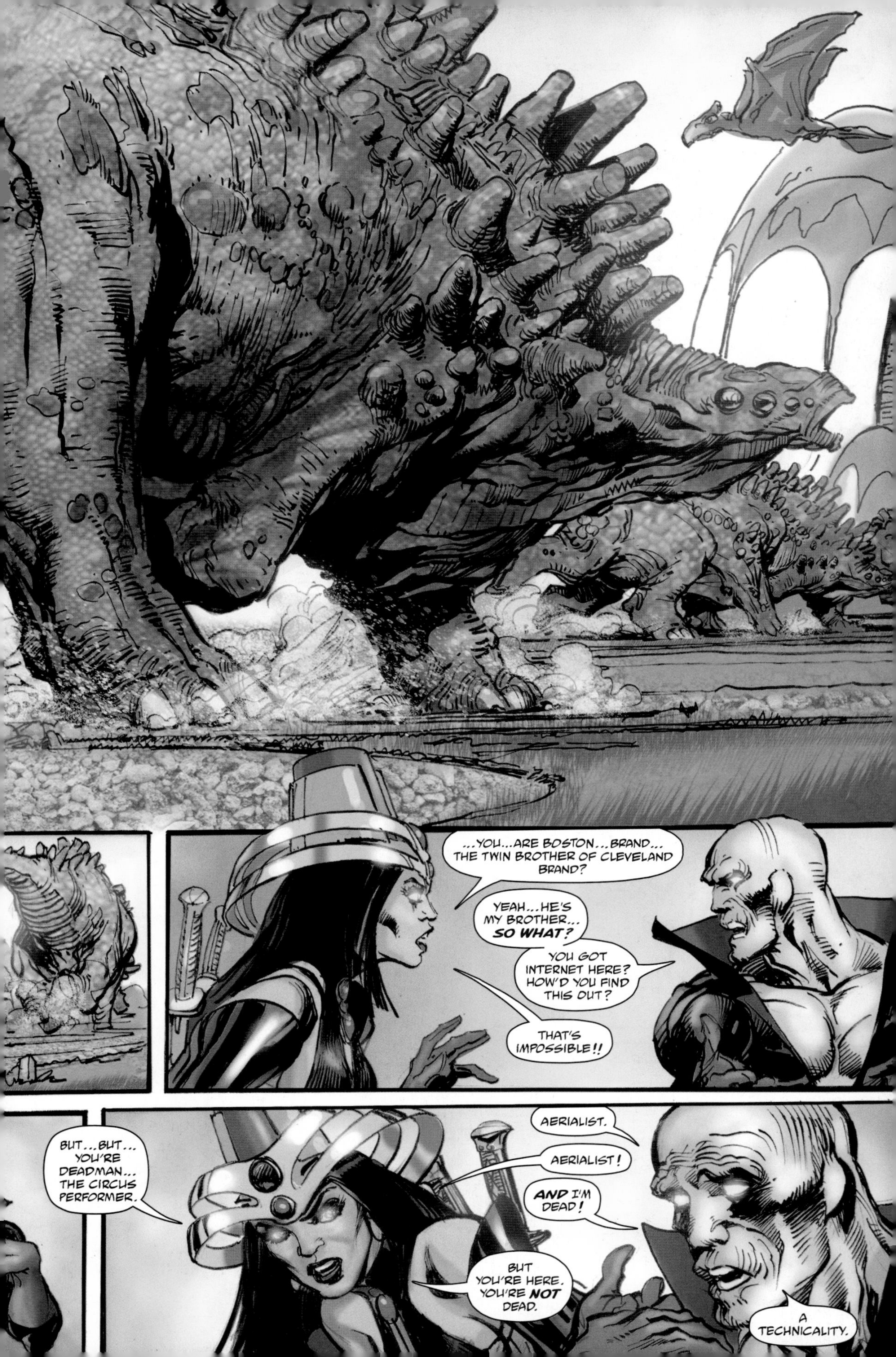
...YOU...ARE BOSTON...BRAND... THE TWIN BROTHER OF CLEVELAND BRAND?
YEAH...HE'S MY BROTHER... **SO WHAT?**
YOU GOT INTERNET HERE? HOW'D YOU FIND THIS OUT?
THAT'S IMPOSSIBLE!!
BUT...BUT... YOU'RE DEADMAN... THE CIRCUS PERFORMER.
AERIALIST.
AERIALIST!
AND I'M DEAD!
BUT YOU'RE HERE. YOU'RE **NOT** DEAD.
A TECHNICALITY.

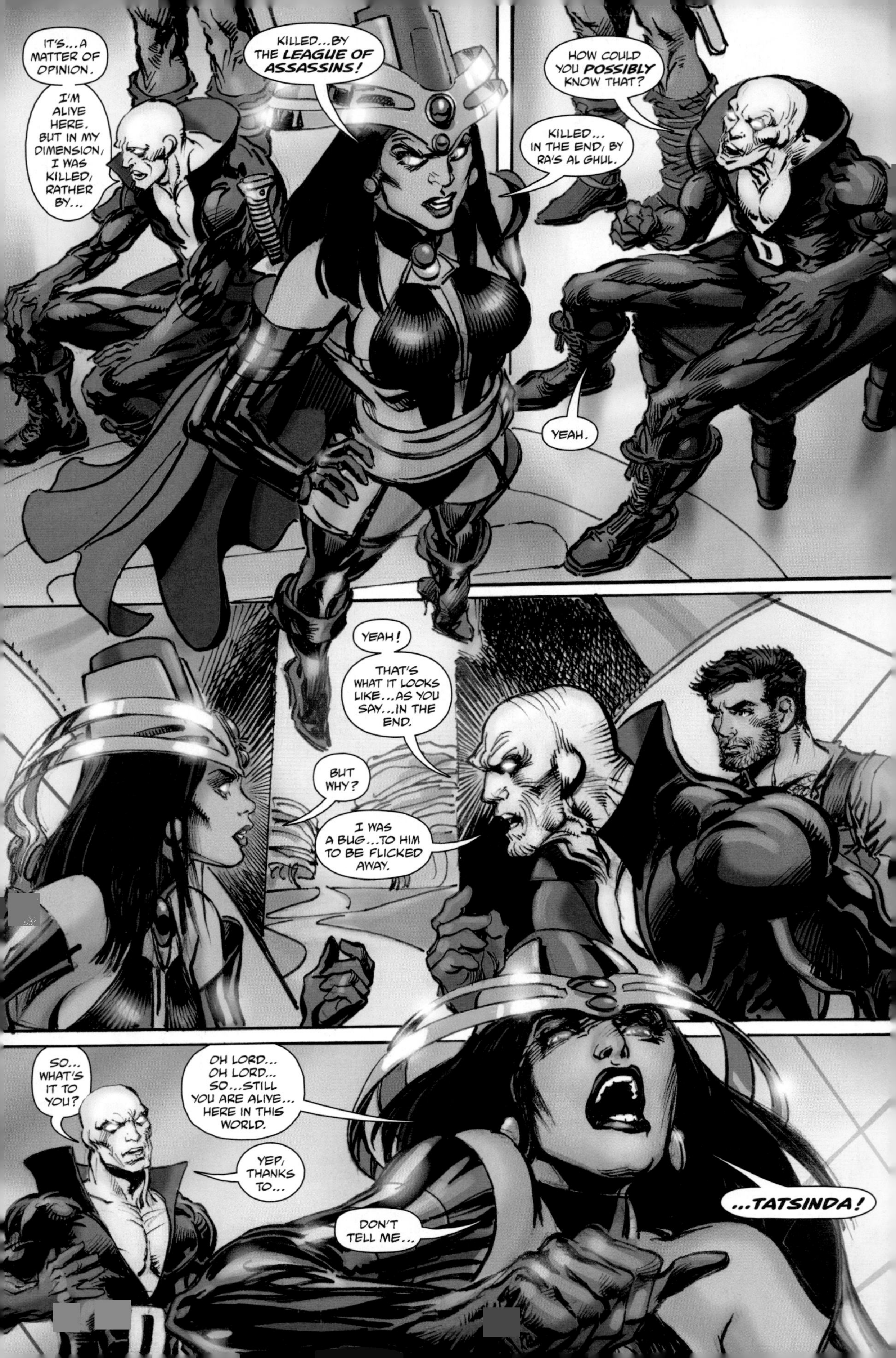
IT'S...A MATTER OF OPINION.
I'M ALIVE HERE. BUT IN MY DIMENSION, I WAS KILLED, RATHER BY...
KILLED...BY THE **LEAGUE OF ASSASSINS!**
HOW COULD YOU **POSSIBLY** KNOW THAT?
KILLED... IN THE END, BY RA'S AL GHUL.
YEAH.
YEAH!
THAT'S WHAT IT LOOKS LIKE...AS YOU SAY...IN THE END.
BUT WHY?
I WAS A BUG...TO HIM TO BE FLICKED AWAY.
SO... WHAT'S IT TO YOU?
OH LORD... OH LORD... SO...STILL YOU ARE ALIVE... HERE IN THIS WORLD.
YEP, THANKS TO...
DON'T TELL ME...
...TATSINDA!

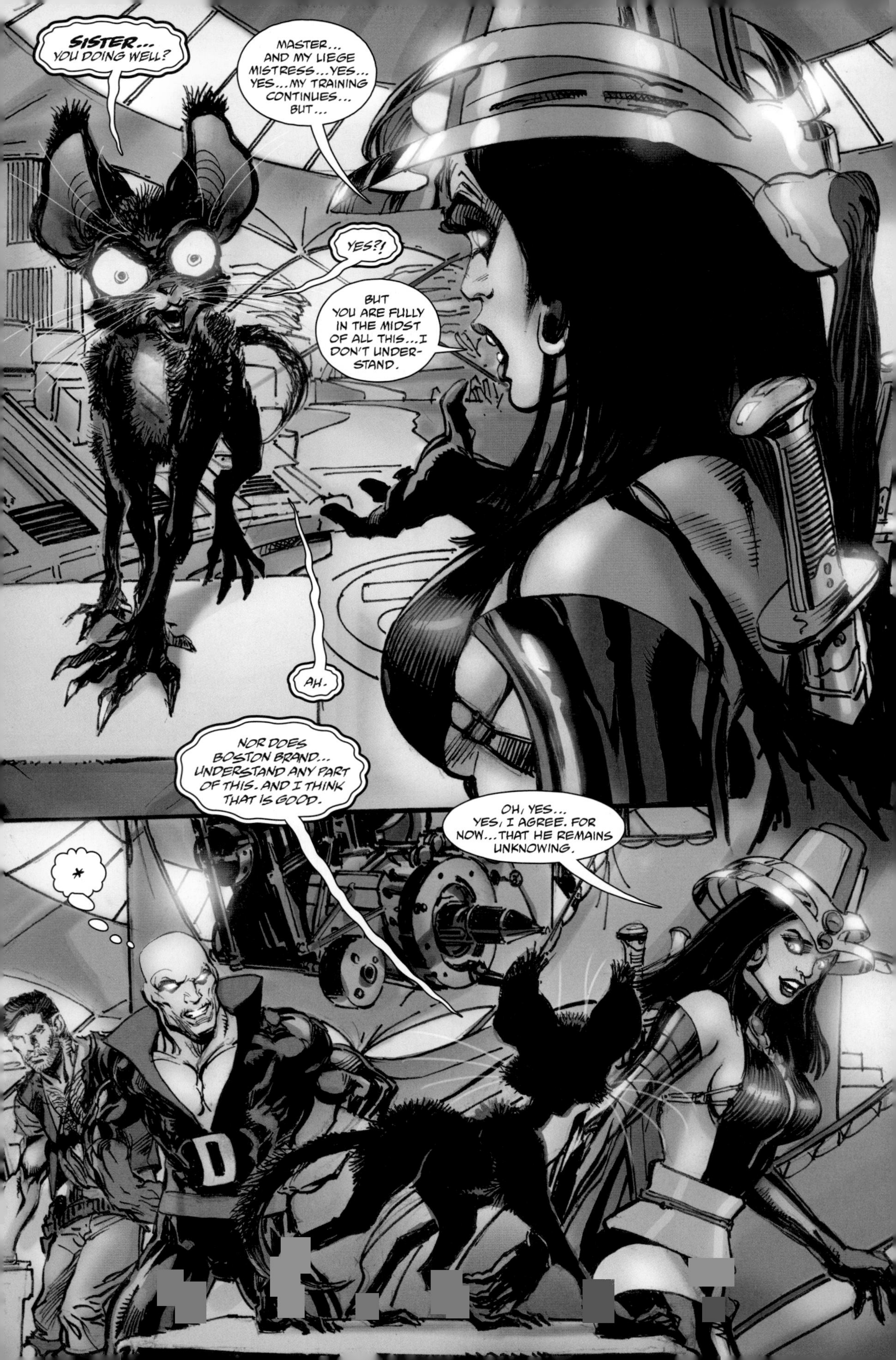
SISTER... YOU DOING WELL?
MASTER... AND MY LIEGE MISTRESS...YES... YES...MY TRAINING CONTINUES... BUT...
YES?!
BUT YOU ARE FULLY IN THE MIDST OF ALL THIS...I DON'T UNDER-STAND.
AH.
NOR DOES BOSTON BRAND... UNDERSTAND ANY PART OF THIS. AND I THINK THAT IS GOOD.
OH, YES... YES, I AGREE. FOR NOW...THAT HE REMAINS UNKNOWING.
*

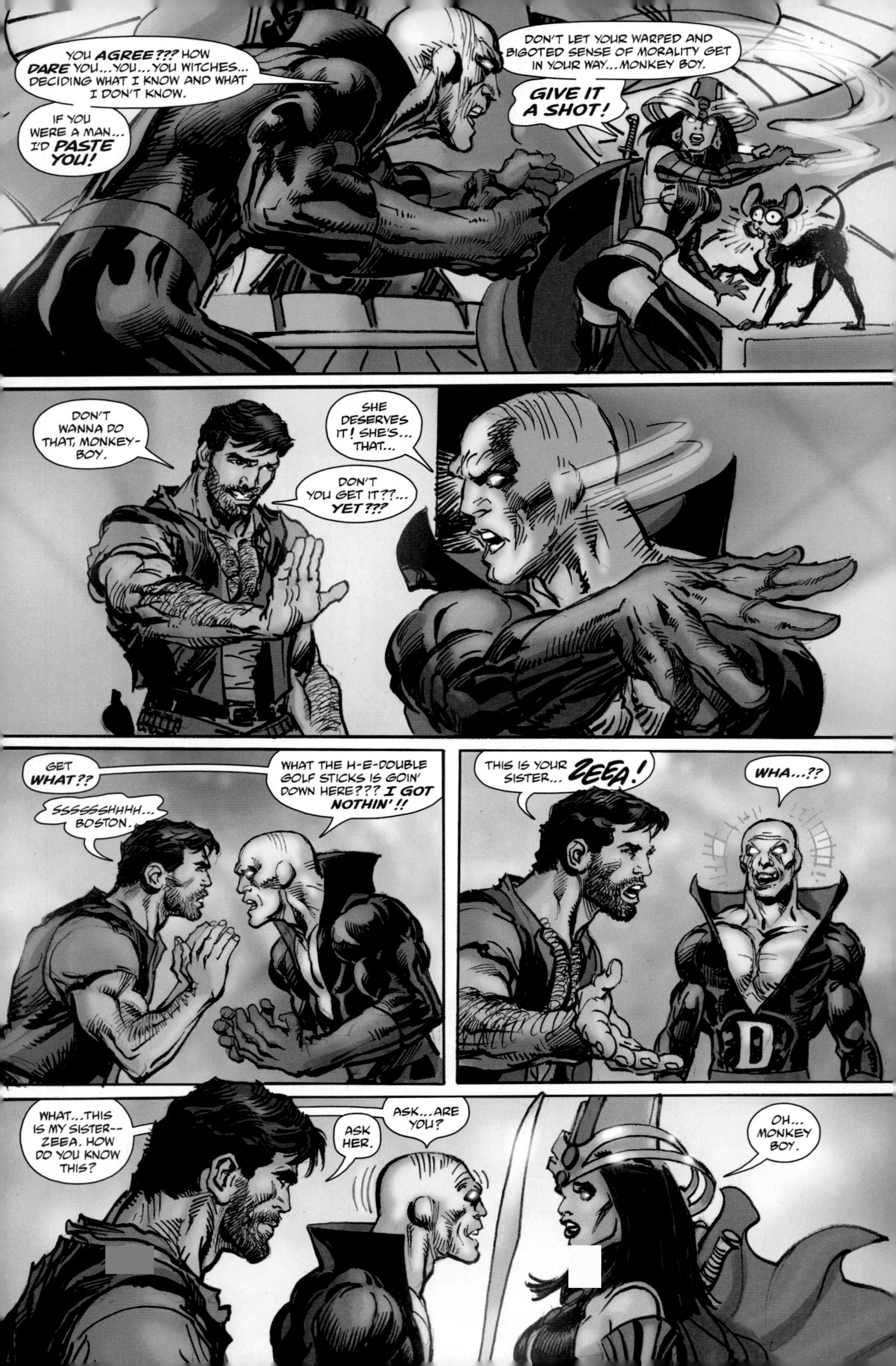
YOU AGREE??? HOW DARE YOU...YOU...YOU WITCHES... DECIDING WHAT I KNOW AND WHAT I DON'T KNOW.
IF YOU WERE A MAN... I'D PASTE YOU!
DON'T LET YOUR WARPED AND BIGOTED SENSE OF MORALITY GET IN YOUR WAY...MONKEY BOY.
GIVE IT A SHOT!
DON'T WANNA DO THAT, MONKEY-BOY.
SHE DESERVES IT! SHE'S... THAT...
DON'T YOU GET IT??... YET???
GET WHAT??
WHAT THE H-E-DOUBLE GOLF STICKS IS GOIN' DOWN HERE??? I GOT NOTHIN'!!
SSSSSSHHHH... BOSTON.
THIS IS YOUR SISTER... ZEEA!
WHA...??
WHAT...THIS IS MY SISTER-- ZEEA. HOW DO YOU KNOW THIS?
ASK HER.
ASK...ARE YOU?
OH... MONKEY BOY.

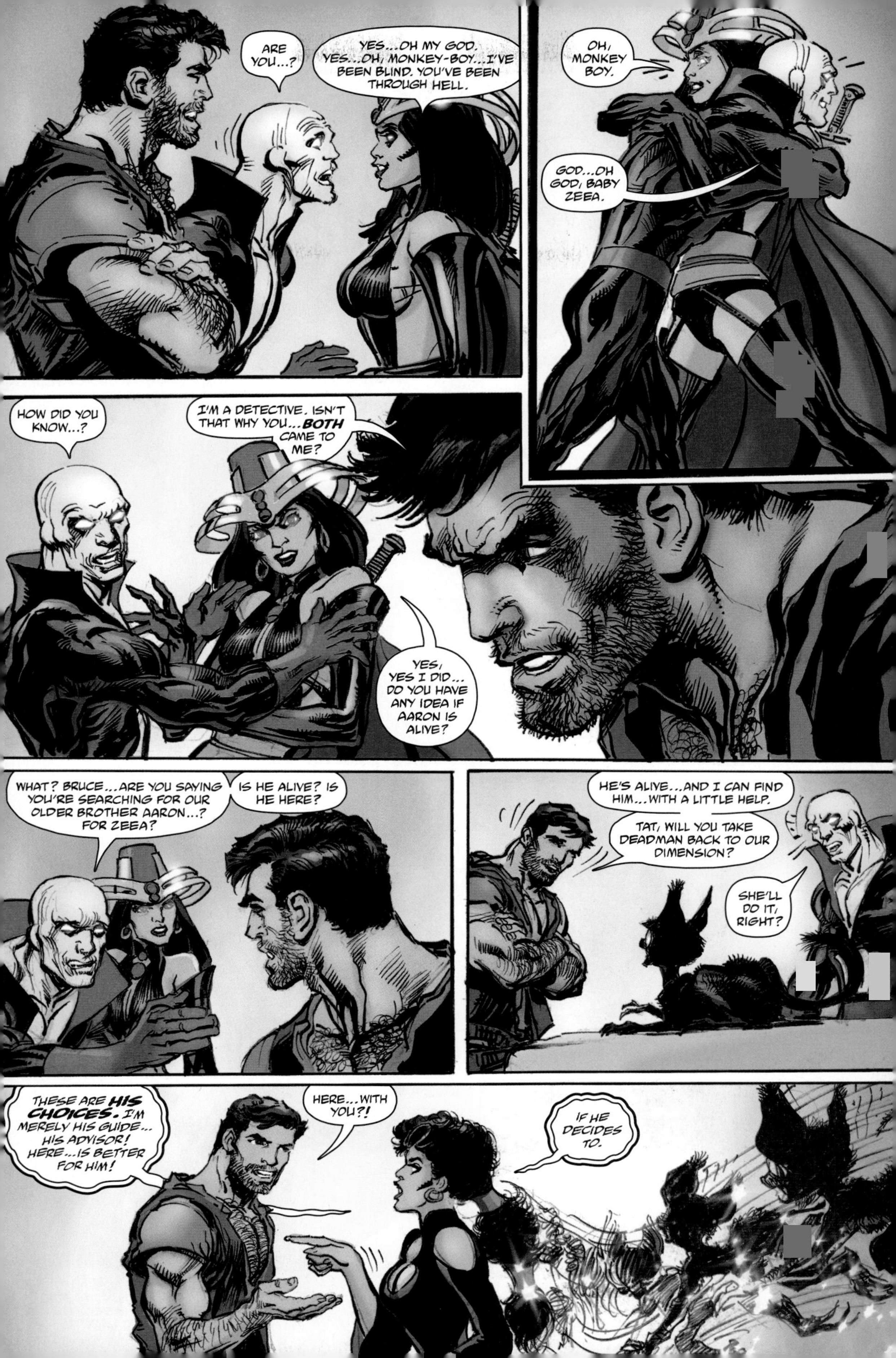
ARE YOU...?
YES...OH MY GOD. YES...OH, MONKEY-BOY...I'VE BEEN BLIND. YOU'VE BEEN THROUGH HELL.
OH, MONKEY BOY.
GOD...OH GOD, BABY ZEEA.
HOW DID YOU KNOW...?
I'M A DETECTIVE. ISN'T THAT WHY YOU...BOTH CAME TO ME?
YES, YES I DID... DO YOU HAVE ANY IDEA IF AARON IS ALIVE?
WHAT? BRUCE...ARE YOU SAYING YOU'RE SEARCHING FOR OUR OLDER BROTHER AARON...? FOR ZEEA?
IS HE ALIVE? IS HE HERE?
HE'S ALIVE...AND I CAN FIND HIM...WITH A LITTLE HELP.
TAT, WILL YOU TAKE DEADMAN BACK TO OUR DIMENSION?
SHE'LL DO IT, RIGHT?
THESE ARE HIS CHOICES. I'M MERELY HIS GUIDE... HIS ADVISOR! HERE...IS BETTER FOR HIM!
HERE...WITH YOU?!
IF HE DECIDES TO.

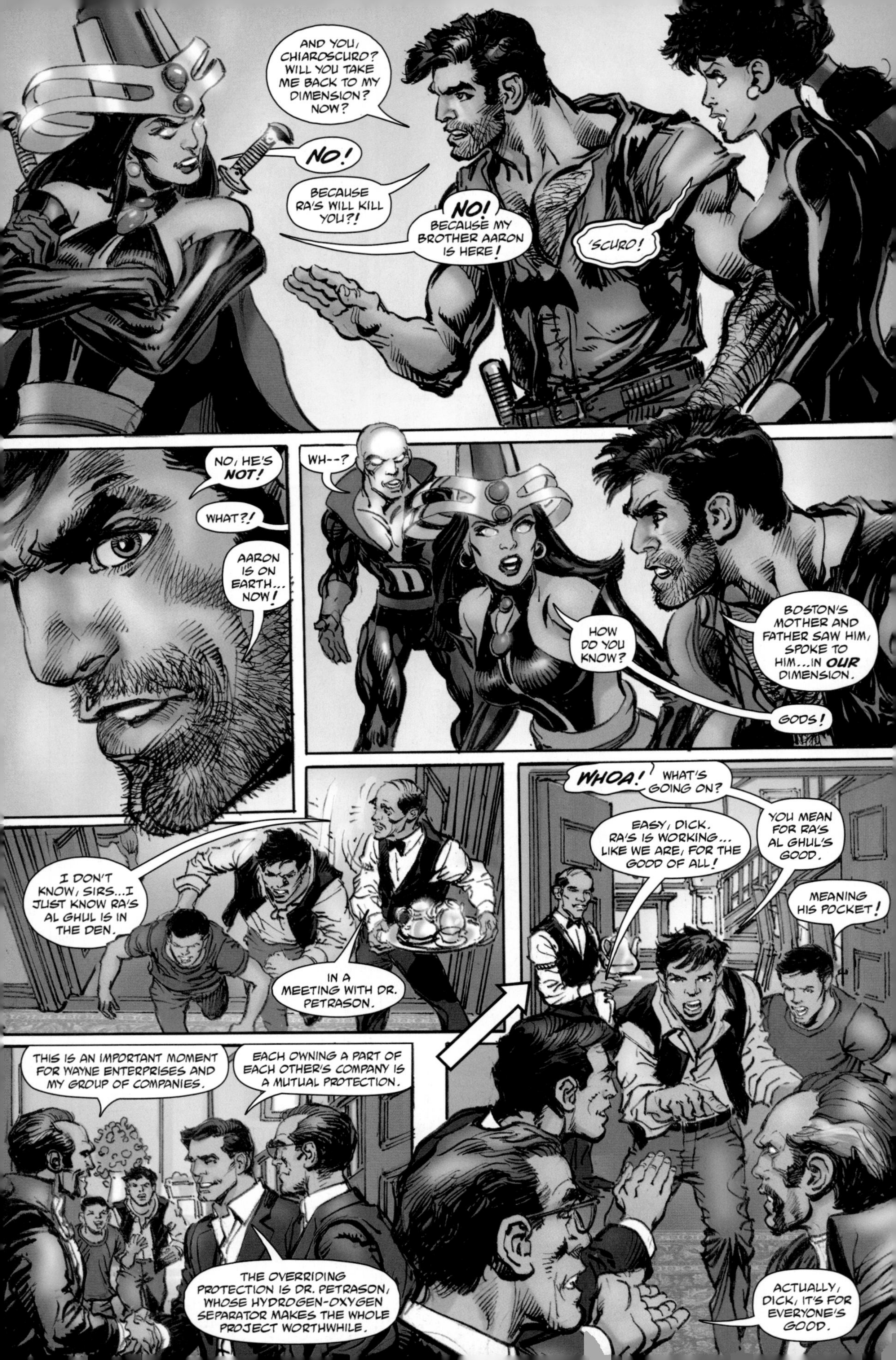
AND YOU, CHIAROSCURO? WILL YOU TAKE ME BACK TO MY DIMENSION? NOW?
NO!
BECAUSE RA'S WILL KILL YOU?!
NO! BECAUSE MY BROTHER AARON IS HERE!
'SCURO!
NO, HE'S NOT!
WHAT?!
AARON IS ON EARTH... NOW!
WH--?
HOW DO YOU KNOW?
BOSTON'S MOTHER AND FATHER SAW HIM, SPOKE TO HIM...IN OUR DIMENSION.
GODS!
I DON'T KNOW, SIRS...I JUST KNOW RA'S AL GHUL IS IN THE DEN.
IN A MEETING WITH DR. PETRASON.
WHOA! WHAT'S GOING ON?
EASY, DICK. RA'S IS WORKING... LIKE WE ARE, FOR THE GOOD OF ALL!
YOU MEAN FOR RA'S AL GHUL'S GOOD.
MEANING HIS POCKET!
THIS IS AN IMPORTANT MOMENT FOR WAYNE ENTERPRISES AND MY GROUP OF COMPANIES.
EACH OWNING A PART OF EACH OTHER'S COMPANY IS A MUTUAL PROTECTION.
THE OVERRIDING PROTECTION IS DR. PETRASON, WHOSE HYDROGEN-OXYGEN SEPARATOR MAKES THE WHOLE PROJECT WORTHWHILE.
ACTUALLY, DICK, IT'S FOR EVERYONE'S GOOD.

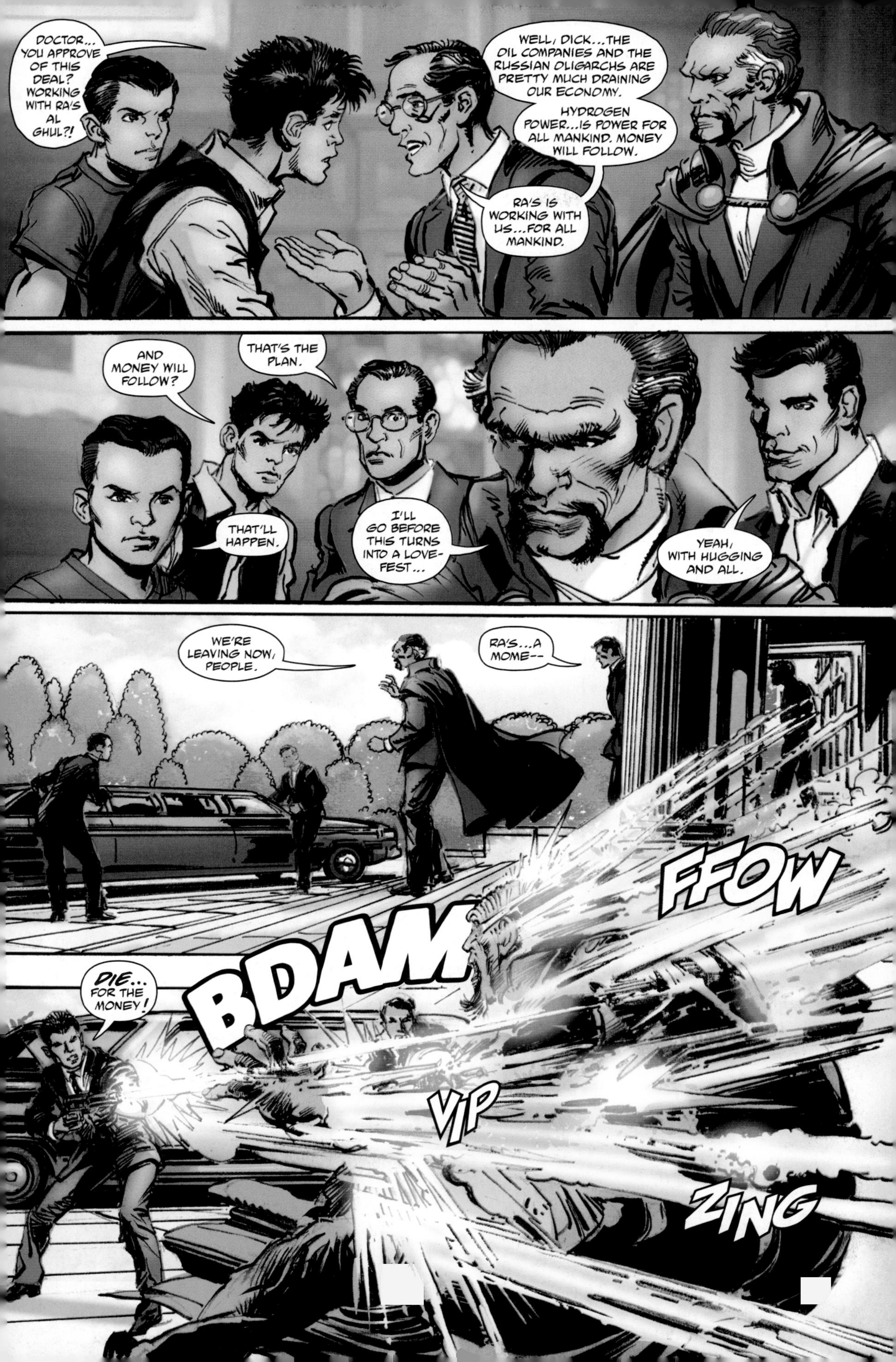

DOCTOR... YOU APPROVE OF THIS DEAL? WORKING WITH RA'S AL GHUL?!
WELL, DICK...THE OIL COMPANIES AND THE RUSSIAN OLIGARCHS ARE PRETTY MUCH DRAINING OUR ECONOMY.
HYDROGEN POWER...IS POWER FOR ALL MANKIND. MONEY WILL FOLLOW.
RA'S IS WORKING WITH US...FOR ALL MANKIND.
AND MONEY WILL FOLLOW?
THAT'S THE PLAN.
THAT'LL HAPPEN.
I'LL GO BEFORE THIS TURNS INTO A LOVE-FEST...
YEAH, WITH HUGGING AND ALL.
WE'RE LEAVING NOW, PEOPLE.
RA'S...A MOME--
FFOW
DIE... FOR THE MONEY!
BDAM
VIP
ZING

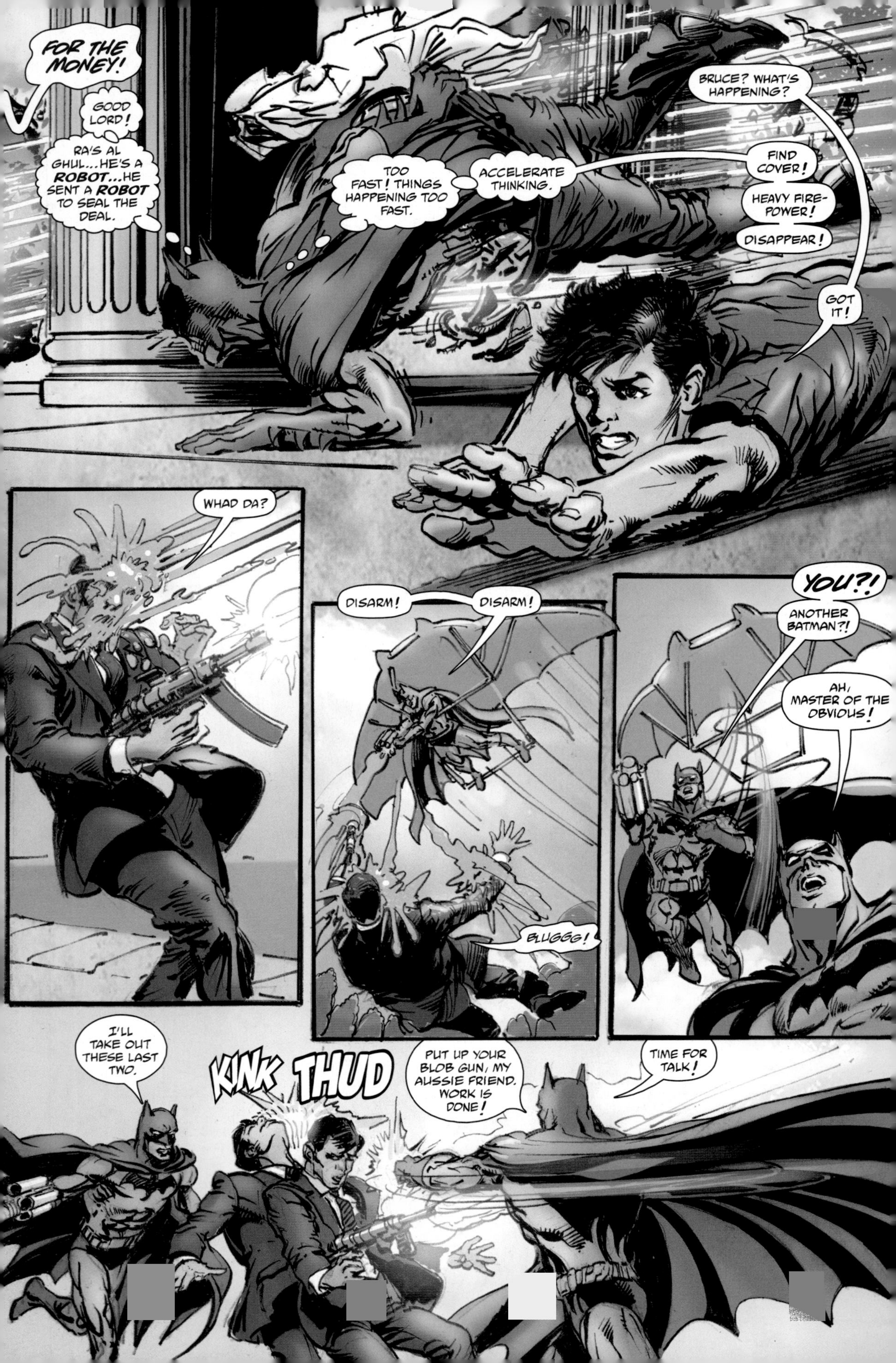
FOR THE MONEY!
GOOD LORD!
RA'S AL GHUL...HE'S A ROBOT...HE SENT A ROBOT TO SEAL THE DEAL.
TOO FAST! THINGS HAPPENING TOO FAST.
ACCELERATE THINKING.
BRUCE? WHAT'S HAPPENING?
FIND COVER!
HEAVY FIRE-POWER!
DISAPPEAR!
GOT IT!
WHAD DA?
DISARM!
DISARM!
BLUGGG!
YOU?!
ANOTHER BATMAN?!
AH, MASTER OF THE OBVIOUS!
I'LL TAKE OUT THESE LAST TWO.
KINK
THUD
PUT UP YOUR BLOB GUN, MY AUSSIE FRIEND. WORK IS DONE!
TIME FOR TALK!

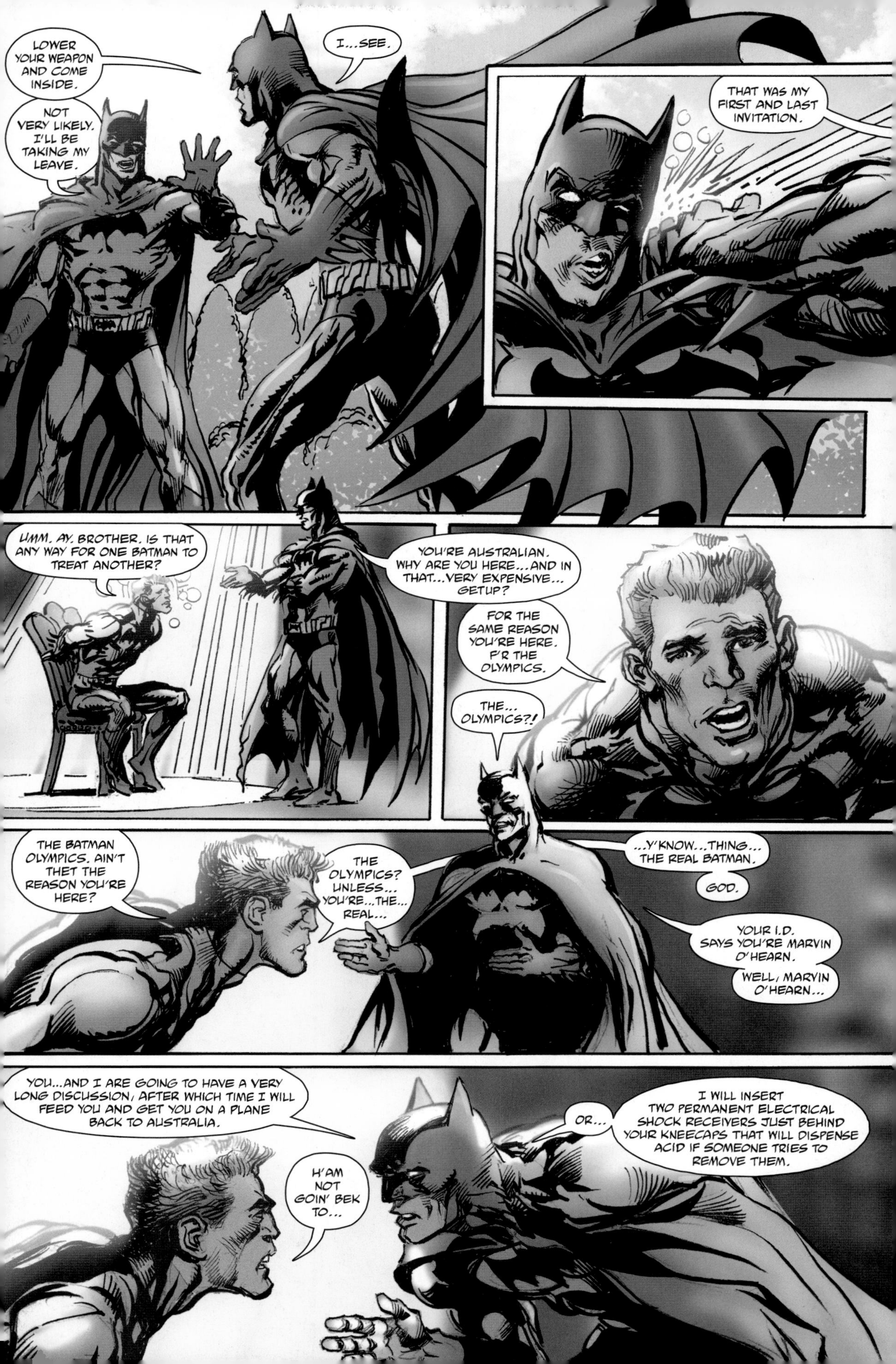
LOWER YOUR WEAPON AND COME INSIDE.
NOT VERY LIKELY. I'LL BE TAKING MY LEAVE.
I...SEE.
THAT WAS MY FIRST AND LAST INVITATION.
UMM. AY. BROTHER. IS THAT ANY WAY FOR ONE BATMAN TO TREAT ANOTHER?
YOU'RE AUSTRALIAN. WHY ARE YOU HERE...AND IN THAT...VERY EXPENSIVE... GETUP?
FOR THE SAME REASON YOU'RE HERE. F'R THE OLYMPICS.
THE... OLYMPICS?!
THE BATMAN OLYMPICS. AIN'T THET THE REASON YOU'RE HERE?
THE OLYMPICS? UNLESS... YOU'RE...THE... REAL...
...Y'KNOW...THING... THE REAL BATMAN.
GOD.
YOUR I.D. SAYS YOU'RE MARVIN O'HEARN.
WELL, MARVIN O'HEARN...
YOU...AND I ARE GOING TO HAVE A VERY LONG DISCUSSION, AFTER WHICH TIME I WILL FEED YOU AND GET YOU ON A PLANE BACK TO AUSTRALIA.
OR...
I WILL INSERT TWO PERMANENT ELECTRICAL SHOCK RECEIVERS JUST BEHIND YOUR KNEECAPS THAT WILL DISPENSE ACID IF SOMEONE TRIES TO REMOVE THEM.
H'AM NOT GOIN' BEK TO...

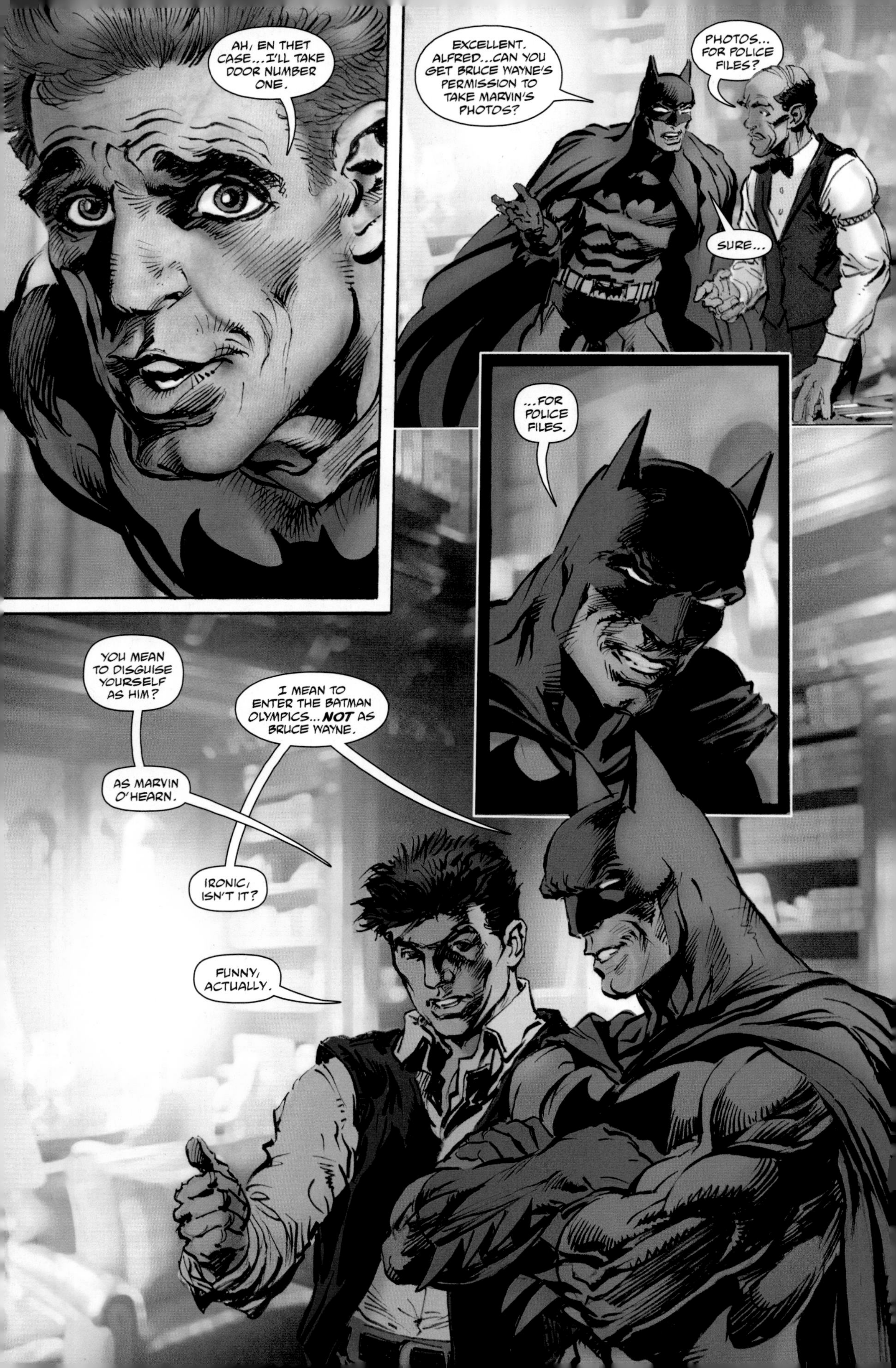
AH, EN THET CASE...I'LL TAKE DOOR NUMBER ONE.
EXCELLENT. ALFRED...CAN YOU GET BRUCE WAYNE'S PERMISSION TO TAKE MARVIN'S PHOTOS?
PHOTOS... FOR POLICE FILES?
SURE...
...FOR POLICE FILES.
YOU MEAN TO DISGUISE YOURSELF AS HIM?
I MEAN TO ENTER THE BATMAN OLYMPICS...**NOT** AS BRUCE WAYNE.
AS MARVIN O'HEARN.
IRONIC, ISN'T IT?
FUNNY, ACTUALLY.

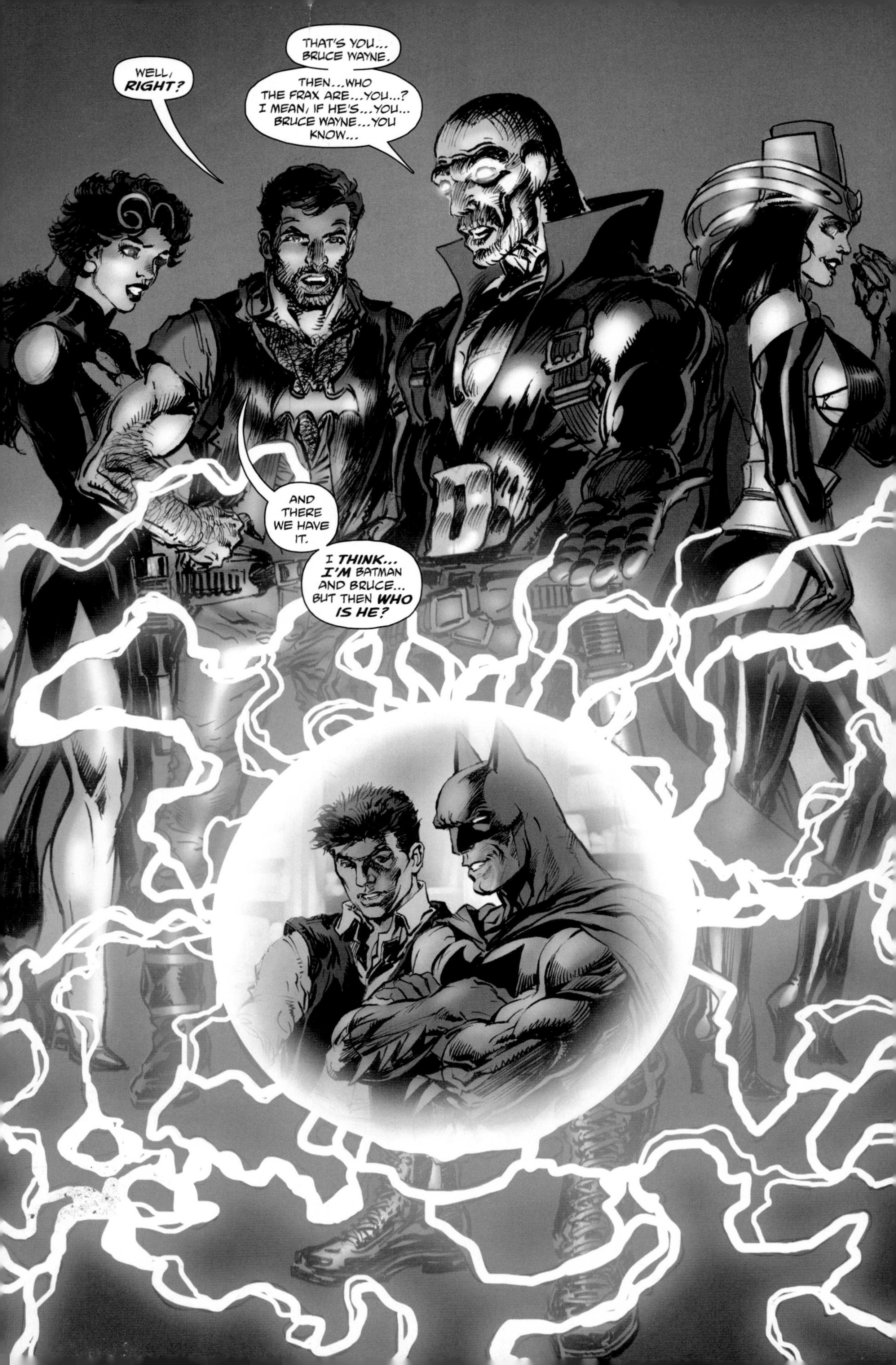
WELL, **RIGHT?**
THAT'S YOU... BRUCE WAYNE.
THEN...WHO THE FRAX ARE...YOU...? I MEAN, IF HE'S...YOU... BRUCE WAYNE...YOU KNOW...
AND THERE WE HAVE IT.
I **THINK... I'M** BATMAN AND BRUCE... BUT THEN **WHO IS HE?**

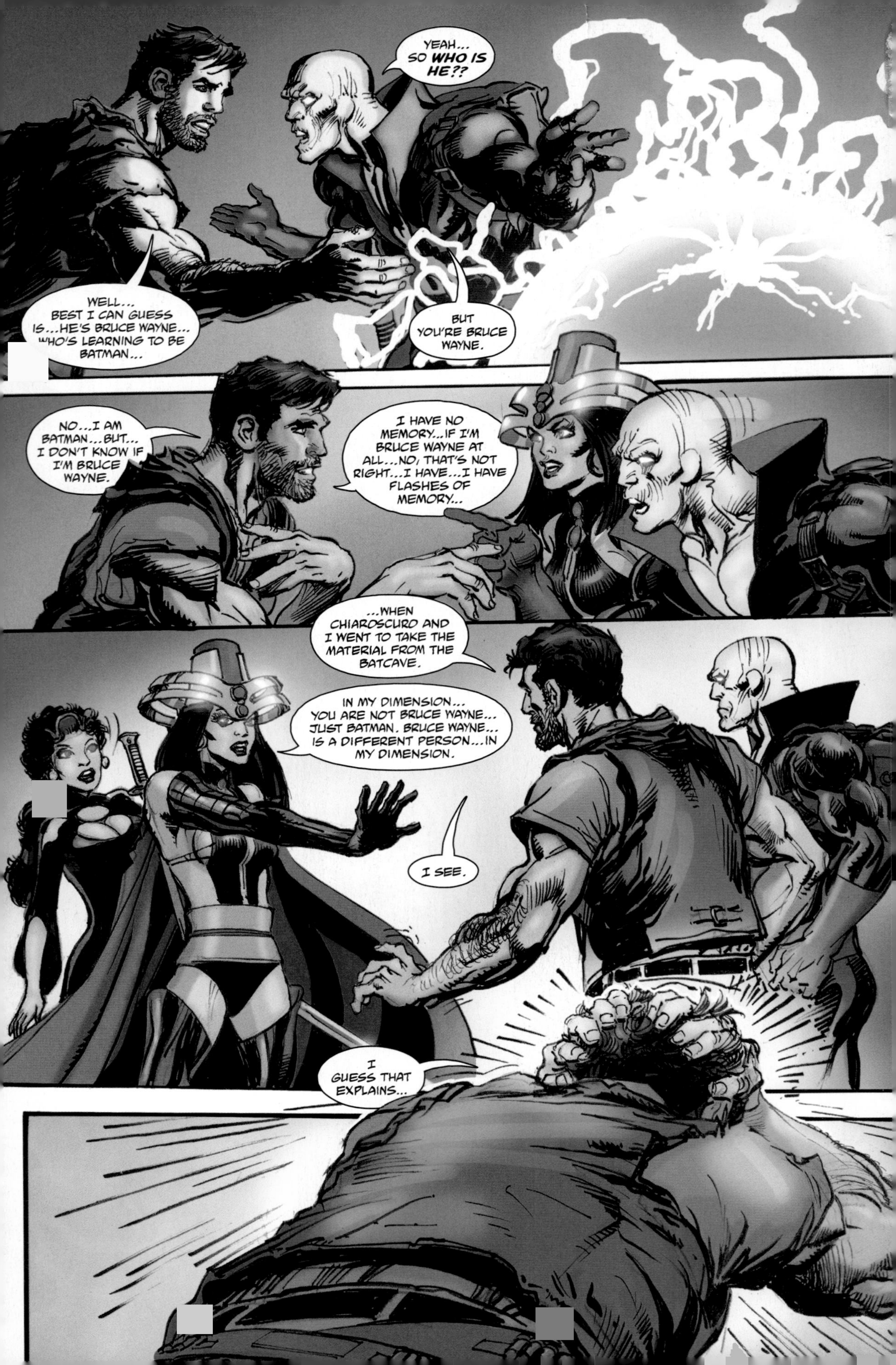
YEAH... SO **WHO IS HE??**
WELL... BEST I CAN GUESS IS...HE'S BRUCE WAYNE... WHO'S LEARNING TO BE BATMAN...
BUT YOU'RE BRUCE WAYNE.
NO...I AM BATMAN...BUT... I DON'T KNOW IF I'M BRUCE WAYNE.
I HAVE NO MEMORY...IF I'M BRUCE WAYNE AT ALL...NO, THAT'S NOT RIGHT...I HAVE...I HAVE FLASHES OF MEMORY...
...WHEN CHIAROSCURO AND I WENT TO TAKE THE MATERIAL FROM THE BATCAVE.
IN MY DIMENSION... YOU ARE NOT BRUCE WAYNE... JUST BATMAN. BRUCE WAYNE... IS A DIFFERENT PERSON...IN MY DIMENSION.
I SEE.
I GUESS THAT EXPLAINS...

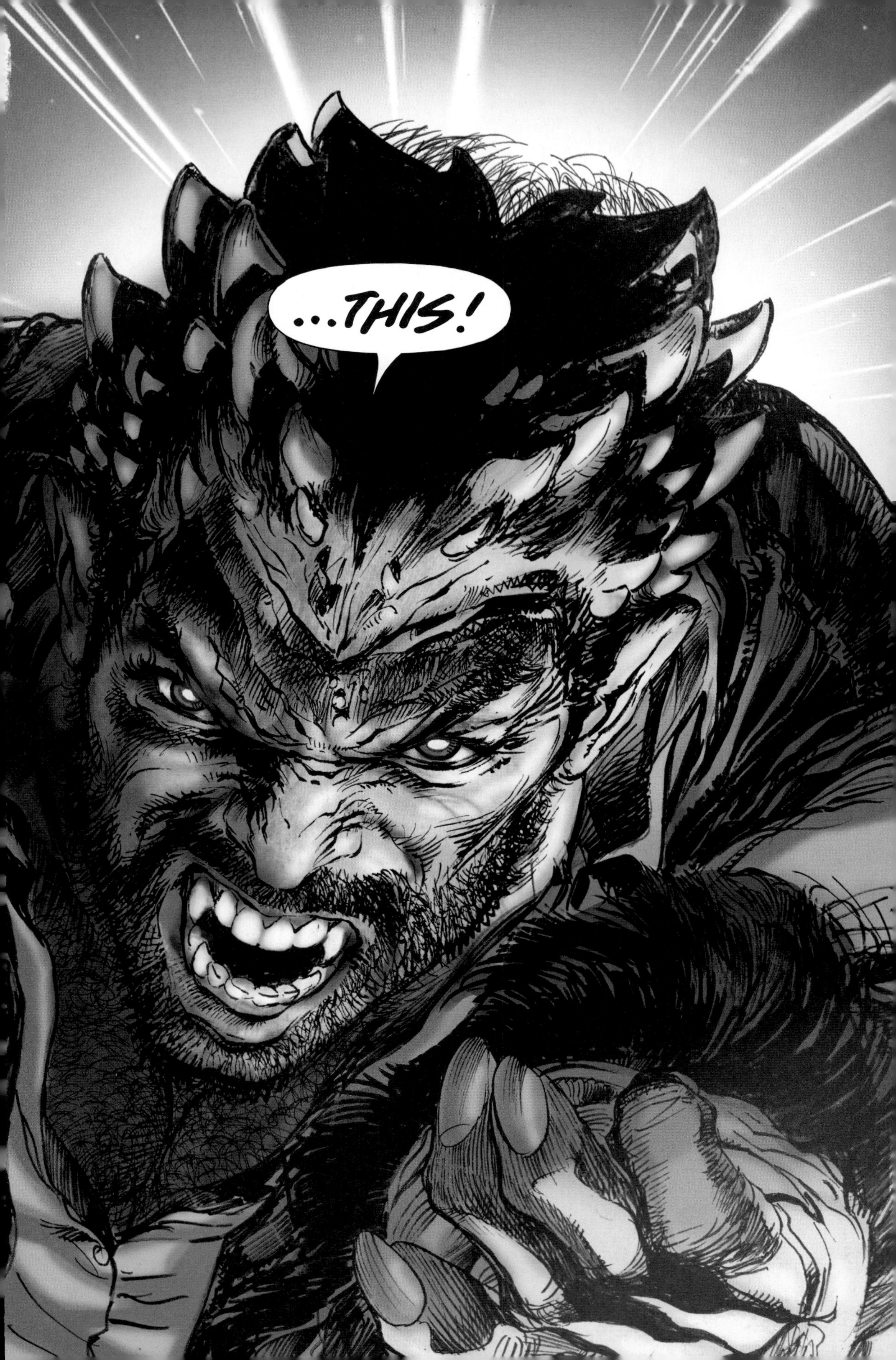
...THIS!

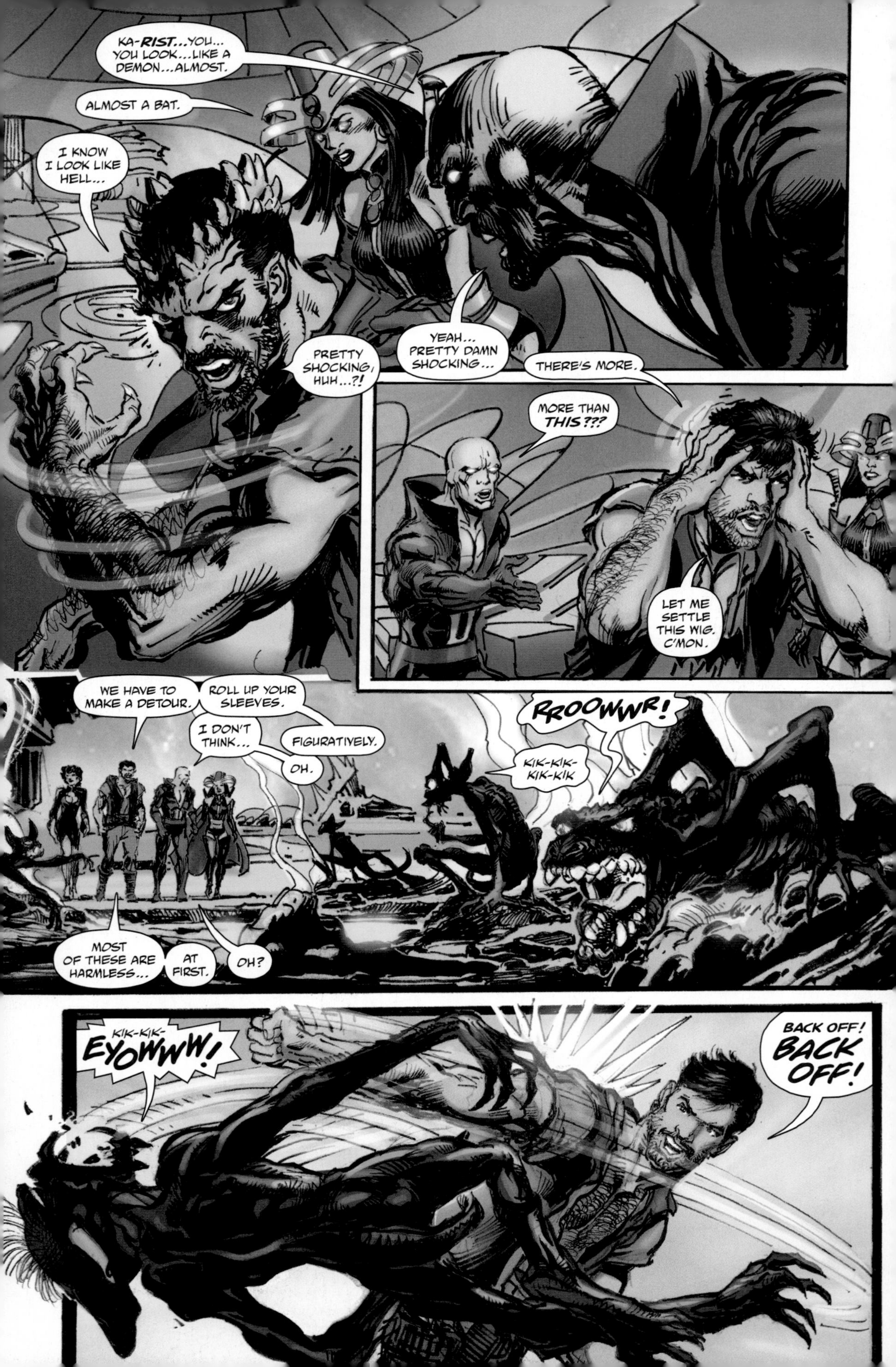
KA-RIST...YOU... YOU LOOK...LIKE A DEMON...ALMOST.
ALMOST A BAT.
I KNOW I LOOK LIKE HELL...
PRETTY SHOCKING, HUH...?!
YEAH... PRETTY DAMN SHOCKING...
THERE'S MORE.
MORE THAN THIS???
LET ME SETTLE THIS WIG. C'MON.
WE HAVE TO MAKE A DETOUR.
ROLL UP YOUR SLEEVES.
I DON'T THINK...
FIGURATIVELY.
OH.
RROOWWR!
KIK-KIK-KIK-KIK
MOST OF THESE ARE HARMLESS...
AT FIRST.
OH?
KIK-KIK-EYOWWW!
BACK OFF! BACK OFF!

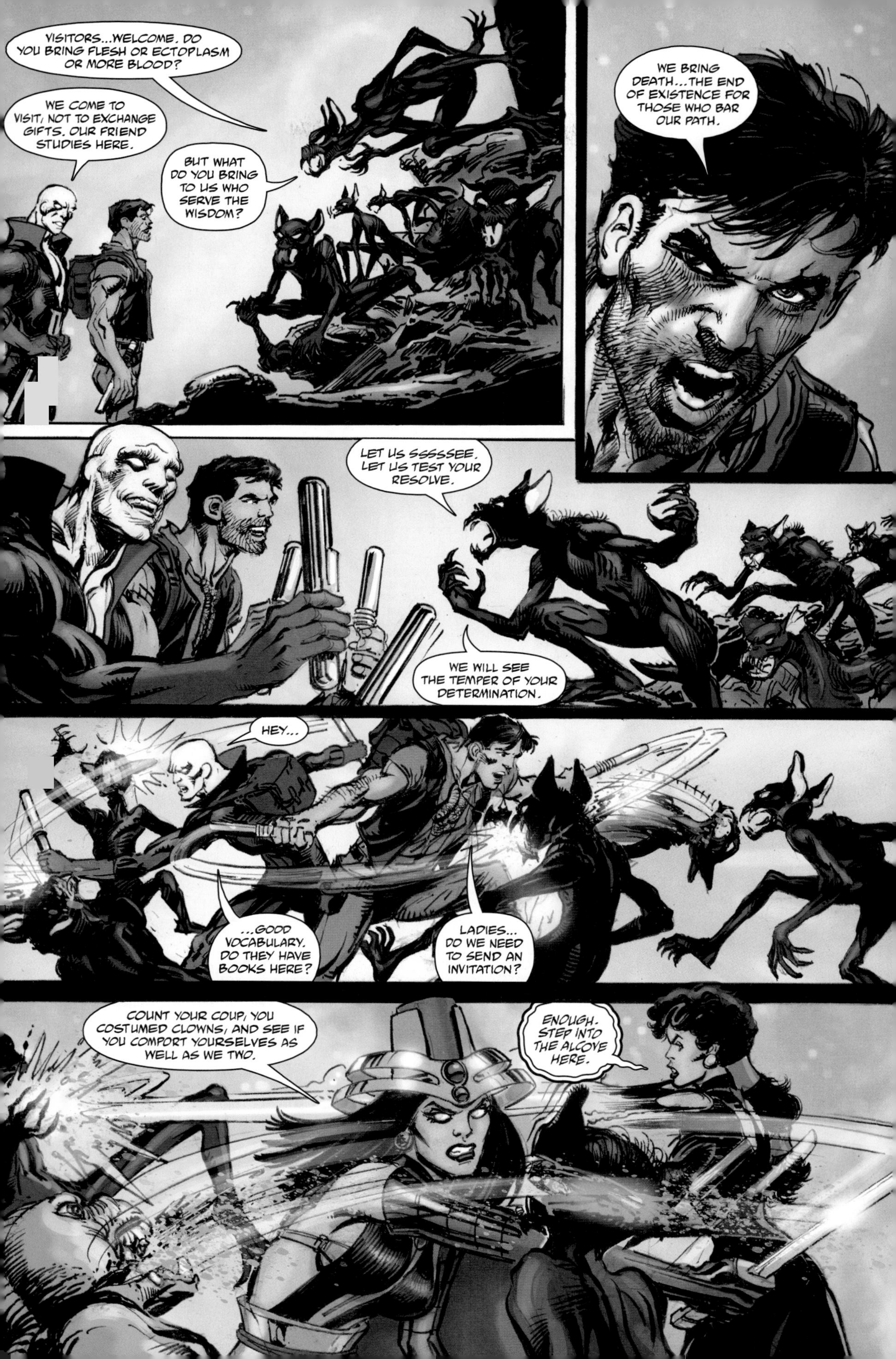
VISITORS...WELCOME. DO YOU BRING FLESH OR ECTOPLASM OR MORE BLOOD?
WE COME TO VISIT, NOT TO EXCHANGE GIFTS. OUR FRIEND STUDIES HERE.
BUT WHAT DO YOU BRING TO US WHO SERVE THE WISDOM?
WE BRING DEATH...THE END OF EXISTENCE FOR THOSE WHO BAR OUR PATH.
LET US SSSSSEE. LET US TEST YOUR RESOLVE.
WE WILL SEE THE TEMPER OF YOUR DETERMINATION.
HEY...
...GOOD VOCABULARY. DO THEY HAVE BOOKS HERE?
LADIES... DO WE NEED TO SEND AN INVITATION?
COUNT YOUR COUP, YOU COSTUMED CLOWNS, AND SEE IF YOU COMPORT YOURSELVES AS WELL AS WE TWO.
ENOUGH. STEP INTO THE ALCOVE HERE.

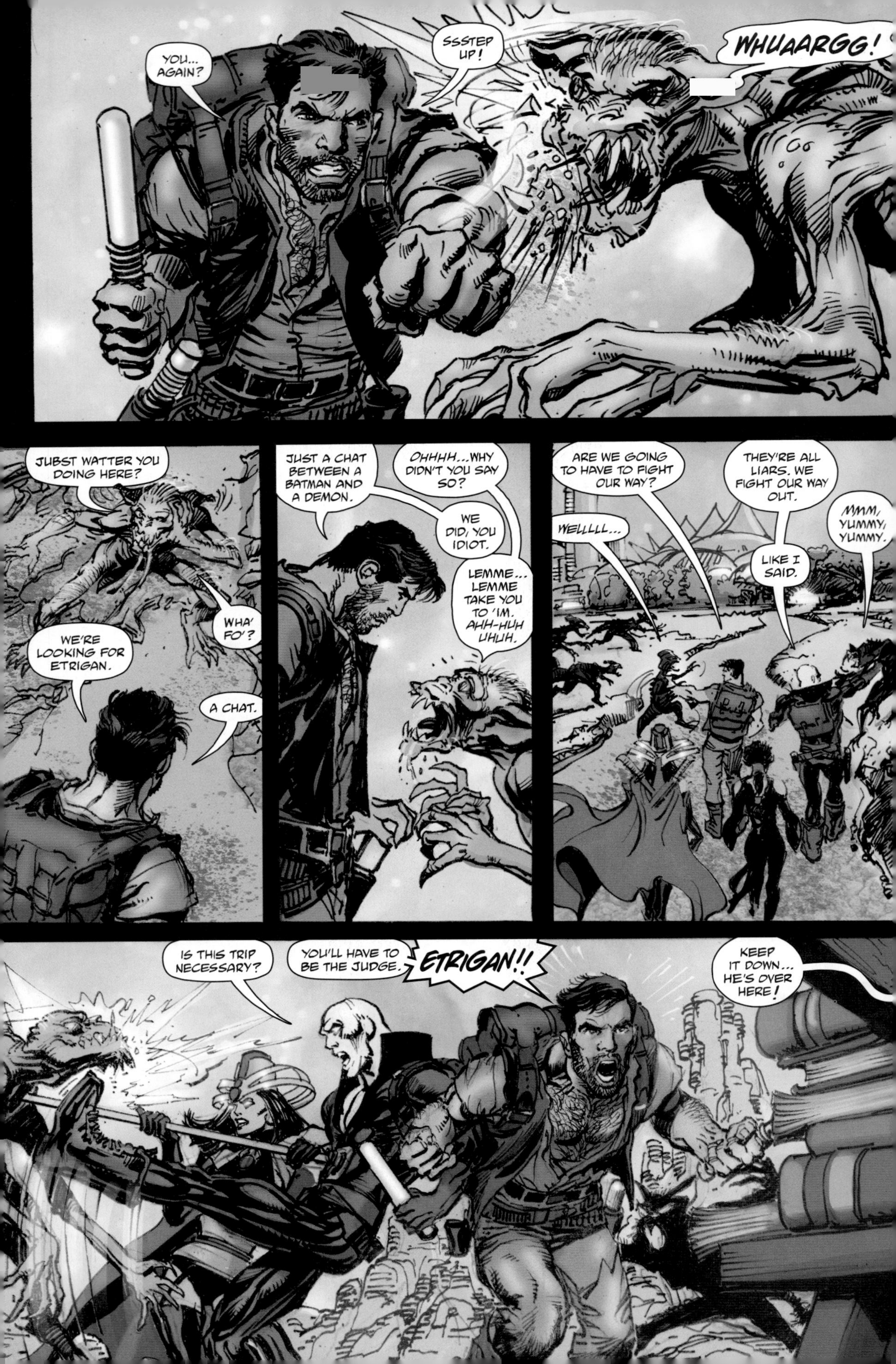

YOU... AGAIN?
SSSTEP UP!
WHUAARGG!
JUBST WATTER YOU DOING HERE?
WE'RE LOOKING FOR ETRIGAN.
WHA' FO'?
A CHAT.
JUST A CHAT BETWEEN A BATMAN AND A DEMON.
OHHHH...WHY DIDN'T YOU SAY SO?
WE DID, YOU IDIOT.
LEMME... LEMME TAKE YOU TO 'IM. AHH-HUH UHUH.
ARE WE GOING TO HAVE TO FIGHT OUR WAY?
WELLLLL...
THEY'RE ALL LIARS. WE FIGHT OUR WAY OUT.
LIKE I SAID.
MMM, YUMMY, YUMMY.
IS THIS TRIP NECESSARY?
YOU'LL HAVE TO BE THE JUDGE.
ETRIGAN!!
KEEP IT DOWN... HE'S OVER HERE!

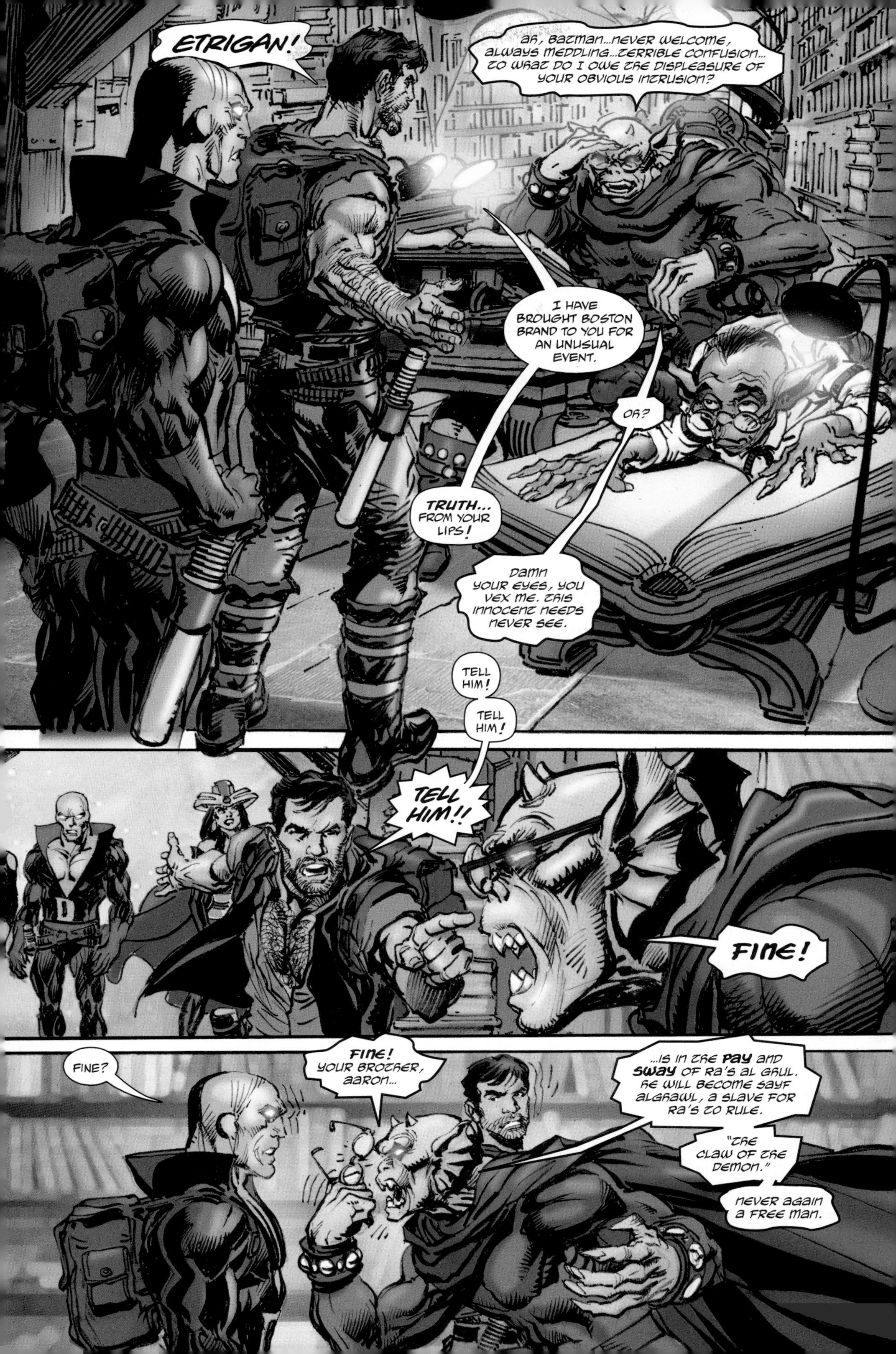
ETRIGAN!
AH, BATMAN...NEVER WELCOME, ALWAYS MEDDLING...TERRIBLE CONFUSION... TO WHAT DO I OWE THE DISPLEASURE OF YOUR OBVIOUS INTRUSION?
I HAVE BROUGHT BOSTON BRAND TO YOU FOR AN UNUSUAL EVENT.
OR?
TRUTH... FROM YOUR LIPS!
DAMN YOUR EYES, YOU VEX ME. THIS INNOCENT NEEDS NEVER SEE.
TELL HIM!
TELL HIM!
TELL HIM!!
FINE!
FINE?
FINE! YOUR BROTHER, AARON...
...IS IN THE PAY AND SWAY OF RA'S AL GHUL. HE WILL BECOME SAYF ALGHAWL, A SLAVE FOR RA'S TO RULE.
"THE CLAW OF THE DEMON."
NEVER AGAIN A FREE MAN.

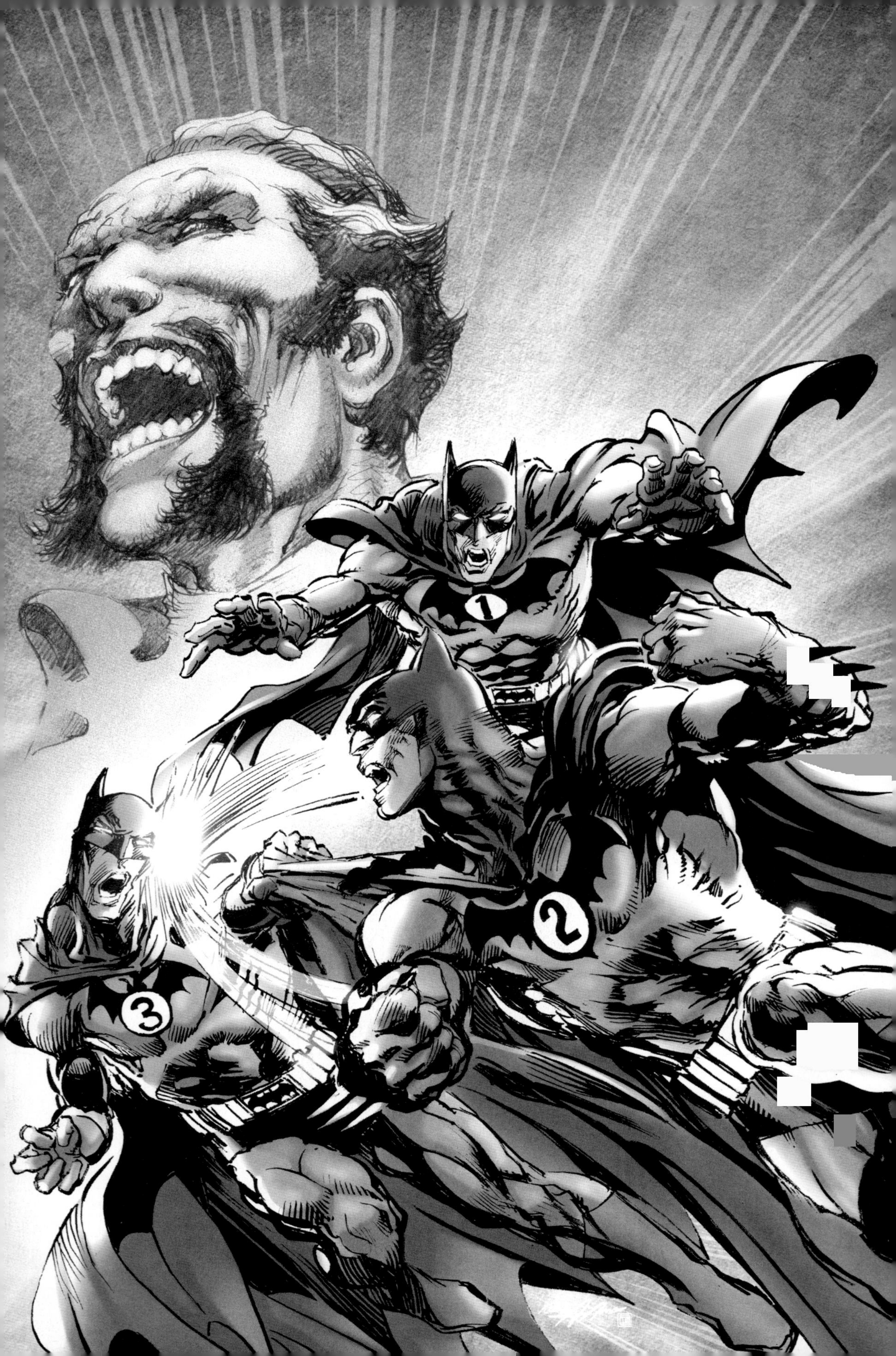

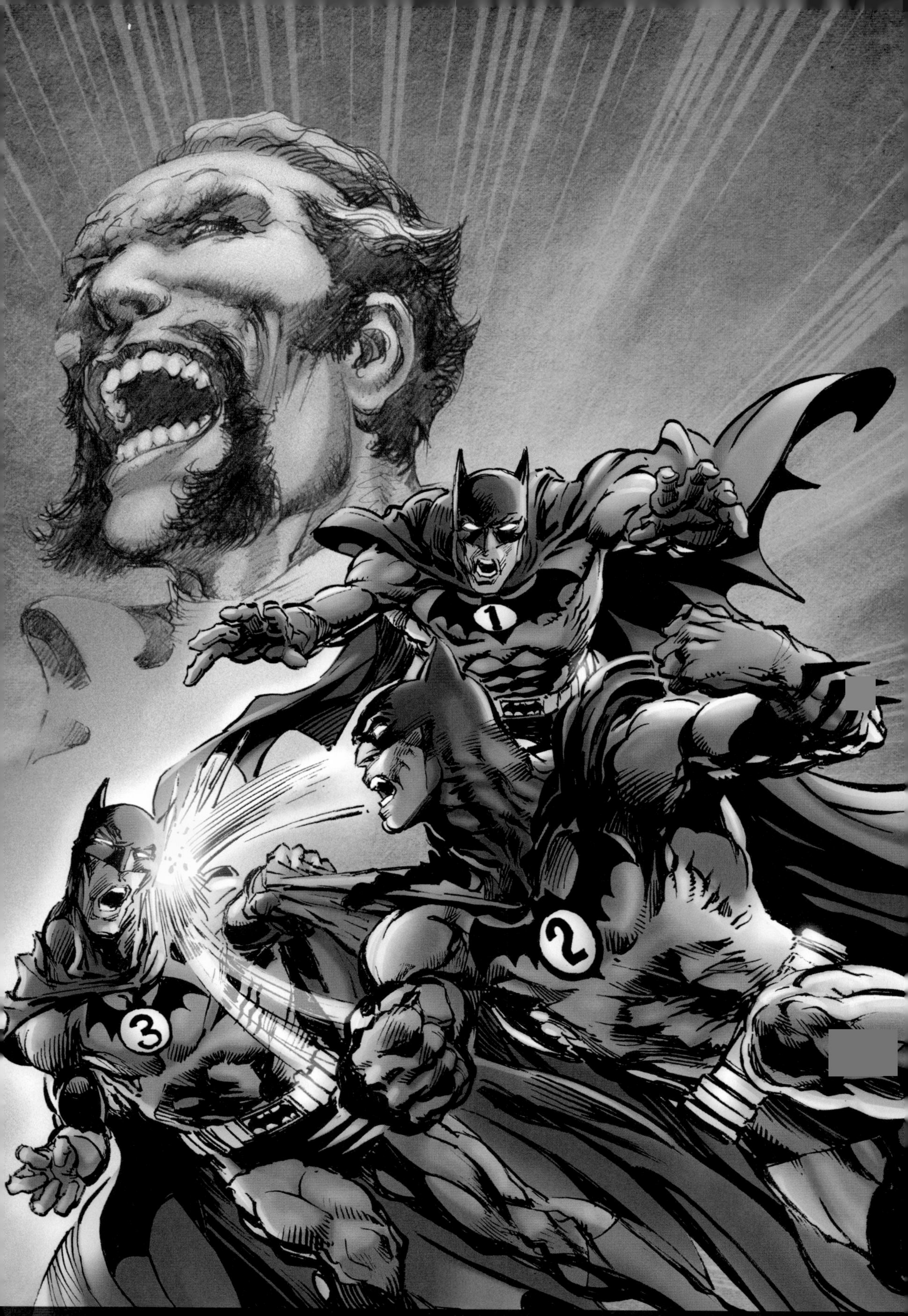

Chapter 5

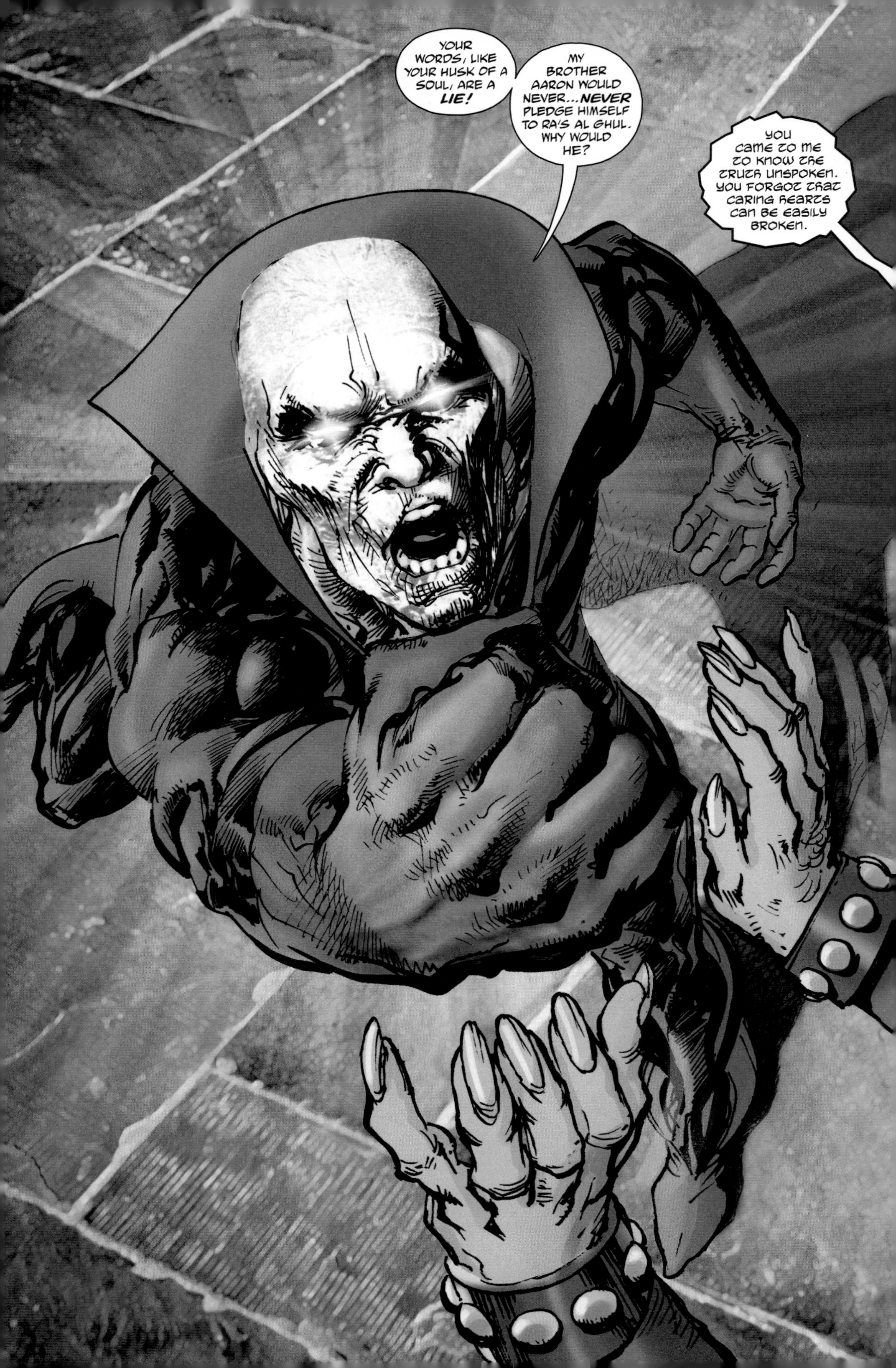
YOUR WORDS, LIKE YOUR HUSK OF A SOUL, ARE A **LIE!**
MY BROTHER AARON WOULD NEVER... **NEVER** PLEDGE HIMSELF TO RA'S AL GHUL. WHY WOULD HE?
YOU CAME TO ME TO KNOW THE TRUTH UNSPOKEN. YOU FORGOT THAT CARING HEARTS CAN BE EASILY BROKEN.

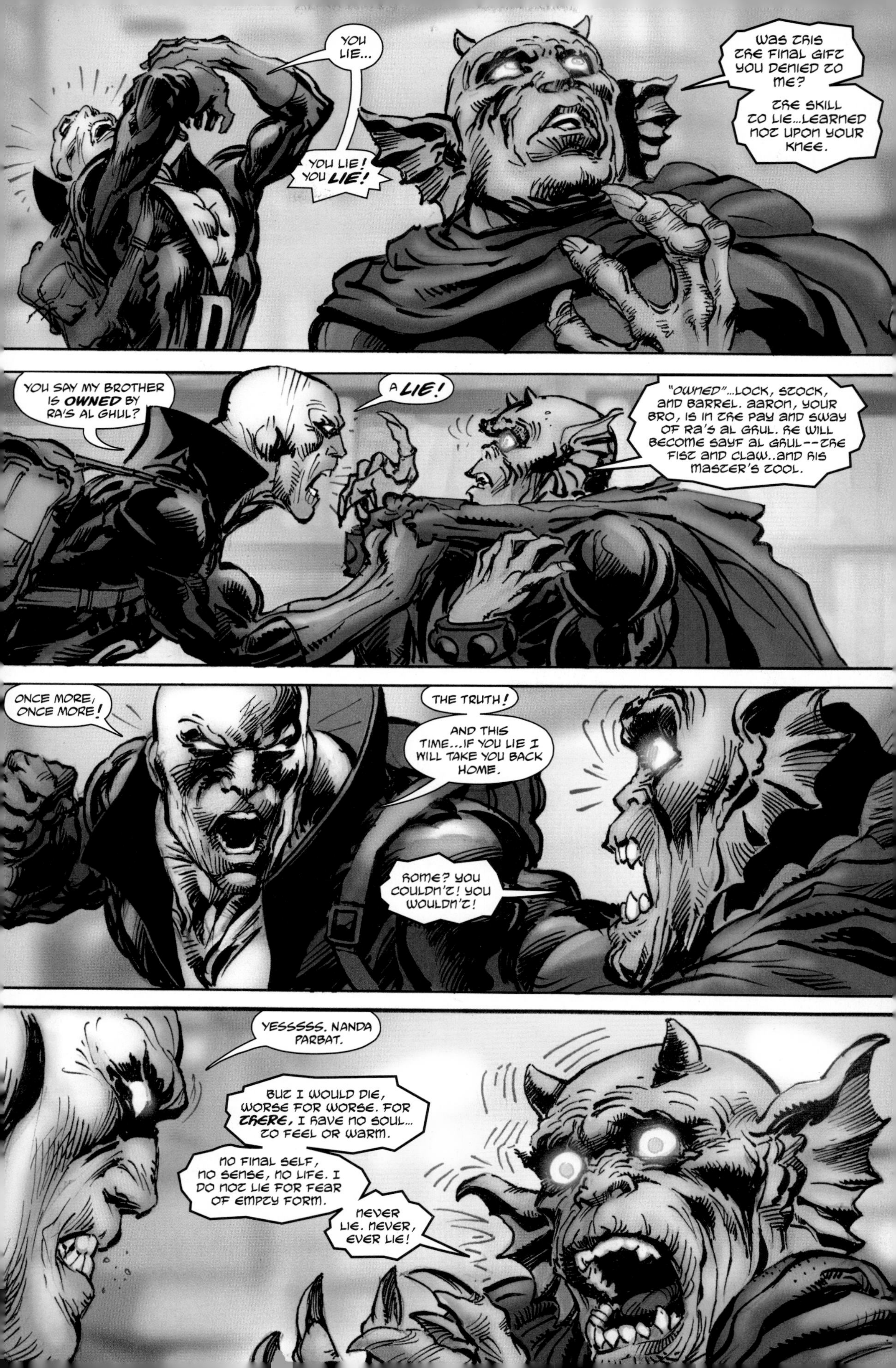

YOU LIE...
YOU LIE! YOU LIE!
WAS THIS THE FINAL GIFT YOU DENIED TO ME?
THE SKILL TO LIE...LEARNED NOT UPON YOUR KNEE.
YOU SAY MY BROTHER IS OWNED BY RA'S AL GHUL?
A LIE!
"OWNED"...LOCK, STOCK, AND BARREL. AARON, YOUR BRO, IS IN THE PAY AND SWAY OF RA'S AL GHUL. HE WILL BECOME SAYF AL GHUL--THE FIST AND CLAW..AND HIS MASTER'S TOOL.
ONCE MORE, ONCE MORE!
THE TRUTH!
AND THIS TIME...IF YOU LIE I WILL TAKE YOU BACK HOME.
HOME? YOU COULDN'T! YOU WOULDN'T!
YESSSSS. NANDA PARBAT.
BUT I WOULD DIE, WORSE FOR WORSE. FOR THERE, I HAVE NO SOUL... TO FEEL OR WARM.
NO FINAL SELF, NO SENSE, NO LIFE. I DO NOT LIE FOR FEAR OF EMPTY FORM.
NEVER LIE. NEVER, EVER LIE!

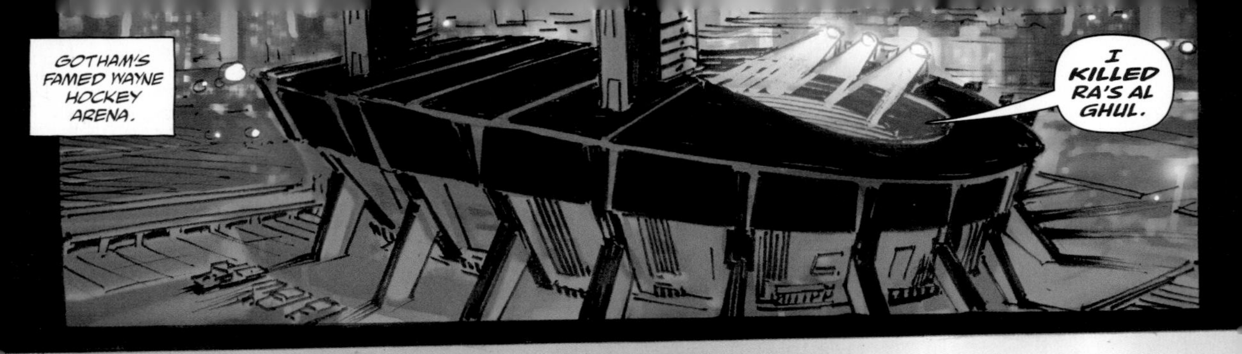
GOTHAM'S FAMED WAYNE HOCKEY ARENA.
I KILLED RA'S AL GHUL.
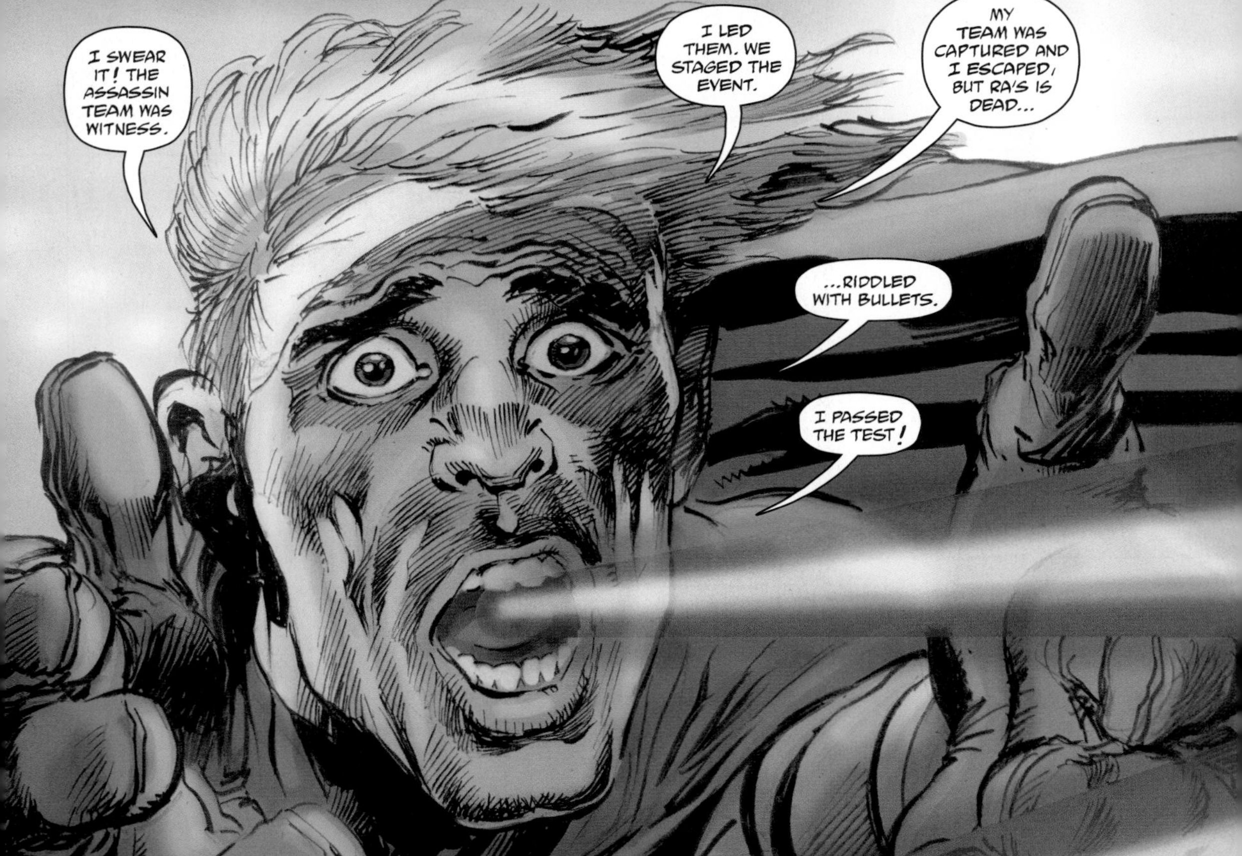
I SWEAR IT! THE ASSASSIN TEAM WAS WITNESS.
I LED THEM. WE STAGED THE EVENT.
MY TEAM WAS CAPTURED AND I ESCAPED, BUT RA'S IS DEAD...
...RIDDLED WITH BULLETS.
I PASSED THE TEST!
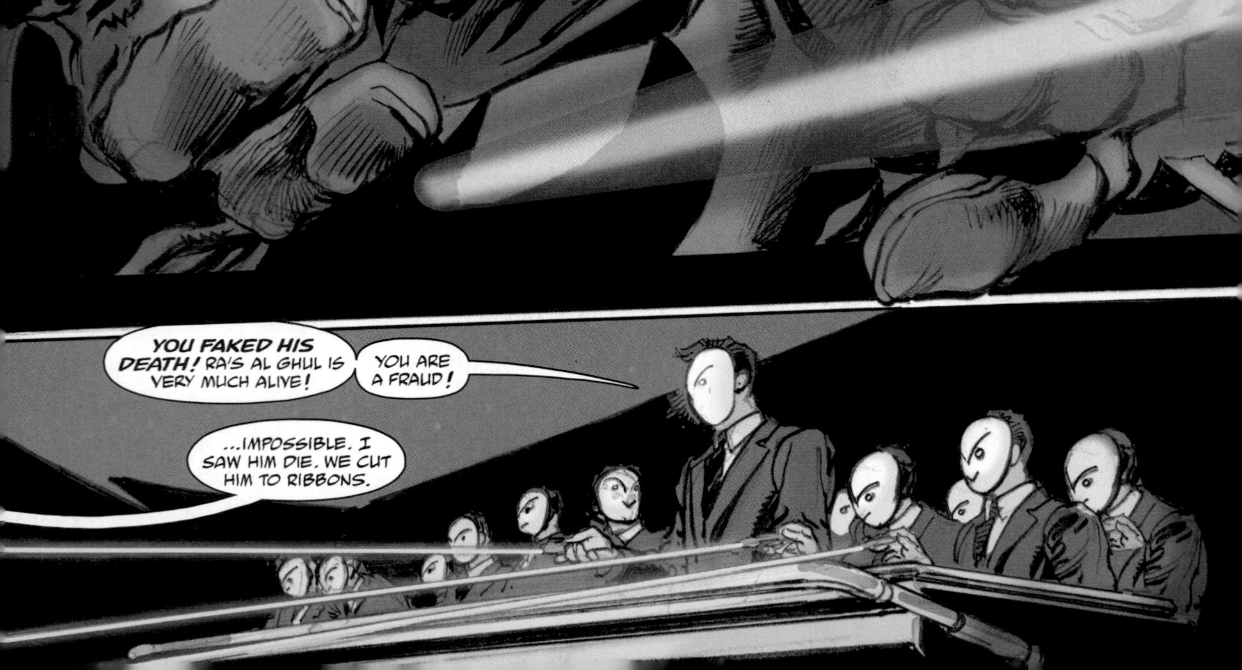
YOU FAKED HIS DEATH! RA'S AL GHUL IS VERY MUCH ALIVE!
YOU ARE A FRAUD!
...IMPOSSIBLE. I SAW HIM DIE. WE CUT HIM TO RIBBONS.

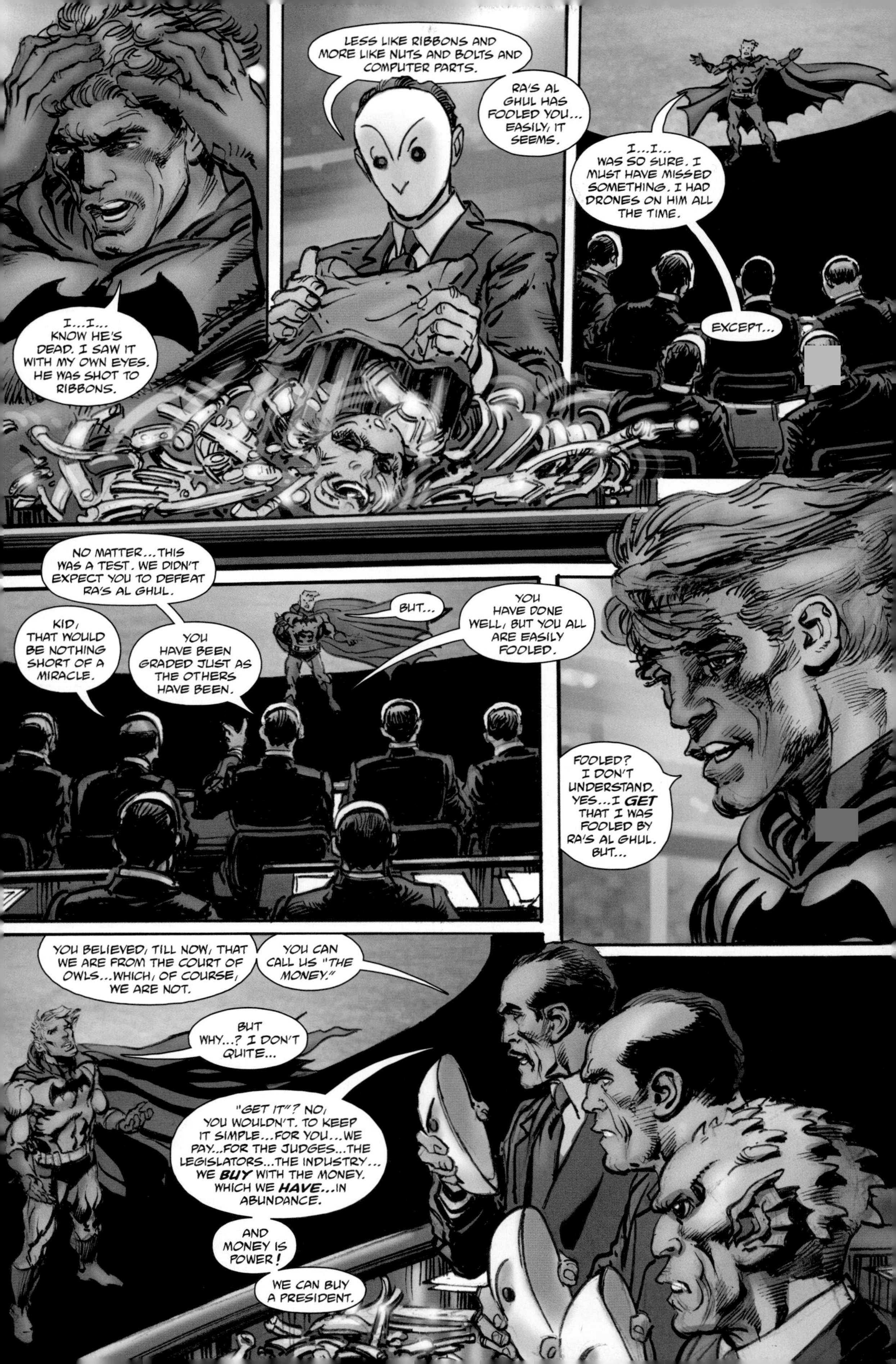
I...I... KNOW HE'S DEAD. I SAW IT WITH MY OWN EYES. HE WAS SHOT TO RIBBONS.
LESS LIKE RIBBONS AND MORE LIKE NUTS AND BOLTS AND COMPUTER PARTS.
RA'S AL GHUL HAS FOOLED YOU... EASILY, IT SEEMS.
I...I... WAS SO SURE. I MUST HAVE MISSED SOMETHING. I HAD DRONES ON HIM ALL THE TIME.
EXCEPT...
NO MATTER...THIS WAS A TEST. WE DIDN'T EXPECT YOU TO DEFEAT RA'S AL GHUL.
KID, THAT WOULD BE NOTHING SHORT OF A MIRACLE.
YOU HAVE BEEN GRADED JUST AS THE OTHERS HAVE BEEN.
BUT...
YOU HAVE DONE WELL, BUT YOU ALL ARE EASILY FOOLED.
FOOLED? I DON'T UNDERSTAND. YES...I **GET** THAT I WAS FOOLED BY RA'S AL GHUL. BUT...
YOU BELIEVED, TILL NOW, THAT WE ARE FROM THE COURT OF OWLS...WHICH, OF COURSE, WE ARE NOT.
YOU CAN CALL US "THE MONEY."
BUT WHY...? I DON'T QUITE...
"GET IT"? NO, YOU WOULDN'T. TO KEEP IT SIMPLE...FOR YOU...WE PAY...FOR THE JUDGES...THE LEGISLATORS...THE INDUSTRY... WE **BUY** WITH THE MONEY. WHICH WE **HAVE...**IN ABUNDANCE.
AND MONEY IS POWER!
WE CAN BUY A PRESIDENT.

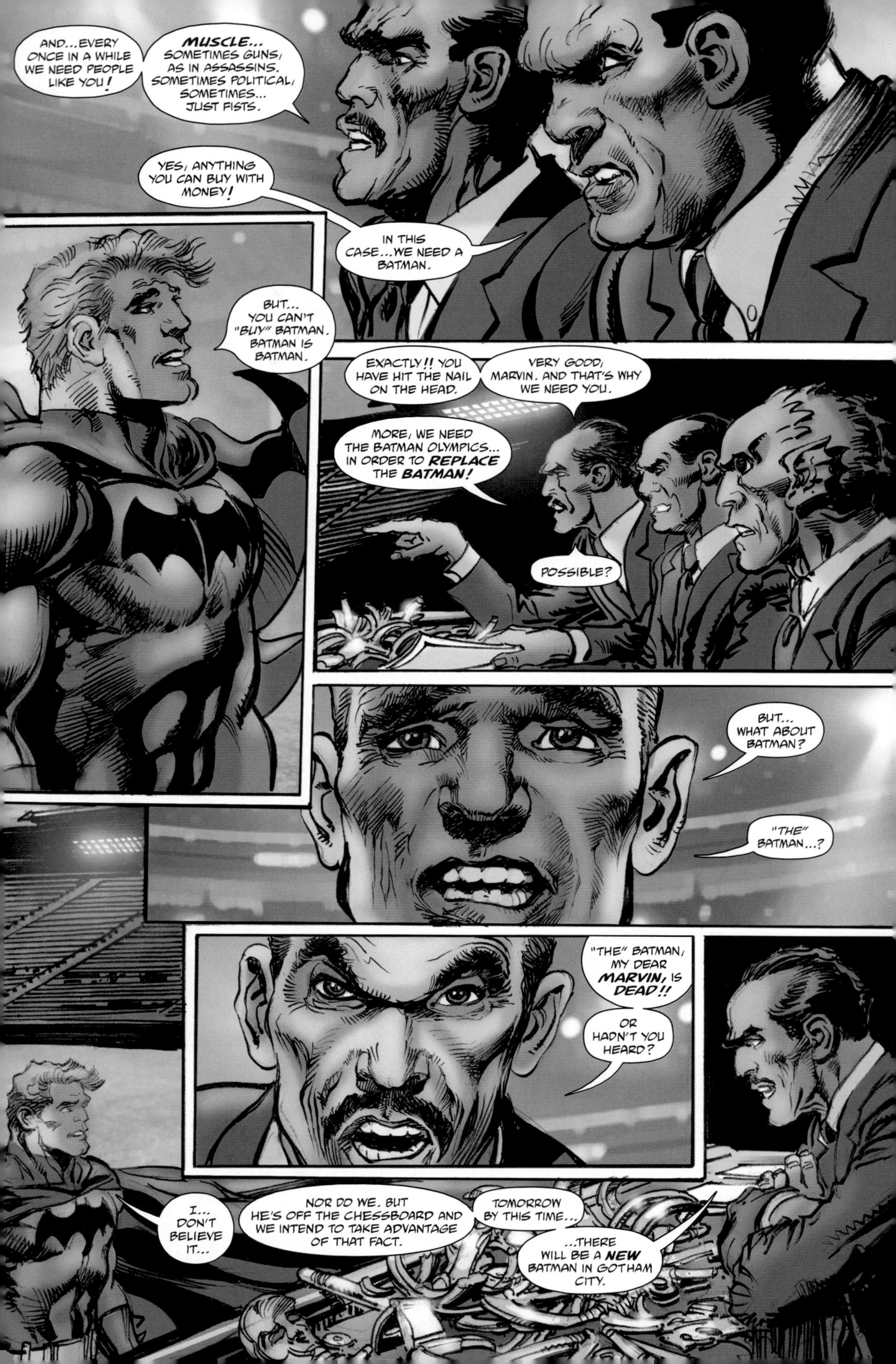
AND...EVERY ONCE IN A WHILE WE NEED PEOPLE LIKE YOU!
MUSCLE... SOMETIMES GUNS, AS IN ASSASSINS. SOMETIMES POLITICAL, SOMETIMES... JUST FISTS.
YES, ANYTHING YOU CAN BUY WITH MONEY!
IN THIS CASE...WE NEED A BATMAN.
BUT... YOU CAN'T "BUY" BATMAN. BATMAN IS BATMAN.
EXACTLY!! YOU HAVE HIT THE NAIL ON THE HEAD.
VERY GOOD, MARVIN. AND THAT'S WHY WE NEED YOU.
MORE, WE NEED THE BATMAN OLYMPICS... IN ORDER TO REPLACE THE BATMAN!
POSSIBLE?
BUT... WHAT ABOUT BATMAN?
"THE" BATMAN...?
"THE" BATMAN, MY DEAR MARVIN, IS DEAD!!
OR HADN'T YOU HEARD?
I... DON'T BELIEVE IT...
NOR DO WE. BUT HE'S OFF THE CHESSBOARD AND WE INTEND TO TAKE ADVANTAGE OF THAT FACT.
TOMORROW BY THIS TIME...
...THERE WILL BE A NEW BATMAN IN GOTHAM CITY.

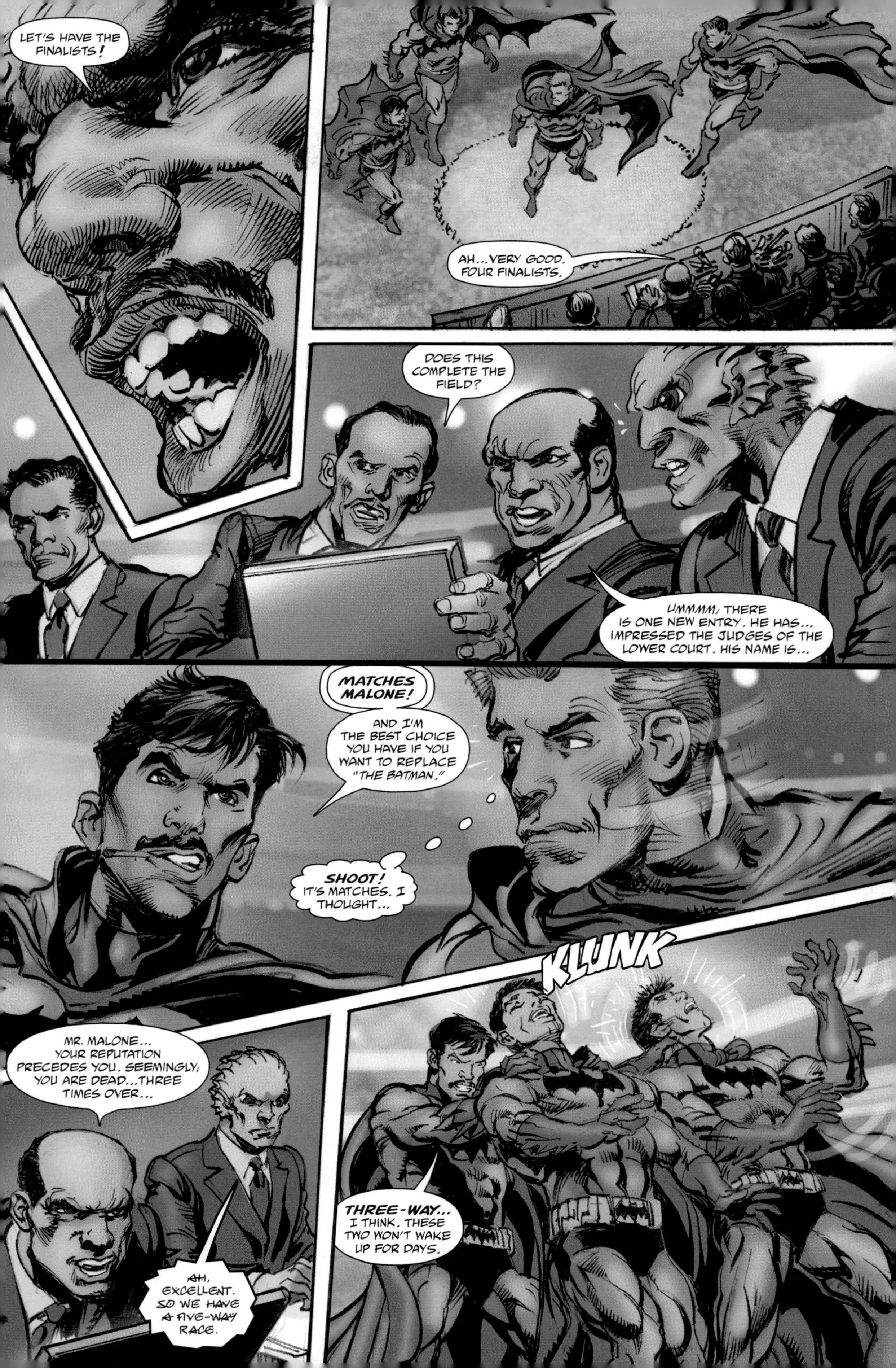
LET'S HAVE THE FINALISTS!
AH...VERY GOOD. FOUR FINALISTS.
DOES THIS COMPLETE THE FIELD?
UMMMM, THERE IS ONE NEW ENTRY. HE HAS... IMPRESSED THE JUDGES OF THE LOWER COURT. HIS NAME IS...
MATCHES MALONE!
AND I'M THE BEST CHOICE YOU HAVE IF YOU WANT TO REPLACE "THE BATMAN."
SHOOT! IT'S MATCHES. I THOUGHT...
KLUNK
MR. MALONE... YOUR REPUTATION PRECEDES YOU. SEEMINGLY, YOU ARE DEAD...THREE TIMES OVER...
AH, EXCELLENT. SO WE HAVE A FIVE-WAY RACE.
THREE-WAY... I THINK. THESE TWO WON'T WAKE UP FOR DAYS.

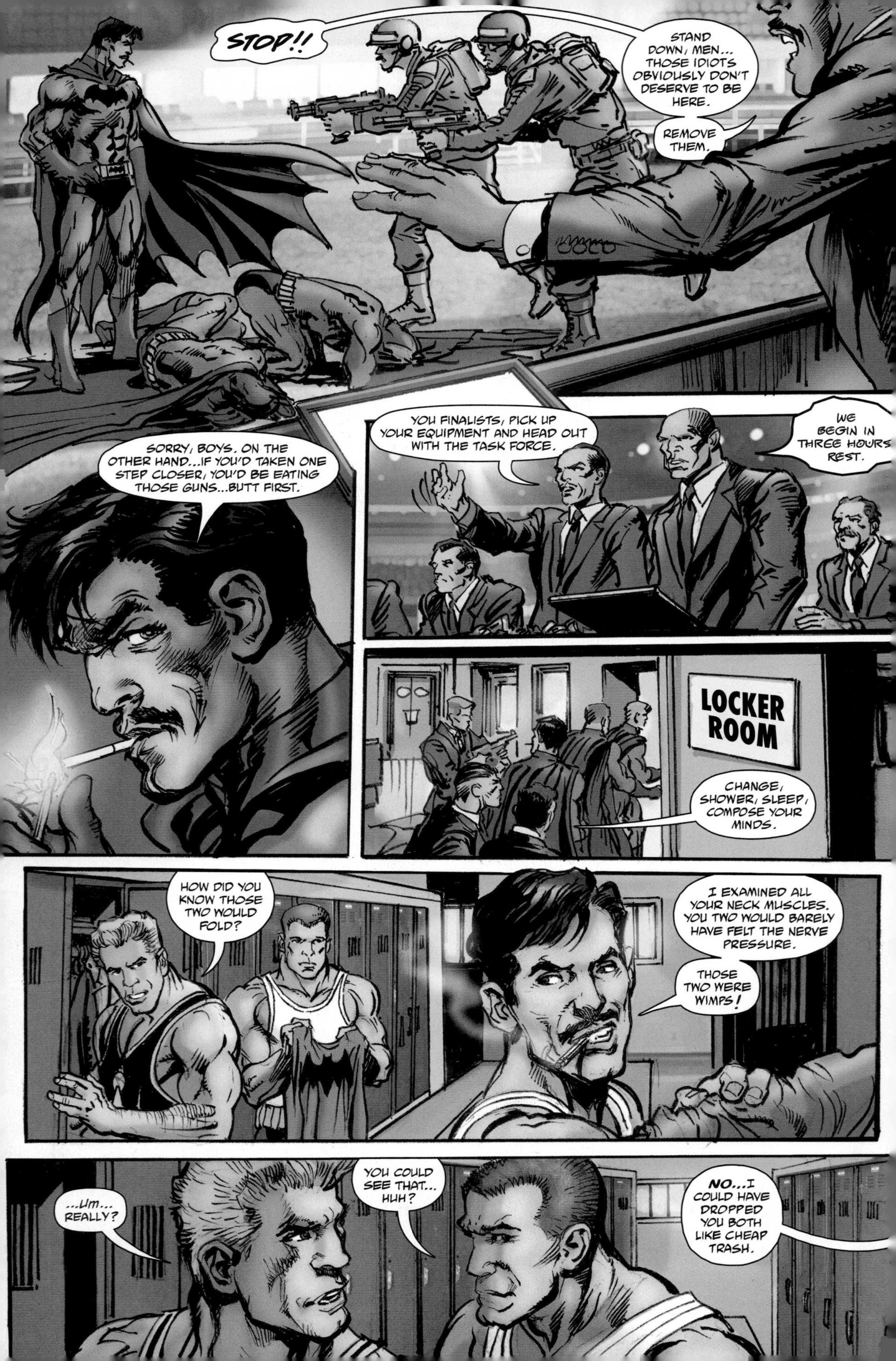

STOP!!
STAND DOWN, MEN... THOSE IDIOTS OBVIOUSLY DON'T DESERVE TO BE HERE.
REMOVE THEM.
SORRY, BOYS. ON THE OTHER HAND...IF YOU'D TAKEN ONE STEP CLOSER, YOU'D BE EATING THOSE GUNS...BUTT FIRST.
YOU FINALISTS, PICK UP YOUR EQUIPMENT AND HEAD OUT WITH THE TASK FORCE.
WE BEGIN IN THREE HOURS REST.
LOCKER ROOM
CHANGE, SHOWER, SLEEP, COMPOSE YOUR MINDS.
HOW DID YOU KNOW THOSE TWO WOULD FOLD?
I EXAMINED ALL YOUR NECK MUSCLES. YOU TWO WOULD BARELY HAVE FELT THE NERVE PRESSURE.
THOSE TWO WERE WIMPS!
...UM... REALLY?
YOU COULD SEE THAT... HUH?
NO...I COULD HAVE DROPPED YOU BOTH LIKE CHEAP TRASH.

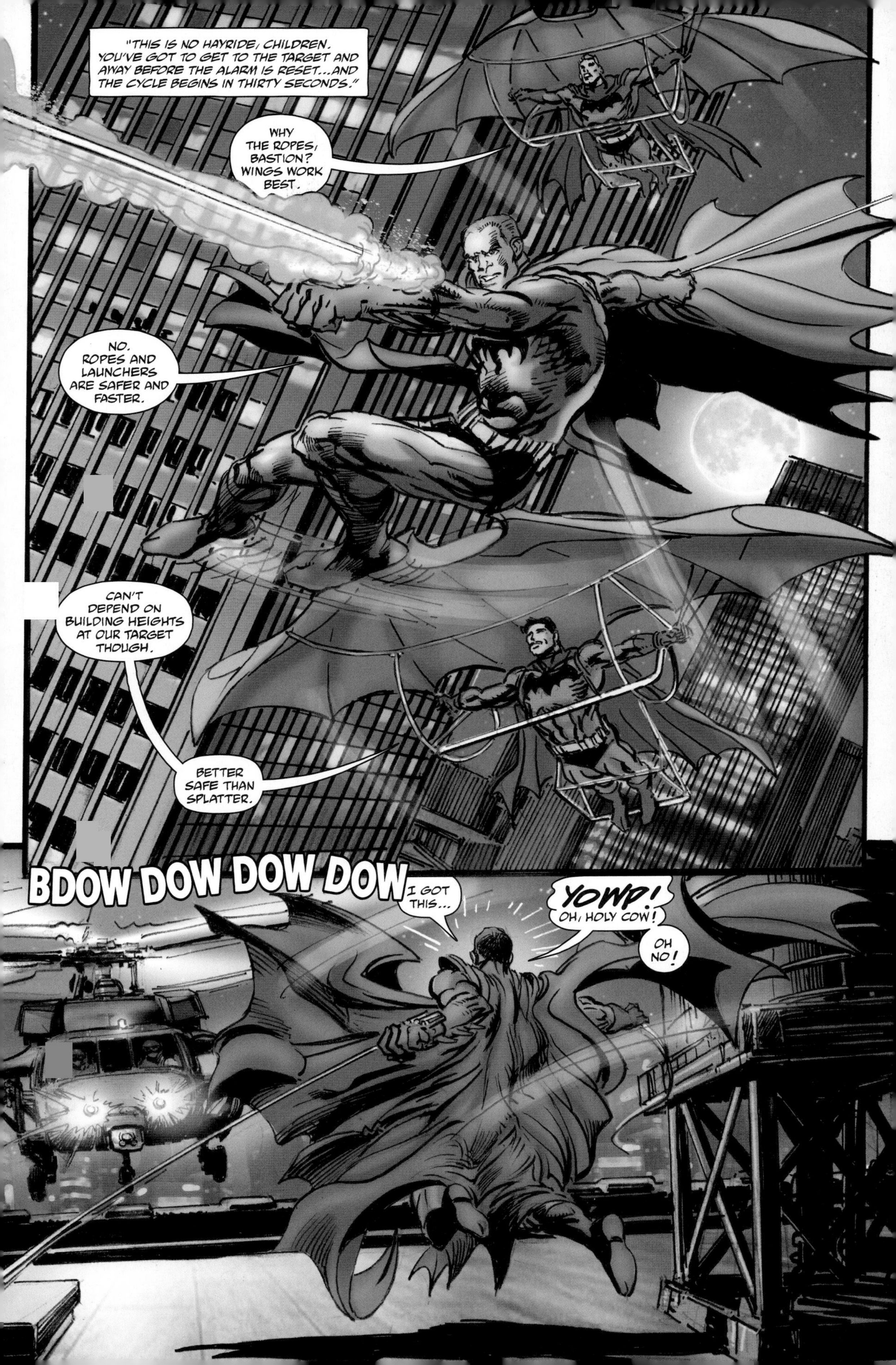
"THIS IS NO HAYRIDE, CHILDREN. YOU'VE GOT TO GET TO THE TARGET AND AWAY BEFORE THE ALARM IS RESET...AND THE CYCLE BEGINS IN THIRTY SECONDS."
WHY THE ROPES, BASTION? WINGS WORK BEST.
NO. ROPES AND LAUNCHERS ARE SAFER AND FASTER.
CAN'T DEPEND ON BUILDING HEIGHTS AT OUR TARGET THOUGH.
BETTER SAFE THAN SPLATTER.
BDOW DOW DOW DOW
I GOT THIS...
YOWP! OH, HOLY COW!
OH NO!

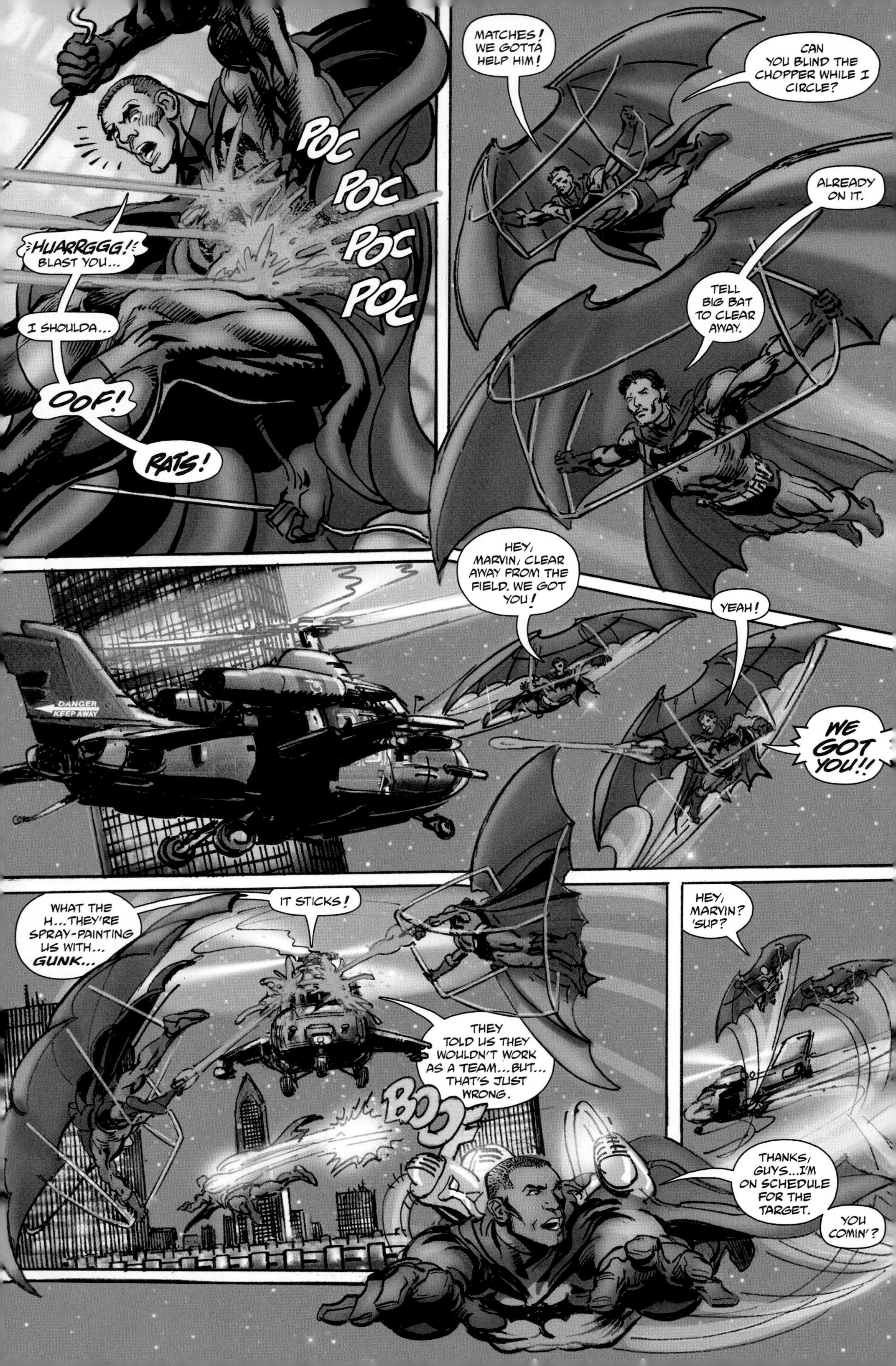
POC
POC
POC
POC
HUARRGGG! BLAST YOU...
I SHOULDA...
OOF!
RATS!
MATCHES! WE GOTTA HELP HIM!
CAN YOU BLIND THE CHOPPER WHILE I CIRCLE?
ALREADY ON IT.
TELL BIG BAT TO CLEAR AWAY.
HEY, MARVIN, CLEAR AWAY FROM THE FIELD. WE GOT YOU!
YEAH!
WE GOT YOU!!
DANGER
KEEP AWAY
WHAT THE H...THEY'RE SPRAY-PAINTING US WITH... GUNK...
IT STICKS!
THEY TOLD US THEY WOULDN'T WORK AS A TEAM...BUT... THAT'S JUST WRONG.
BOOF
HEY, MARVIN? 'SUP?
THANKS, GUYS...I'M ON SCHEDULE FOR THE TARGET.
YOU COMIN'?

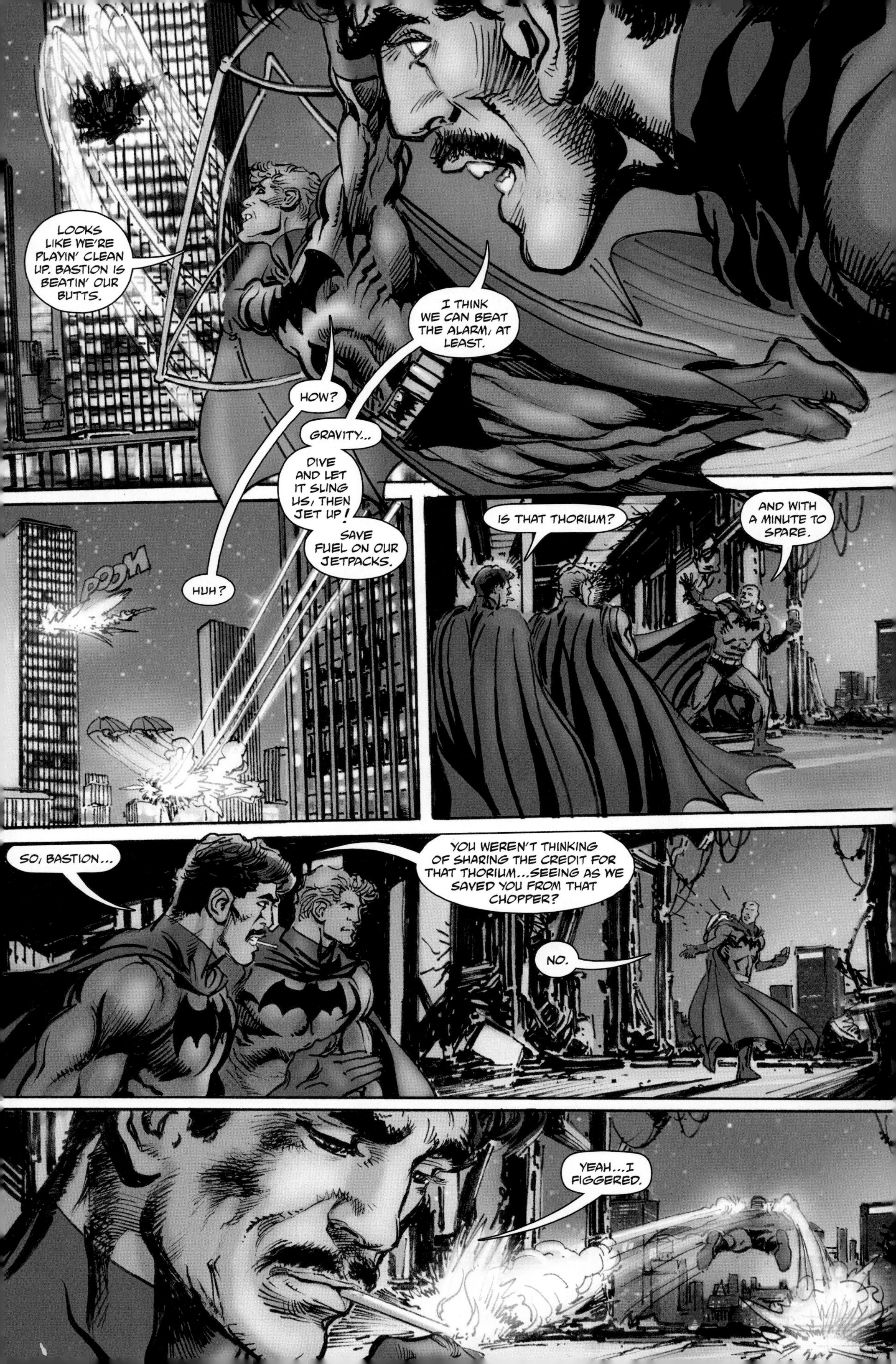
LOOKS LIKE WE'RE PLAYIN' CLEAN UP. BASTION IS BEATIN' OUR BUTTS.
I THINK WE CAN BEAT THE ALARM, AT LEAST.
HOW?
GRAVITY...
DIVE AND LET IT SLING US, THEN JET UP!
SAVE FUEL ON OUR JETPACKS.
HUH?
BOOM
IS THAT THORIUM?
AND WITH A MINUTE TO SPARE.
SO, BASTION...
YOU WEREN'T THINKING OF SHARING THE CREDIT FOR THAT THORIUM...SEEING AS WE SAVED YOU FROM THAT CHOPPER?
NO.
YEAH...I FIGGERED.

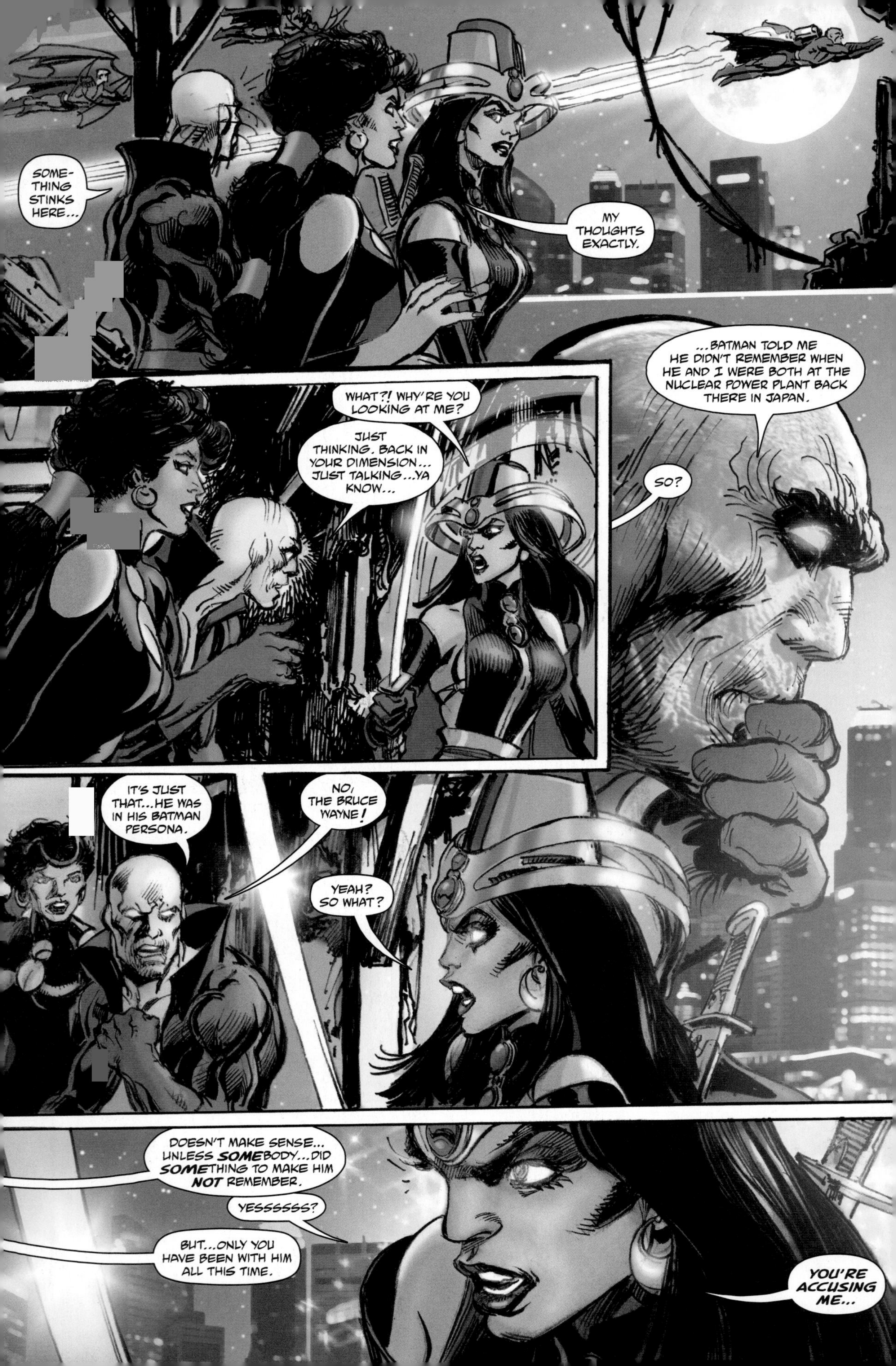
SOME-THING STINKS HERE...
MY THOUGHTS EXACTLY.
...BATMAN TOLD ME HE DIDN'T REMEMBER WHEN HE AND I WERE BOTH AT THE NUCLEAR POWER PLANT BACK THERE IN JAPAN.
SO?
WHAT?! WHY'RE YOU LOOKING AT ME?
JUST THINKING. BACK IN YOUR DIMENSION... JUST TALKING...YA KNOW...
IT'S JUST THAT...HE WAS IN HIS BATMAN PERSONA.
NO, THE BRUCE WAYNE!
YEAH? SO WHAT?
DOESN'T MAKE SENSE... UNLESS SOMEBODY...DID SOMETHING TO MAKE HIM NOT REMEMBER.
YESSSSSS?
BUT...ONLY YOU HAVE BEEN WITH HIM ALL THIS TIME.
YOU'RE ACCUSING ME...

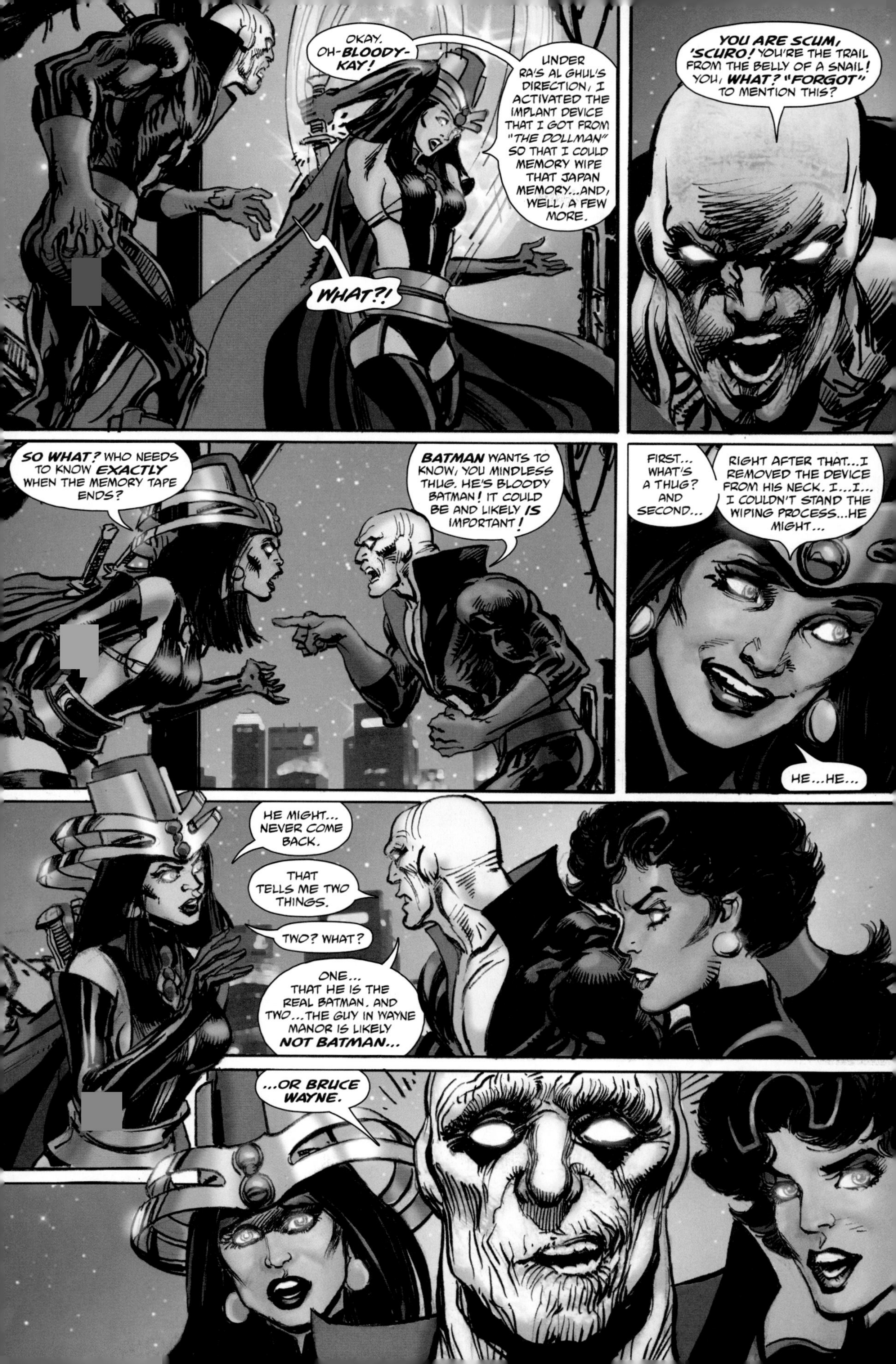
OKAY. OH-BLOODY-KAY!
UNDER RA'S AL GHUL'S DIRECTION, I ACTIVATED THE IMPLANT DEVICE THAT I GOT FROM "THE DOLLMAN" SO THAT I COULD MEMORY WIPE THAT JAPAN MEMORY...AND, WELL, A FEW MORE.
WHAT?!
YOU ARE SCUM, 'SCURO! YOU'RE THE TRAIL FROM THE BELLY OF A SNAIL! YOU, WHAT? "FORGOT" TO MENTION THIS?
SO WHAT? WHO NEEDS TO KNOW EXACTLY WHEN THE MEMORY TAPE ENDS?
BATMAN WANTS TO KNOW, YOU MINDLESS THUG. HE'S BLOODY BATMAN! IT COULD BE AND LIKELY IS IMPORTANT!
FIRST... WHAT'S A THUG? AND SECOND...
RIGHT AFTER THAT...I REMOVED THE DEVICE FROM HIS NECK. I...I... I COULDN'T STAND THE WIPING PROCESS...HE MIGHT...
HE...HE...
HE MIGHT... NEVER COME BACK.
THAT TELLS ME TWO THINGS.
TWO? WHAT?
ONE... THAT HE IS THE REAL BATMAN. AND TWO...THE GUY IN WAYNE MANOR IS LIKELY NOT BATMAN...
...OR BRUCE WAYNE.

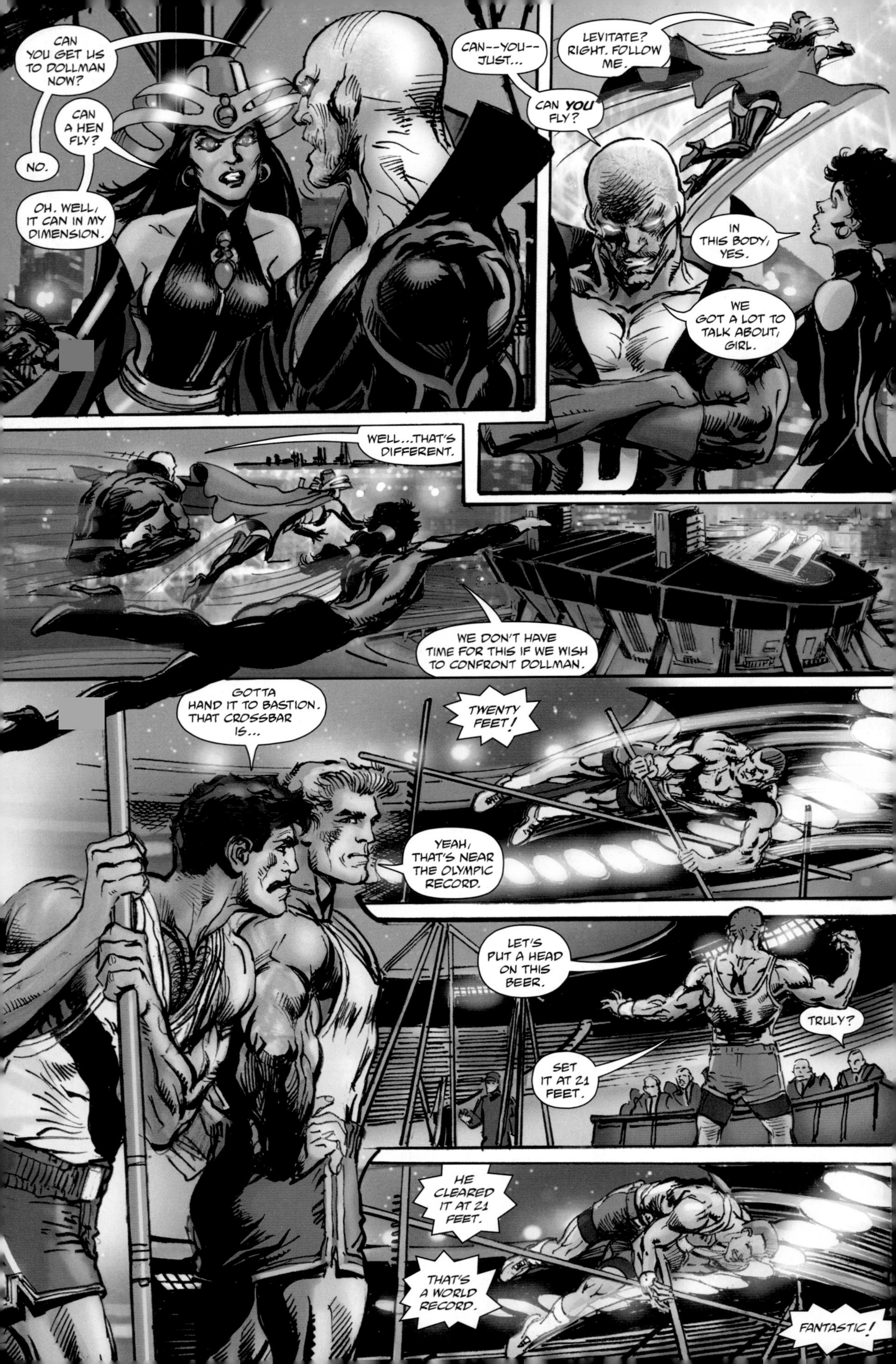
CAN YOU GET US TO DOLLMAN NOW?
NO.
CAN A HEN FLY?
OH. WELL, IT CAN IN MY DIMENSION.
CAN--YOU--JUST...
CAN YOU FLY?
LEVITATE? RIGHT. FOLLOW ME.
IN THIS BODY, YES.
WE GOT A LOT TO TALK ABOUT, GIRL.
WELL...THAT'S DIFFERENT.
WE DON'T HAVE TIME FOR THIS IF WE WISH TO CONFRONT DOLLMAN.
GOTTA HAND IT TO BASTION. THAT CROSSBAR IS...
TWENTY FEET!
YEAH, THAT'S NEAR THE OLYMPIC RECORD.
LET'S PUT A HEAD ON THIS BEER.
TRULY?
SET IT AT 21 FEET.
HE CLEARED IT AT 21 FEET.
THAT'S A WORLD RECORD.
FANTASTIC!

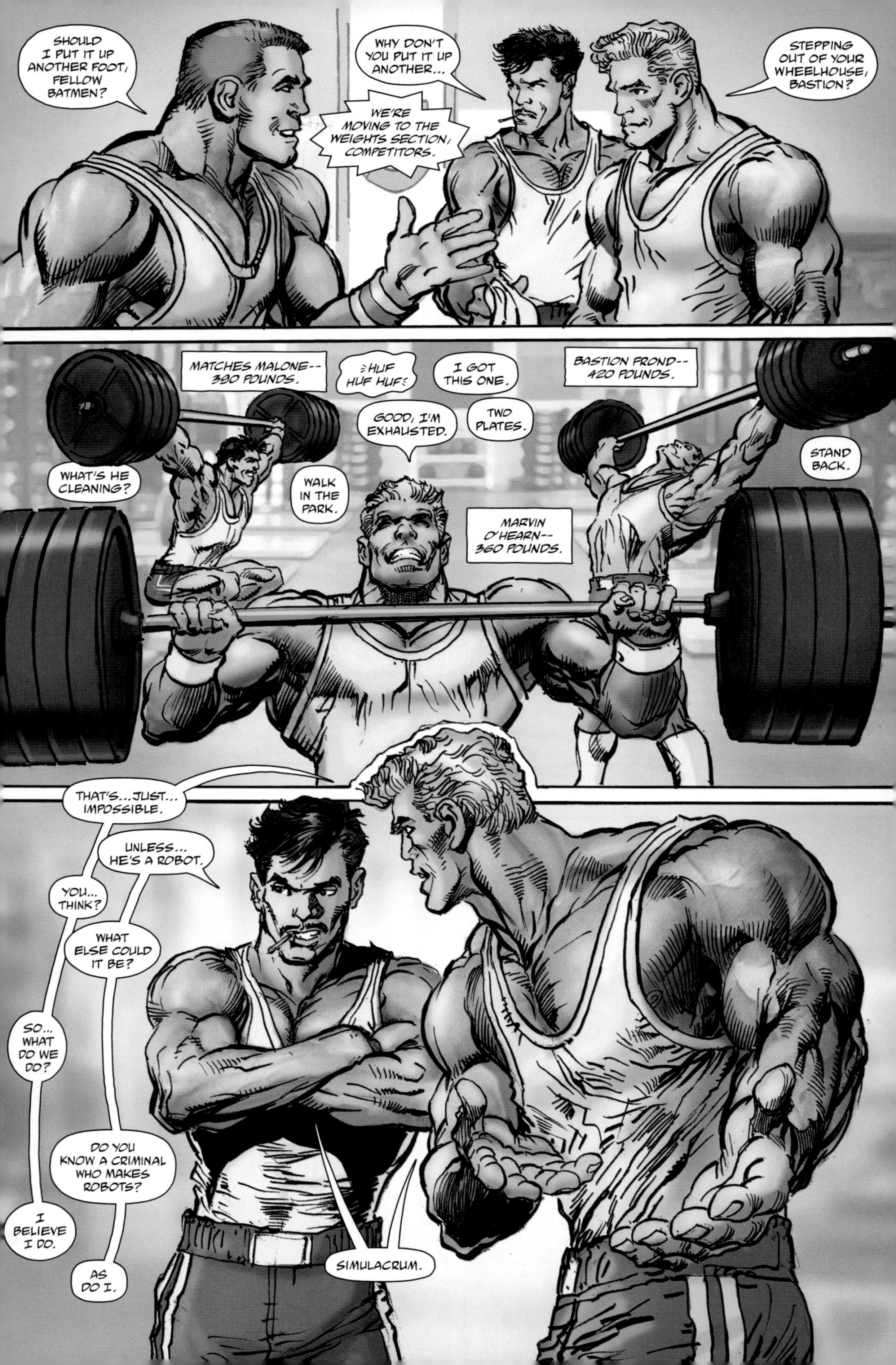
SHOULD I PUT IT UP ANOTHER FOOT, FELLOW BATMEN?
WHY DON'T YOU PUT IT UP ANOTHER...
WE'RE MOVING TO THE WEIGHTS SECTION, COMPETITORS.
STEPPING OUT OF YOUR WHEELHOUSE, BASTION?
MATCHES MALONE-- 390 POUNDS.
WHAT'S HE CLEANING?
HUF HUF HUF
GOOD, I'M EXHAUSTED.
WALK IN THE PARK.
I GOT THIS ONE.
TWO PLATES.
BASTION FROND-- 420 POUNDS.
STAND BACK.
MARVIN O'HEARN-- 360 POUNDS.
THAT'S...JUST... IMPOSSIBLE.
UNLESS... HE'S A ROBOT.
YOU... THINK?
WHAT ELSE COULD IT BE?
SO... WHAT DO WE DO?
DO YOU KNOW A CRIMINAL WHO MAKES ROBOTS?
I BELIEVE I DO.
AS DO I.
SIMULACRUM.

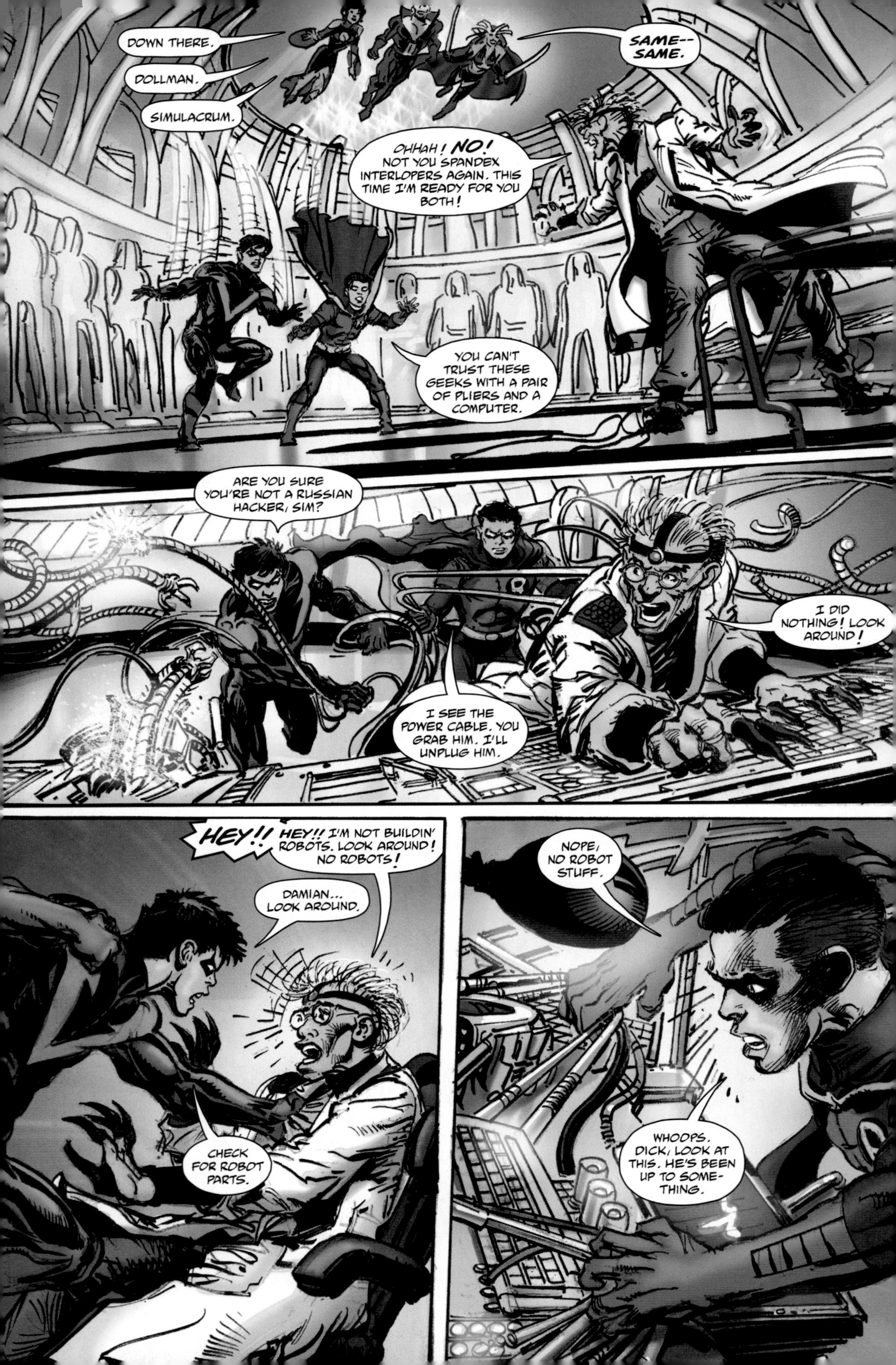
DOWN THERE.
DOLLMAN.
SIMULACRUM.
SAME--SAME.
OHHAH! NO! NOT YOU SPANDEX INTERLOPERS AGAIN. THIS TIME I'M READY FOR YOU BOTH!
YOU CAN'T TRUST THESE GEEKS WITH A PAIR OF PLIERS AND A COMPUTER.
ARE YOU SURE YOU'RE NOT A RUSSIAN HACKER, SIM?
I DID NOTHING! LOOK AROUND!
I SEE THE POWER CABLE. YOU GRAB HIM. I'LL UNPLUG HIM.
HEY!!
HEY!! I'M NOT BUILDIN' ROBOTS. LOOK AROUND! NO ROBOTS!
DAMIAN... LOOK AROUND.
CHECK FOR ROBOT PARTS.
NOPE, NO ROBOT STUFF.
WHOOPS. DICK, LOOK AT THIS. HE'S BEEN UP TO SOME-THING.

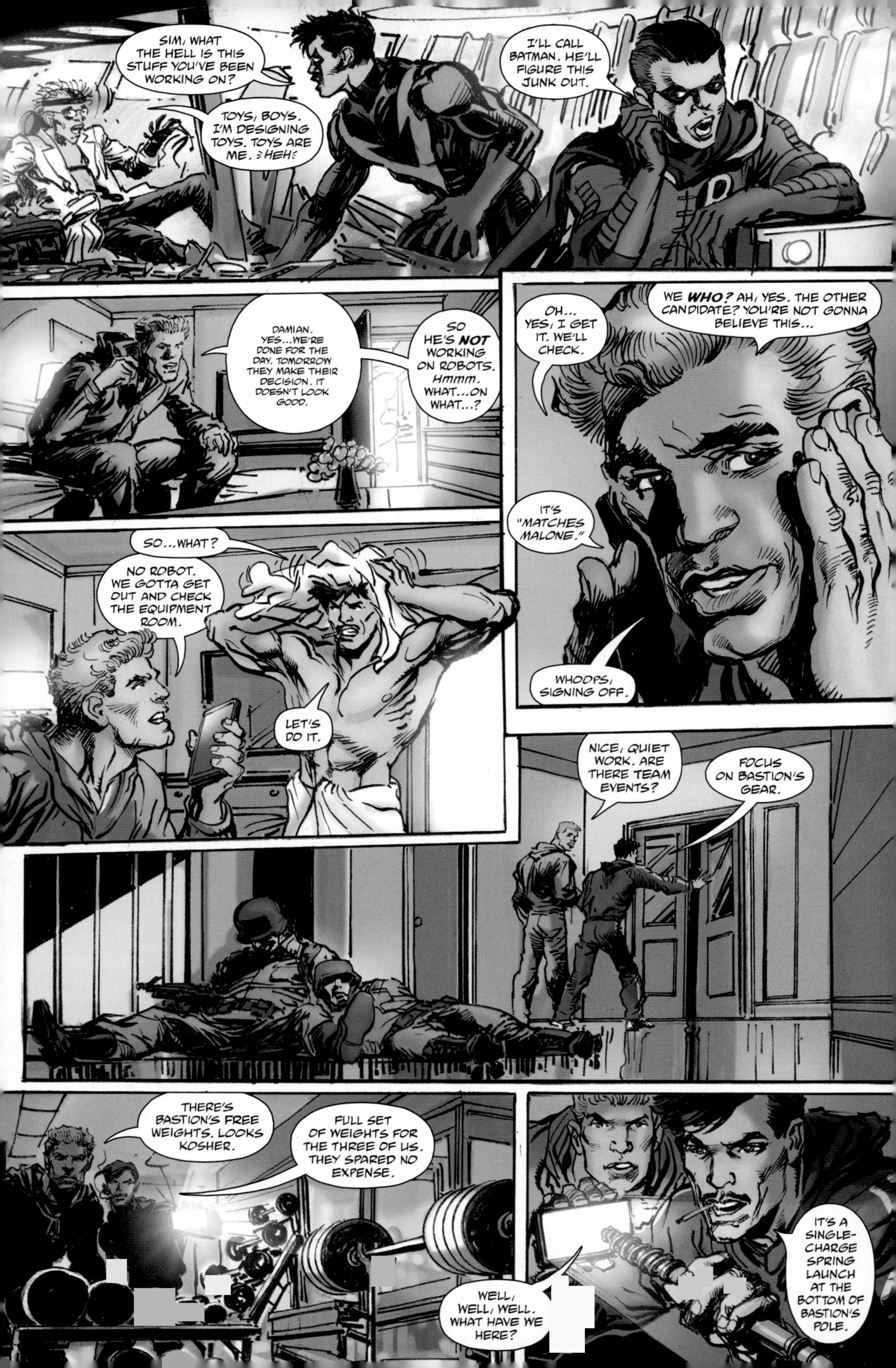
SIM, WHAT THE HELL IS THIS STUFF YOU'VE BEEN WORKING ON?
TOYS, BOYS. I'M DESIGNING TOYS. TOYS ARE ME. HEH
I'LL CALL BATMAN. HE'LL FIGURE THIS JUNK OUT.
DAMIAN. YES...WE'RE DONE FOR THE DAY. TOMORROW THEY MAKE THEIR DECISION. IT DOESN'T LOOK GOOD.
SO HE'S **NOT** WORKING ON ROBOTS. *Hmmm.* WHAT...ON WHAT...?
WE ***WHO?*** AH, YES. THE OTHER CANDIDATE? YOU'RE NOT GONNA BELIEVE THIS...
OH... YES, I GET IT. WE'LL CHECK.
IT'S "MATCHES MALONE."
WHOOPS, SIGNING OFF.
SO...WHAT?
NO ROBOT. WE GOTTA GET OUT AND CHECK THE EQUIPMENT ROOM.
LET'S DO IT.
NICE, QUIET WORK. ARE THERE TEAM EVENTS?
FOCUS ON BASTION'S GEAR.
THERE'S BASTION'S FREE WEIGHTS. LOOKS KOSHER.
FULL SET OF WEIGHTS FOR THE THREE OF US. THEY SPARED NO EXPENSE.
WELL, WELL, WELL. WHAT HAVE WE HERE?
IT'S A SINGLE-CHARGE SPRING LAUNCH AT THE BOTTOM OF BASTION'S POLE.

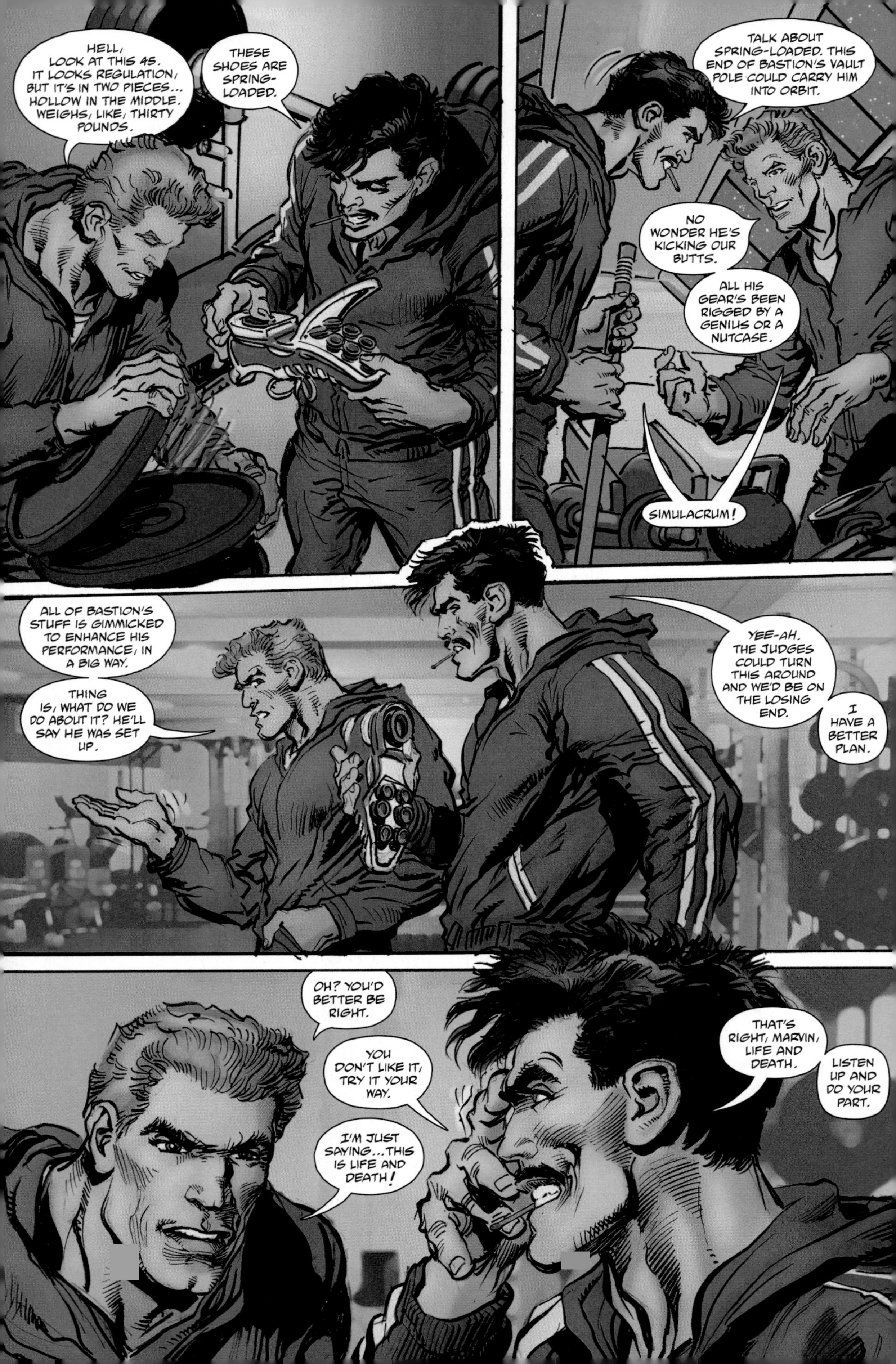

HELL, LOOK AT THIS 45. IT LOOKS REGULATION, BUT IT'S IN TWO PIECES... HOLLOW IN THE MIDDLE. WEIGHS, LIKE, THIRTY POUNDS.
THESE SHOES ARE SPRING-LOADED.
TALK ABOUT SPRING-LOADED. THIS END OF BASTION'S VAULT POLE COULD CARRY HIM INTO ORBIT.
NO WONDER HE'S KICKING OUR BUTTS.
ALL HIS GEAR'S BEEN RIGGED BY A GENIUS OR A NUTCASE.
SIMULACRUM!
ALL OF BASTION'S STUFF IS GIMMICKED TO ENHANCE HIS PERFORMANCE, IN A BIG WAY.
THING IS, WHAT DO WE DO ABOUT IT? HE'LL SAY HE WAS SET UP.
YEE-AH. THE JUDGES COULD TURN THIS AROUND AND WE'D BE ON THE LOSING END.
I HAVE A BETTER PLAN.
OH? YOU'D BETTER BE RIGHT.
YOU DON'T LIKE IT, TRY IT YOUR WAY.
I'M JUST SAYING...THIS IS LIFE AND DEATH!
THAT'S RIGHT, MARVIN, LIFE AND DEATH.
LISTEN UP AND DO YOUR PART.

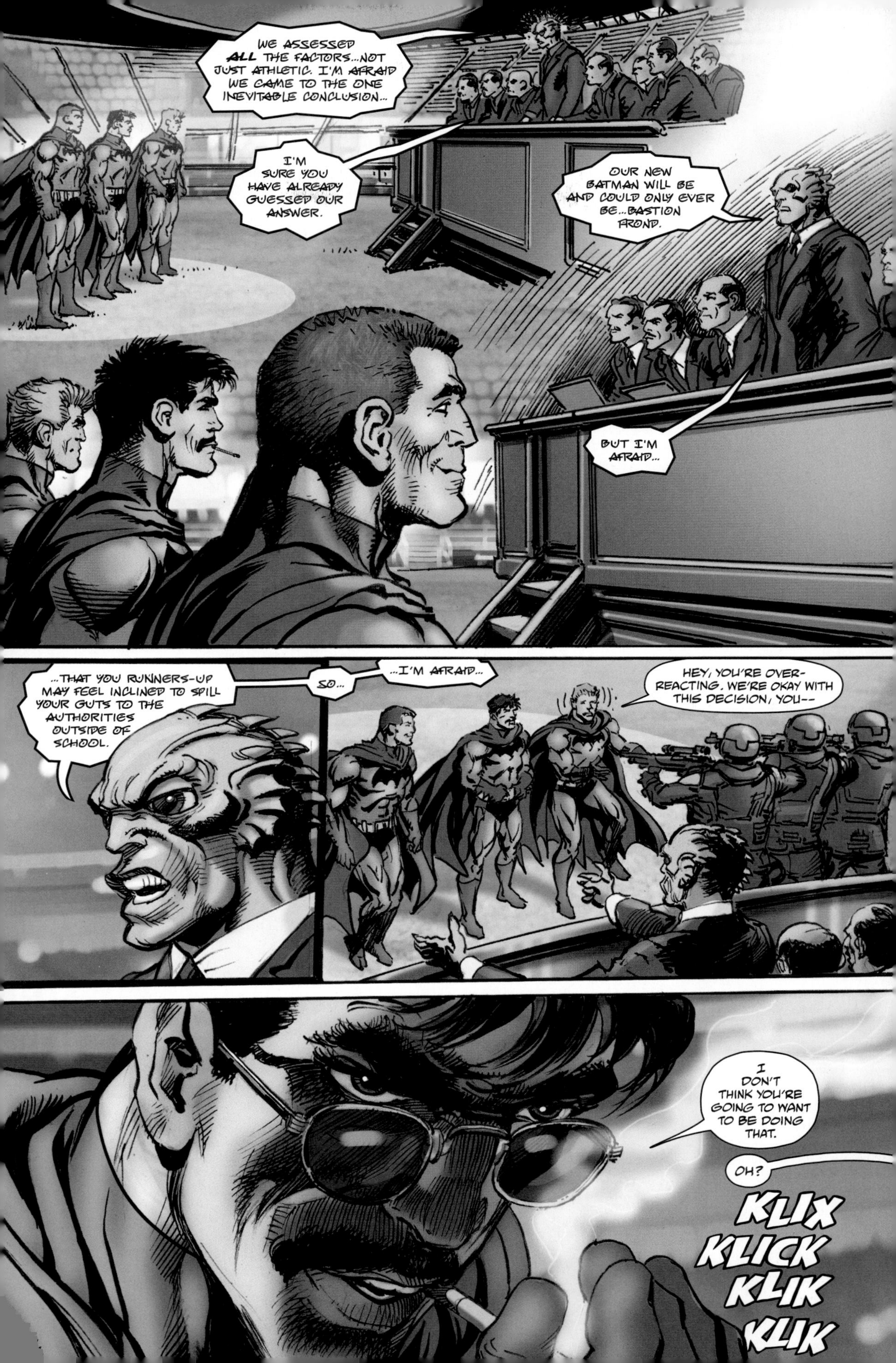
WE ASSESSED ALL THE FACTORS...NOT JUST ATHLETIC. I'M AFRAID WE CAME TO THE ONE INEVITABLE CONCLUSION...
I'M SURE YOU HAVE ALREADY GUESSED OUR ANSWER.
OUR NEW BATMAN WILL BE AND COULD ONLY EVER BE...BASTION FROND.
BUT I'M AFRAID...
...THAT YOU RUNNERS-UP MAY FEEL INCLINED TO SPILL YOUR GUTS TO THE AUTHORITIES OUTSIDE OF SCHOOL.
SO...
...I'M AFRAID...
HEY, YOU'RE OVER-REACTING. WE'RE OKAY WITH THIS DECISION, YOU--
I DON'T THINK YOU'RE GOING TO WANT TO BE DOING THAT.
OH?
KLIX
KLICK
KLIK
KLIK

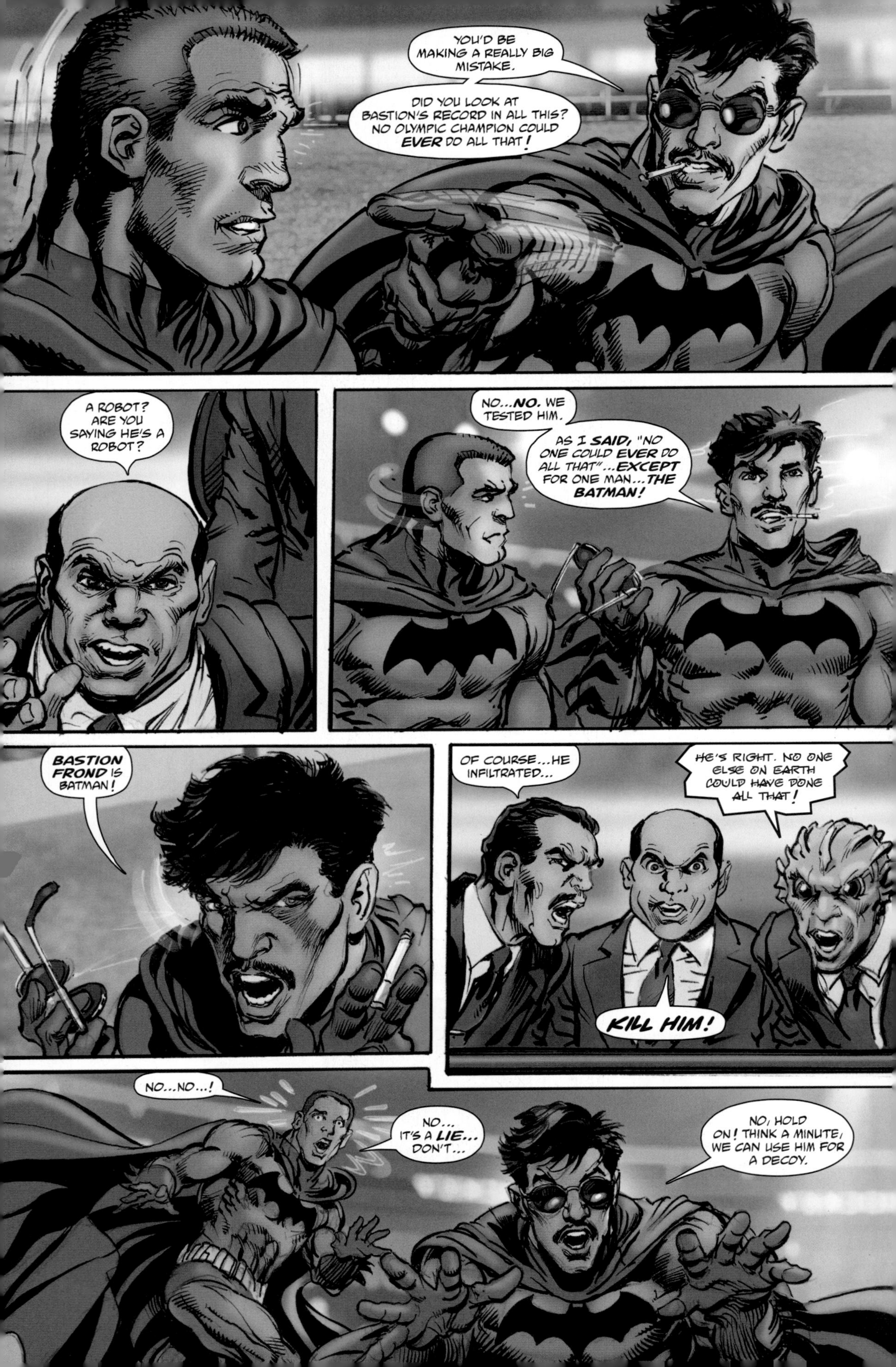
YOU'D BE MAKING A REALLY BIG MISTAKE.
DID YOU LOOK AT BASTION'S RECORD IN ALL THIS? NO OLYMPIC CHAMPION COULD EVER DO ALL THAT!
A ROBOT? ARE YOU SAYING HE'S A ROBOT?
NO...NO. WE TESTED HIM.
AS I SAID, "NO ONE COULD EVER DO ALL THAT"...EXCEPT FOR ONE MAN...THE BATMAN!
BASTION FROND IS BATMAN!
OF COURSE...HE INFILTRATED...
HE'S RIGHT. NO ONE ELSE ON EARTH COULD HAVE DONE ALL THAT!
KILL HIM!
NO...NO...!
NO... IT'S A LIE... DON'T...
NO, HOLD ON! THINK A MINUTE, WE CAN USE HIM FOR A DECOY.

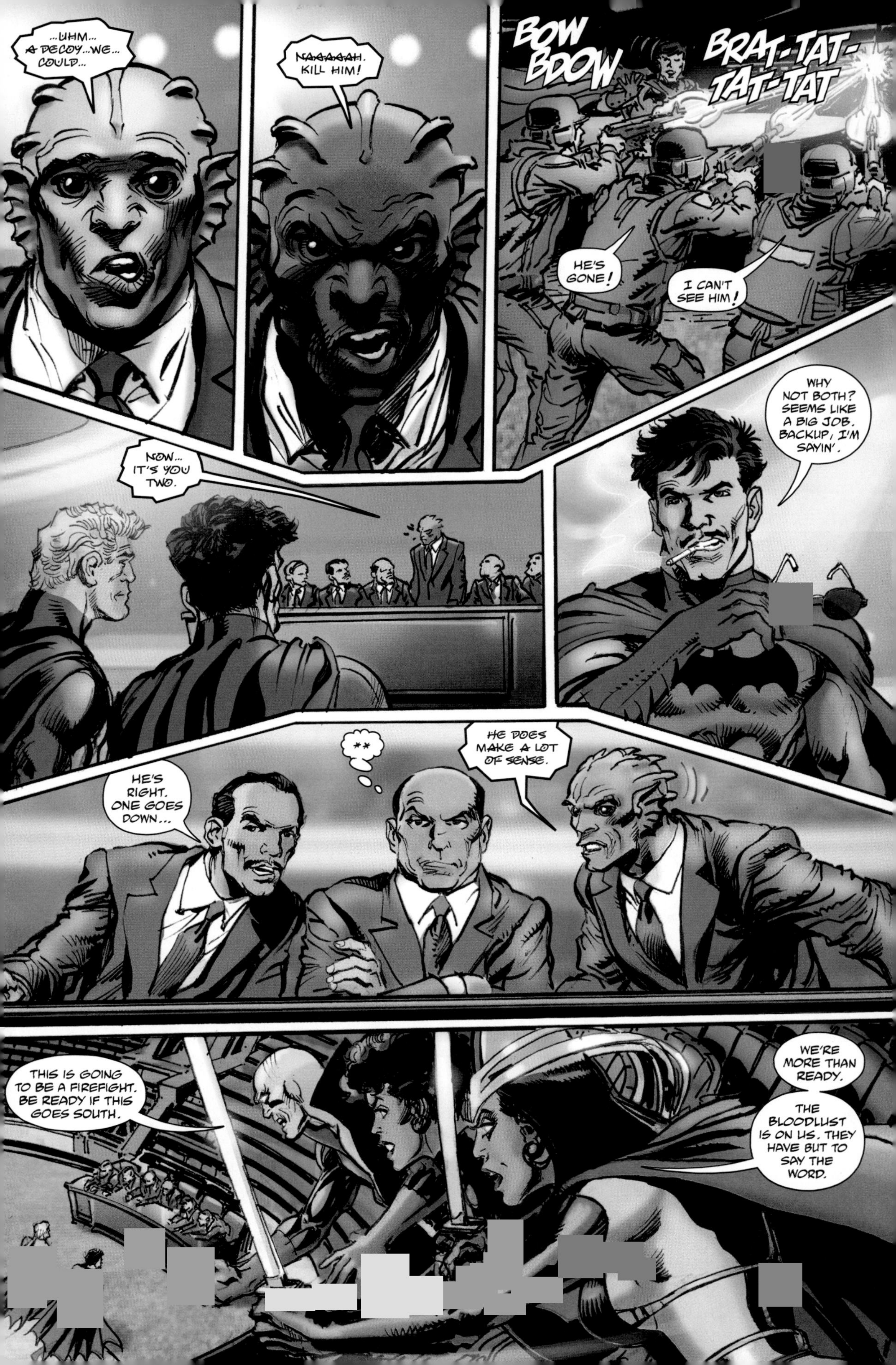
...UHM... A DECOY...WE... COULD...
NAAAAAH. KILL HIM!
BOW BDOW
BRAT-TAT-TAT-TAT
HE'S GONE!
I CAN'T SEE HIM!
NOW... IT'S YOU TWO.
WHY NOT BOTH? SEEMS LIKE A BIG JOB. BACKUP, I'M SAYIN'.
HE'S RIGHT. ONE GOES DOWN...
**
HE DOES MAKE A LOT OF SENSE.
THIS IS GOING TO BE A FIREFIGHT. BE READY IF THIS GOES SOUTH.
WE'RE MORE THAN READY.
THE BLOODLUST IS ON US. THEY HAVE BUT TO SAY THE WORD.

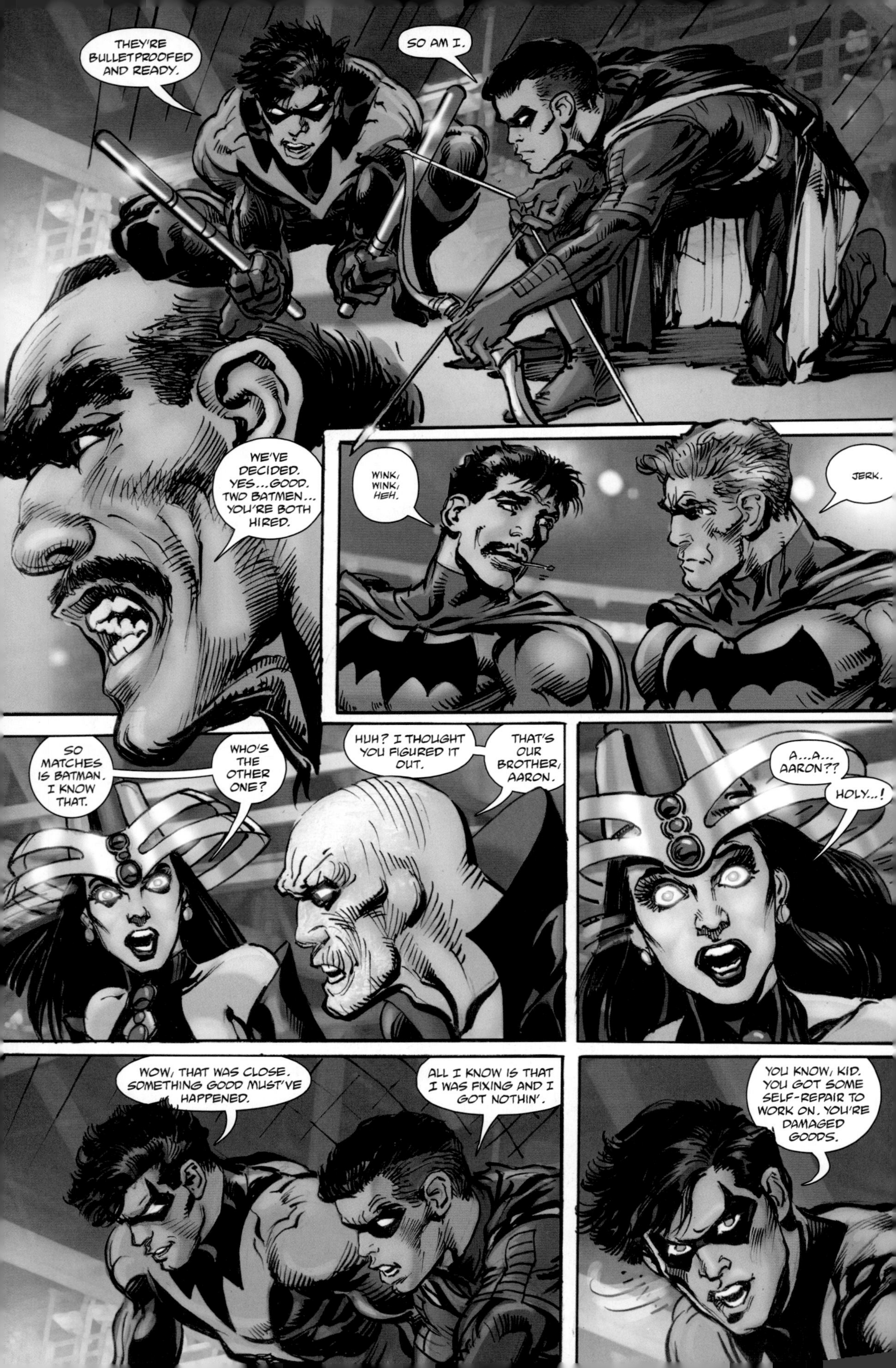
THEY'RE BULLETPROOFED AND READY.
SO AM I.
WE'VE DECIDED. YES...GOOD. TWO BATMEN... YOU'RE BOTH HIRED.
WINK, WINK, HEH.
JERK.
SO MATCHES IS BATMAN. I KNOW THAT.
WHO'S THE OTHER ONE?
HUH? I THOUGHT YOU FIGURED IT OUT.
THAT'S OUR BROTHER, AARON.
A...A... AARON??
HOLY...!
WOW, THAT WAS CLOSE. SOMETHING GOOD MUST'VE HAPPENED.
ALL I KNOW IS THAT I WAS FIXING AND I GOT NOTHIN'.
YOU KNOW, KID. YOU GOT SOME SELF-REPAIR TO WORK ON. YOU'RE DAMAGED GOODS.

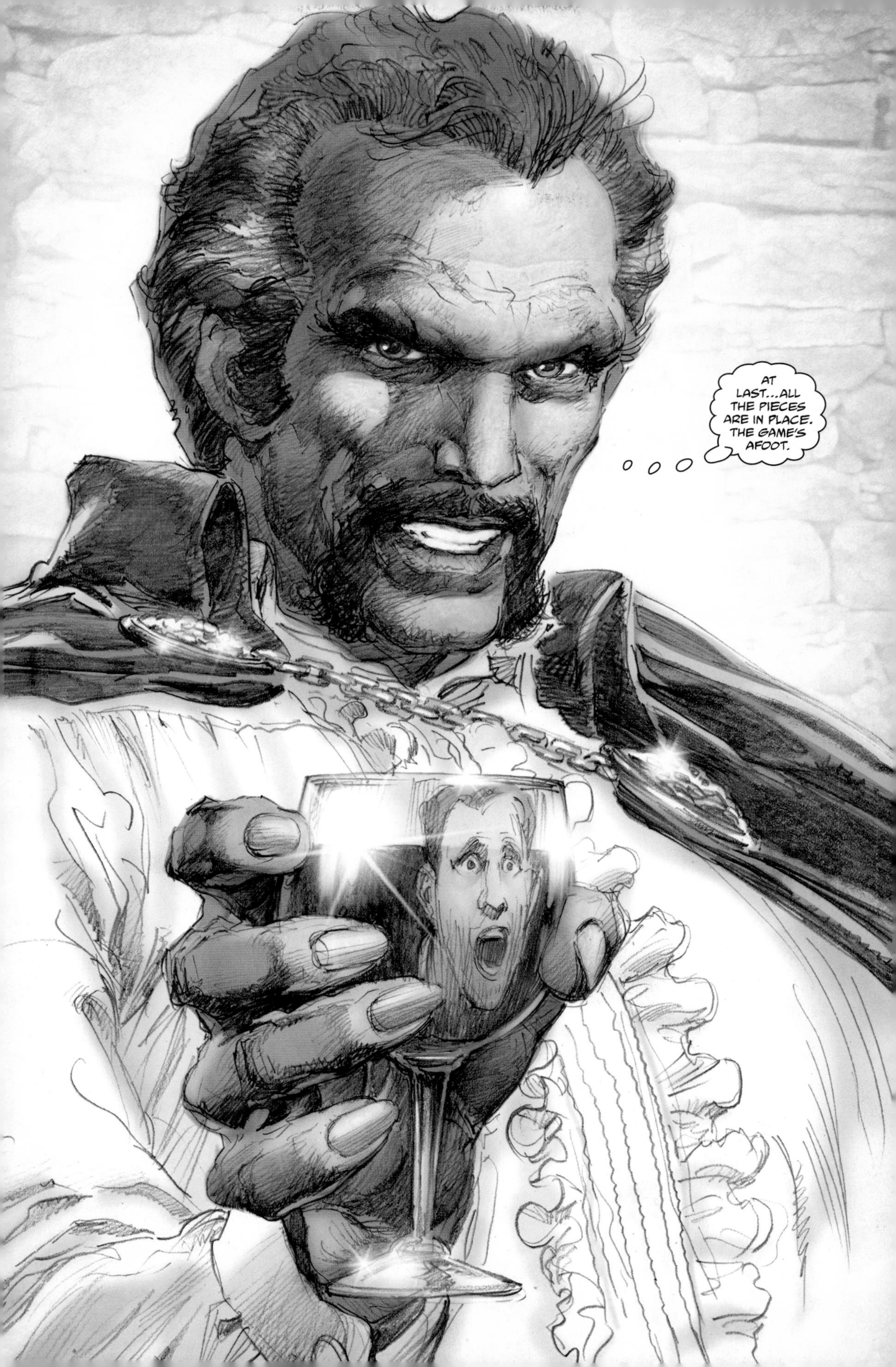
AT LAST...ALL THE PIECES ARE IN PLACE. THE GAME'S AFOOT.

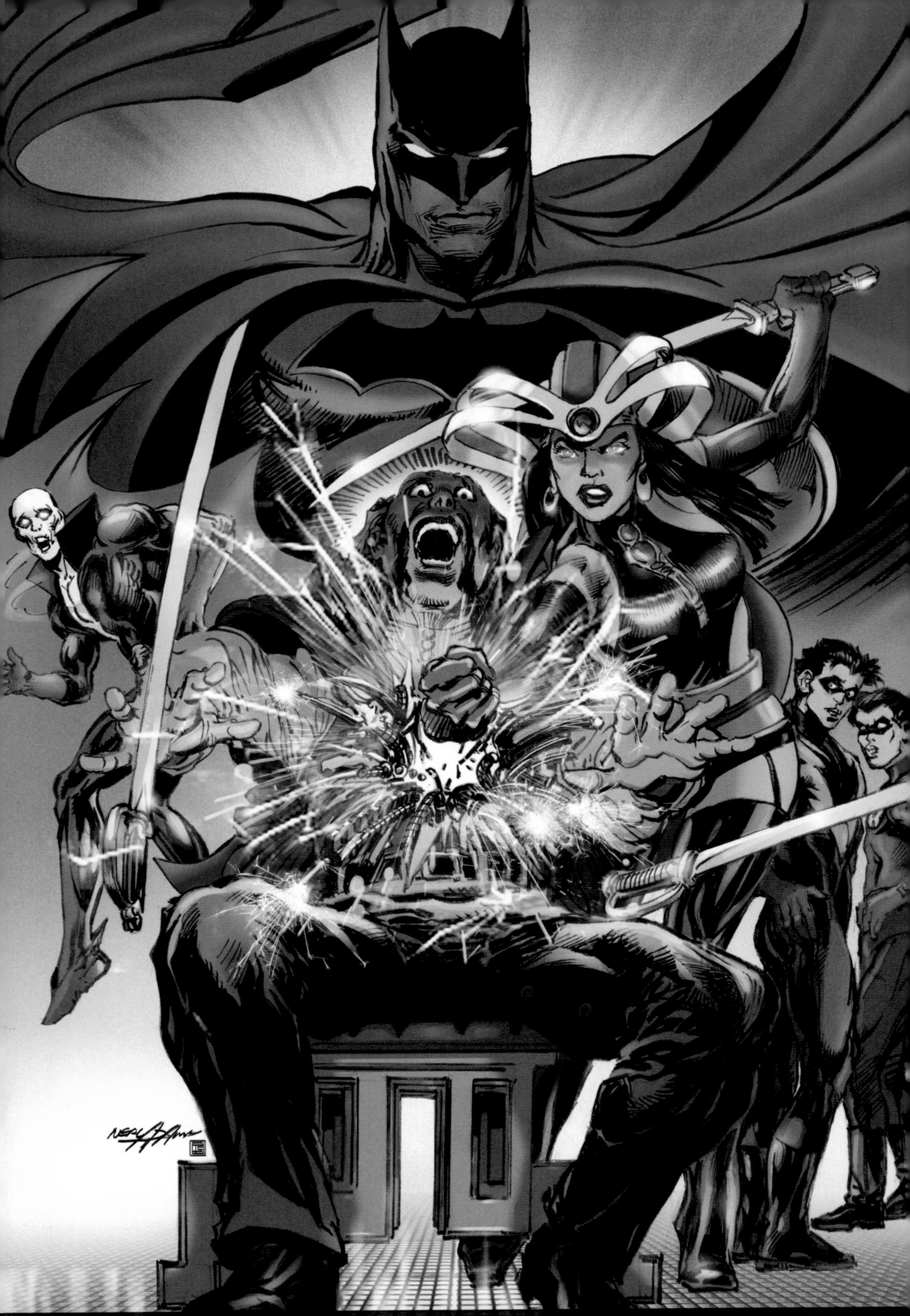

Chapter 6

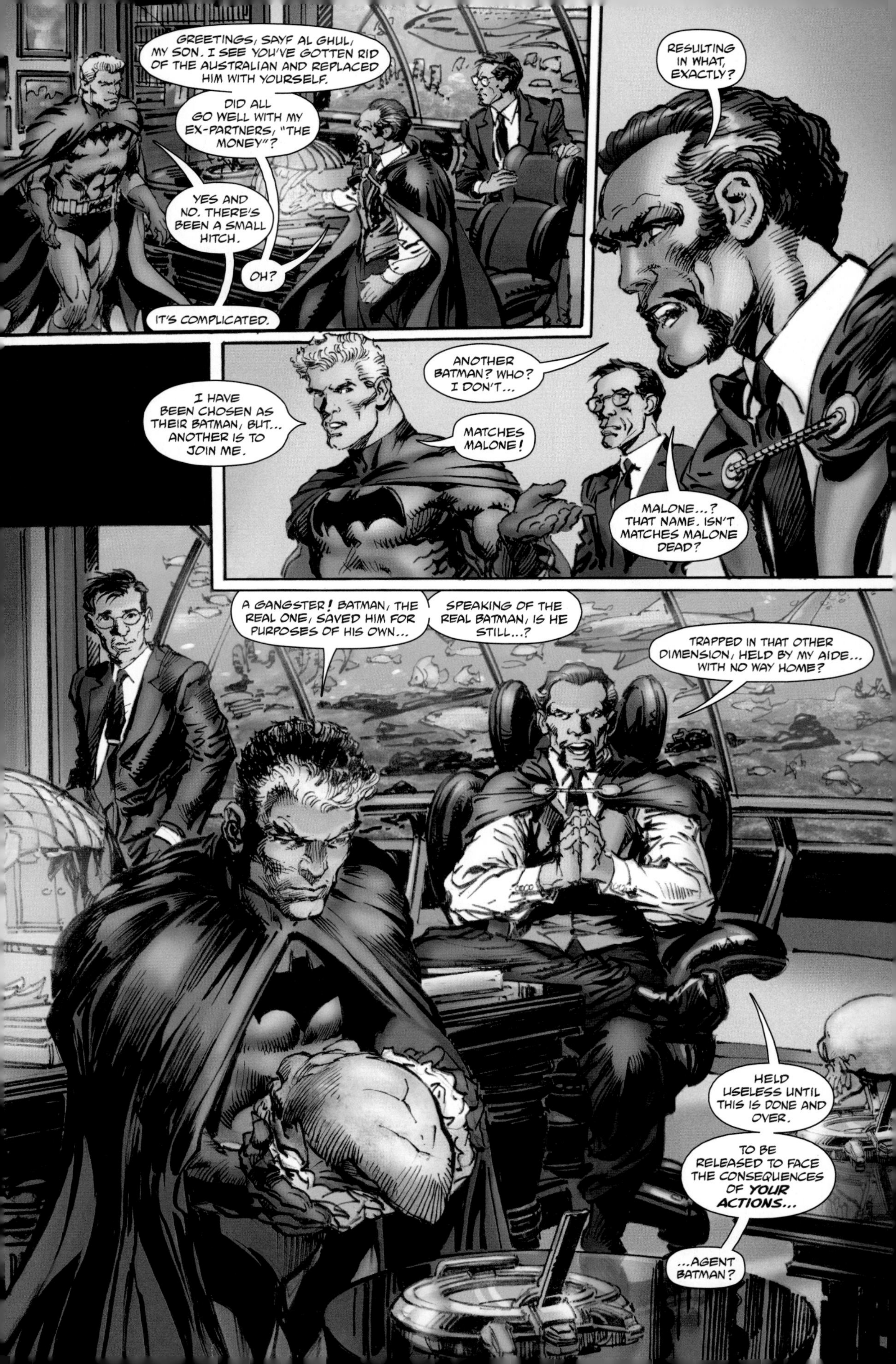
GREETINGS, SAYF AL GHUL, MY SON. I SEE YOU'VE GOTTEN RID OF THE AUSTRALIAN AND REPLACED HIM WITH YOURSELF.
DID ALL GO WELL WITH MY EX-PARTNERS, "THE MONEY"?
YES AND NO. THERE'S BEEN A SMALL HITCH.
OH?
IT'S COMPLICATED.
RESULTING IN WHAT, EXACTLY?
I HAVE BEEN CHOSEN AS THEIR BATMAN, BUT... ANOTHER IS TO JOIN ME.
ANOTHER BATMAN? WHO? I DON'T...
MATCHES MALONE!
MALONE...? THAT NAME. ISN'T MATCHES MALONE DEAD?
A GANGSTER! BATMAN, THE REAL ONE, SAVED HIM FOR PURPOSES OF HIS OWN...
SPEAKING OF THE REAL BATMAN, IS HE STILL...?
TRAPPED IN THAT OTHER DIMENSION, HELD BY MY AIDE... WITH NO WAY HOME?
HELD USELESS UNTIL THIS IS DONE AND OVER.
TO BE RELEASED TO FACE THE CONSEQUENCES OF YOUR ACTIONS...
...AGENT BATMAN?

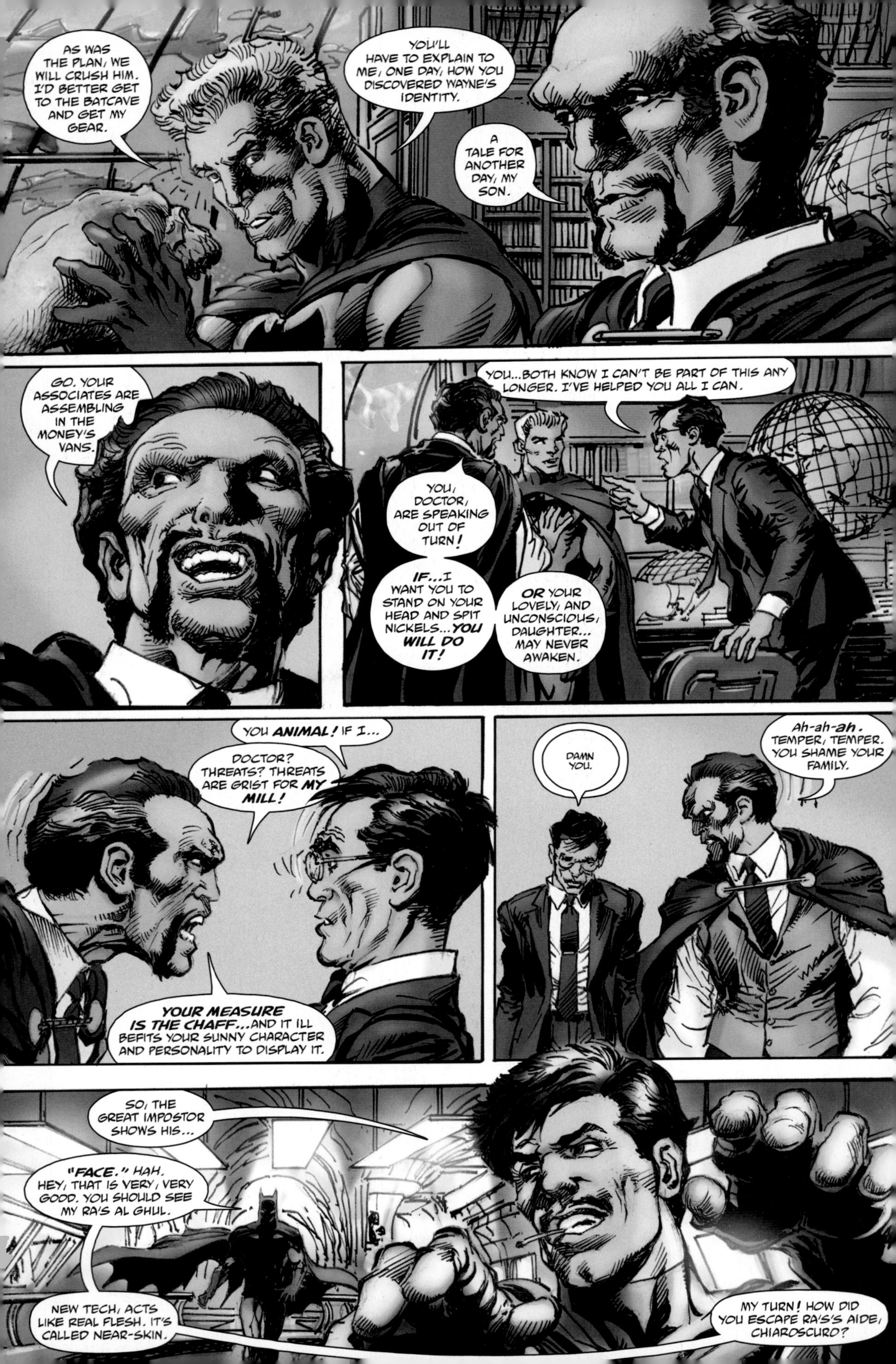

AS WAS THE PLAN, WE WILL CRUSH HIM. I'D BETTER GET TO THE BATCAVE AND GET MY GEAR.
YOU'LL HAVE TO EXPLAIN TO ME, ONE DAY, HOW YOU DISCOVERED WAYNE'S IDENTITY.
A TALE FOR ANOTHER DAY, MY SON.
GO. YOUR ASSOCIATES ARE ASSEMBLING IN THE MONEY'S VANS.
YOU...BOTH KNOW I CAN'T BE PART OF THIS ANY LONGER. I'VE HELPED YOU ALL I CAN.
YOU, DOCTOR, ARE SPEAKING OUT OF TURN!
IF...I WANT YOU TO STAND ON YOUR HEAD AND SPIT NICKELS...YOU WILL DO IT!
OR YOUR LOVELY, AND UNCONSCIOUS, DAUGHTER... MAY NEVER AWAKEN.
YOU ANIMAL! IF I...
DOCTOR? THREATS? THREATS ARE GRIST FOR MY MILL!
YOUR MEASURE IS THE CHAFF...AND IT ILL BEFITS YOUR SUNNY CHARACTER AND PERSONALITY TO DISPLAY IT.
DAMN YOU.
Ah-ah-ah. TEMPER, TEMPER. YOU SHAME YOUR FAMILY.
SO, THE GREAT IMPOSTOR SHOWS HIS...
"FACE." HAH. HEY, THAT IS VERY, VERY GOOD. YOU SHOULD SEE MY RA'S AL GHUL.
NEW TECH, ACTS LIKE REAL FLESH. IT'S CALLED NEAR-SKIN.
MY TURN! HOW DID YOU ESCAPE RA'S'S AIDE, CHIAROSCURO?

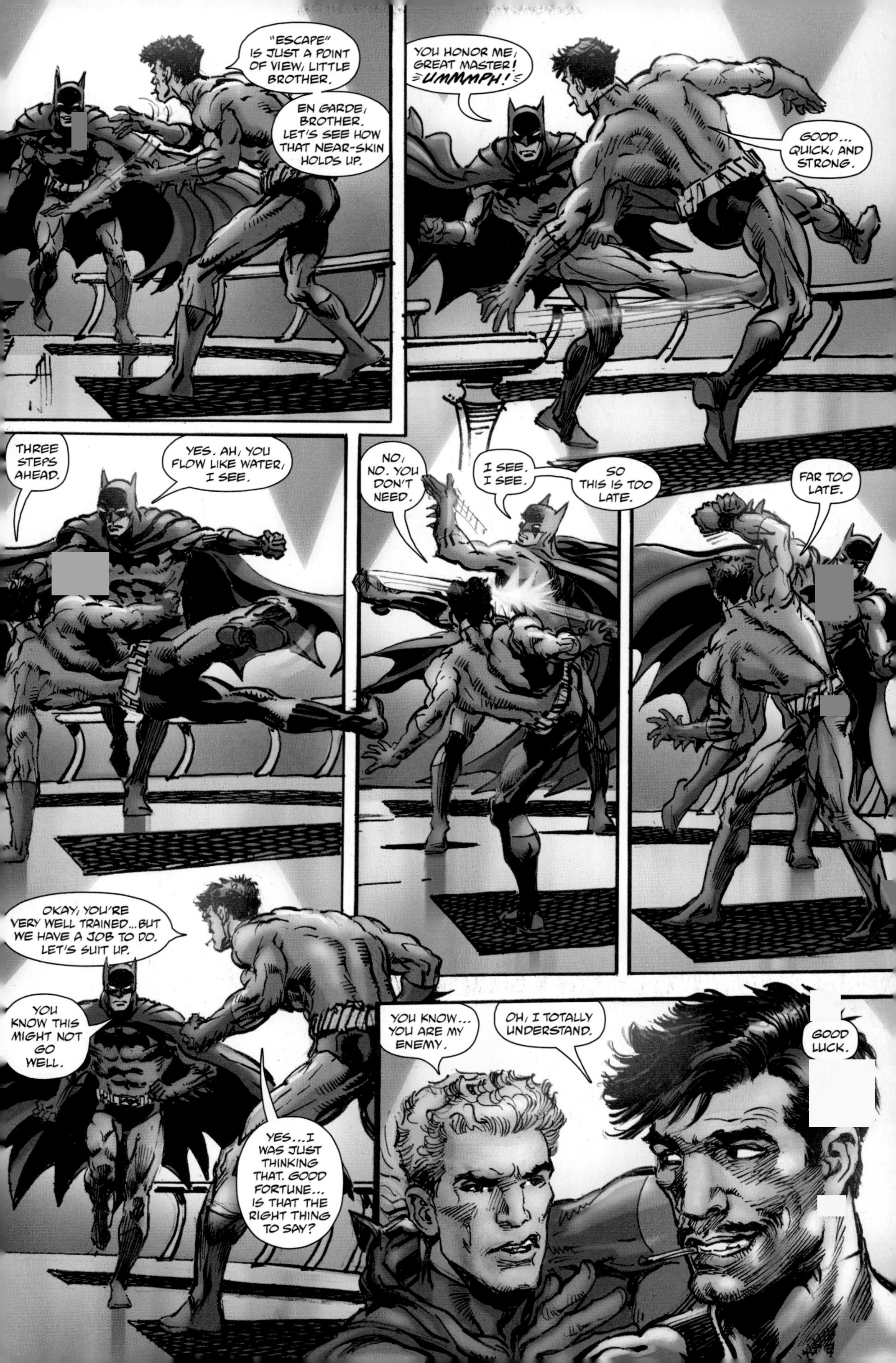
"ESCAPE" IS JUST A POINT OF VIEW, LITTLE BROTHER.
EN GARDE, BROTHER. LET'S SEE HOW THAT NEAR-SKIN HOLDS UP.
YOU HONOR ME, GREAT MASTER!
UMMMPH!
GOOD... QUICK, AND STRONG.
THREE STEPS AHEAD.
YES. AH, YOU FLOW LIKE WATER, I SEE.
NO, NO. YOU DON'T NEED.
I SEE. I SEE.
SO THIS IS TOO LATE.
FAR TOO LATE.
OKAY, YOU'RE VERY WELL TRAINED... BUT WE HAVE A JOB TO DO. LET'S SUIT UP.
YOU KNOW THIS MIGHT NOT GO WELL.
YES... I WAS JUST THINKING THAT. GOOD FORTUNE... IS THAT THE RIGHT THING TO SAY?
YOU KNOW... YOU ARE MY ENEMY.
OH, I TOTALLY UNDERSTAND.
GOOD LUCK.

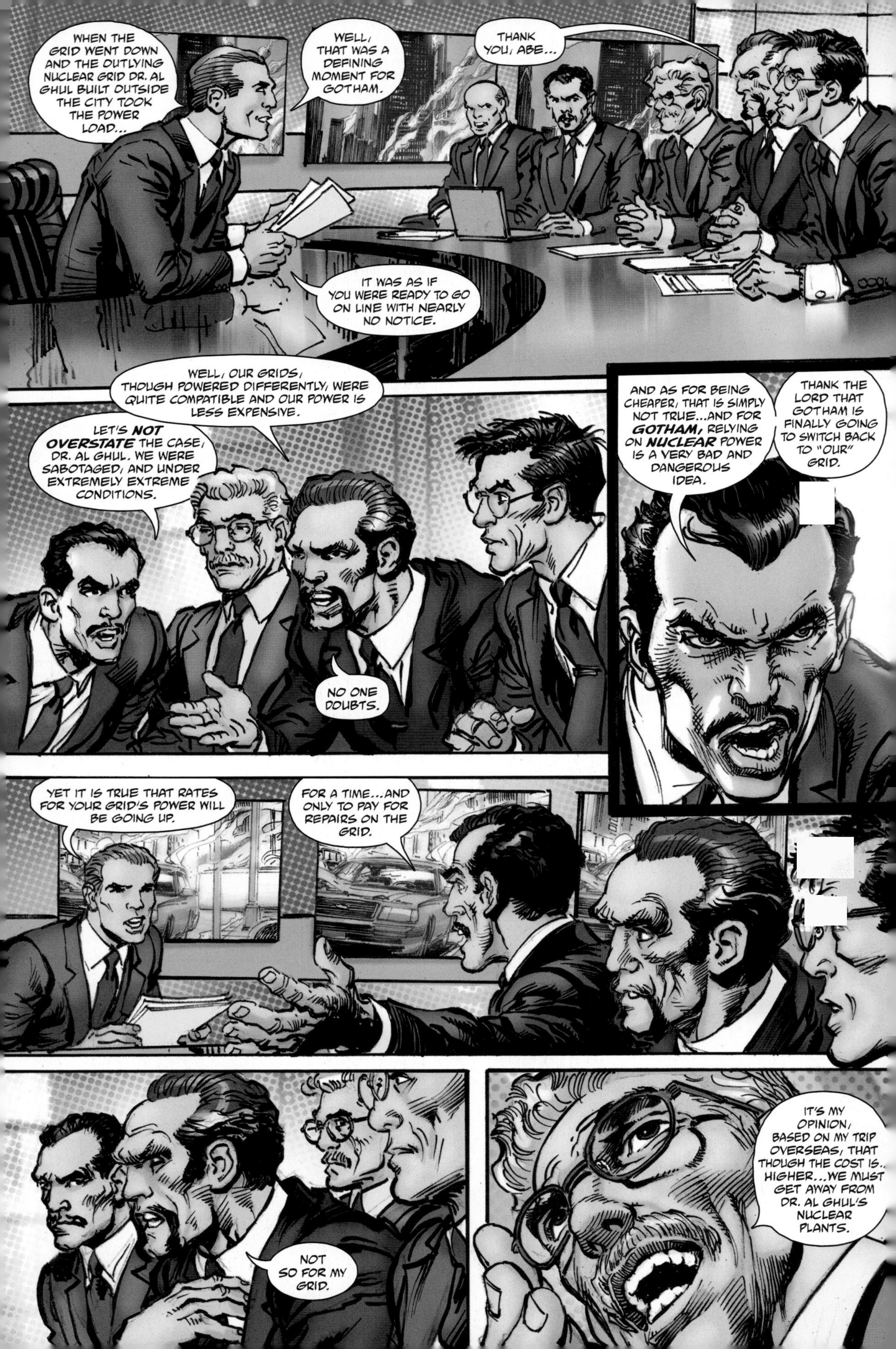
WHEN THE GRID WENT DOWN AND THE OUTLYING NUCLEAR GRID DR. AL GHUL BUILT OUTSIDE THE CITY TOOK THE POWER LOAD...
WELL, THAT WAS A DEFINING MOMENT FOR GOTHAM.
THANK YOU, ABE...
IT WAS AS IF YOU WERE READY TO GO ON LINE WITH NEARLY NO NOTICE.
WELL, OUR GRIDS, THOUGH POWERED DIFFERENTLY, WERE QUITE COMPATIBLE AND OUR POWER IS LESS EXPENSIVE.
LET'S **NOT OVERSTATE** THE CASE, DR. AL GHUL. WE WERE SABOTAGED, AND UNDER EXTREMELY EXTREME CONDITIONS.
NO ONE DOUBTS.
AND AS FOR BEING CHEAPER, THAT IS SIMPLY NOT TRUE...AND FOR ***GOTHAM,*** RELYING ON ***NUCLEAR*** POWER IS A VERY BAD AND DANGEROUS IDEA.
THANK THE LORD THAT GOTHAM IS FINALLY GOING TO SWITCH BACK TO "OUR" GRID.
YET IT IS TRUE THAT RATES FOR YOUR GRID'S POWER WILL BE GOING UP.
FOR A TIME...AND ONLY TO PAY FOR REPAIRS ON THE GRID.
NOT SO FOR MY GRID.
IT'S MY OPINION, BASED ON MY TRIP OVERSEAS, THAT THOUGH THE COST IS.. HIGHER...WE MUST GET AWAY FROM DR. AL GHUL'S NUCLEAR PLANTS.

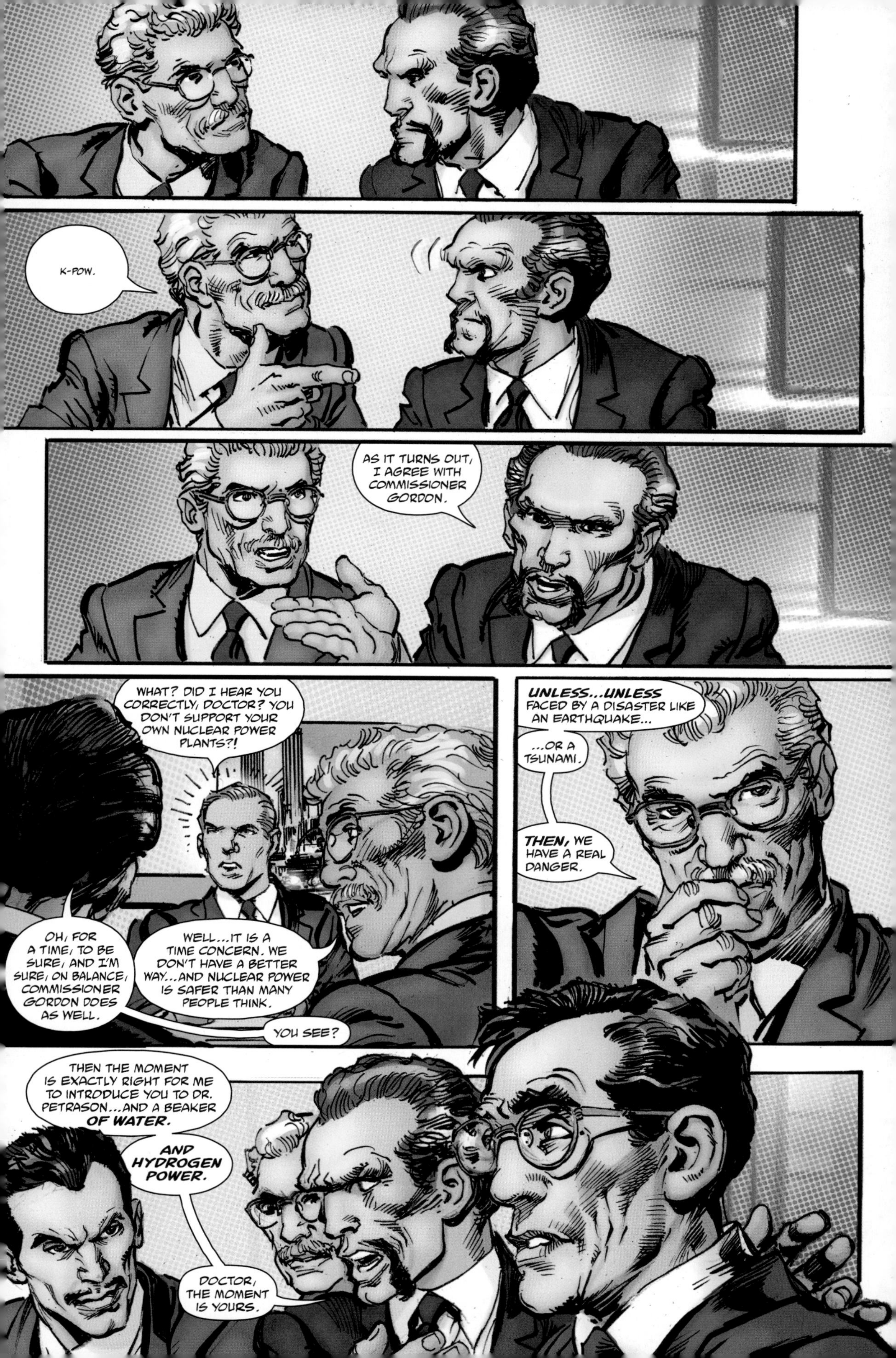
K-POW.
AS IT TURNS OUT, I AGREE WITH COMMISSIONER GORDON.
WHAT? DID I HEAR YOU CORRECTLY, DOCTOR? YOU DON'T SUPPORT YOUR OWN NUCLEAR POWER PLANTS?!
OH, FOR A TIME, TO BE SURE, AND I'M SURE, ON BALANCE, COMMISSIONER GORDON DOES AS WELL.
WELL...IT IS A TIME CONCERN. WE DON'T HAVE A BETTER WAY...AND NUCLEAR POWER IS SAFER THAN MANY PEOPLE THINK.
YOU SEE?
UNLESS...UNLESS FACED BY A DISASTER LIKE AN EARTHQUAKE...
...OR A TSUNAMI.
THEN, WE HAVE A REAL DANGER.
THEN THE MOMENT IS EXACTLY RIGHT FOR ME TO INTRODUCE YOU TO DR. PETRASON...AND A BEAKER OF WATER.
AND HYDROGEN POWER.
DOCTOR, THE MOMENT IS YOURS.

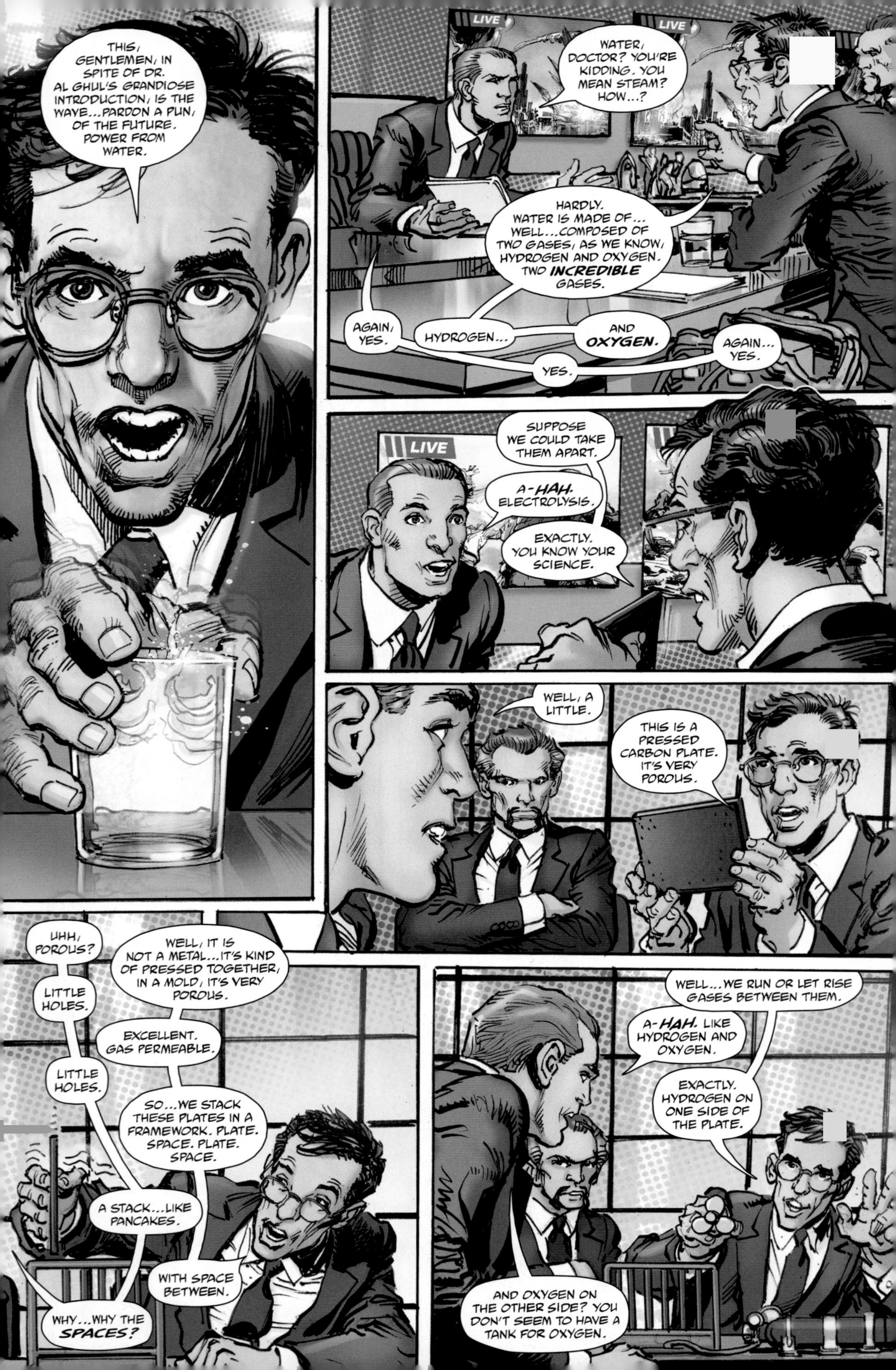
THIS, GENTLEMEN, IN SPITE OF DR. AL GHUL'S GRANDIOSE INTRODUCTION, IS THE WAVE...PARDON A PUN, OF THE FUTURE. POWER FROM WATER.
WATER, DOCTOR? YOU'RE KIDDING. YOU MEAN STEAM? HOW...?
HARDLY. WATER IS MADE OF... WELL...COMPOSED OF TWO GASES, AS WE KNOW, HYDROGEN AND OXYGEN. TWO **INCREDIBLE** GASES.
AGAIN, YES.
HYDROGEN...
YES.
AND **OXYGEN.**
AGAIN... YES.
SUPPOSE WE COULD TAKE THEM APART.
A-**HAH.** ELECTROLYSIS.
EXACTLY. YOU KNOW YOUR SCIENCE.
WELL, A LITTLE.
THIS IS A PRESSED CARBON PLATE. IT'S VERY POROUS.
UHH, POROUS?
WELL, IT IS NOT A METAL...IT'S KIND OF PRESSED TOGETHER, IN A MOLD, IT'S VERY POROUS.
LITTLE HOLES.
EXCELLENT. GAS PERMEABLE.
LITTLE HOLES.
SO...WE STACK THESE PLATES IN A FRAMEWORK. PLATE. SPACE. PLATE. SPACE.
A STACK...LIKE PANCAKES.
WITH SPACE BETWEEN.
WHY...WHY THE **SPACES?**
WELL...WE RUN OR LET RISE GASES BETWEEN THEM.
A-**HAH.** LIKE HYDROGEN AND OXYGEN.
EXACTLY. HYDROGEN ON ONE SIDE OF THE PLATE.
AND OXYGEN ON THE OTHER SIDE? YOU DON'T SEEM TO HAVE A TANK FOR OXYGEN.

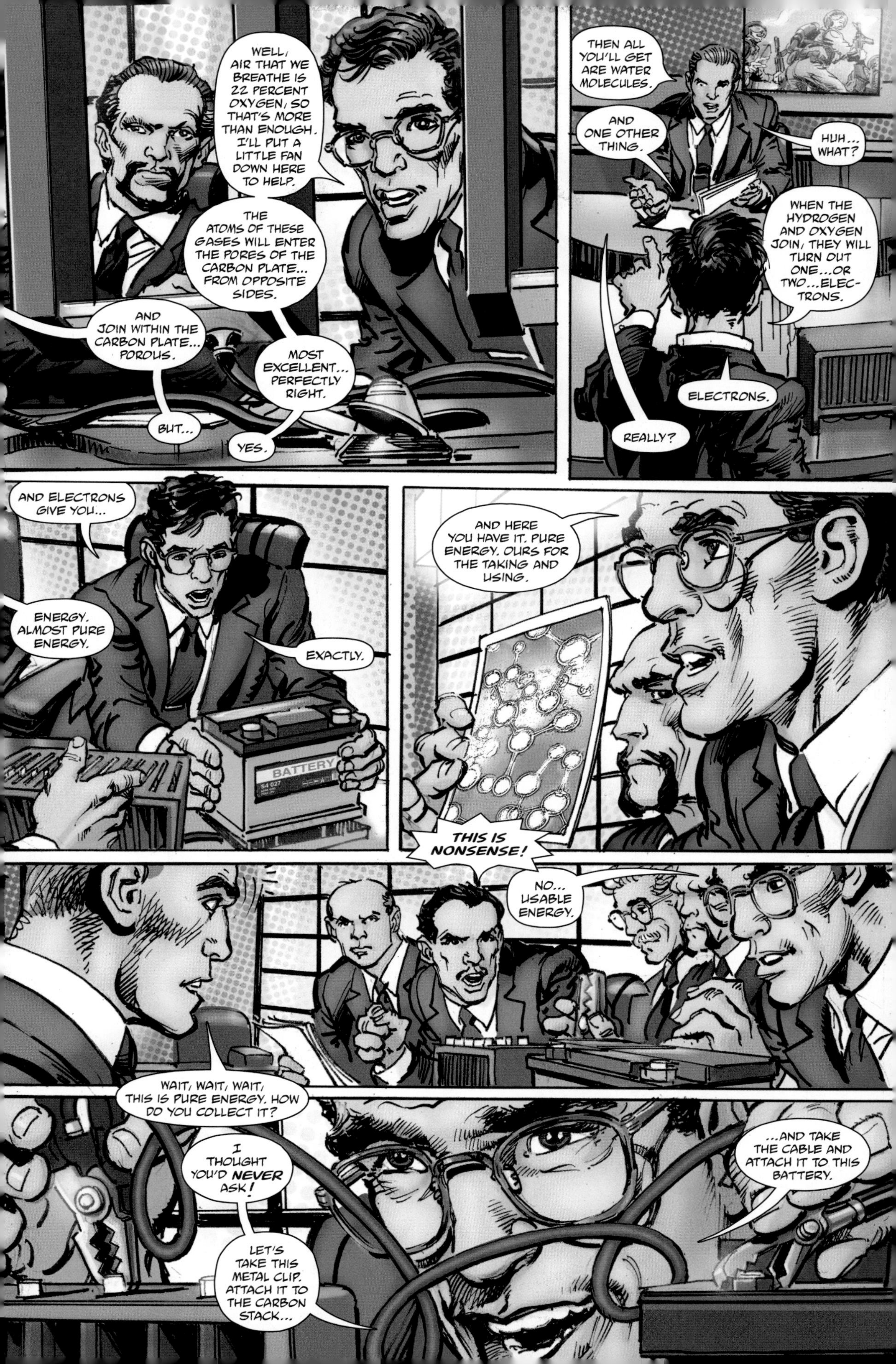
WELL, AIR THAT WE BREATHE IS 22 PERCENT OXYGEN, SO THAT'S MORE THAN ENOUGH. I'LL PUT A LITTLE FAN DOWN HERE TO HELP.
THE ATOMS OF THESE GASES WILL ENTER THE PORES OF THE CARBON PLATE... FROM OPPOSITE SIDES.
AND JOIN WITHIN THE CARBON PLATE... POROUS.
MOST EXCELLENT... PERFECTLY RIGHT.
BUT...
YES.
THEN ALL YOU'LL GET ARE WATER MOLECULES.
AND ONE OTHER THING.
HUH... WHAT?
WHEN THE HYDROGEN AND OXYGEN JOIN, THEY WILL TURN OUT ONE...OR TWO...ELEC-TRONS.
ELECTRONS.
REALLY?
AND ELECTRONS GIVE YOU...
ENERGY. ALMOST PURE ENERGY.
EXACTLY.
BATTERY
AND HERE YOU HAVE IT. PURE ENERGY. OURS FOR THE TAKING AND USING.
THIS IS NONSENSE!
NO... USABLE ENERGY.
WAIT, WAIT, WAIT, THIS IS PURE ENERGY. HOW DO YOU COLLECT IT?
I THOUGHT YOU'D NEVER ASK!
LET'S TAKE THIS METAL CLIP. ATTACH IT TO THE CARBON STACK...
...AND TAKE THE CABLE AND ATTACH IT TO THIS BATTERY.

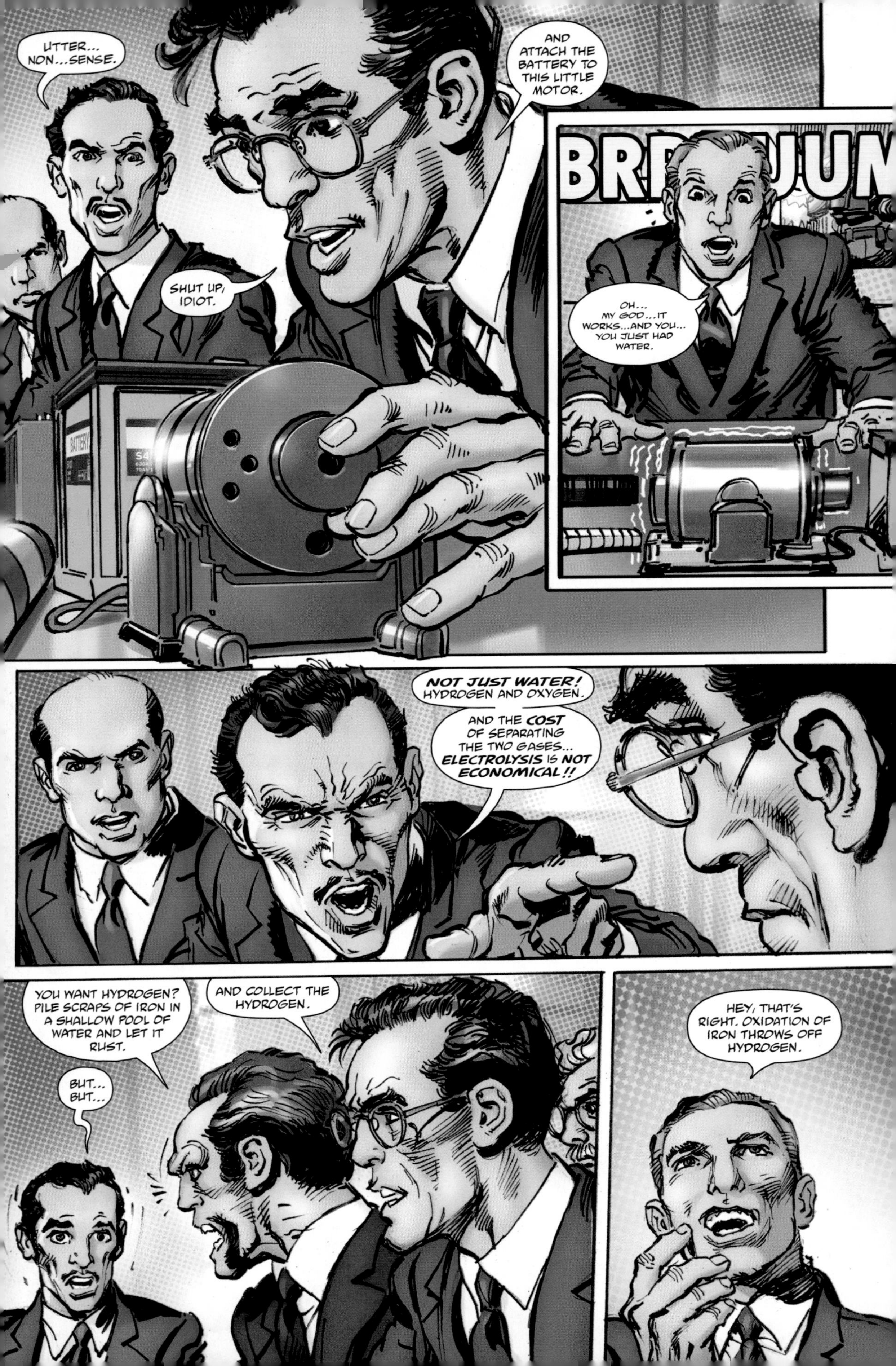
UTTER... NON...SENSE.
AND ATTACH THE BATTERY TO THIS LITTLE MOTOR.
SHUT UP, IDIOT.
BATTERY
BRRRUUUM
OH... MY GOD...IT WORKS...AND YOU... YOU JUST HAD WATER.
NOT JUST WATER! HYDROGEN AND OXYGEN.
AND THE COST OF SEPARATING THE TWO GASES... ELECTROLYSIS IS NOT ECONOMICAL!!
YOU WANT HYDROGEN? PILE SCRAPS OF IRON IN A SHALLOW POOL OF WATER AND LET IT RUST.
AND COLLECT THE HYDROGEN.
BUT... BUT...
HEY, THAT'S RIGHT. OXIDATION OF IRON THROWS OFF HYDROGEN.

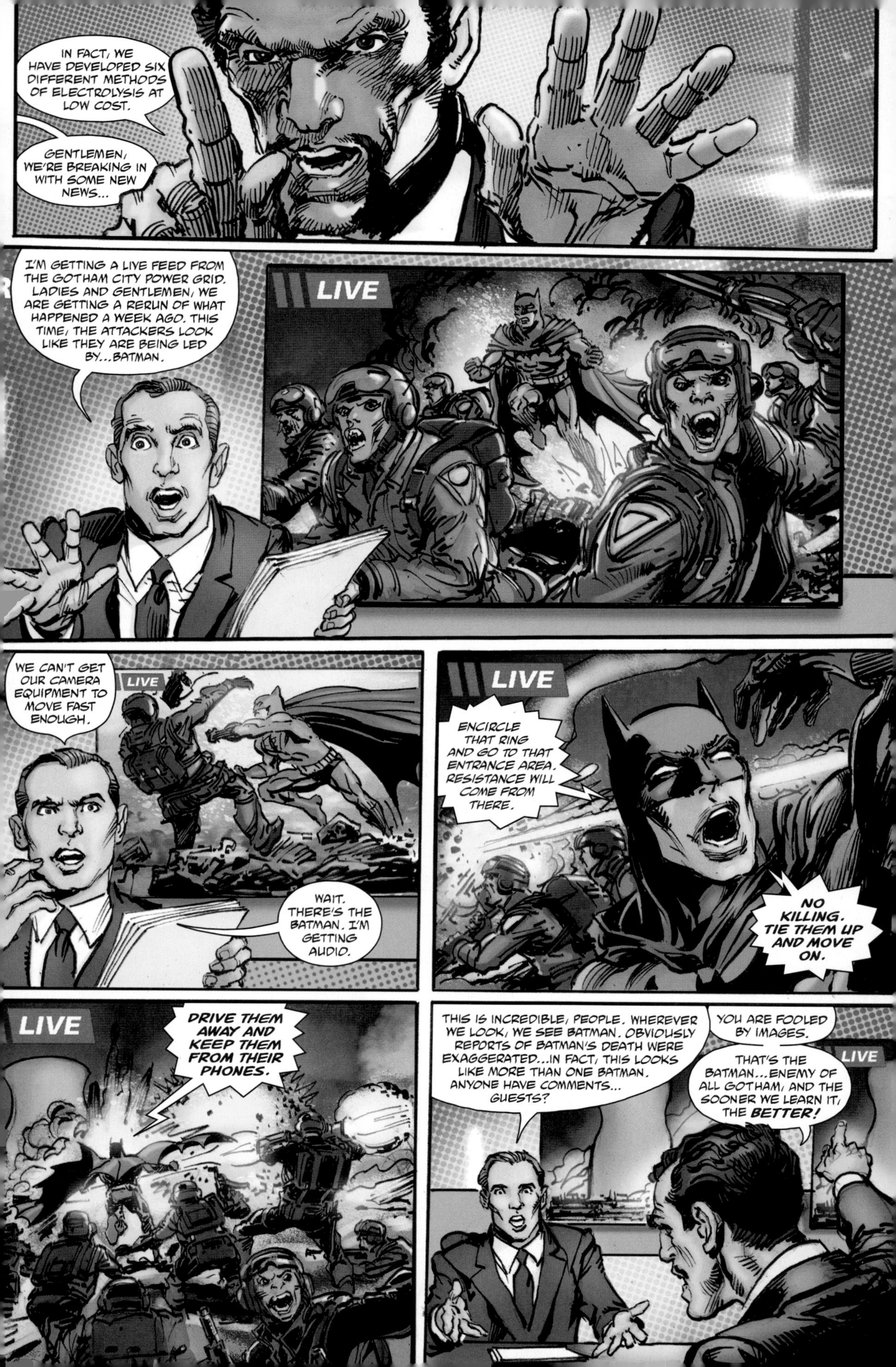
IN FACT, WE HAVE DEVELOPED SIX DIFFERENT METHODS OF ELECTROLYSIS AT LOW COST.
GENTLEMEN, WE'RE BREAKING IN WITH SOME NEW NEWS...
I'M GETTING A LIVE FEED FROM THE GOTHAM CITY POWER GRID. LADIES AND GENTLEMEN, WE ARE GETTING A RERUN OF WHAT HAPPENED A WEEK AGO. THIS TIME, THE ATTACKERS LOOK LIKE THEY ARE BEING LED BY...BATMAN.
LIVE
WE CAN'T GET OUR CAMERA EQUIPMENT TO MOVE FAST ENOUGH.
LIVE
WAIT. THERE'S THE BATMAN. I'M GETTING AUDIO.
LIVE
ENCIRCLE THAT RING AND GO TO THAT ENTRANCE AREA. RESISTANCE WILL COME FROM THERE.
NO KILLING. TIE THEM UP AND MOVE ON.
LIVE
DRIVE THEM AWAY AND KEEP THEM FROM THEIR PHONES.
THIS IS INCREDIBLE, PEOPLE. WHEREVER WE LOOK, WE SEE BATMAN. OBVIOUSLY REPORTS OF BATMAN'S DEATH WERE EXAGGERATED...IN FACT, THIS LOOKS LIKE MORE THAN ONE BATMAN. ANYONE HAVE COMMENTS... GUESTS?
YOU ARE FOOLED BY IMAGES.
LIVE
THAT'S THE BATMAN...ENEMY OF ALL GOTHAM, AND THE SOONER WE LEARN IT, THE BETTER!

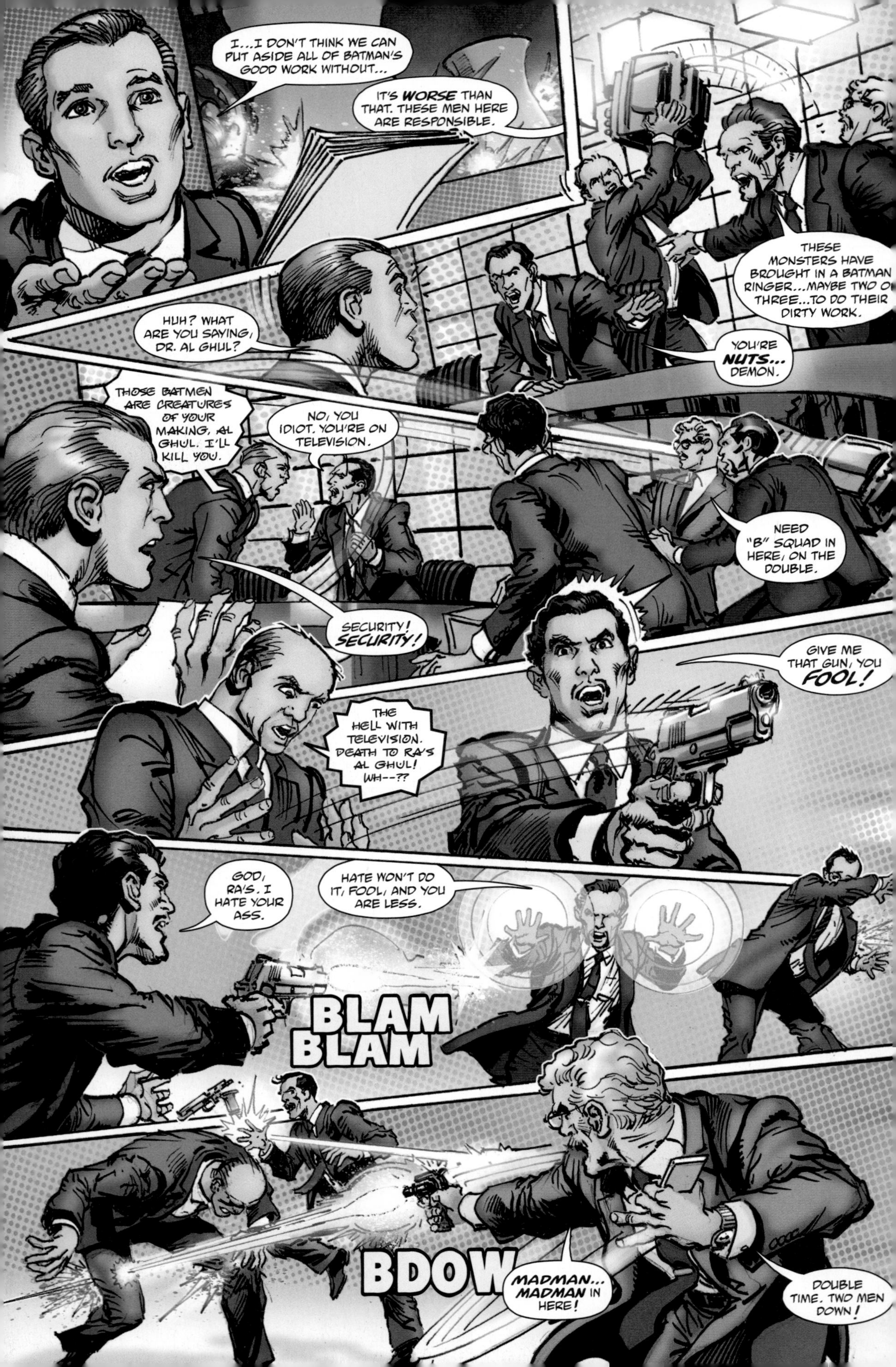
I...I DON'T THINK WE CAN PUT ASIDE ALL OF BATMAN'S GOOD WORK WITHOUT...
IT'S WORSE THAN THAT. THESE MEN HERE ARE RESPONSIBLE.
THESE MONSTERS HAVE BROUGHT IN A BATMAN RINGER...MAYBE TWO OR THREE...TO DO THEIR DIRTY WORK.
HUH? WHAT ARE YOU SAYING, DR. AL GHUL?
YOU'RE NUTS... DEMON.
THOSE BATMEN ARE CREATURES OF YOUR MAKING, AL GHUL. I'LL KILL YOU.
NO, YOU IDIOT. YOU'RE ON TELEVISION.
NEED "B" SQUAD IN HERE, ON THE DOUBLE.
SECURITY! SECURITY!
GIVE ME THAT GUN, YOU FOOL!
THE HELL WITH TELEVISION. DEATH TO RA'S AL GHUL! WH--??
GOD, RA'S. I HATE YOUR ASS.
HATE WON'T DO IT, FOOL, AND YOU ARE LESS.
BLAM
BLAM
BDOW
MADMAN... MADMAN IN HERE!
DOUBLE TIME. TWO MEN DOWN!

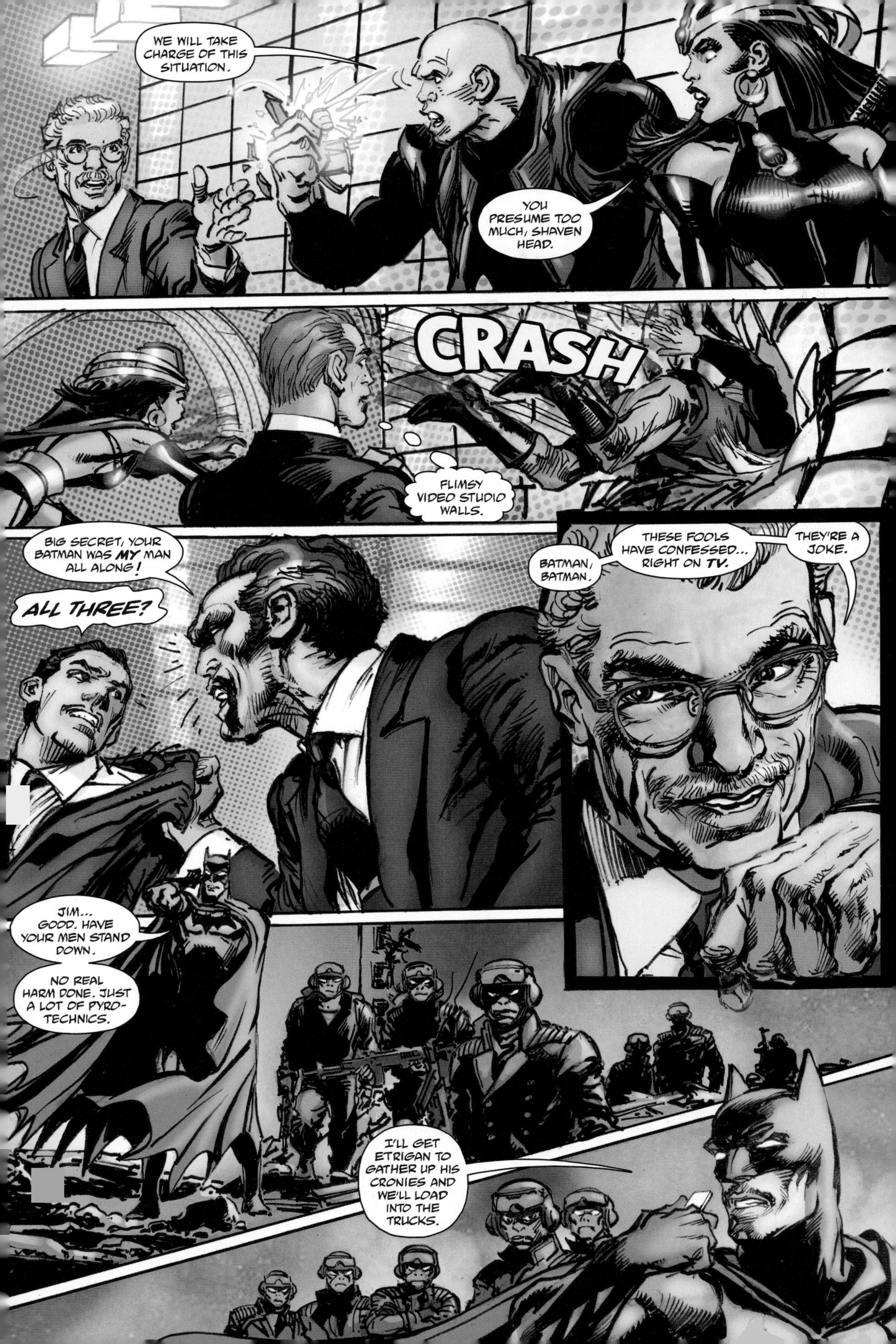
WE WILL TAKE CHARGE OF THIS SITUATION.
YOU PRESUME TOO MUCH, SHAVEN HEAD.
CRASH
FLIMSY VIDEO STUDIO WALLS.
BIG SECRET, YOUR BATMAN WAS MY MAN ALL ALONG!
ALL THREE?
BATMAN, BATMAN.
THESE FOOLS HAVE CONFESSED... RIGHT ON TV.
THEY'RE A JOKE.
JIM... GOOD. HAVE YOUR MEN STAND DOWN.
NO REAL HARM DONE. JUST A LOT OF PYRO-TECHNICS.
I'LL GET ETRIGAN TO GATHER UP HIS CRONIES AND WE'LL LOAD INTO THE TRUCKS.

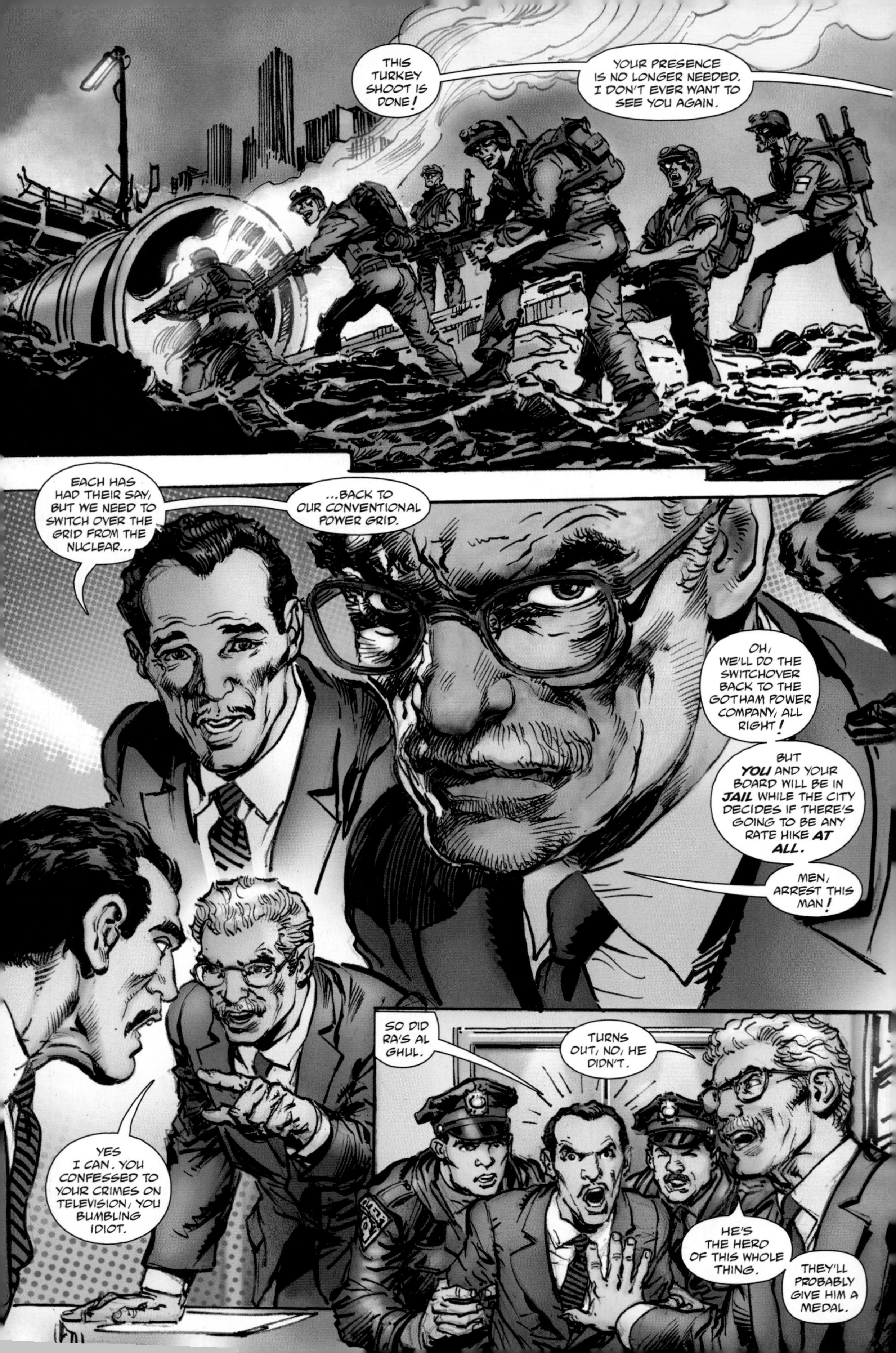
THIS TURKEY SHOOT IS DONE!
YOUR PRESENCE IS NO LONGER NEEDED. I DON'T EVER WANT TO SEE YOU AGAIN.
EACH HAS HAD THEIR SAY, BUT WE NEED TO SWITCH OVER THE GRID FROM THE NUCLEAR...
...BACK TO OUR CONVENTIONAL POWER GRID.
OH, WE'LL DO THE SWITCHOVER BACK TO THE GOTHAM POWER COMPANY, ALL RIGHT!
BUT YOU AND YOUR BOARD WILL BE IN JAIL WHILE THE CITY DECIDES IF THERE'S GOING TO BE ANY RATE HIKE AT ALL.
MEN, ARREST THIS MAN!
YES I CAN. YOU CONFESSED TO YOUR CRIMES ON TELEVISION, YOU BUMBLING IDIOT.
SO DID RA'S AL GHUL.
TURNS OUT, NO, HE DIDN'T.
HE'S THE HERO OF THIS WHOLE THING.
THEY'LL PROBABLY GIVE HIM A MEDAL.

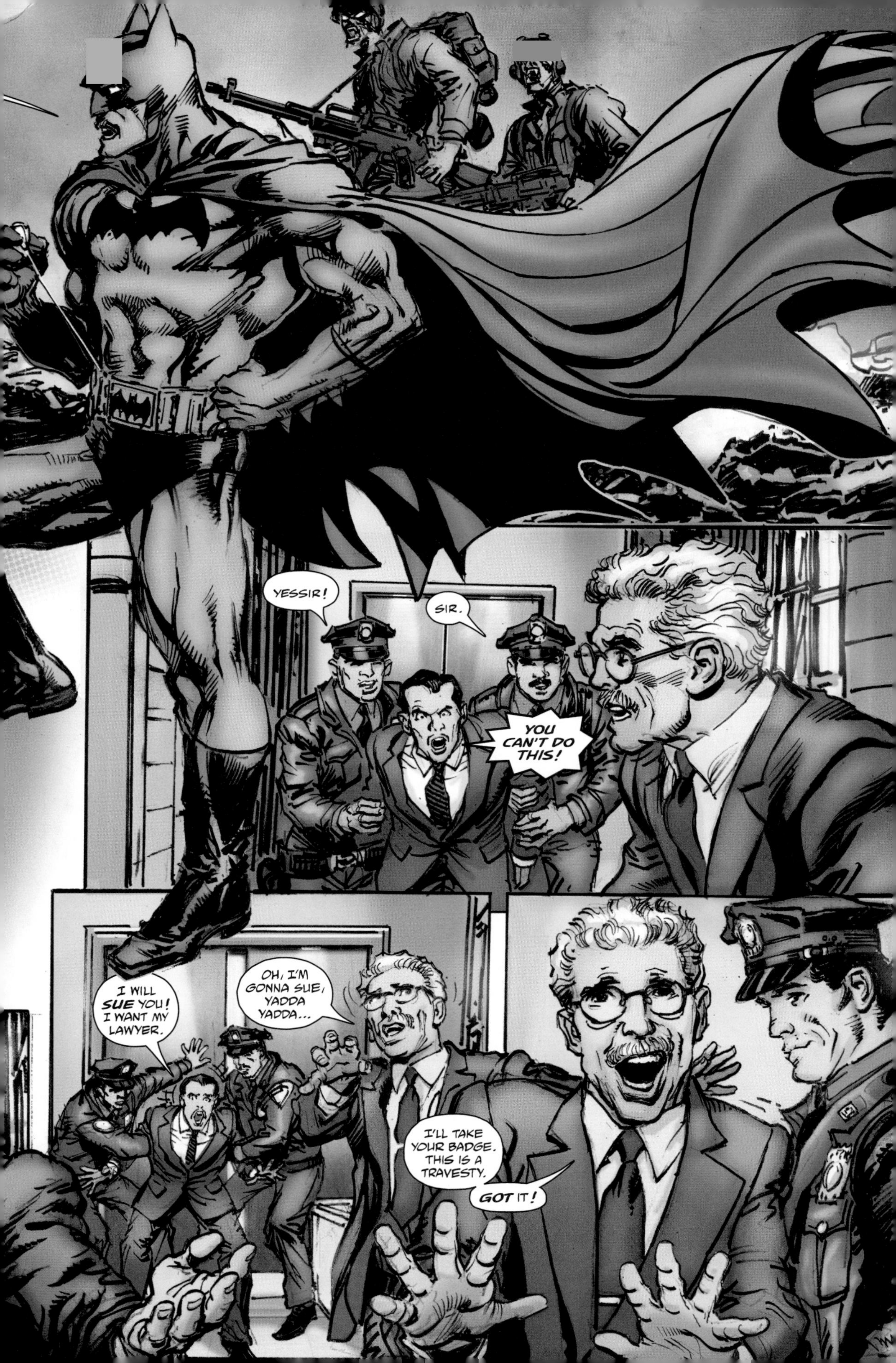
YESSIR!
SIR.
YOU CAN'T DO THIS!
I WILL SUE YOU! I WANT MY LAWYER.
OH, I'M GONNA SUE, YADDA YADDA...
I'LL TAKE YOUR BADGE. THIS IS A TRAVESTY.
GOT IT!

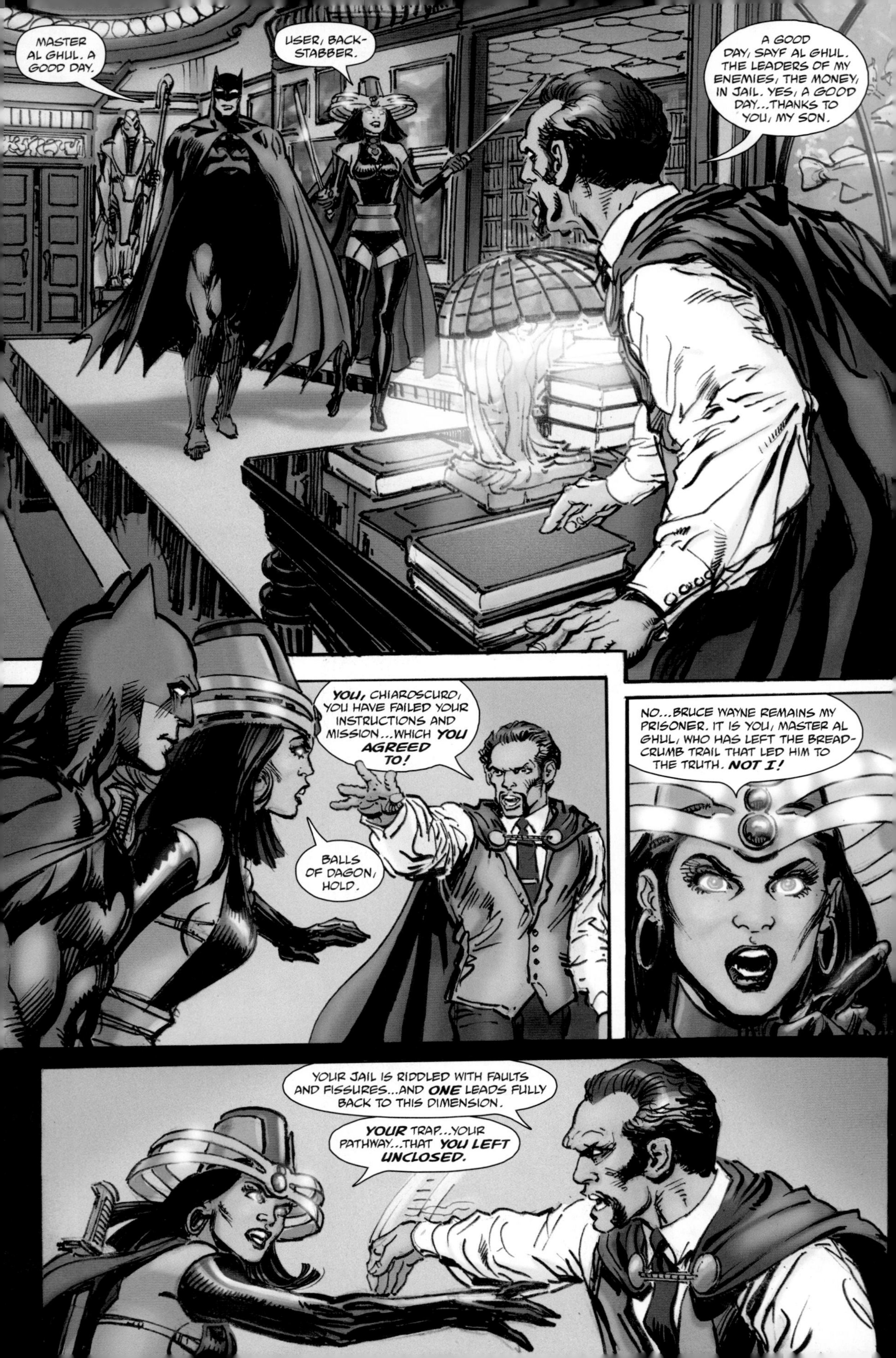

MASTER AL GHUL. A GOOD DAY.
USER, BACK-STABBER.
A GOOD DAY, SAYF AL GHUL. THE LEADERS OF MY ENEMIES, THE MONEY, IN JAIL. YES, A GOOD DAY...THANKS TO YOU, MY SON.
YOU, CHIAROSCURO, YOU HAVE FAILED YOUR INSTRUCTIONS AND MISSION...WHICH YOU AGREED TO!
BALLS OF DAGON, HOLD.
NO...BRUCE WAYNE REMAINS MY PRISONER. IT IS YOU, MASTER AL GHUL, WHO HAS LEFT THE BREAD-CRUMB TRAIL THAT LED HIM TO THE TRUTH. NOT I!
YOUR JAIL IS RIDDLED WITH FAULTS AND FISSURES...AND ONE LEADS FULLY BACK TO THIS DIMENSION.
YOUR TRAP...YOUR PATHWAY...THAT YOU LEFT UNCLOSED.

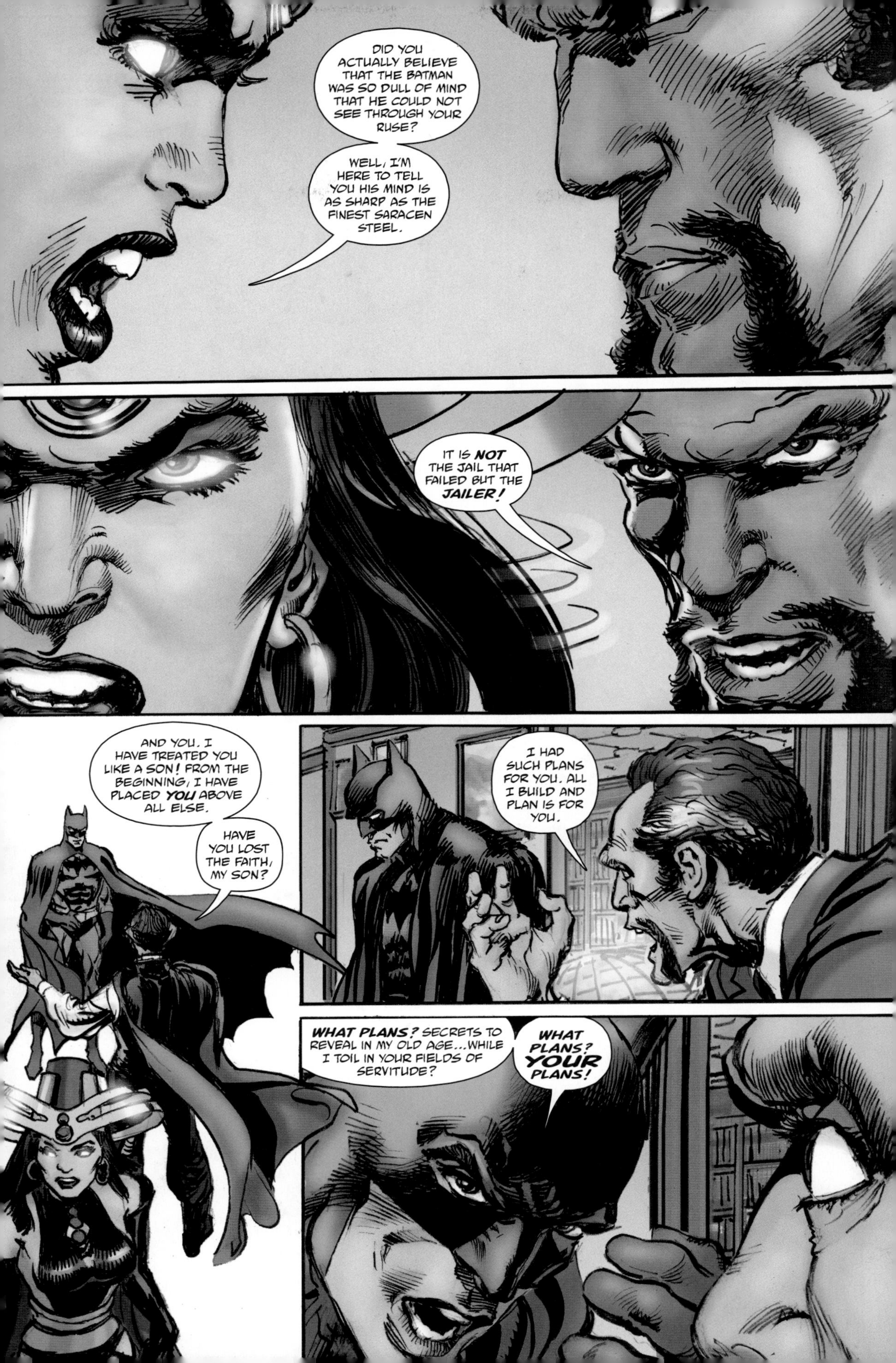
DID YOU ACTUALLY BELIEVE THAT THE BATMAN WAS SO DULL OF MIND THAT HE COULD NOT SEE THROUGH YOUR RUSE?
WELL, I'M HERE TO TELL YOU HIS MIND IS AS SHARP AS THE FINEST SARACEN STEEL.
IT IS **NOT** THE JAIL THAT FAILED BUT THE **JAILER!**
AND YOU. I HAVE TREATED YOU LIKE A SON! FROM THE BEGINNING, I HAVE PLACED **YOU** ABOVE ALL ELSE.
HAVE YOU LOST THE FAITH, MY SON?
I HAD SUCH PLANS FOR YOU. ALL I BUILD AND PLAN IS FOR YOU.
WHAT PLANS? SECRETS TO REVEAL IN MY OLD AGE...WHILE I TOIL IN YOUR FIELDS OF SERVITUDE?
WHAT PLANS? YOUR PLANS!

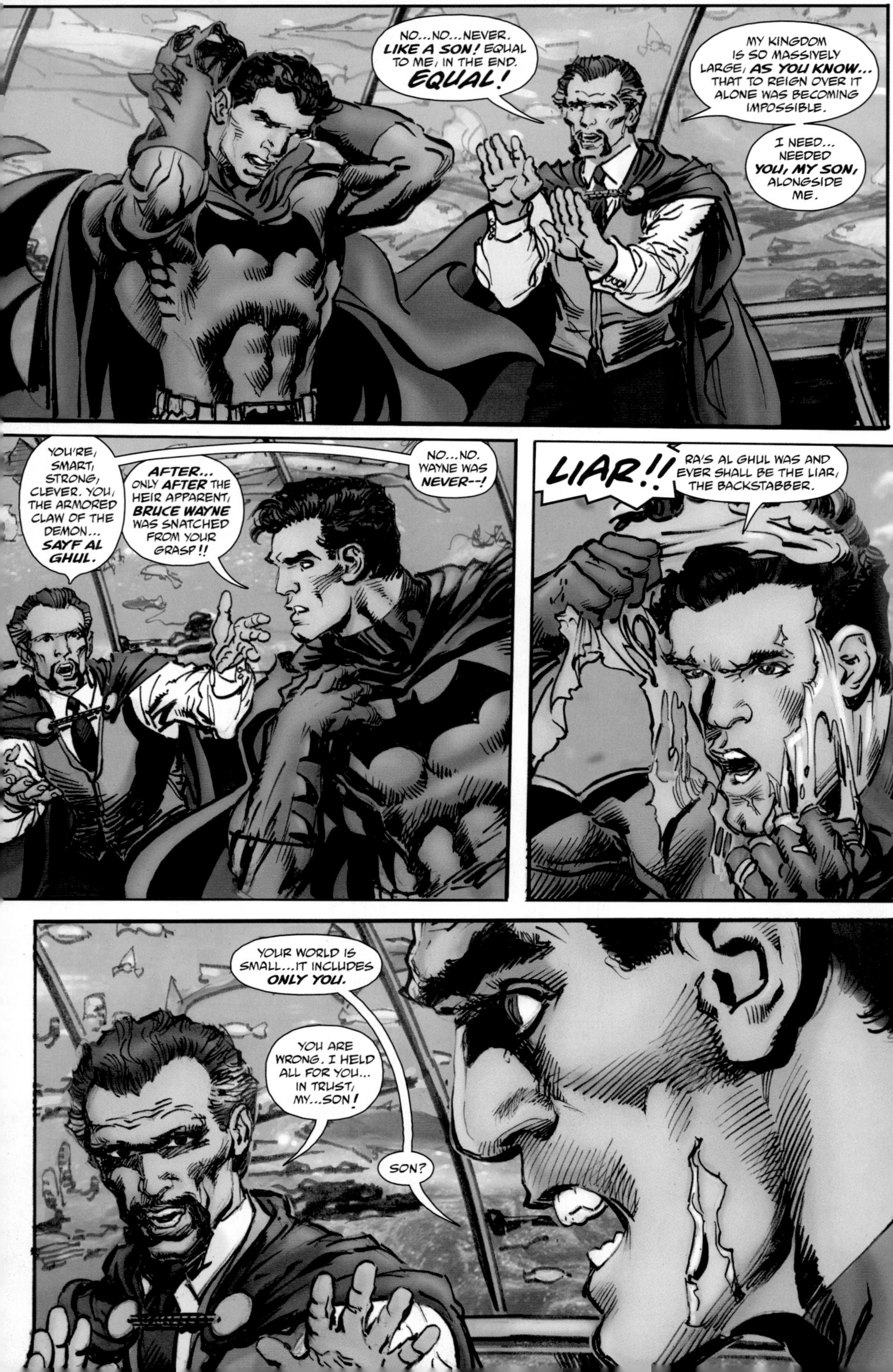

NO...NO...NEVER. LIKE A SON! EQUAL TO ME, IN THE END. EQUAL!
MY KINGDOM IS SO MASSIVELY LARGE, AS YOU KNOW... THAT TO REIGN OVER IT ALONE WAS BECOMING IMPOSSIBLE.
I NEED... NEEDED YOU, MY SON, ALONGSIDE ME.
YOU'RE, SMART, STRONG, CLEVER. YOU, THE ARMORED CLAW OF THE DEMON... SAYF AL GHUL.
NO...NO. WAYNE WAS NEVER--!
AFTER... ONLY AFTER THE HEIR APPARENT, BRUCE WAYNE WAS SNATCHED FROM YOUR GRASP!!
LIAR!!
RA'S AL GHUL WAS AND EVER SHALL BE THE LIAR, THE BACKSTABBER.
YOUR WORLD IS SMALL...IT INCLUDES ONLY YOU.
YOU ARE WRONG. I HELD ALL FOR YOU... IN TRUST, MY...SON!
SON?

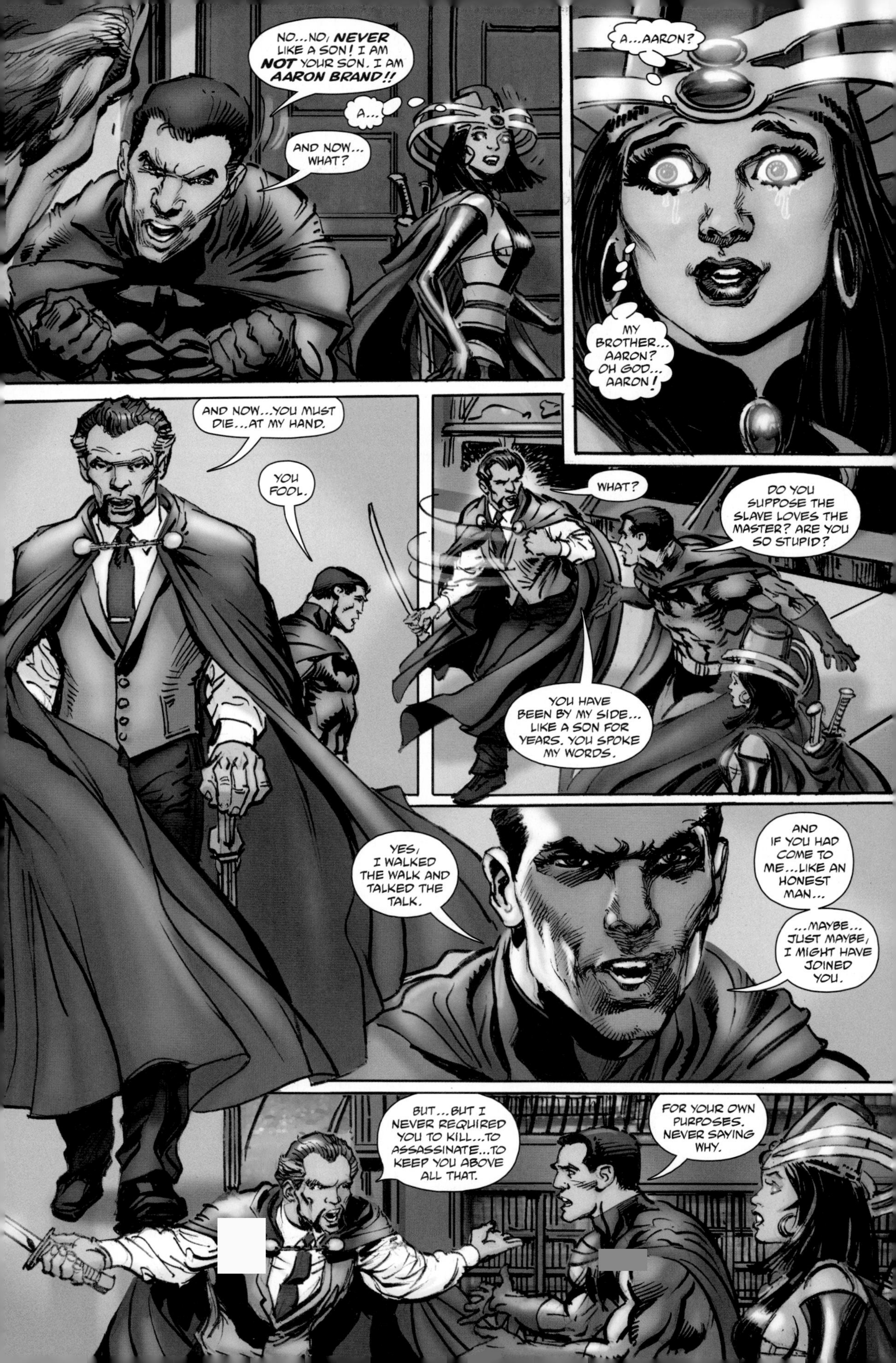
NO...NO, NEVER LIKE A SON! I AM NOT YOUR SON. I AM AARON BRAND!!
A...
AND NOW... WHAT?
A...AARON?
MY BROTHER... AARON? OH GOD... AARON!
AND NOW...YOU MUST DIE...AT MY HAND.
YOU FOOL.
WHAT?
DO YOU SUPPOSE THE SLAVE LOVES THE MASTER? ARE YOU SO STUPID?
YOU HAVE BEEN BY MY SIDE... LIKE A SON FOR YEARS. YOU SPOKE MY WORDS.
YES, I WALKED THE WALK AND TALKED THE TALK.
AND IF YOU HAD COME TO ME...LIKE AN HONEST MAN...
...MAYBE... JUST MAYBE, I MIGHT HAVE JOINED YOU.
BUT...BUT I NEVER REQUIRED YOU TO KILL...TO ASSASSINATE...TO KEEP YOU ABOVE ALL THAT.
FOR YOUR OWN PURPOSES. NEVER SAYING WHY.

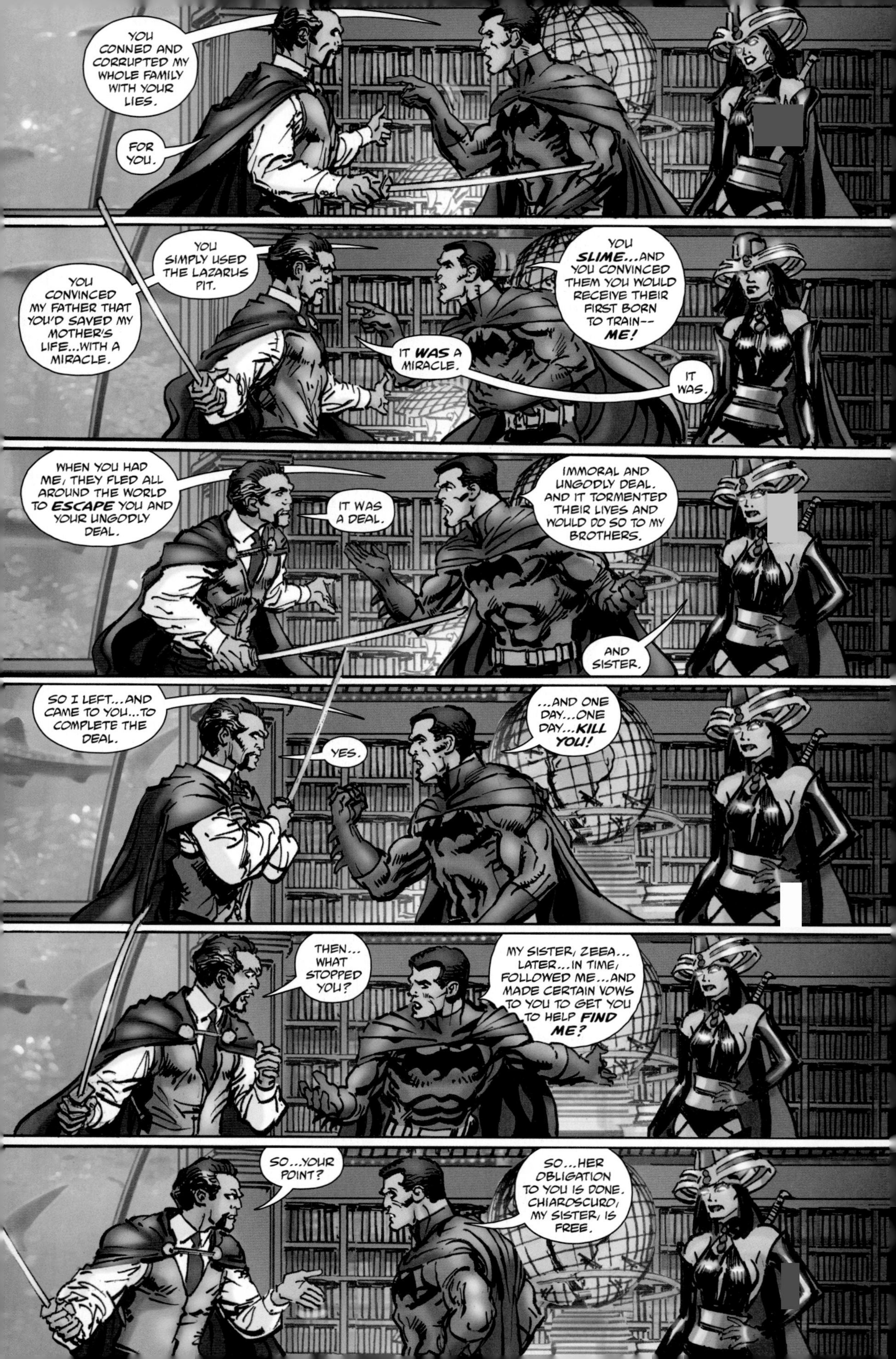
YOU CONNED AND CORRUPTED MY WHOLE FAMILY WITH YOUR LIES.
FOR YOU.
YOU CONVINCED MY FATHER THAT YOU'D SAVED MY MOTHER'S LIFE...WITH A MIRACLE.
YOU SIMPLY USED THE LAZARUS PIT.
YOU SLIME...AND YOU CONVINCED THEM YOU WOULD RECEIVE THEIR FIRST BORN TO TRAIN--ME!
IT WAS A MIRACLE.
IT WAS.
WHEN YOU HAD ME, THEY FLED ALL AROUND THE WORLD TO ESCAPE YOU AND YOUR UNGODLY DEAL.
IT WAS A DEAL.
IMMORAL AND UNGODLY DEAL. AND IT TORMENTED THEIR LIVES AND WOULD DO SO TO MY BROTHERS.
AND SISTER.
SO I LEFT...AND CAME TO YOU...TO COMPLETE THE DEAL.
YES.
...AND ONE DAY...ONE DAY...KILL YOU!
THEN... WHAT STOPPED YOU?
MY SISTER, ZEEA... LATER...IN TIME, FOLLOWED ME...AND MADE CERTAIN VOWS TO YOU TO GET YOU TO HELP FIND ME?
SO...YOUR POINT?
SO...HER OBLIGATION TO YOU IS DONE. CHIAROSCURO, MY SISTER, IS FREE.

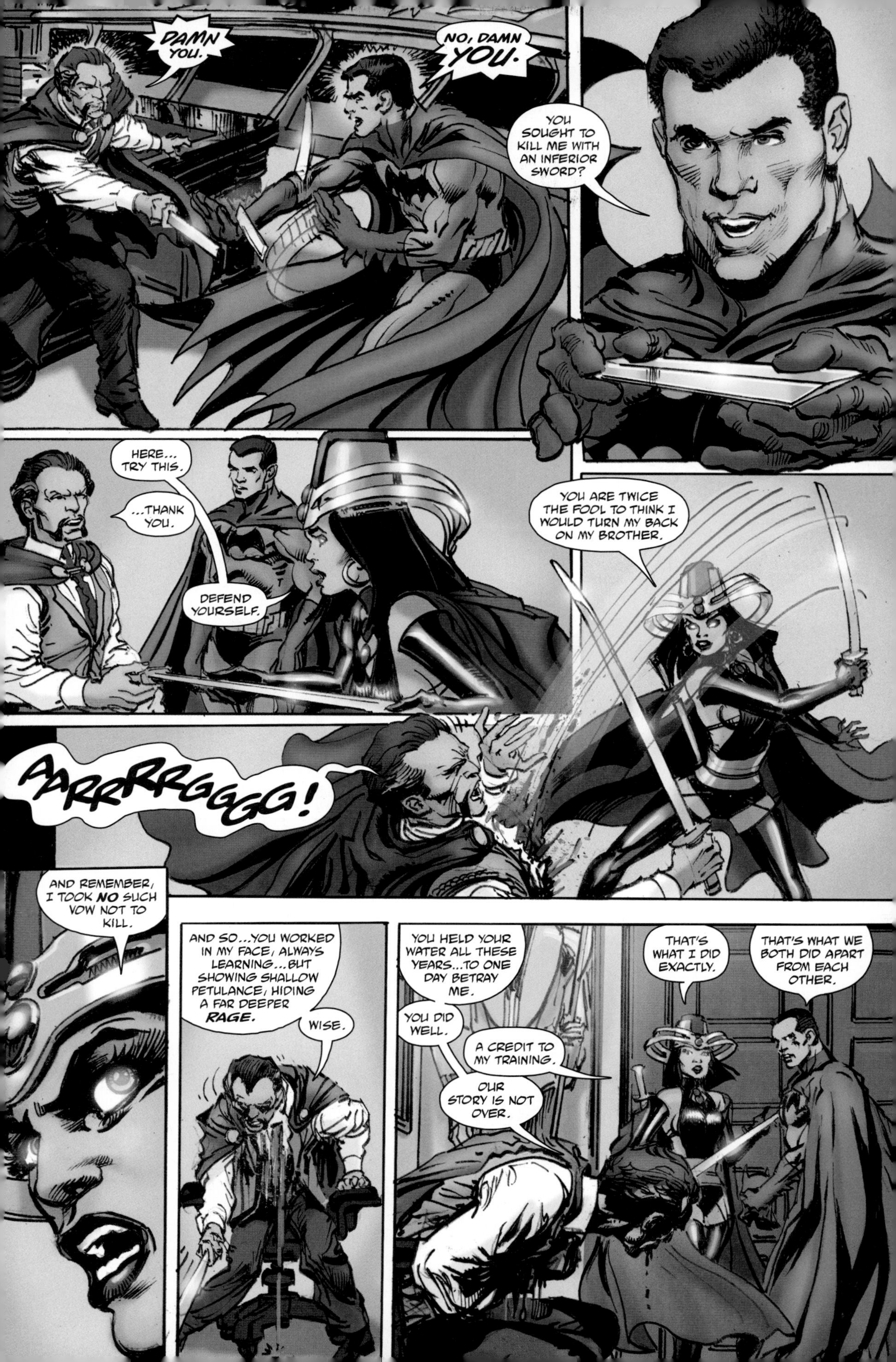
DAMN YOU.
NO, DAMN YOU.
YOU SOUGHT TO KILL ME WITH AN INFERIOR SWORD?
HERE... TRY THIS.
...THANK YOU.
DEFEND YOURSELF.
YOU ARE TWICE THE FOOL TO THINK I WOULD TURN MY BACK ON MY BROTHER.
AARRRRGGGG!
AND REMEMBER, I TOOK NO SUCH VOW NOT TO KILL.
AND SO...YOU WORKED IN MY FACE, ALWAYS LEARNING...BUT SHOWING SHALLOW PETULANCE, HIDING A FAR DEEPER RAGE.
WISE.
YOU HELD YOUR WATER ALL THESE YEARS...TO ONE DAY BETRAY ME.
YOU DID WELL.
A CREDIT TO MY TRAINING.
OUR STORY IS NOT OVER.
THAT'S WHAT I DID EXACTLY.
THAT'S WHAT WE BOTH DID APART FROM EACH OTHER.

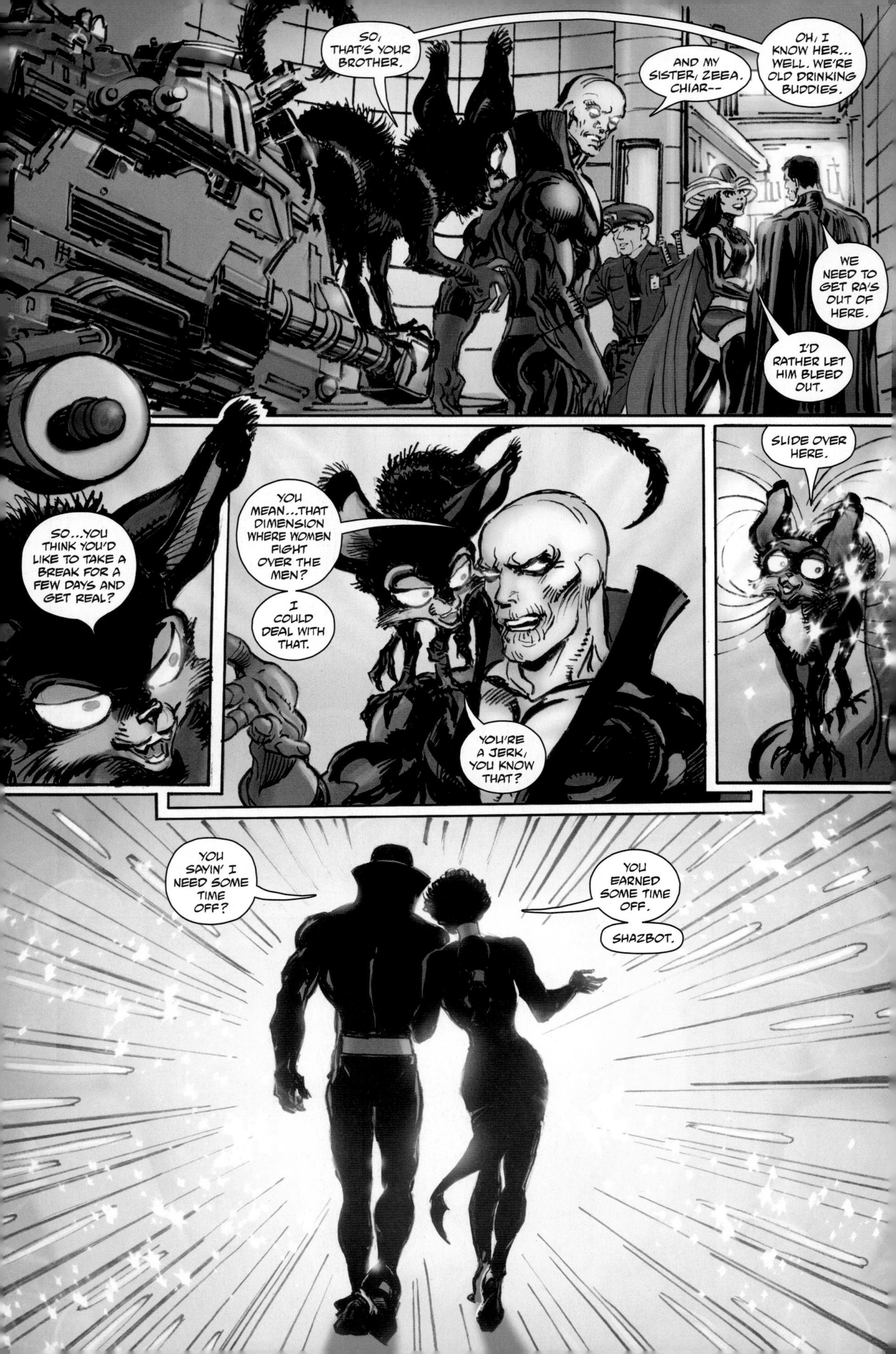
SO, THAT'S YOUR BROTHER.
AND MY SISTER, ZEEA. CHIAR--
OH, I KNOW HER... WELL. WE'RE OLD DRINKING BUDDIES.
WE NEED TO GET RA'S OUT OF HERE.
I'D RATHER LET HIM BLEED OUT.
SO...YOU THINK YOU'D LIKE TO TAKE A BREAK FOR A FEW DAYS AND GET REAL?
YOU MEAN...THAT DIMENSION WHERE WOMEN FIGHT OVER THE MEN?
I COULD DEAL WITH THAT.
YOU'RE A JERK, YOU KNOW THAT?
SLIDE OVER HERE.
YOU SAYIN' I NEED SOME TIME OFF?
YOU EARNED SOME TIME OFF.
SHAZBOT.

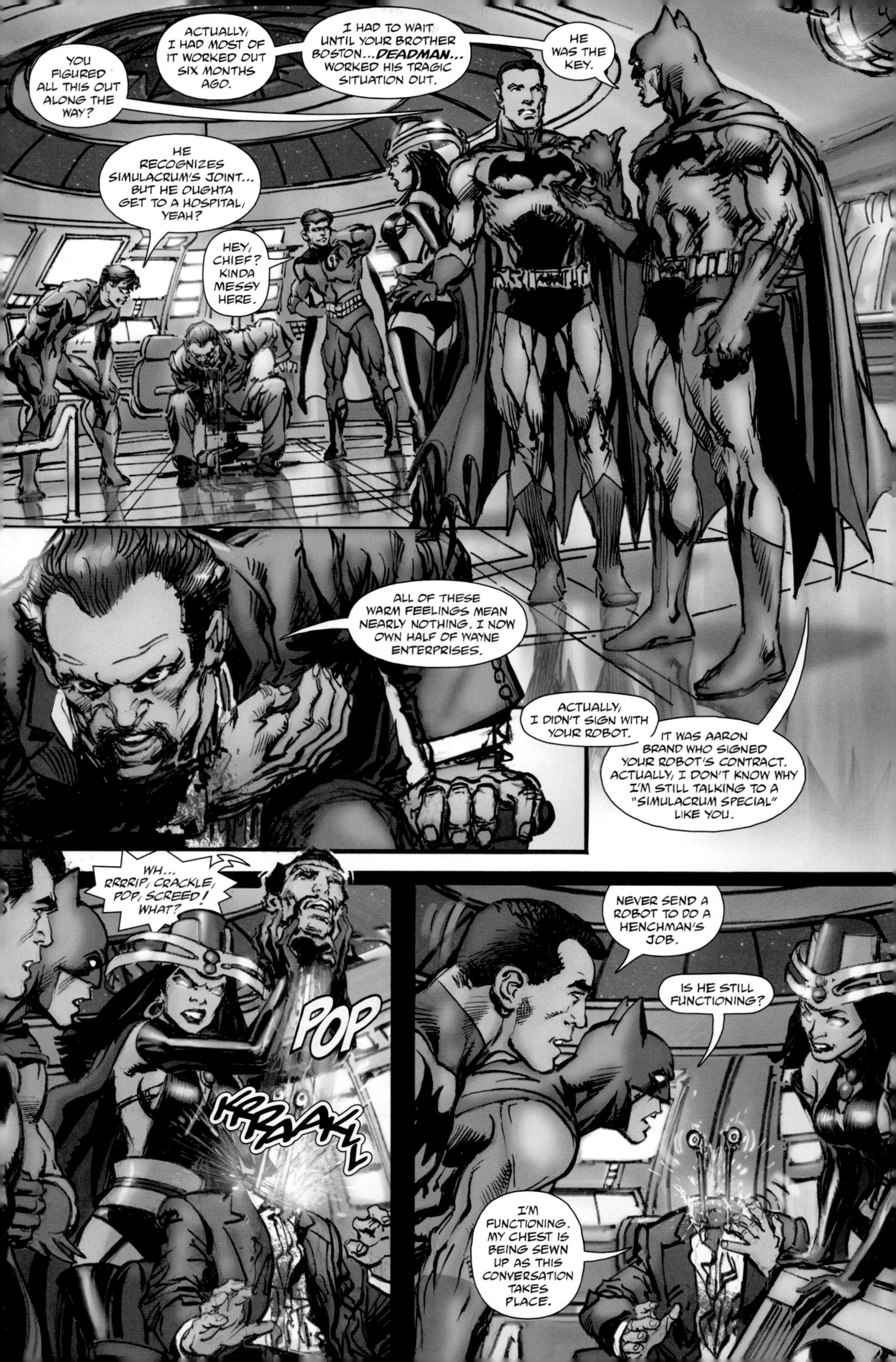
YOU FIGURED ALL THIS OUT ALONG THE WAY?
ACTUALLY, I HAD MOST OF IT WORKED OUT SIX MONTHS AGO.
I HAD TO WAIT UNTIL YOUR BROTHER BOSTON...DEADMAN... WORKED HIS TRAGIC SITUATION OUT.
HE WAS THE KEY.
HE RECOGNIZES SIMULACRUM'S JOINT... BUT HE OUGHTA GET TO A HOSPITAL, YEAH?
HEY, CHIEF? KINDA MESSY HERE.
ALL OF THESE WARM FEELINGS MEAN NEARLY NOTHING. I NOW OWN HALF OF WAYNE ENTERPRISES.
ACTUALLY, I DIDN'T SIGN WITH YOUR ROBOT.
IT WAS AARON BRAND WHO SIGNED YOUR ROBOT'S CONTRACT. ACTUALLY, I DON'T KNOW WHY I'M STILL TALKING TO A "SIMULACRUM SPECIAL" LIKE YOU.
WH... RRRRIP, CRACKLE, POP, SCREED! WHAT?
POP
KRAAKL
NEVER SEND A ROBOT TO DO A HENCHMAN'S JOB.
IS HE STILL FUNCTIONING?
I'M FUNCTIONING. MY CHEST IS BEING SEWN UP AS THIS CONVERSATION TAKES PLACE.

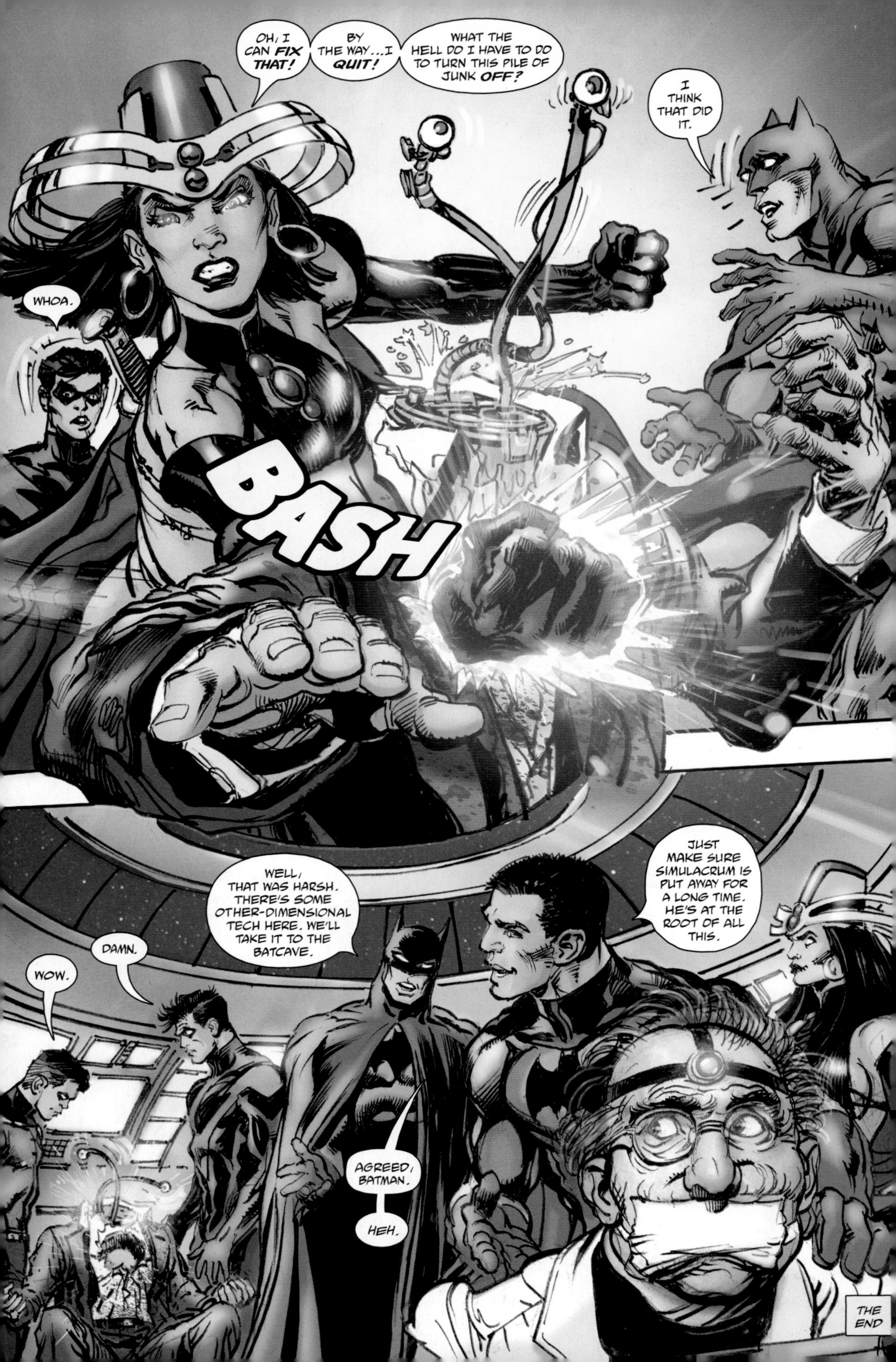
OH, I CAN FIX THAT!
BY THE WAY...I QUIT!
WHAT THE HELL DO I HAVE TO DO TO TURN THIS PILE OF JUNK OFF?
I THINK THAT DID IT.
WHOA.
BASH
WELL, THAT WAS HARSH. THERE'S SOME OTHER-DIMENSIONAL TECH HERE. WE'LL TAKE IT TO THE BATCAVE.
JUST MAKE SURE SIMULACRUM IS PUT AWAY FOR A LONG TIME. HE'S AT THE ROOT OF ALL THIS.
DAMN.
WOW.
AGREED, BATMAN.
HEH.
THE END

Issue #1 variant cover by Neal Adams

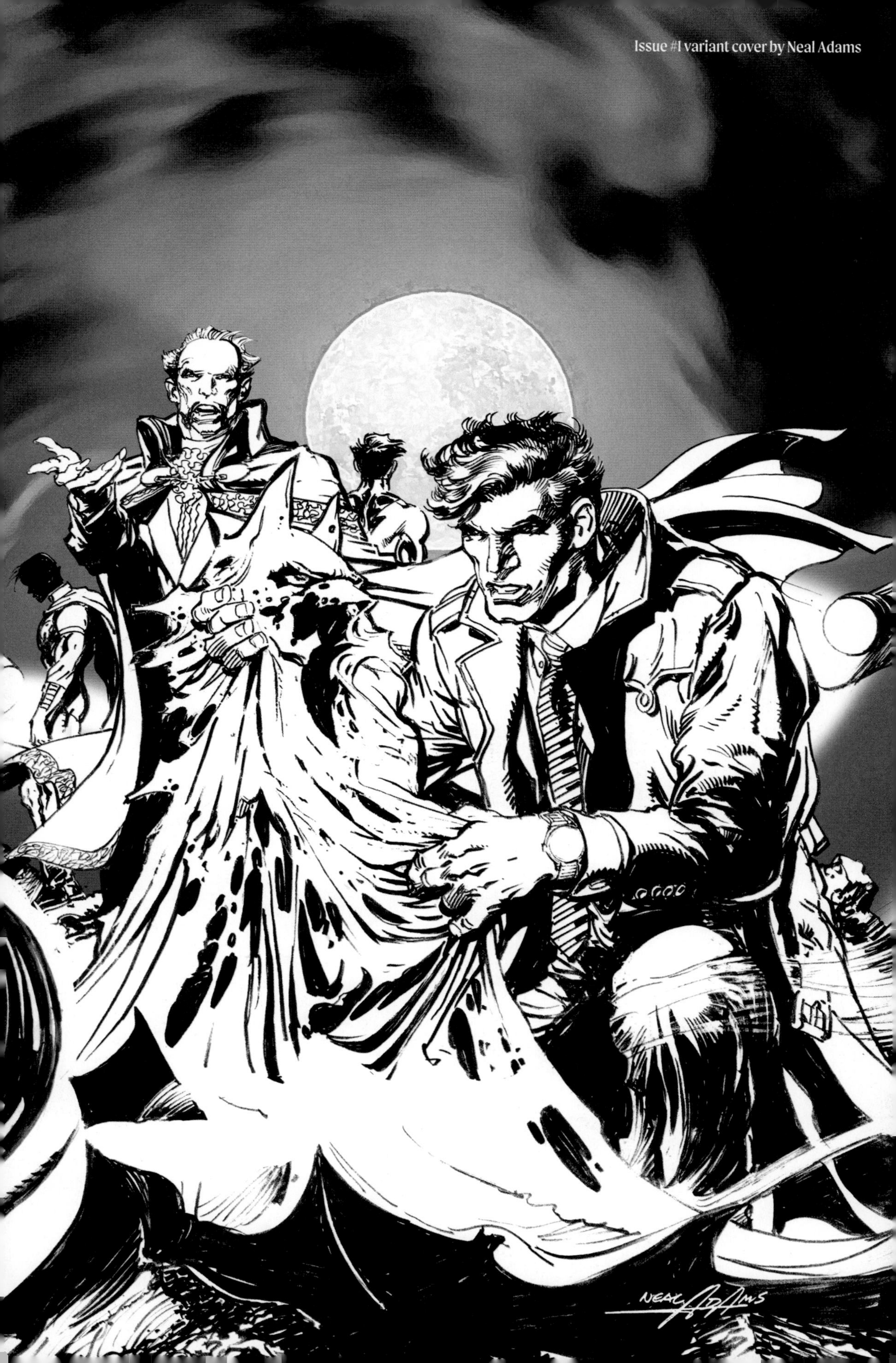

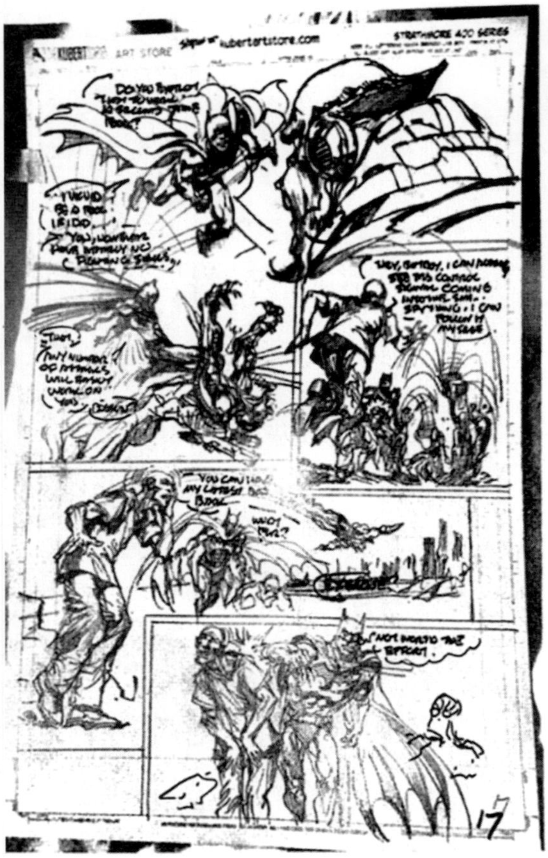
NOT WORTH THE EFFORT.

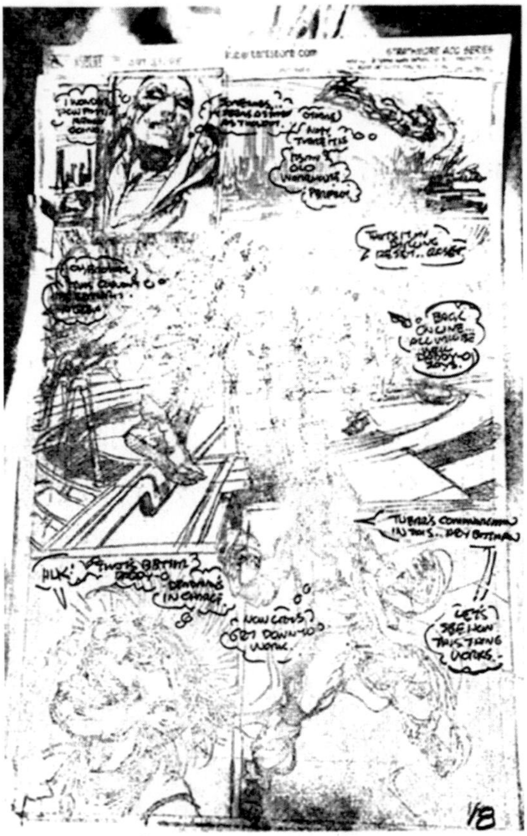
NOW LET'S GET DOWN TO WORK.
LET'S SEE HOW THIS THING WORKS.

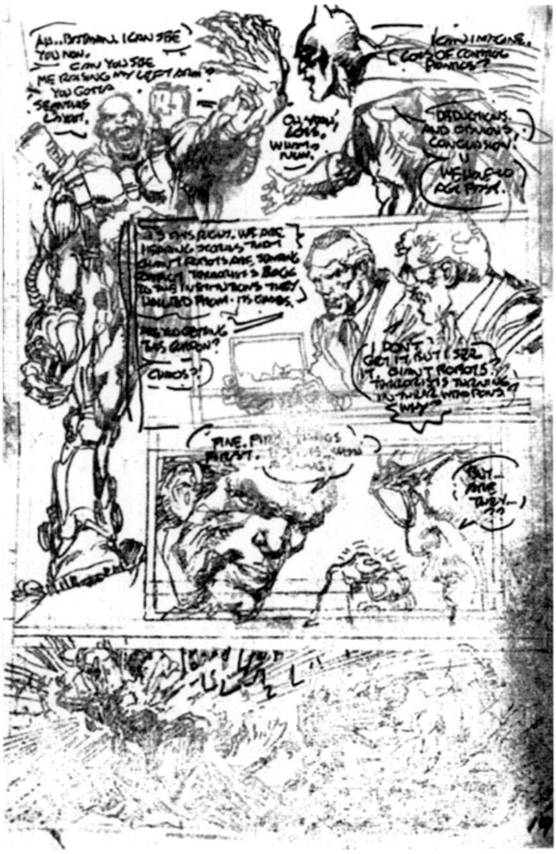
CHAOS?

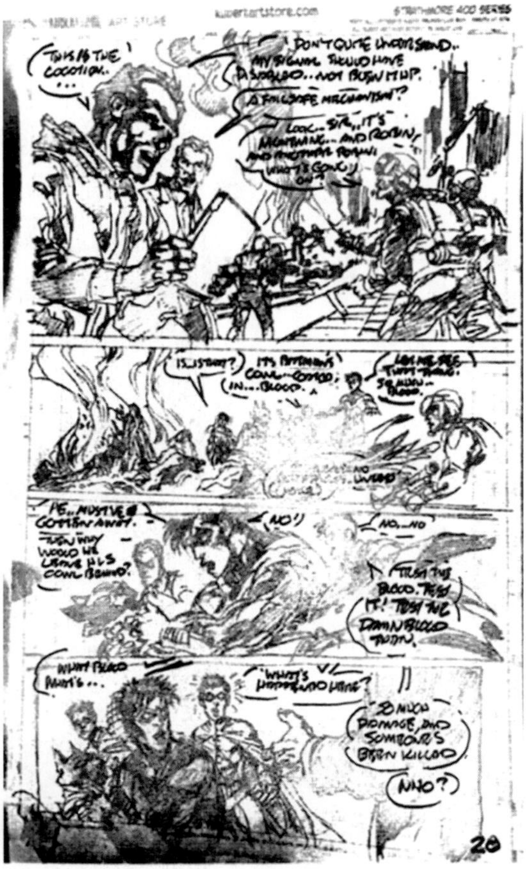
THIS IS THE COCOON...
A FAILSAFE MECHANISM?
NO!
NO...NO
WHAT'S HAPPENING HERE?
SO MUCH DAMAGE, AND SOMEONE'S BEEN KILLED.
WHO?

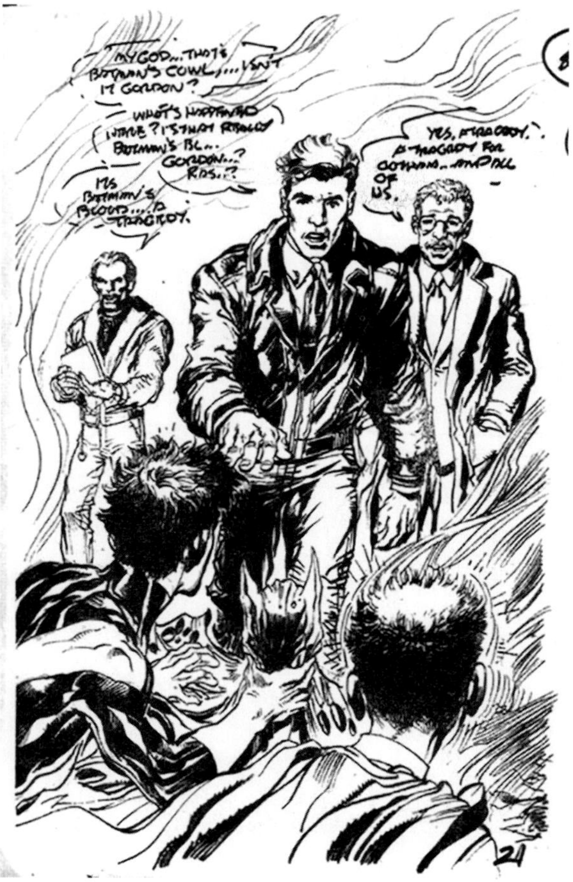
MY GOD... THAT'S BATMAN'S COWL, ...ISN'T IT GORDON?
YES, A TRAGEDY. A TRAGEDY FOR GOTHAM... AND ALL OF US.
21

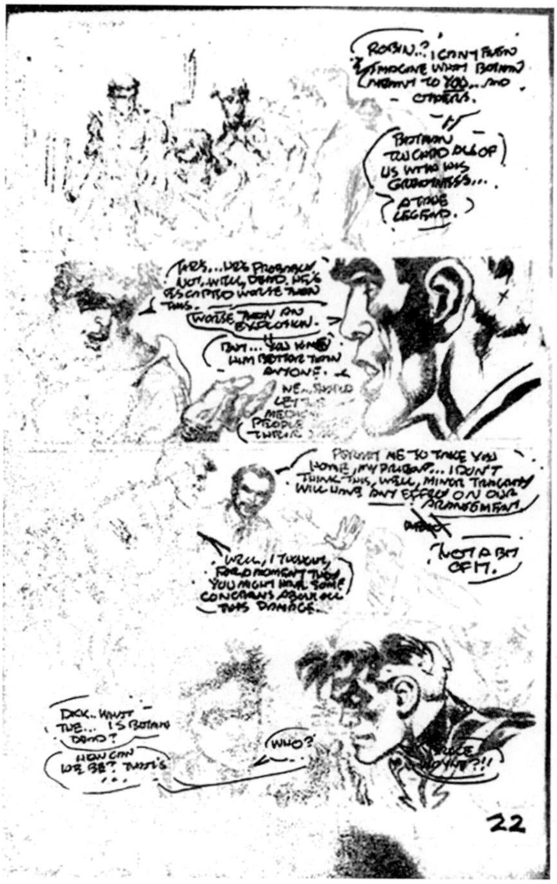
ROBIN..? I CAN'T EVEN IMAGINE WHAT BATMAN MEANT TO YOU... AND OTHERS.
BATMAN TOUCHED ALL OF US WITH HIS GREATNESS... A TRUE LEGEND.
WORSE THAN AN EXPLOSION.
PERMIT ME TO TAKE YOU HOME, MY FRIEND... I DON'T THINK THIS, WELL, MINOR TRAGEDY WILL HAVE ANY EFFECT ON OUR ARRANGEMENT.
WELL, I THOUGHT, FOR A MOMENT THERE YOU MIGHT HAVE SOME CONCERNS ABOUT ALL THIS DAMAGE.
NOT A BIT OF IT.
WHO?
22

With every issue, as he's finalizing dialogue, Neal hand-letters the balloon guides over his pencils. We treat this as our bible. Our much-missed assistant editor Liz Erickson would take the original script, update it to match the exact wording employed on the Jpegs, and compile the documents for letterer Clem Robins. I always appreciated her, but after she left and I had to read the text myself, I also missed her keen eyesight!

Clem would take the clean files from the inks stage and the updated script, and use the guides to set up the correct styles for balloons (shouting, whispering, or talking are all very clear in the guides) and then start on the sound effects. Clem is truly a master of the craft, and I was always thrilled to have him to geek out over these stories with.

Finally, we send the lettered PDF back to Neal and see how we did!

—**Kristy Quinn**

Issue #1 page 19 inks and colors

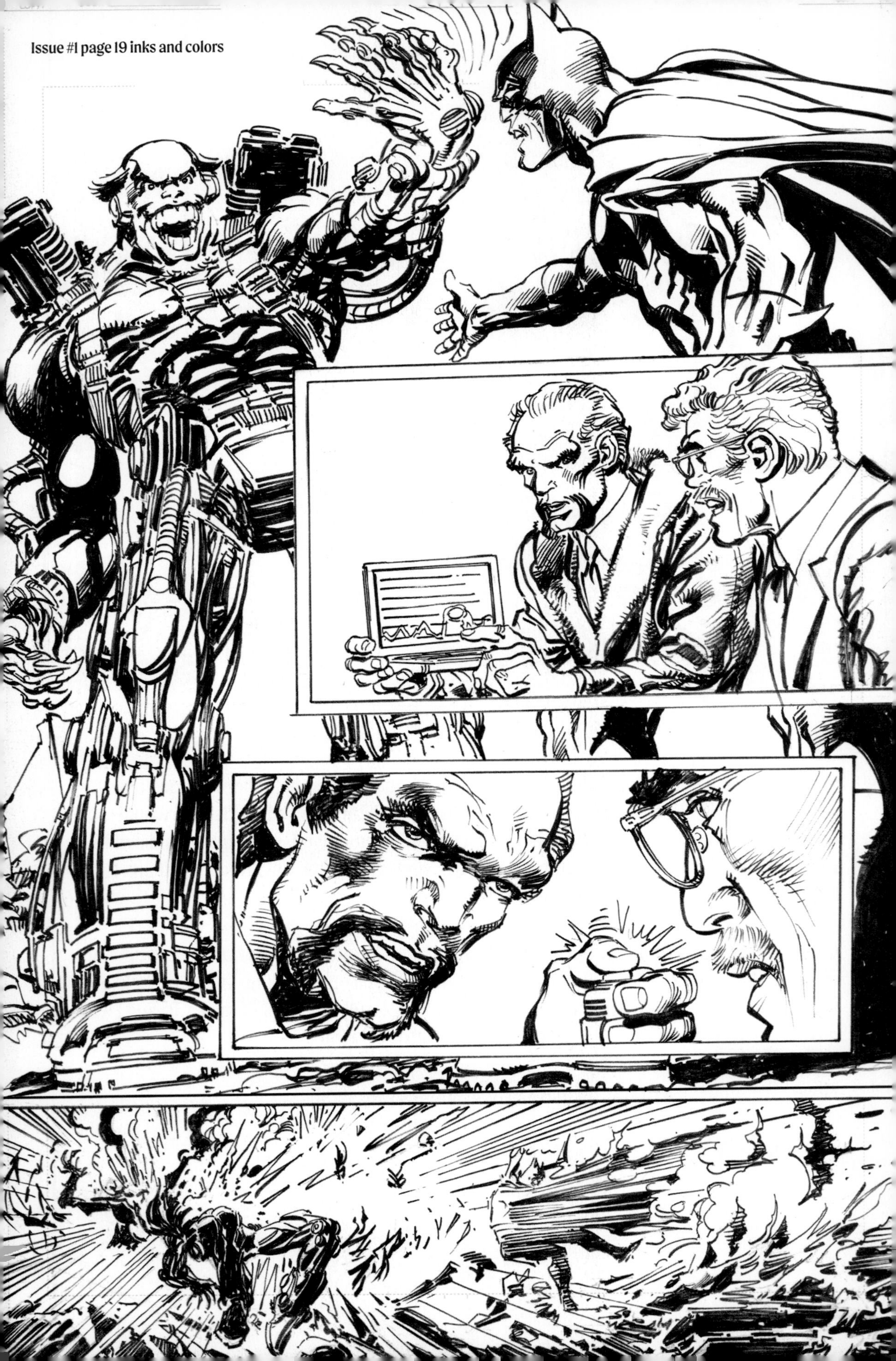

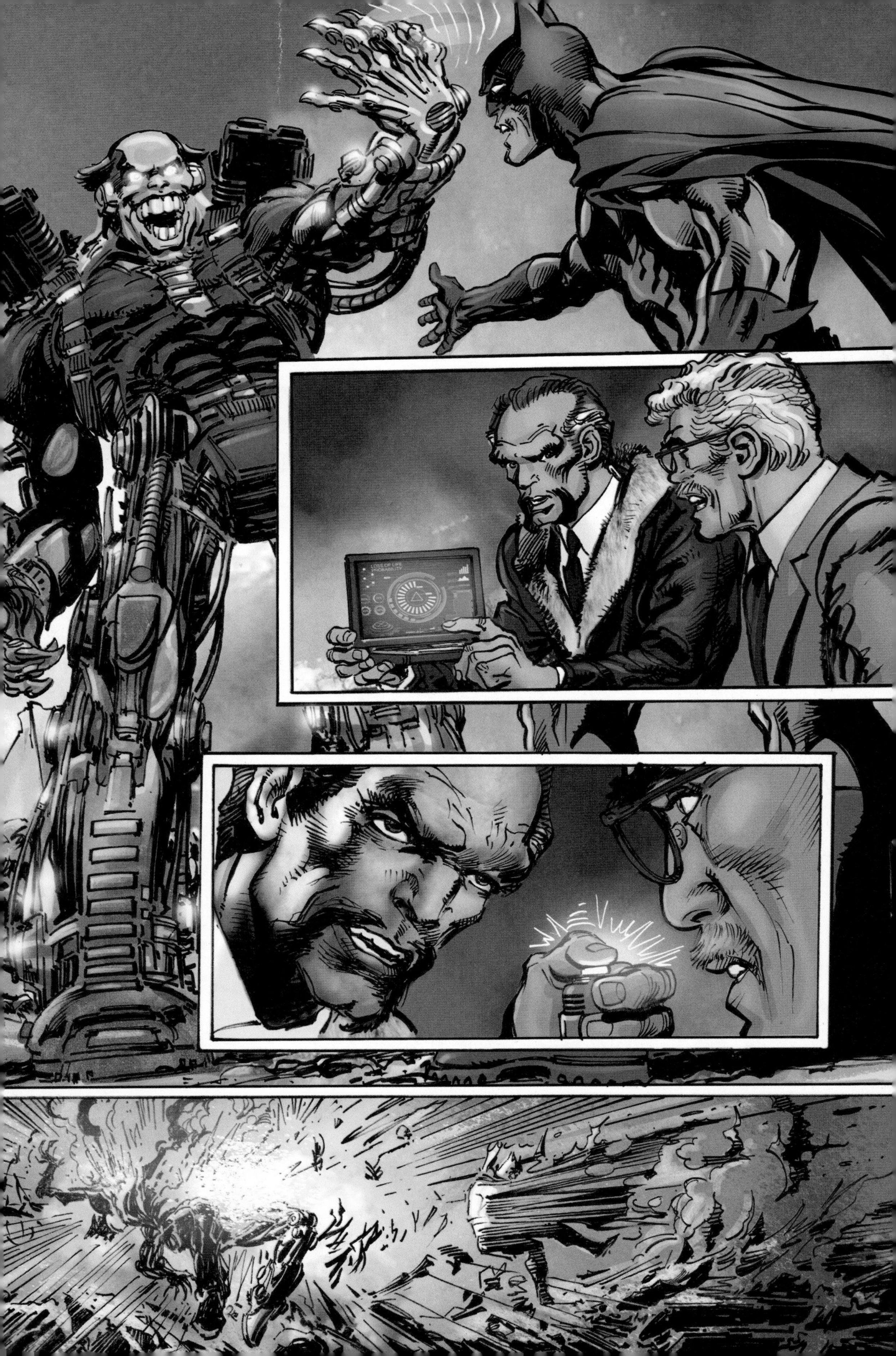
LOSS OF LIFE
PROBABILITY

Issue #1 page 20 inks and colors

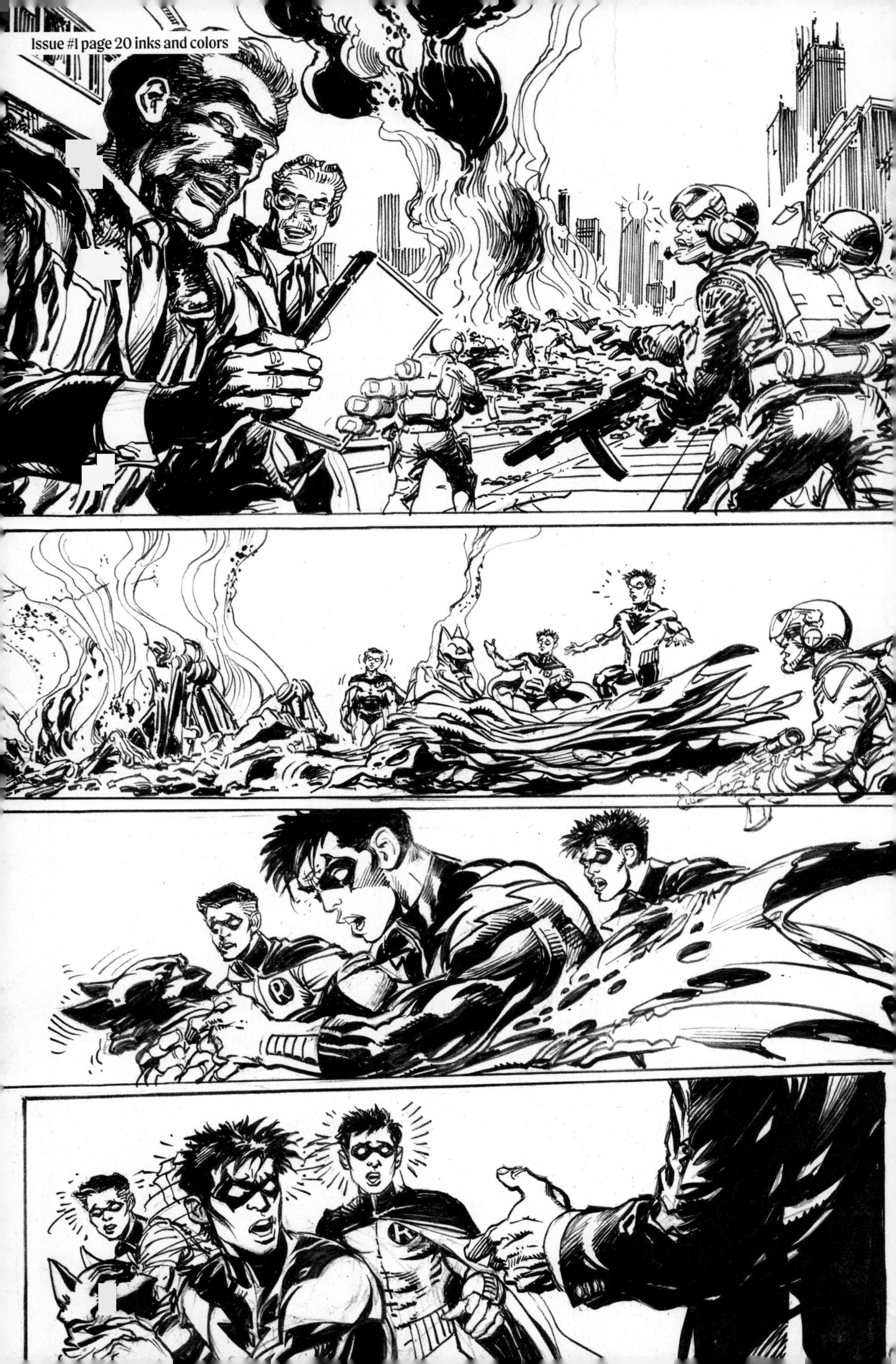

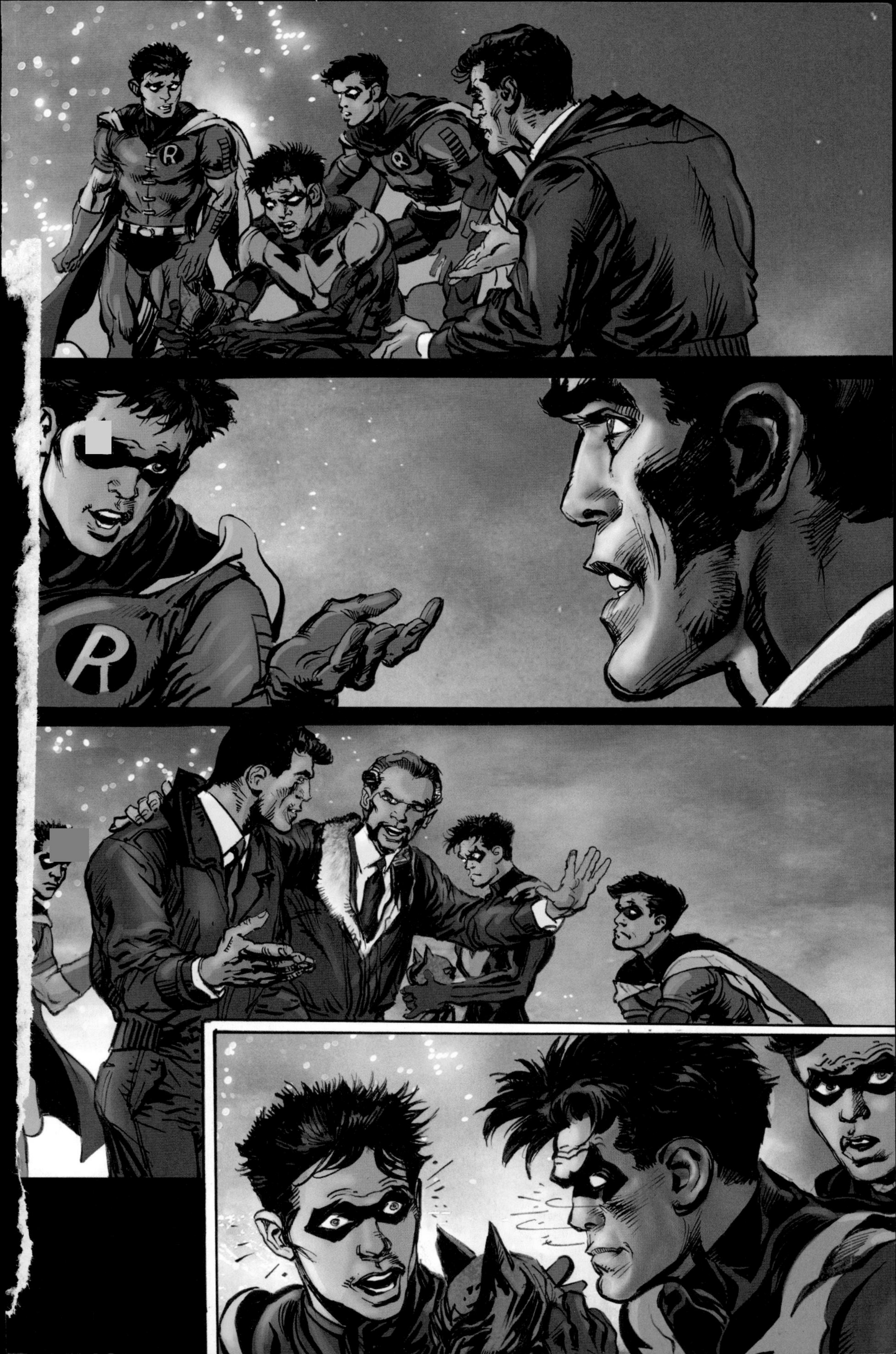

NEAL ADAMS

Born on June 15, 1941, in New York City, Neal Adams began his career in comics and illustration immediately after high school and worked in the field from then on. He first began freelancing for DC Comics in 1965, and he quickly became one of their top cover artists, contributing radical and dynamic illustrations to nearly every series the company published. His first interior work was done for editor Robert Kanigher's war titles, but it was his celebrated run on a new book called *Deadman* that began to build his reputation as a revolutionary creative force.

That reputation was cemented in the early 1970s with DC's publication of a series of collaborations between Adams, writer Dennis O'Neil, and inker Dick Giordano starring Batman, Green Lantern, and Green Arrow. These stories revolutionized a struggling industry and flew in the face of—and finally removed the teeth from—the repressive Comics Code, while breaking new ground for mainstream comics and attracting major (and overwhelmingly positive) national media attention to the art form. Years later, Adams opened Continuity Associates (which would become Continuity Studios) and invited Giordano to join. Capitalizing on their comics experience, they produced advertising artwork for clients around the world.

In addition to his pivotal artistic and business roles, Adams was also one of the founders of the movement for creators' rights in the comics industry, which has worked to establish as standard practices the return of original art, the payment of royalties, and the use of better-quality color separation and printing methodologies, as well as helping individual creators and their families in protecting and asserting their rights. Neal Adams passed away in April 2022.

Issue #1 page 22 inks and colors

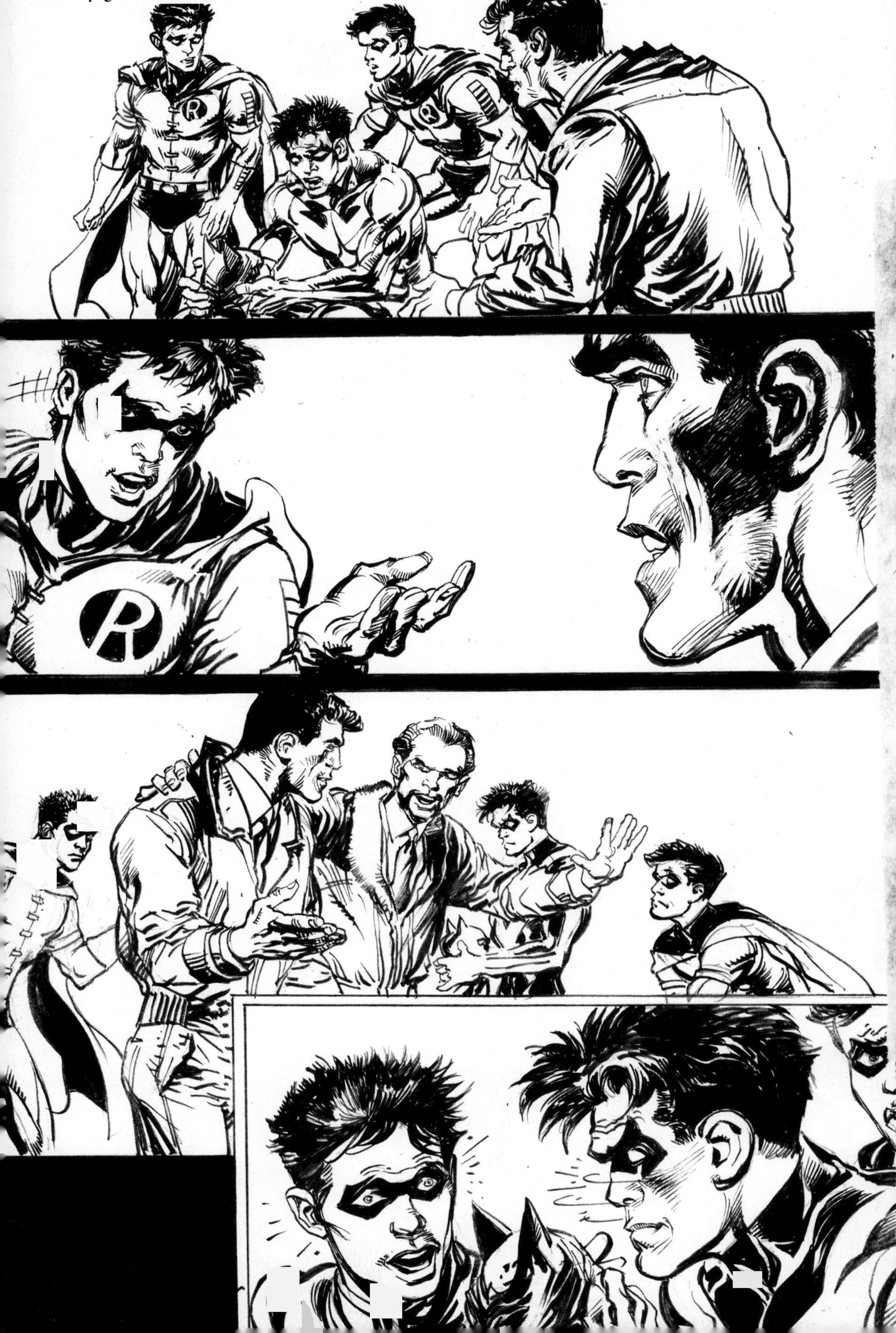

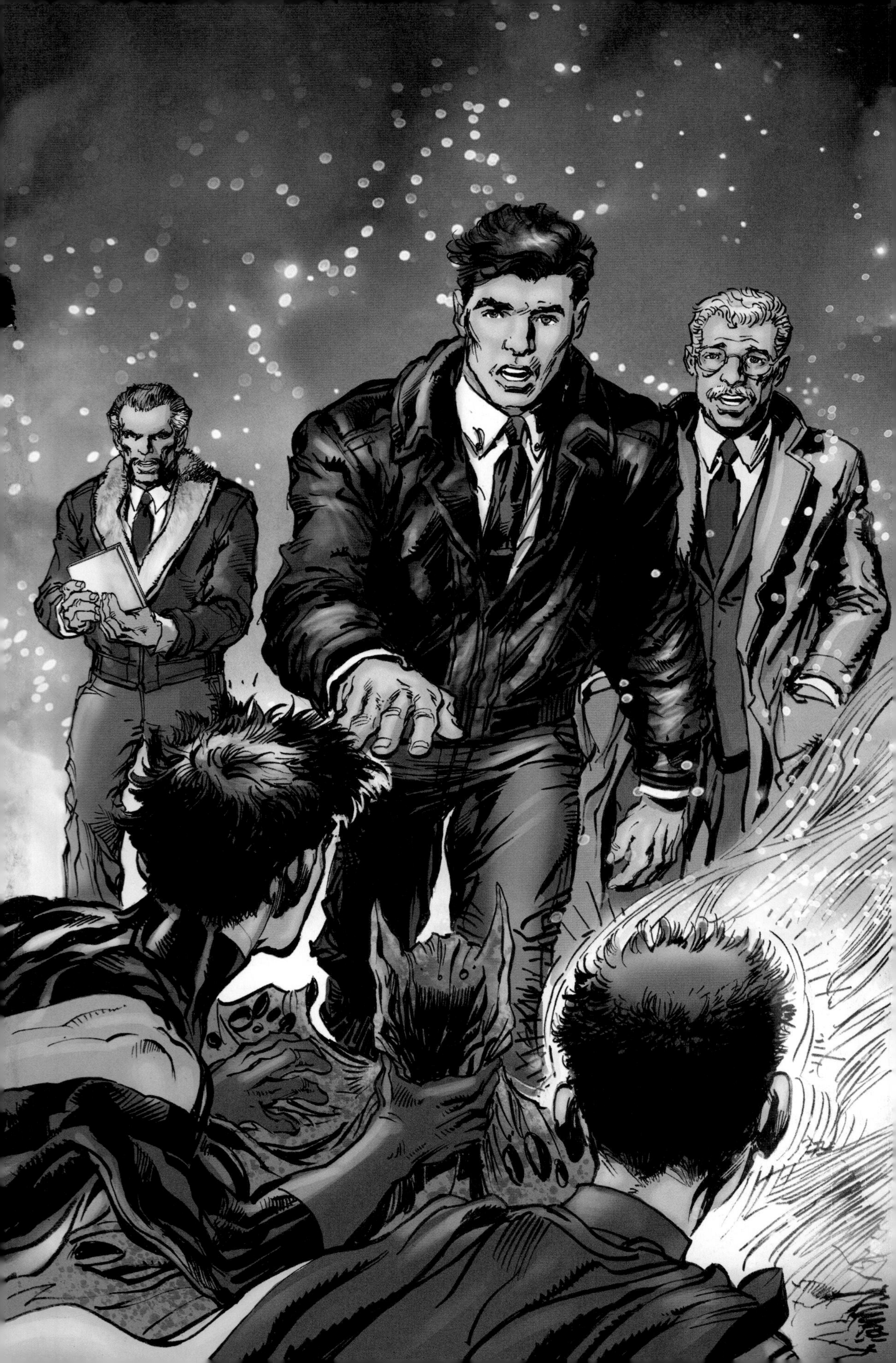

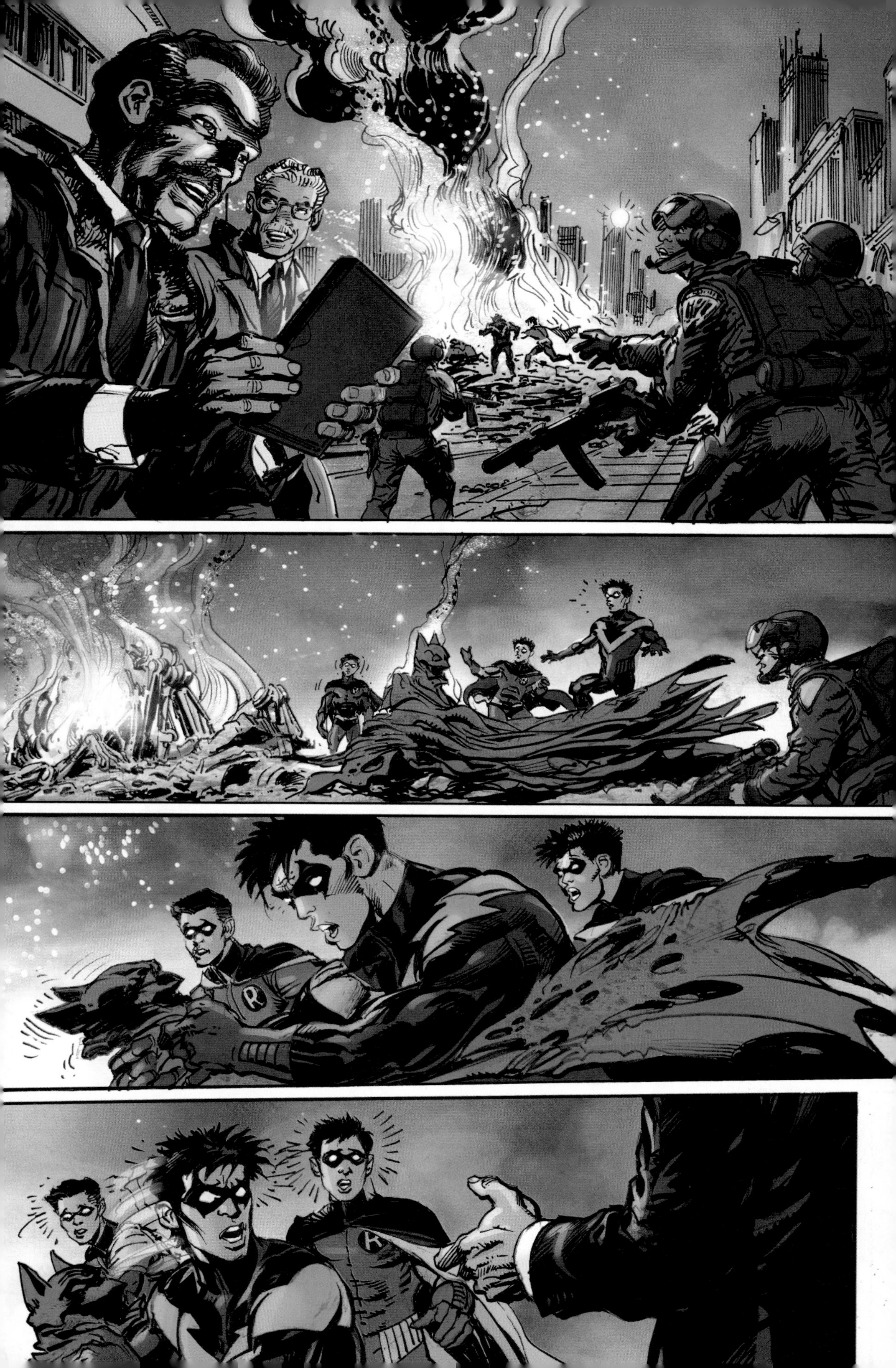

Issue #1 page 21 inks and colors

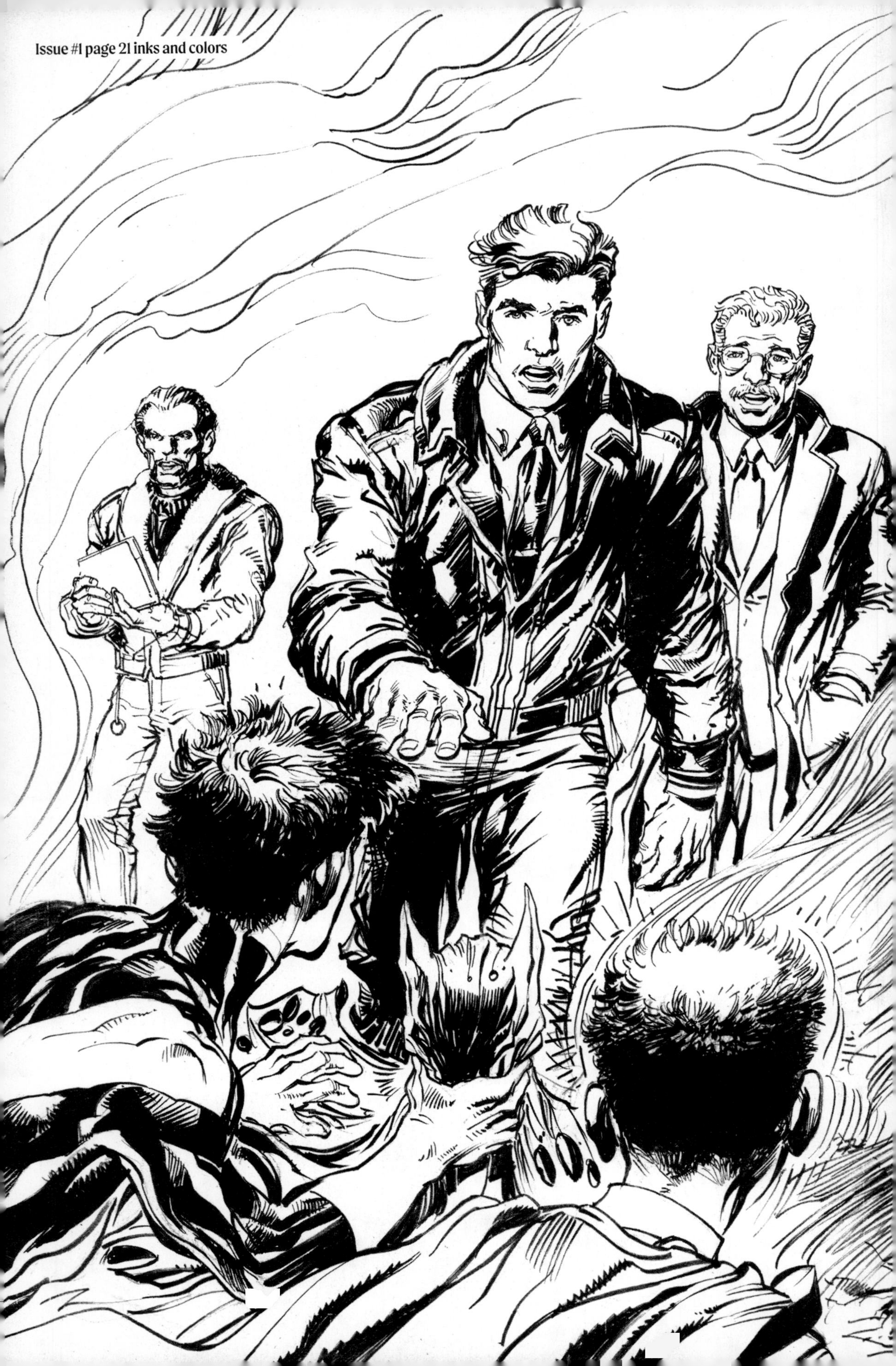